A History in Indigenous Voices

A History in
Indigenous Voices

Menominee, Ho-Chunk, Oneida,
Stockbridge, and Brothertown
Interactions in the Removal Era

Carol Cornelius

WISCONSIN HISTORICAL SOCIETY PRESS

Published by the Wisconsin Historical Society Press
Publishers since 1855

The Wisconsin Historical Society helps people connect to the past by collecting, preserving, and sharing stories. Founded in 1846, the Society is one of the nation's finest historical institutions. *Join the Wisconsin Historical Society*: wisconsinhistory.org/membership

Publication of this book was made possible thanks to the generous support of the Wisconsin Historical Society Press Readers Circle. For more information and to join, visit support.wisconsinhistory.org/readerscircle.

For permission to reuse material from *A History in Indigenous Voices* (ISBN 978-1-9766-0009-8; e-book ISBN 978-1-9766-0010-4), please access www.copyright.com or contact the Copyright Clearance Center, Inc. (CCC), 222 Rosewood Drive, Danvers, MA 01923, 978-750-8400. CCC is a not-for-profit organization that provides licenses and registration for a variety of users.

Photographs identified with WHi or WHS are from the Society's collections; address requests to reproduce these photos to the Visual Materials Archivist at the Wisconsin Historical Society, 816 State Street, Madison, WI 53706.

Printed in the United States of America
Cover design by Mayfly Design
Typesetting by Sara DeHaan

27 26 25 24 23   1 2 3 4 5

Library of Congress Cataloging-in-Publication Data available.

∞ The paper used in this publication meets the minimum requirements of the American National Standard for Information Sciences—Permanence of Paper for Printed Library Materials, ANSI Z39.48–1992.

Contents

Notes on Terminology

It is always difficult in writing about Indigenous nations to deal with the variety of identifications used in documents. A wide range of identifying verbiage—from the generalized term *Indian* to the specific Indigenous nation's name for itself—was used.

In addition to transcription errors and simplification by European writers, the nations themselves have changed what they prefer to be called. The Mu-he-con-ne-ok Nation, whose name means "the people who live by the waters that are never still," referring to the Hudson River, would later be called the Stockbridge. The Onyote^aka, whose name means "people of the standing stone," are now known as the Oneida. In recent times, the Winnebago Nation has returned to its original name for itself, HoChungra (or Ho-Chunk).

In source documents, the Indigenous nations are often grouped under one name, then listed as individual nations. Documents during the time period discussed in this book, 1820 to 1838, referred to Indigenous nations both by their chosen names and as "New York Indians." The specific Indigenous nations that made up the "New York Indians" varied throughout the treaties.

It is important to acknowledge that Indigenous nations were recognized by the US government as a "nation or tribe of Indians"—for example, "Oneida Nation or tribe of Indians." This nation status clearly indicated that the treaties were between nations.

In this book, I have used the terms and proper names as they appear in the documents, always with the acknowledgment of Indigenous nations as nations. This section offers definitions for some of the most frequently confused names and terms found in the documents.

Brothertown: The Brothertown (frequently spelled Brotherton) Nation consists of seven nations from along the East Coast and Long Island that were so devastated by the invasion of settlers, disease, and war that they joined together in 1785 to form the Brothertown Nation: Mohegan, Montaukett, Narragansett, Niantic, Tunxis, Mashantucket Pequot, and Stonington Pequot.

Indian: The term *Indian* was used by the US government throughout the documents in this book, and I have kept that term when found in the original documents. Every Indigenous nation has its own name for itself, in its own language. The US used the original names of Indigenous nations in a few of the early treaties and documents but generally used *Indian*.

Indigenous nations: The Indigenous nations are the original peoples who populated the western hemisphere. In this book I have used *Indigenous nations* in the more contemporary history and *Indians* as found in documents.

Menominee Nation: The name of the Menominee Nation, or "people of the wild rice," is spelled several different ways throughout the documents. I've left the spelling as it occurs.

New York Indians: This name has been applied to many groupings of the various tribes from New York State. As used in this book, the term includes the Stockbridge, Oneida, and Brothertown Nations.

Oneida: Onyote^aka, or "people of the standing stone." After 1934, the United States identified the Oneida as the Oneida Tribe of Indians of Wisconsin. In a 2015 Oneida Nation referendum, we changed this to Oneida Nation.

Six Nations and Iroquois Confederacy: The original five nations of the Iroquois Confederacy were Mohawk, Oneida, Onondaga, Cayuga, and Seneca. The Tuscarora were included after the 1700s, which made it the Six Nations. The Haudenosaunee, or "people of the longhouse," have returned to using Haudenosaunee.

Stockbridge-Munsee: Mu-he-con-ne-ok, or "the people who live by the waters (Hudson River) that are never still." The Munsee Nation was absorbed into the Stockbridge Nation. Today the Stockbridge are known as the Mohican Nation and/or the Stockbridge-Munsee Band of Mohican Indians.

Winnebago Nation: Winnebago Nation is the name used in the historical documents that appear in this book. The Winnebago have moved forward using their original name for their nation, HoChungra (also Ho-Chunk), meaning "people of the big (or sacred) voice."

INTRODUCTION

Hearing the Voices of Native Nations

This book began with my wanting to find and record, if possible, the discussions, negotiations, and understandings between Indigenous nations in the words of the Menominee, the Ho-Chunk (Winnebago), and the Oneida, Stockbridge, and Brothertown Nations (New York Indians). What did the Menominee, Ho-Chunk, and New York Indians say to one another during and after the treaty negotiations of the early nineteenth century, and what did they understand to be in those treaties? What role did US government policies play during treaties made between 1821 and 1838? Why would the New York Indians agree to emigrate to what is now Wisconsin? What other entities were involved that influenced the treaty process?

The treaty negotiations between these Indigenous nations are mentioned by researchers and authors, but to date, no one has presented the actual statements of the Menominee, Ho-Chunk, and New York Indians. Most often, when researchers refer to an Indigenous person involved in the negotiations, they quote only a few sentences. However, primary sources—including treaty negotiations, speeches, petitions, journals of US commissioners assigned to a treaty, and memorials (written formal requests)—provide detailed descriptions and often complete texts. In addition, many letters were written by Indigenous peoples during this time period, addressed directly to the president of the United States or the secretary of war on a nation-to-nation basis. Many of these sources are now preserved on microfilm. Therefore, we can access the words and thoughts of the Native people with whom they originated.

As a Stockbridge, Brothertown, and enrolled Oneida person, it has always been my wish to understand, from our own ancestors, why they would agree to such a dramatic move from our homelands in what is now New York State to Green Bay. As the Oneida of Wisconsin, we have generally been taught that our ancestors became Christians and followed Reverend Eleazer Williams to Wisconsin. Historic documents present quite

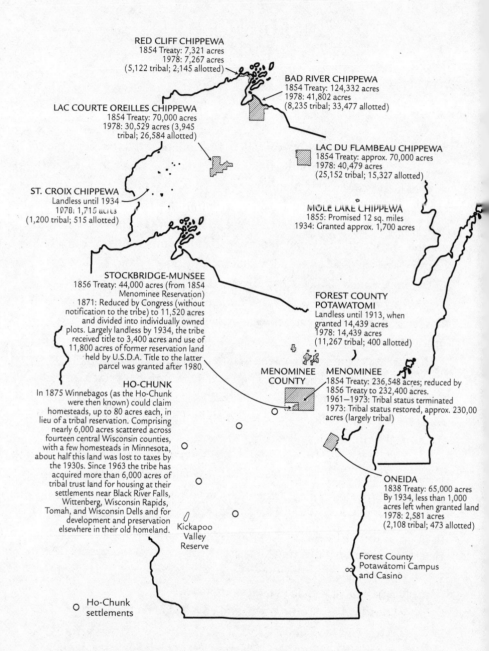

RED CLIFF CHIPPEWA
1854 Treaty: 7,321 acres
1978: 7,267 acres
(5,122 tribal; 2,145 allotted)

BAD RIVER CHIPPEWA
1854 Treaty: 124,332 acres
1978: 41,802 acres
(8,235 tribal; 33,477 allotted)

LAC COURTE OREILLES CHIPPEWA
1854 Treaty: 70,000 acres
1978: 30,529 acres (3,945
tribal; 26,584 allotted)

LAC DU FLAMBEAU CHIPPEWA
1854 Treaty: approx. 70,000 acres
1978: 40,479 acres
(25,152 tribal; 15,327 allotted)

ST. CROIX CHIPPEWA
Landless until 1934
1978: 1,715 acres
(1,200 tribal; 515 allotted)

MOLE LAKE CHIPPEWA
1855: Promised 12 sq. miles
1934: Granted approx. 1,700 acres

STOCKBRIDGE-MUNSEE
1856 Treaty: 44,000 acres (from 1854
Menominee Reservation)
1871: Reduced by Congress (without
notification to the tribe) to 11,520 acres
and divided into individually owned
plots. Largely landless by 1934, the tribe
received title to 3,400 acres and use of
11,800 acres of former reservation land
held by U.S.D.A. Title to the latter
parcel was granted after 1980.

**FOREST COUNTY
POTAWATOMI**
Landless until 1913, when
granted 14,439 acres
1978: 14,439 acres
(11,267 tribal; 400 allotted)

HO-CHUNK
In 1875 Winnebagos (as the Ho-Chunk
were then known) could claim
homesteads, up to 80 acres each, in
lieu of a tribal reservation. Comprising
nearly 6,000 acres scattered across
fourteen central Wisconsin counties,
with a few homesteads in Minnesota,
about half this land was lost to taxes by
the 1930s. Since 1963 the tribe has
acquired more than 6,000 acres of
tribal trust land for housing at their
settlements near Black River Falls,
Wittenberg, Wisconsin Rapids,
Tomah, and Wisconsin Dells and for
development and preservation
elsewhere in their old homeland.

**MENOMINEE
COUNTY**

MENOMINEE
1854 Treaty: 236,548 acres; reduced by
1856 Treaty to 232,400 acres.
1961–1973: Tribal status terminated
1973: Tribal status restored, approx. 230,00
acres (largely tribal)

ONEIDA
1838 Treaty: 65,000 acres
By 1934, less than 1,000
acres left when granted land
1978: 2,581 acres
(2,108 tribal; 473 allotted)

Kickapoo
Valley
Reserve

Forest County
Potawatomi Campus
and Casino

o   Ho-Chunk
    settlements

Native nations in Wisconsin today
AMELIA JANES/MIKE GALLAGHER, MIDWEST EDUCATIONAL GRAPHICS, BASED ON A MAP BY
JUDY PATENAUDE

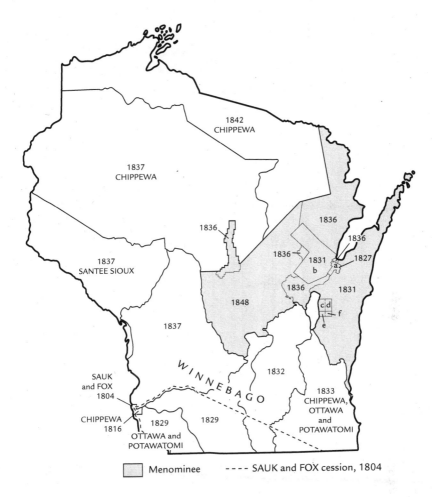

| Menominee | ---- SAUK and FOX cession, 1804 |

Native land cessions in Wisconsin. (a) Land ceded by the Ojibwe, Menominee, and Ho-Chunk in 1827 for use by the New York Indians; because of irregularities in the treaty, the Menominee who were actually resident in the area in 1827 repudiated any claim by the New York Indians. In 1831, the area marked (b) was ceded by the Menominee for use by the New York Indians. The present Oneida reservation was granted in the southeastern end of this same tract in 1838. Meanwhile, in 1831, the Stockbridge-Munsee and Brothertown were granted areas (c) and (d). In 1839, they ceded the eastern half (e) of their total holdings; in 1848 they ceded the western half (f). At that time, the Brothertown opted for citizenship, but the Stockbridge-Munsee chose to remain under federal jurisdiction. Like a number of other Wisconsin tribes, they were supposed to move to a reservation in Minnesota, but this plan was not carried out, and in 1856 the Stockbridge received their present reservation. (The dates of cession are those when treaties were signed; ratification by the US Senate often occurred a year or more later.)
AMELIA JANES/MIKE GALLAGHER, MIDWEST EDUCATIONAL GRAPHICS, BASED ON A MAP BY
JUDY PATENAUDE

a different picture of the forces and events impacting the Oneida's move to Wisconsin, in which Williams was only one factor. These documents are found in the journals of Euro-American treaty negotiators, Senate documents, and letters submitted to the secretary of war and the president. The documents have been preserved, generally on microfilm, and are essential to this book.

The purpose of this research was not to take sides nor to create controversy, but to show the interactions and what happened in the voices of the Indigenous nations involved, in their own words whenever possible.

In rendering the speeches of the Indigenous nations, I have included the complete text. Some of the speeches and letters are handwritten, which made them difficult to decipher. An ellipsis (. . .) indicates where the writing is illegible; a bracketed question mark [?] indicates cases where handwriting or flaws in the documents made transcribing challenging. I have captured dashes and surrounding space and instances of underlining as true to the original documents as possible. I have left spelling and capitalization errors and inconsistencies as they appear in the documents, making corrections or bracketed insertions only where needed for comprehension. The names of many of the Native people mentioned were spelled a variety of ways (for example, Oshkosh, Oash-kosh, Oush-kosh, etc.); I have left them as they were spelled in the source documents.

STRUCTURE OF THE BOOK

This book begins by identifying the Indigenous nations involved in making Indian nation–to–Indian nation treaties in 1821, 1822, 1824, and 1825. From there, I identify the removal policies of both New York State and the US government, the conditions impacting the move of Indigenous nations from New York State to the Green Bay area, the parties involved, and the details in Indigenous nation–to–Indigenous nation treaties of 1821, 1822, 1824, and 1825.

The focus then shifts to the years of controversy regarding the 1821 and 1822 treaties, as the United States continued making treaties with other Native nations that basically ignored the Indian nation–to–Indian nation treaties that had been made for the same lands. The Menominee thought they had agreed to *share* the land with the New York Indians, but the New York Indians believed they had *purchased* the land in these treaties. This intense controversy was addressed in the United State treaties with the Menominee in 1825 (Treaty of Prairie du Chien), 1827 (Treaty of Butte des Morts), 1831 (Treaty of Washington), and 1832.

Next I document more treaties with the United States that made provisions for the New York Indians to remove west into Indian Territory. The unratified *Schermerhorn* treaties in 1836 and the ratified United States treaty with the Six Nations at Buffalo Creek in 1838 were made to remove all the New York Indians west of the Mississippi River.

Finally, I cover the US treaties that define the current reservations in Wisconsin. The treaty of February 3, 1838 (Treaty with the Oneida), established the Oneida reservation in Wisconsin, but pressures to move west continued. Treaties established the current reservations in Wisconsin for the Menominee in 1854, the Oneida in 1838, and the Stockbridge in 1856.

THE ISSUES AND CONTROVERSIES

The Menominee and Ho-Chunk (Winnebago) Nations are among the Indigenous peoples of what is now called Wisconsin. In 1821, a treaty was made between the Menominee and Winnebago and the New York Indians granting the New York Indians a small area of land. In 1822, a similar treaty was made between the Menominee and the New York Indians granting a larger area of land. There was considerable tension between the Menominee and Ho-Chunk on the one side and the New York Indians on the other, because they held two completely different perspectives and beliefs on the land transactions in the treaties of 1821 and 1822.

The Menominee and Ho-Chunk were willing to *share* some of their land with the New York Indians, but the New York Indians understood the directions from the US government to mean that they would *purchase* lands from the Menominee and Ho-Chunk for a permanent homeland. This disagreement lasted for years until the land dispute ended in treaties made in 1838.

TREATIES

Treaties are legal documents made between two or more nations. The US Constitution states, in Article VI, paragraph 2:

> This Constitution, and the Laws of the United States which shall be made in Pursuance Thereof; and all Treaties made, or which shall be made, under the Authority of the United States; shall be the supreme Law of the Land; and the Judges in every State shall be bound Thereby, any Thing in the Constitution or Laws of any State to the Contrary notwithstanding.

The Six Nations (Mohawk, Oneida, Onondaga, Cayuga, Seneca, and Tuscarora) made treaties with the British, the Dutch, and the colonies of Pennsylvania, Maryland, and Virginia prior to the American Revolution and the formation of the United States. The New York Indians had vast experience making treaties with the thirteen colonies, dating back to the mid-1700s. The first treaty, the Two Row Wampum, was made in the early 1600s between the Six Nations and the Dutch. The Dutch had proposed they would be the fathers and the Six Nations would be the children. The Six Nations rejected this proposal and explained to the Dutch that their relationship would be as equal brothers.

Treaties with Indigenous nations required interpreters to bridge language barriers. As such, much was either intentionally or unintentionally lost in translation, such as the different understandings of *share* versus *purchase*. Treaties with Indigenous nations usually began with a statement of who was present. Early treaties began with the Indigenous delegate's Indigenous name and the nation they represented. Then an expression of greeting and friendship was usually stated. Next came descriptions of the boundaries of land to be ceded and the terms of payment for those lands in money and goods. The boundaries of the land to be reserved by the Indigenous nation were then outlined. This is significant because so often it is believed that the United States gave land to Indian nations; however, Indigenous leaders always reserved land for their nations through the treaties.

Articles in a treaty make further provisions for annuity payments, reserving hunting and gathering rights in the ceded territory, and funds for schools, churches, saw mills, and grain mills. Despite the United States' purported belief in the separation of church and state, US treaties with Indigenous nations often provided funds to build a Christian church, which supported assimilation policies. Treaties between the US and Indigenous nations were always written by the US and did not always reflect what Indigenous nations thought they had agreed to in negotiations. The signatures on the treaties are fascinating; they were written phonetically by the person writing the treaty, and an X was placed behind or in the middle of the name by the signer. The signers were typically listed under their specific nation.

Indian Nation–to–Indian Nation Treaties: 1821, 1822, 1824, and 1825

In the early twentieth century, Charles Kappler, an attorney and clerk for the US Senate Committee on Indian Affairs, compiled an extensive collection of Indian treaties. He focused on ratified treaties, meaning those treaties approved first by Congress and then signed by the US president. What makes the 1821 treaty between the Menominee and Ho-Chunk and the New York Indians and the 1822 treaty between the Menominee and the New York Indians unique is that they are classified as "unratified" because they were between Indigenous nations. President James Monroe signed his approval of these two treaties, stating the treaties did not have to go to Congress because they were between Indian nations. His decision was questioned in later treaties and became a point of controversy.

There were other Indian nation–to–Indian nation treaties made between the Brothertown and the Mu-he-con-ne-ok, or Stockbridge Nation, and the St. Regis Nation (1824) and between the First Christian Party of the Oneida Nation and the Tuscarora Nation and Munsee Nation of Indians (1825). Because the Brothertown Nation was not part of the 1821 and 1822 treaties, the 1824 and 1825 treaties were written to include lands for the Brothertown. Like those earlier Indian nation–to–Indian nation treaties, the 1824 and 1825 treaties were not ratified by the US government.

Treaties with New York State and the United States

After the American Revolution, New York State continued to make treaties with individual Native nations. The Oneida lost the bulk of their land, millions of acres, in the 1785 and 1788 treaties with New York State. The United States passed the Trade and Non-Intercourse Act in 1790 to stop the individual states from making treaties. This act stated that only the federal government could make treaties with Indian nations. New York State defied this federal law and continued making treaties with the Oneida after 1790. The Oneida filed land claims in 1970 based on the illegality of the 1795 Treaty with New York State for one hundred thousand acres. The case went to the US Supreme Court, and the Oneida won the case in 1985.

After the 1821, 1822, 1824, and 1825 Indian nation–to–Indian nation treaties, treaties were made with New York State and the United States. All treaties relating to these Indian nations made by the United States were submitted to Congress for ratification. The treaties between the Menominee and the United States in 1825, 1827, 1831, and 1832 were the major treaties to establish boundaries and obtain land.

The Oneida had divided largely into factions by 1820: the First Christian Party and Second Christian Party (also called the Orchard Party), who wanted to move west, and the Pagan Party, who resisted removal and maintained traditions. These opposing forces were often found in Native nations as resistance by those who wanted to keep the culture, land, and traditions versus those who were Christianized and followed European and American ways.

The so-called New York Indians, although negotiating treaties together, signed treaties with their names under the heading for their separate nations. In later years, these nations would once again conduct transactions and treaties as separate nations. The Oneida sent a letter from Duck Creek on August 29, 1836, from Daniel Bread, a leading Oneida voice, to US commissioners and the governor of Wisconsin Territory, Henry Dodge, stating they would no longer conduct business with the New York Indians, but would conduct their own agreements.[1]

REMOVAL

United States Indian policy in the 1820s and 1830s was to remove all Indigenous nations west of the Mississippi River, and treaties were used to facilitate this policy. The official Indian Removal Act was passed in 1830. However, the removal of the New York Indians to the west began in the

1820s. New York State wanted *all* the Six Nations removed from the state. Of these Indigenous nations, only the Oneida actually removed to what is now Wisconsin. The Oneida, Stockbridge, and Brothertown Nations migrated to Menominee and Ho-Chunk lands near Green Bay. The Ogden Land Company (a prominent land speculation company), the US government, New York State, and missionaries colluded to implement the removal of the Oneida, Stockbridge, and Brothertown Nations.

Brief Histories of the Nations

New York Indians

"New York Indians" was a label the US government used to lump together the Indigenous nations it wanted to remove from the state of New York to a permanent homeland on the Menominee and Ho-Chunk lands near Green Bay. In historical documents, the specific Indigenous nations are listed for each transaction, and they signed as individual nations despite the United States' effort to lump them together to negotiate treaties for land. When the New York Indians are listed in documents, the term refers to different combinations of these Indigenous nations: Oneida, Stockbridge-Munsee, Brothertown, St. Regis (Mohawk), Cayuga, Seneca, Onondaga, and Tuscarora.

From examining the signatures on documents, it is apparent that when the Six Nations is referenced it generally means the Oneida. Of these Indigenous nations, only the Oneida, Stockbridge-Munsee, and Brothertown, who were the targets of the US government removal policy, removed to Menominee lands near Green Bay.

On-kwe-hon-weh, the Hotenishoni, our name for ourselves in our language, means "people of the longhouse." We were called the Five Nations by the British and the Iroquois Confederacy by the French. The original nations were the Mohawk, Oneida, Onondaga, Cayuga, and Seneca. The Tuscarora became part of the Iroquois Confederacy in the 1700s after being displaced from the Carolinas, and the Iroquois Confederacy also became known as the Six Nations. At first, several of these nations of the confederacy were involved in the move to what is now Wisconsin, but in the end only the Oneida actually emigrated.

Menominee and Ho-Chunk Nations

The Menominee (people of the wild rice) and the Ho-Chunk (people of the sacred voice, or big voice) are the aboriginal inhabitants of central and southern Wisconsin and have been here, according to their creation stories, since the beginning of time. Menominee lands consisted of approximately ten million acres that stretched from the Menominee River in the north to Milwaukee in the south, and from the Door Peninsula in the east to the Mississippi River in the west. The Menominee had many villages, and each village had head chiefs who would meet in council to make decisions. When there was an issue that impacted the entire Menominee Nation, the head chiefs who were responsible for government gathered to make decisions.[2] In later years, the US disregarded the Menominee government by making treaties without all the designated chiefs; in some cases the United States appointed people to be chiefs who would sign their treaties. In 1820, Reverend Jedidiah Morse described the Menominee as living in "ten villages, north-west of Green Bay, on Menomine river, which is their north-east boundary, but chiefly on Fox river, on and near Winebago Lake. A few were scattered at Prairie du Chien, Upper and Lower Mississippi, and at Milwakie, on the west shore of Lake Michigan." Morse counted 3,900 Menominee at that time and noted,

> The Menominee claim the whole of the waters of Green Bay, with its islands. On its north-west shores, and on Fox river, they claim from the entrance of Menomine river, in length, one hundred and twenty miles, south-west and north-east; and in breadth sixty miles. On the south-east shore of the Bay, and on Fox River, from the river Rouge, or Red River, to the Grand Cockalaw, a distance of forty-five miles, and twenty-four in breadth.[3]

The Menominee had made only one treaty of peace and friendship with the United States by 1817. The next treaty that would have relinquished their lands was made in 1820 by the Indian agent John Bowyer. This treaty was never ratified. When the first treaty of 1821 was made between the Menominee and Winnebago and the New York Indians, both the Menominee and Winnebago participated, which shows a governmental relationship between these Indigenous nations. The second treaty, made in 1822, was between the Menominee and the New York Indians.

Members of the Menominee made speeches stating their opposition to the treaties. Afterward, they expressed their belief that they did not sell the land, stating that the proper chiefs were not present at the treaty making, and their understanding was they were *sharing the land* with the New York Indians. The Menominee have a word in their language that means to "sit down upon," which indicates sharing. Another perspective was that the Menominee and Winnebago thought they got a good deal just for sharing lands with the New York Indians. They had no notion that the treaties, as written, said they had ceded the land in sale.

Andy Thundercloud, a Ho-Chunk elder, describes the Ho-Chunk as "one of two of the First nations of Wisconsin with an oral history that places their origin in Wisconsin at Moogasuc, or the Red Banks," which is just north of Green Bay. "The Ho-Chunk Nation's ten million acres of ancestral land, between the Mississippi and Rock Rivers," Thundercloud says, "were recognized in treaties between the United States and the Ho-Chunk Nation." Thundercloud describes Ho-Chunk land as stretching from the Door County peninsula south to Chicago and west to the Mississippi. The United States forcibly removed the Ho-Chunk west, to Minnesota, South Dakota, and Nebraska, but they always came back to their lands in Wisconsin. Thundercloud explains that today, "The Ho-Chunk Nation is not located on a reservation or a single continuous land base in Wisconsin but rather, the Ho-Chunk Nation owns land in 14 counties is Wisconsin." [4]

The Ho-Chunk played a major role in the negotiation with the Menominee and the New York Indians in 1821. They would be negotiators in later treaties alongside US commissioners, as the US insisted on establishing land boundaries between the First Nations in what would become Wisconsin.

Oneida Nation

The Oneida Nation is one of the six member nations of the Haudenosaunee (Six Nations/Iroquois Confederacy), along with the Mohawk, Onondaga, Cayuga, Seneca, and Tuscarora. The fifty chiefs of the confederacy hold Grand Council meetings at Onondaga. The Oneida have nine chiefs, three from the Turtle Clan, three from the Bear Clan, and three from the Wolf

Clan. Their homelands once covered approximately six million acres in central New York State from the St. Lawrence River to the Pennsylvania border.

Today, there are three places where the Oneida live due to the impact of treaties and US Indian policies: New York State, Wisconsin, and Canada. The Oneida Nation in Wisconsin is the largest, with seventeen thousand people. The Canadian Oneida are next with about five thousand people, and those in New York State are the smallest in number, with about a thousand. Cultural continuity is evident in the documents that show we did not leave our traditions, our language, nor our culture behind. Historical documents verify that after our move we continued to govern our nation with chiefs, we had our clans, and we continued speaking our language. Our economy continued with growing corn, beans, and squash. The impact of moving to lands near Green Bay created a division between the people who wanted to remove and those who wanted to stay in New York State.

Stockbridge and Munsee Nations

The Muh-he-con-ne-ok Nation, from the New England area along the Hudson River, became known as the Stockbridge-Munsee Band of Mohican Indians. They have also been called the Mohican, Mahikan, Housatonic Indians, and River Indians. The Munsee Nation was a band of the Delaware Nation.

After the American Revolution, in which the Stockbridge sided with the colonists, and with pressure from white settlers, they moved to lands that were part of the Oneida Nation. According to one scholar, "The Stockbridges decided to move because of the terrible losses during the war, the takeover of Stockbridge by whites, and the Stockbridges' susceptibility to the vices of their white neighbors. At the invitation of the Oneidas, they moved to Oneida Creek, New York, in the mid-1780s and established New Stockbridge."[5] The land granted to the Stockbridge by the Oneida consisted of an area five to seven miles square.[6]

In 1817 and 1818, a group of Stockbridge, under the leadership of John Metoxen, emigrated to Miami Indian lands in White River, Indiana, only to find that the Miami had made a treaty with the United States for the lands on which the Stockbridge were to settle.[7] Due to these events, the Stockbridge were ready, and encouraged by the federal government, to join the New York Indians in efforts to obtain land near Green Bay. Accordingly, "in 1821, [Hendrick] Aupaumut's son, Solomon, took a small group to Wisconsin, where they settled on Menominee lands and were joined by others from Indiana and New York. In 1828, land was purchased for them on the Fox River, and in 1829, the year before Aupaumut's death, the last Stockbridges, including Aupaumut himself, removed to the West."[8] The Stockbridge continued making treaties for lands in Wisconsin until 1856.

Brothertown Nation

The Brothertown Nation consists of six nations from along the East Coast and Long Island that were so devasted by the invasion of white settlers, disease, and war that they joined together to form the Brothertown Nation. The nations and their original locations were

> Mohegan—Mohegan, Connecticut
> Montaukett—Montauk, New York (Long Island)
> Narragansett—Charleston, Rhode Island
> Niantic—Rhode Island and Connecticut
> Pequot—Mashantucket and Stonington, Connecticut
> Tunxis—Farmington, Connecticut

The Brothertown Nation moved to New York State in 1785 to lands granted to them by the Oneida. The Brothertown then purchased a small tract of land from the lands the Oneida had ceded to the Stockbridge.

Decades later, the Brothertown became one of the Indigenous nations to emigrate to Wisconsin. Under pressure from the United States to remove west, the Brothertown became US citizens in 1839 "to prevent removal and establish their community" as a permanent "resting place for [themselves] and posterity."[9] Doing this meant that the Brothertown were no longer recognized as an Indian nation by the US government. On March 3, 1839, they were made citizens by congressional legislation, which allotted their lands to individuals. To this day, the Brothertown have been seeking federal recognition as an Indian nation, but they have never lost their identity as the Brothertown Nation, as they continue to hold tribal council meetings and function as a nation.

Relationships among the New York Indian Nations

The specific nations of New York Indians varied as delegates from several nations were involved in different trips and treaties. As land was acquired in the Green Bay area, these nations settled as separate nations on lands acquired in treaties.

It is interesting to know that these nations had been separately conducting their own treaties until 1821, when the United States and New York State began calling them the New York Indians for the purposes of removal. They negotiated treaties as the New York Indians, yet kept their identities as distinct, separate nations. The Oneida had been making treaties with New York State from 1785 into the 1840s that were illegal and took millions of acres, eventually reducing Oneida lands to only thirty-two acres. The Stockbridge had been negotiating for land on their own up to June 9, 1821, when they requested delegates to go to Green Bay to procure land. The Stockbridge thought they had obtained land and began to move to White River, Indiana, only to discover the land had been sold before they arrived.

A relationship among the Oneida, Stockbridge, and Brothertown had been established in New York State, as the Oneida shared their lands with the Stockbridge and Brothertown after the American Revolution. In the 1788 Oneida treaty with New York State, provisions were made for the Stockbridge and Brothertown:

> and further notwithstanding any reservations of lands to the
> Oneidas for their own use, the New England Indians (now settled
> at Brothertown under the pastoral care of the Rev. Samson Occom)
> and their posterity forever, and the Stockbridge Indians and their
> posterity forever are to enjoy their settlements on the lands heretofore
> given to them by the Oneida for that purpose, that is to say, a tract
> two miles in breadth and three miles in length for the New England
> Indians, and a tract of six miles square for the Stockbridge Indians.[10]

On December 2, 1794, the United States made a treaty with the Oneida, the Tuscarora, and the Stockbridge dwelling in Oneida country. This treaty was based on the recognition that these nations had been allies to the colonists during the American Revolution, and the United States acknowledged "their obligation to these faithful friends and promised to reward them." The amount of five thousand dollars was to be distributed among the Oneida, Tuscarora, and Stockbridge Nations. Provisions were made to build a grist mill and saw mill with teachers for three years. One thousand dollars was applied to build a church at Oneida. This treaty ended any further claims.

The signatures on this treaty are significant because the Wolf, Turtle, and Bear are the clans of the Oneida, and the chiefs signed the treaty by clan.

Wolf Tribe
Odotsaihte, his x mark
Konnoquenyau, his x mark
Head sachems of the Oneidas
John Skenendo, eldest war chief, his x mark

Bear Tribe
Lodowik Kohsauwetau, his x mark
Cornelius Kauhiktoton, his x mark
Thos. Osauhataugaunlot, his x mark
War chiefs

Turtle Tribe
Shonohleyo, his x mark
Peter Konnauterlook, sachem, his x mark
Daniel Teouneslees, son of Skenendo, war chief, his x mark

Tuscaroras
Thaulondauwaugon, sachem, his x mark
Kanatjogh, or Nichols Cusick, war chief, his x mark

Witness to the signing and sealing of the agent of the United States, and of the chiefs of the Oneida and Tuscarora nations: S. Kirkland, James Dean, Interpreter

Witnesses to the signing and sealing of the four chiefs of the
Stockbridge Indians, whose names are below: Saml. Kirkland, John
Sergeant.

Stockbridge Indians
Hendrick Aupaumut (L.S.)
Joseph Quonney (L.S.)
John Konkapot (L.S.)
Jacob Konkapot (L.S.)[11]

INDIGENOUS DIPLOMACY AND PROTOCOL

Indigenous diplomacy and diplomatic protocol were required at the signing of treaties made between Indian nations, and later with the Dutch, the
English, the British colonies, and the United States. Generally, writers have
glossed over the diplomacy used to conduct meetings with Native nations
and dismissed the protocols as not important, but there are references to
Indigenous diplomatic protocol that clearly illustrate Indigenous protocols continued. The early colonists and governmental officials did adapt
to the proper procedures for conducting meetings with Native nations, as
evidenced in Benjamin Franklin's account of treaties from 1736 to 1762.

Two Row Wampum
The first treaty, the Two Row Wampum, the Six Nations made with the
Dutch in the early 1600s. The metaphors used in this agreement continue
to be used to this day.

The Friendship Between the Indian and His White Brother

The On-kwe-hon-weh of the Hotenishoni made a treaty with the
early Dutch people when they came to this continent. The On-
kwehon-weh lived very happy enjoying life the way the Creator
intended. The On-kwe-hon-weh was wholly dependent on nature
until the coming of the Dutch people. The Dutch people learned
the customs, art work, and how to get along with the On-kwe-hon-
weh. The Dutch and the On-kwe-hon-weh became friends so they

decided to make a treaty and agreed to continue in friendship. Then the time came when the Dutch said, we shall pronounce ourselves in friendship.

The On-kwe-hon-weh called the Dutch "white people." The Onkwe-hon-weh held a special council informing the people that the time has come for the white race and the On-kwe-hon-weh to continue as friends so that all the people may walk upon this earth in peace and love one another. When the On-kwe-hon-weh and the white people understood this kind of friendship it was made known by both races that the day has come to make friendship.

The On-kwe-hon-weh said, we now have an understanding about our friendship so that the generations to come will also know about our friendship. The whiteman replied, I will put our friendship in writing. The On-kwe-hon-weh replied, this is good, but one thing we must remember which will be passed on to the next generation to come. They agreed.

The whiteman said, how is the On-kwe-hon-weh going to describe our friendship? The On-kwe-hon-weh replied, we must thank the Creator for all his creations, and greet one another by holding hands to show the covenant chain that binds our friendship so that we may walk upon this earth in peace, trust, love, and friendship, and we may smoke the sacred tobacco in a pipe which is a symbol of peace.

The whiteman said he would respect the On-kwe-hon-weh's belief and pronounce him as a son. The On-kwe-hon-weh replied, I respect you, your belief, and what you say; you pronounced yourself as my father and this I do not agree because the father can tell his son what

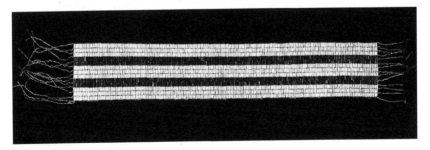

A Two Row Wampum belt
TWO ROW WAMPUM BELT REPLICA BY FORREST BROOKS

to do and also can punish him. I suggest that you pronounce me as your brother.

The whiteman said, the symbol of this covenant is a three-link chain which binds this agreement made by us, and there is nothing that will come between us to break the links of this chain. The Onkwe-hon-weh replied, the first link shall stand for friendship, the second link will stand for our good minds, and the third link shall mean there will always be peace between us. This is confirmed by us. The On-kwe-hon weh said, this friendship shall be everlasting and the younger generation will know and the rising faces from Mother Earth will benefit by our agreement.

The whiteman said, what symbols will you go by? The On-kwehon-weh replied, we will go by these symbols: when the Creator made Mother Earth, man was created to walk upon this earth to enjoy all nature's fruits, saying no one shall claim Mother Earth except the rising faces which are to be born. (1) As long as the sun shines upon this earth, that is how long our agreement will stand; (2) as long as the water still flows; and (3) as long as the grass grows green at a certain time of the year. Now we have symbolized this agreement and it shall be binding forever as long as Mother Earth is still in motion. We have finished and we understand what we have confirmed and this is what our generation should know and learn not to forget.

The whiteman said, I confirm what you have said and this we shall always remember. What we do about our own ways of belief, we shall both respect having our own rights and power. The Onkwe-hon-weh replied, I have a canoe and you have a vessel with sails and this is what we shall do: I will put in my canoe my belief and laws; in your vessel you will put your belief and laws; all of my people in my canoe, your people in your vessel; we shall put these boats in the water and they shall always be parallel; as long as there is Mother Earth, this will be everlasting.

The whiteman said, what will happen supposing your people will like to go into my vessel? The On-kwe-hon-weh replied, if this happens, then they will have to be guided by my canoe. Now the whiteman understands this agreement.

The whiteman said, what will happen if any of our people may someday want to have one foot in each of the boats that we placed parallel? The On-kwe-hon-weh replied, if this so happens that my people may wish to have their feet in each of the two boats, there will be a high wind and the boats will separate and the person that has his feet in each of the boats shall fall between the boats; and there is no living soul who will be able to bring him back to the right way given by the Creator but only one: the Creator himself.

The On-kwe-hon-weh called the wampum belt "Gus-when-ta." The two paths signifies the whiteman's laws and beliefs and the other signifies the On-kwe-hon-weh's laws and beliefs. The white wampum background signifies purity, good minds and peace, and they should not interfere with one another's way.

The whiteman said, I understand. I confirm what you have said, that this will be everlasting as long as there is Mother Earth. We have confirmed this and our generation to come shall never forget what we have agreed. Now it is understood that we shall never interfere with one another's belief or laws for generations to come.

The On-kwe-hon-weh said, what we agreed upon we shall renew this every so often so that the covenant chain made between us shall always be clean from dust and rust. We shall renew our agreements and polish the covenant and when we get together to renew our agreements, we shall have interpreters; we will dress the same way as when we met so that our people will know who we are. I will put on my buckskin clothing, you will dress the same way you dressed when you first came to our people, the On-kwe-hon-weh. They both confirmed this. So they completed the treaty of the two partied.[12]

The so-called silver chain treaty of April 21, 1613, was written by the Dutch to document the same meeting. This agreement focused on trade between the nations, purchase of land and goods, and disputes that would be heard by their commissioners. There are only two references similar to the Two Row Wampum. First, "that we the participants will keep one another in case of lack of food and if this is not sufficient will help one another necessaries." The second reference says this agreement will "continue and to maintain as long as the grass will be green and as proof of honour and affection we exchange a silver chain to fathom of sailor's cloth."

The metaphors of the Two Row Wampum, brothers, peace and friendship, and "as long as the grass is green" continued to be cited in treaty negotiations and historical documents. Because silver tends to rust, many meetings began with "polishing the chain" and renewing the chain of friendship as part of the purpose of the negotiation. Franklin documented the extensive use of these metaphors in *Indian Treaties printed by Ben Franklin, 1736–1762*.

Diplomatic Protocol

As participants arrived at the meeting place, they were fed and provided a place to rest, as was the custom of many Indigenous nations. The process of conducting meetings began with opening the meeting with the thanksgiving address, which gives thanks to all of creation. There could also be a burning of sacred tobacco. The nations formally greeted each other and acknowledged all of those present. During the meeting, one person stood up to speak and no one interrupted the presentation. Once the speaker completed his statement, there was an exchange of wampum and/or hides to confirm the truth of the statements made and the honesty of the speaker. Then the issue and purpose of the meeting was stated, and the proper person from each side responded. This discussion went back and forth, with the receiver of the statement reiterating the speaker's main points to confirm the message was understood correctly. Once decisions were reached, the decision was restated to affirm understanding, and wampum was used to confirm the agreement. The meeting was closed with the thanksgiving address, and everyone ate.

This protocol was documented in early treaties between the Six Nations and the colonists, but it began to fade after the American Revolution, though the Covenant Chain is mentioned in the journal of Thomas L. McKenney, the superintendent of Indian Affairs, regarding the treaty of 1827. The reference indicates a long-ago agreement between the Six Nations and the Chippewa.

Each of the Indigenous nations involved in the treaties had well-established creation stories, clans, governments, and diplomacy. The lands to which the New York Indians were to be removed were the Indigenous lands of the Menominee and Ho-Chunk Nations.

The conditions that impacted all of the New York Indian nations prior to emigration included loss of land through treaty, invasions by white settlers, missionary influence, a desire to get their people away from the effects of liquor, and a desire to have permanent lands for a home for their people. Both New York State and the United States wanted to remove all of the Six Nations to the west.

1

Before the First
Journey West

By the 1820s, the New York Indians had lost much of their land in treaties with New York State and the US government. In 1788 alone, the
Oneidas signed a treaty with New York State that ceded millions of acres
and left them a land base of only 250,000 acres. Oneida perspectives on
relocation and removal speak to the loss of land in this treaty and others
like it, in addition to the loss of the natural environment the Oneida needed
for survival and the selling of alcohol to Indians by white traders. The
Oneida and the Six Nations made their views on relocation widely known,
with some arguing for and some arguing against relocation and removal.[1]

Requests to Move West

There are differing, sometimes conflicting accounts chronicling the New
York Indians and their move west. Arguments for relocation were generally made by the US government, land speculators, and missionaries. The
New York Indians (mostly the First Christian Party) asked to move west to
secure a more permanent land base and to get away from alcohol and the
Euro-Americans who traded it. Eleazer Williams wrote of the New York Indians, "The Chiefs and sensible men among these tribes, to a great extent,
feel that a change in their situation has become necessary, that they must
quit the hunter, and adopt the agricultural state."[2] In a letter to Secretary
of War William H. Crawford, several chiefs of the Six Nations asked the

1

secretary, among other questions, if the government would consent to their move. The chiefs wrote:

> The Sachems and Chiefs of the Six Nations are however aware of the impropriety of forming any definitive resolutions on a measure so materially affecting the future condition or welfare of their people without the advice and approbation of the government of the US that has so long cherished and protected them, and to which they are closely united by the brightest chain of peace and friendship.
>
> The object of this memorial is therefore to enquire. First, whether the government will consent to our leaving our present habitations, and removing into the neighborhood of our western Brethren? Secondly, whether if we should obtain either by gift or purchase, from our western friends, a seat on their lands, the government will acknowledge our title in the same manner as it now acknowledges it in those from whom we may receive it? And thirdly, whether our removal will be considered as changing in any manner the relations now subsisting between our Tribes and the Government, or whether they will be permitted to continue the same; and existing treaties still remain in force, and annuities paid as heretofore? We send this by our approved friends, Gen. Porter, and Mr. Granger, and Capt. Parish.
>
> After the strong and repeated proofs given by the Six Nations of their friendship and attachment for the US, the Sachems and Chiefs feel assured that their wish of removing to a more distant part of the country will not be attributed to any dissatisfaction towards their white Brethren. – And they are persuaded that no political consequences injurious to the US will result from such removal. On the contrary they cannot but hope that the representations they will be able to make to their western brethren of the friendly disposition of the people towards the natives under their protection, and of the honor and good faith always observed by the Government in its dealings with us, will greatly tend to render their friendship permanent and their fidelity secure.[3]

Crawford responded that their "Great Father the President" approved the Six Nations' requests. Crawford as well relayed that in petitioning for land in the west, the Six Nations should "define limits of the seats which you are about to obtain from your brethren in the west, and furnish the government with its metes and bounds so that in treaties to be held hereafter with other tribes, your land may not be granted away by them."[4] That Crawford and President James Madison specifically instructed the Six Nations to track the "metes and bounds" of whatever land they obtained so that it might be secured is important. Most Indian treaties established vague land boundaries that led to future confusion, dissatisfaction, and the removal of Indigenous peoples from lands they were promised by the government and held legally.

Crawford authorized the Six Nations' move west in a letter. He wrote to the Six Nations:

The friends of the New York Indians have presented a long "appeal" in support of the "rights" of those tribes, for the consideration of the President and Senate of the United States. They have dated their determination to remove from the State of New York as early as 1810. The evidence they have produced then goes to show, that their "wants and wishes" were expressed to President Madison in 1815, through their friends Gen. Porter, Mr. Granger, and Capt. Parish, of the State of New York, which solicited permission to remove "into the neighborhood of their western brethren." This appeal elicited a reply, signed by Mr. Crawford, as Secretary of War, dated Feb. 12, 1816, granting their request.[5]

THE OGDEN LAND COMPANY

The Ogden Land Company of New York State purchased the preemptory rights to Six Nations lands in 1810. This meant that the Ogden Land Company had first rights to buy land from the Six Nations, which the company intended to do.[6] Hoping to make a large profit, the Ogden Land Company had every incentive, then, to push the New York Indians westward, and they had approval from the War Department to do it. As A. G. Ellis wrote of the plan, it "was pondered with great care, thoroughly matured, decided and acted upon by the Ogden company, with equal skill and vigor."[7]

In the early 1800s, companies began to exert more pressure on tribes to sell their lands, aiming to take over what remained of the Six Nations' territories in New York. In 1810, the Holland Land Company, which had secured the preemptory rights to purchase millions of acres of Indian land in Massachusetts and New York State, sold its preemptory rights to David A. Ogden of the Ogden Land Company for fifty cents an acre. By 1817, the Ogden Land Company had succeeded in extinguishing the New York Indians' title to all but the reservations in Cattaraugus, Alleghany, Tonawanda, Tuscarora, and Buffalo. Efforts were then made by the Ogden Land Company, with the consent and cooperation of the War Department, to persuade the New York Indians to vacate and move west.[8]

Government Officials and Missionaries Support the Move West

Lewis Cass, the governor of Michigan Territory, supported the New York Indians in their move to Green Bay, believing that the "civilized" New York Indians would stand as a buffer against the western tribes, including the Menominee and Winnebago. Yet for all the enthusiasm that men such as Cass and Ogden showed in the forced relocation of the New York Indians, many Indigenous nations in Wisconsin expressed some hesitation. John Kinzie, an Indian agent based in Chicago, wrote Cass to explain that the "Potawatomies, Chippeways, & Ottawas, who jointly claim that part of the Territory required for the future residence of the Six Nations of Indians now residing in the State of New York," are not willing to make decisions without the majority of their nation present. This is standard governmental procedure for Native nations. Kinzie added, though, that "I have merely spoken to a few chiefs whom I consider as having the most influence, who appear to be well disposed toward receiving the Six Nations among them."[9]

Like those in government, Christian missionaries encouraged the New York Indians to go west. Many missionaries were convinced that a move to Wisconsin would "civilize" the New York Indians, who would in turn civilize the western tribes. The US government was largely supportive of the missionaries' goals. Reverend Jedidiah Morse, with the American Board of Commissioners of Foreign Missions, who in 1820 was sent to Green Bay, wrote, "The aid given by the government to religious associations, who have made establishments for the improvement of several portions of these Indians, appears to have been judiciously bestowed, and probably is the full proportion of the fund placed at the disposal of the President for the civilization of the Indians."[10] Williams expressed a similar opinion when he wrote

> The plan of collecting the Indians, somewhere in the westward now . . . into one body for the purpose of educating them for religious instruction, would be more convenient & at less expense. The best & most successful means which could be employed by government & religious societies to civilize the Indians, was to born them to cultivate the soil, as the white do.[11]

The policy of civilization included religious instruction and teaching Indian men how to plow fields, build fences, and raise cattle. Gender roles also changed, as men took to agricultural work, which had been the domain of Iroquois women, while women were taught to stay in the house to cook and perform other domestic chores. Traditionally, men provided food from the woods, and women harvested corn, beans, and squash—known as the three sisters. Women also gathered plants for food and medicine. A good example that highlights how labor roles were equally balanced traditionally is found in corn soup, a staple of the New York Indians' diet. Women provided the corn and beans, and men provided the meat, making corn soup a complete protein. Thus, civilization was a blatant attack on the Oneida's way of life and sought to destroy the balance in men's and women's roles.

ELEAZER WILLIAMS

Reverend Eleazer Williams was commissioned in 1816 to be a catechist and lay reader at the Episcopal Church mission serving the Oneida. The son of a reverend and educated in New England, Williams played a significant role in Oneida removal. Ellis writes of Williams that in "1818 he began growing the plan with the Oneida and all of the Six Nations to move westward and form a grand confederacy near Green Bay."[12] Williams estimated that four-fifths of the Oneida, who numbered about fifteen hundred people, were pagan when he arrived in Green Bay in 1816, "and held Christianity in utter

A clergyman of mixed ancestry who often represented the St. Regis (Mohawk) during treaty negotiations, Eleazer Williams colluded with the Ogden Land Company to remove the New York Indians to Green Bay. WHI IMAGE ID 93231

Lewis Cass, governor of Michigan Territory 1813–1831 and US Secretary of War 1831–1836. WHI IMAGE ID 2574

abhorrence."[13] He boasted that within several weeks of his arrival, many of the Oneida had become converts. Williams had more influence on the younger men, who were more willing to relocate.[14] When he applied to the War Department seeking approval for a journey to Green Bay with twenty men from the Six Nations, he did so "by holding out dazzling promises of future glory and aggrandizement," and the government granted him its support.[15]

Williams had grandiose plans to move the Six Nations west. There he planned to "unite them in one grand confederacy of cantons, but all under one federal head; the government to be a mixture of civil, military, and ecclesiastic, the latter to be pre-eminent."[16] He saw himself as the leader of this new confederacy and presented his plan to the chiefs, but the older chiefs were not impressed, though Williams did capture the interest of several of the younger chiefs. Ellis notes that Williams presented his plan throughout the Six Nations and "enticed a few young men of each tribe to enter into his scheme."[17]

Collusion between the War Department, President Monroe, mission-aries, and the Ogden Land Company is evident in Williams's papers. It is clear from his statements that he was paid by the Ogden Land Company to remove the New York Indians to the Green Bay area. He had full knowl-edge of the complicity between the Ogden Land Company and the War Department, and Williams's writings show that he went to Washington seeking permission to explore the area near Green Bay. In Washington, Williams met

the Hon. Mr. Calhoun then in the War Department. And by whose invitation, I visited Washington during the winter 1820. The various interviews I had with the Secretary of War on the subject of my inquiry were so satisfactory as to relieve my mind from the anxiety which I had . . . on the subject . . . information as to ultimate object of the government upon her present policy of removing the Eastern Indians to the west. I was kindly entertained by President Monroe and the Secretary of War while in Washington, and by several members of Congress.[18]

Williams also wrote that:

On my return to New York, I had several interviews with Thomas L. Ogden, Esq., a gentleman of great respectability, whose land interest was involved with a certain company who had purchased the preemption right to the Senecas lands in the State of New York. . . . The plan of the government of removing the New York Indians to the west, was to them a favorable omen.[19]

A letter from Charles C. Trowbridge provides clear evidence of the collusion among Williams, the US government, the Ogdens, and Cass. Trowbridge was secretary to Cass and was assigned to be the US negotia-tor for the 1821 treaty. In a letter to Lyman C. Draper, Trowbridge wrote of the Six Nations that the government was "desirous to see the remnants of those tribes 'comfortably settled in some fertile spot' so far away from the . . . White men 'that they would never be disturbed.'"[20] Much later, Williams wrote to the Ogden Land Company in 1833 to complain that he had not been paid enough by the company for his part in Oneida removal:

> I have relied much upon the promises of the different trustees ever since in 1819 for assistance in the "great cause" in which I have been engaged and ultimately with a liberal and handsome compensation. I have, however, found to my mortification that instead of receiving that support which I expected, (altho, an interest of their's nearly half-million, as it is aid at stake) I have been compelled to spend all the property I had. To effect the treaty in 1821 and the following year, I expended a little sum of my own money. I have been often surprised that a business of this magnitude of importance to the company should have been transacted for a sum so much less than that which the present Secretary of War stated to the Hon. D.A. Ogden, who in his letter (dated at Detroit January 29, 1829) says, It is all important that four or five thousand dollars should be reserved from the consideration money, to be distributed in presents to the Indians. Without this little can be expected. With it everything may be hoped.
>
> Now instead of this sum of twelve thousand dollars, as it was explicitly stated to me by Mr. Ogden at Utica in June 1820, was the sum anticipated by the company would be necessary to procure a location of the Senecas. . . . And on my part, in consequence of the past promises of the trustees of the assistance which was to be given to me (from time to time) and 'ultimately, a liberal and handsome compensation,' I have endeavored to my utmost to save the expenses of the company by blending the interest of the Senecas with the other branches of the six nations, the expenses of the company have been greatly lessened and their object has been attained at the expense of other tribes. I have endeavored to serve them more than 12 years and actually left the pleasant valley of Oneida for this western wilderness and have suffered much in health and reputation.[21]

As Williams's letter highlights, pressure was exerted on the Oneida by the US government's removal policies, by New York State's efforts to move the Six Nations west, and the use of the treaty process to take Oneida land. The Ogden Land Company, New York State, the federal government, churches, and Williams conspired to remove the Six Nations to Green Bay.

Oneida Perspectives on the Move West

What were the Oneida thinking, discussing, and experiencing that made them decide to move to Wisconsin? Many factors impacted their eventual relocation, three of which are explained in the following pages.

Invitation from the Western Tribes

Before 1812, the western tribes, specifically the Menominee, extended an invitation to the eastern tribes to live in or near their territories. The War of 1812, however, delayed or put an end to any thought the eastern tribes had to move west. Williams provided a brief history of this invitation in a letter addressed to "Respected Madam":

> In regard to the removal somewhere to the westward was not a new subject to the Oneida nor the Six Nations; but that this subject had often been discussed in their general council since 1812. At that time, they had a special invitation from the western tribes to leave their current residence and accept a location which they were ready to present, if they will accept of it. This was received with great cordiality by the confederates [?] but the Declaration of War on the part of the U. States against Great Britain prevented further negotiation. This subject was however revived by them after the war. . . . to it delegation from the Six Nations with the U. States agent met in council with their western Brethren during the years of 1816, 7 & 8. But the interests & policy of the State [of] Indiana & the Territory of Michigan. . . . thawed [?] the view of the two Indian parties.[22]

Loss of Natural Environment and Economy

With the loss of land there was most certainly a loss of the natural environment needed to support the Oneida people both culturally and economically. Euro-Americans were cutting trees in large numbers to build towns, to clear fields for planting, and to send back to Europe. The trees provided the natural environment for plants, animals, fish, and medicines that Oneida people used on a daily basis. The animals were fleeing north where there were more trees, as Williams writes of the Oneida that "their territories had become so limited & scarcity of timber as to foresee that it cannot be long before they must become in want."[23] When a natural environment is disturbed, the entire ecosystem is changed, even destroyed. The natural resources that thrived in those ecosystems were no longer available after colonization, thus negatively impacting the life support systems of the Oneida people.

Oneida Survival

It is very apparent that the Oneidas were worried about having a land base for future generations. By the early 1800s, they had begun to discuss how the Oneida would survive as a nation. Williams wrote his perspective on the survival of the Oneida people to support his plans:

> The novelty of changing the place of residence, which the minds
> of the younger part of the several tribes had been excited, were not
> so easily abated. They saw enough in their present condition, the
> necessity of such a change was impelled by a sense of duty as well
> as interest, to exert, to obtain that which their elders chiefs were
> not able to accomplish in consequence of the policy of the state and
> territorial governments. This subject was actual in agitation among
> them. . . . One thing I had already seen that to save the Oneidas there
> must be change, either the place of residence or their morals. As I had
> already been successful in the latter, so I conjectured they may so still
> be improved as to prevent necessity of the former.[24]

Impact of Alcohol

The sale and consumption of alcohol in the Six Nations was a pressing cause for concern from the onset of settler colonialism. Some Indigenous peoples believed that alcohol was tearing relationships apart and leading to other unwanted behavior. As a result, many felt that the best thing to do would be to stay away from it, as Williams wrote:

> Arrived at Oneida Castle March 23rd, 1816, announced by a crier to
> the Nations. I now discovered for the first time, that the invitation
> my coming thither originated principally from the pagan party of
> the nations whose numbers about six hundred, which is one half of

the nation I had visited back in autumn in 1814. First Christian party more drunkenness than the pagan party at this time. It would seem that the exhortation of the late Allegany Prophet had still restrained the pagan party from running into the same excess with those who bear the honorable name of Christian.[25]

The "Allegany prophet" (Seneca) referred to here is Handsome Lake. In his 1799 vision, he saw what the abuse of alcohol was doing to the people. He established a strict prohibition on drinking alcohol because it was destroying lives. Handsome Lake encouraged people to attend ceremonies, be of a good mind, and not to be involved in negative behaviors. There are many more instructions, and today the Code of Handsome Lake is told over four days among Haudenosaunee nations.[26]

These factors pertaining to quality of life and economics must have driven the Six Nations' decision to move. So often throughout the history of Native peoples along the East Coast of the United States, there is reference to moving farther west to escape the negative impact of the Euro-American ways, including the consumption of alcohol.

Opposition to Removal

On November 11, 1818, some Oneida wrote a petition to the governor of New York State protesting land losses and expressing their opposition to moving west. They reminded the governor that during the American Revolution, the Oneida supported the colonists:

> To his Excellency De Witt Clinton, Esq. Governor of the state of New York.
>
> The Petition of the undersigned Sachems and Warriors of the first and second party of the Oneida nation of Indians,
>
> RESEPCTFULLY SHOWETH,
>
> That for several years past, your petitioners have been much annoyed by the solicitations of interest individuals to sell . . . the remainder of our reservation, and remove to the west. That some individuals of our nation being in favor, but the most respectable part thereof being opposed to this measure, it has become the cause

of much uneasiness, and the source of many quarrels between individuals and the nation; all which your petitioners have submitted to in silence. But latterly the affair has assumed a more serious aspect, as we are indirectly given to understand, that the government of the United States has determined on our removal.

As we have always, since the independence of the United States, supported the character of being faithful friends and allies of the good people of these United States, we feel grieved, that now we should be threatened with expulsion from the contracted remnant of our once extensive reservation – more especially at this time, when we are just beginning to learn the arts of civil society, and taste the sweets of that pure religion which our white brothers have long wished to introduce among us.

We well remember the advice of your excellency's predecessor, the late venerable George Clinton. He, as he knew the service we had rendered the United States in the revolutionary war, respected our nation; and wishing to see us happy, advised us to remain in peace on our reservations, under protection of the state of New York. We venerate his character, as well as his advice: and not feeling at this time ready, or willing to make an immediate removal to the west, we respectfully solicit the patronage and protection of your excellency; and request that (as far as may be proper) you would kindly interfere with the general government, to induce them to allow all reasonable indulgence to your petitions.

And your petitioners, as in duty bound, will every pray, &c.

Oneida Castle, Nov. 11, 1818[27]

Williams was aware of Oneida opposition to relocation. Upon his return from Washington, he described his meeting with the Oneida. He stated in a letter to Right Rev. Jackson Kemper, "As the time of my contemplated departure for the westward, is drawing nigh. . . . You are doubtless apprised of the circumstance of a certain portion of the Oneida being partially opposed to the plan which I had in view. In order, therefore, to give weight to a matter of this importance, and to show them that my going thither has your sanction, it is my wish that you may write to them a friendly letter giving the subject your approbation, and me, orders to proceed."[28]

Williams also wrote:

On my return to the Oneida in a council, I unfolded to them the
views of the General government in regard to their removal to the
west . . . the chiefs and the warriors were divided on the subject.
Many powerful arguments were offered on both sides. The discussion
for two days was animated and interesting in the extreme. The St.
Regis Indians were no less so. The opposition party there were more
powerful, as they were aided by the British agents and romanish
missionaries.[29]

It is clear that much discussion was taking place among the Six Nations
and the Oneida regarding the move west. It seems some of the younger
men, and those of the First Christian Party, were more willing to remove,
but not all the Oneida, nor the Six Nations, were as supportive. Throughout the treaty negotiations, and long after the treaties had been signed,
many continued to oppose relocation and removal.

2

THE FIRST JOURNEY WEST

By 1820, the governor of Michigan Territory, Christian missionaries, and officials in the US government were working together to remove the New York Indians to western lands. An interview with the chiefs and principal men of the Menominee Nation in the summer of 1820 describes their conditions and their wish not to sell their land. Nevertheless, John Bowyer, the Indian agent at Green Bay, was determined to make a treaty to obtain Menominee land and open it to white speculators. Meanwhile, the New York Indians prepared to visit the Green Bay area for the first time.

Lewis Cass was appointed governor of Michigan Territory by President James Monroe in January 1820.[1] In March of that year, Cass wrote to the secretary of war, John C. Calhoun, expressing his opinion that extinguishing Indian title to lands near Green Bay could be accomplished without offering annuities, and he suggested distributing presents. Cass stated it was the policy of the United States to extinguish Indian title to lands before taking resources, as private individuals could not call a council and meet with Indians on their own. Cass suggested that the United States make a treaty with the Menominee to extinguish their land claims because "the application here must be to the tribe, because in all their land, there is a community of interest, which cannot be severed or conveyed by the acts of individuals."[2] He believed, however, that the United States could acquire the land with no annuities and for only a "few trifling presents."[3] Cass understood that the United States needed to make treaties with Indian nations to secure Indian land. Indian nations are and have always been sovereign, and Cass recognized this sovereignty when he noted that a "community of interest" cannot be dealt with economically or politically

14

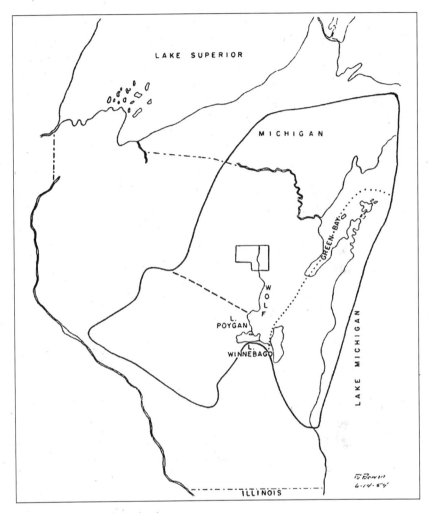

Original Menominee homelands
MENOMINEE HISTORIC PRESERVATION OFFICE

by private citizens. The 1790 Trade and Non-Intercourse Act, which the federal government passed to regulate commerce between Indians and Euro-Americans, established that only the US government could make treaties with Indigenous nations. That Bowyer believed he could obtain Menominee land for far less than its value demonstrates he did not understand or had no regard for the complexities and sovereignty of Indian governments.

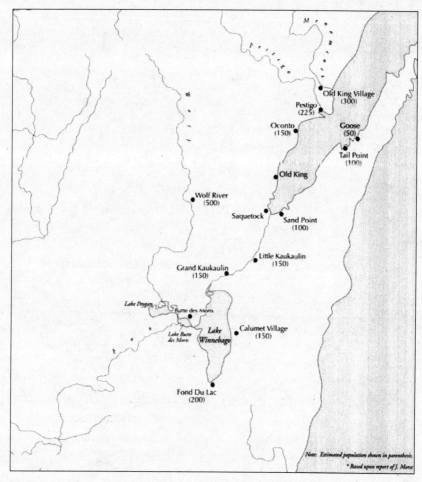

Menominee villages in 1820 (estimated populations shown in parentheses)
ORIGINALLY PUBLISHED *IN FAITH IN PAPER: THE ETHNOHISTORY AND LITIGATION OF UPPER GREAT LAKES INDIAN TREATIES* BY CHARLES CLELAND, COPYRIGHT 2011 UNIVERSITY OF MICHIGAN PRESS

MISSIONARIES AND "CIVILIZATION"

In 1820, Reverend Jedidiah Morse, a geographer and theologian with the American Board of Commissioners of Foreign Missions, applied to the War Department to visit territories in the west to assess the suitability of land there for the New York Indians. Morse stated that his mission was part of a larger attempt by the US government "to attempt the civilization of the Indians generally."[4] Calhoun relayed instructions from Monroe to Morse, who was told to examine the "religious, moral and political view" of the Indian tribes he encountered on his journey.[5] Calhoun further stressed the policy of the US government to open schools for the assimilation and civilization of Indian children.[6] Indeed, Calhoun wrote that "the interesting inquiry remains to be solved, whether such an education would lead them to that state of morality, civilization, and happiness, to which it is the desire of the Government to bring them."[7] Monroe, Calhoun, and Morse each evinced a belief in the superiority and assimilative power of Euro-American civilization that was widely held during the nineteenth century.

That the sovereignty of Indian nations stood as an impediment to civilization was, though perhaps poorly understood by Bowyer and others, a fact Calhoun grasped very well. Referring to Indigenous peoples, he wrote:

> We have always treated them as an independent people; and however insignificant a tribe may become, and however surrounded by a dense white population, so long as there are any remains, it continues independent of our laws and authority. To tribes thus surrounded, nothing can be conceived more opposed to their happiness and civilization than this state of nominal independence.[8]

Calhoun is expressing what was a commonly held opinion, that forcing Native Americans into dependency would lead them to embrace assimilation and civilization. With this attitude often came a sense of racial superiority and blatant condescension, as Calhoun wrote that "it is, however, believed that all difficulties may be surmounted, and this wretched, but in many respects noble race, be ultimately brought within the pale of civilization."[9]

THE BOWYER TREATY

In a letter written to Calhoun on June 10, 1819, Bowyer outlined his attempts to convince the Menominee to sell a portion of their lands. When the Menominee returned from hunting in May, Bowyer called them together and asked "if they were disposed to relinquish their claim to twenty-five or thirty miles square of the lands in the neighbourhood of Fort Howard, for which the United States would Give them a generous price in goods."[10] The Menominee chiefs responded that "they could not at present think of disposing of any of their lands." Moreover, Bowyer told Calhoun, "that I was the first whiteman that had asked their Nation to Sell their lands, that their forefathers had for a long time lived on the lands I had asked them to sell, that they were born on the land & did not like to leave the graves of their forefathers." Bowyer told them the lands he was discussing were now devoid of game and their people were starving and "that every winter since I had been at Green Bay a number of their women and Children had died from hunger and cold, and many more would have died the same way, had I not furnished them with provisions and clothing when they came to me Starving and naked — They acknowledged what I said was very true, but could not agree to sell their lands at this time."[11] Bowyer blamed Menominee opposition to selling land on four chiefs whom he speculated were being influenced by the British. As allies, Bowyer identified eight other chiefs whom he assured Calhoun "are under the protection of the United States" and whom he claimed "are willing to sell some land."[12] That Bowyer adopted this strategy is not surprising, as Indian agents like him often singled out chiefs willing to sign treaties, even if they had no authority to do so.

Calhoun replied on August 24, 1819. "The department is not desirous of obtaining a cession of this tract of country," he told Bowyer, "unless it can be done at a very moderate expense; and you are authorized to treat with the Indians claiming it, only in the event of your being satisfied, that a purchase can be effected for a small consideration." Calhoun complained about the cost of treaty negotiations and instructed Bowyer to restrict expenses to only those spent on the treaty.[13]

Nearly a year later, Bowyer had at last convinced a few Menominee chiefs to sign a treaty for land near Fort Howard. Made on June 23, 1820, just a month before the New York Indians arrived in Detroit, the Bowyer treaty would have exchanged large portions of Menominee land for an annuity of eight hundred dollars. It reserved ten square miles of land for the 236 children of mixed ancestry who had Menominee mothers and English or French fathers. Each child was to receive 160 acres, with the remaining surplus going to the United States. The treaty also reserved 640 acres near "first rapids on Fox River for four children of John Dousman whose property here was destroyed in the late War by the Indians."

Article VI of the treaty secured for the Menominee "the right to hunt on the ceded lands, as stipulated in the treaty of Greenville & gives them leave also to make sugar."[14] The Bowyer treaty clearly favored the US and was specifically written to open Menominee lands to white settlers and traders in the Green Bay area.

The Menominee did not generally favor the Bowyer treaty. Eleazer Williams noted in his journal that "the real chiefs" of the Menominee opposed any loss of land:

Some days previous to our departure from Detroit, Rev. Dr. Noye returned from G. Bay who confirmed the report we had heard as to a tract of land bordering on the mouth of the Fox River. "The real chiefs" says the Rev. Dr. of the nation were so decidedly opposed to the sale of this land, a tract of forty miles square, intersected by the Fox River from its mouth upward that they refused to attend the treaty at the invitation of the agent who, in consequence, was constrained of his own authority to create chiefs to sign his treaty. In this way their lands were sold in opposition to the will of the Nation, though from the face of the treaty, it would appear as if done with their consent. The President in being made acquainted with the facts, laid the treaty aside and it was not ratified.[15]

INTERVIEW WITH THE CHIEFS AND PRINCIPAL MEN OF THE MENOMINEE

Reporting on time spent with the Menominee, Morse empathized that removal would provide the best opportunities and methods to civilize Indigenous peoples. During his journey, Morse met with the Menominee and accounted for one of his meetings in the following passages that recorded an interview conducted in the early summer of 1820:

At this interview, I communicated, at considerable length, the views of the Government, and the design of my mission, and left them to consider my message to them. Two days after, I met them again, and received from the speakers, hereafter named, answers which follow.

The names of three of the Chiefs present are Mau-cau-tau-bee,

aged 22, son of the celebrated Thomaw, a modest, sensible young
man, of good countenance; Sha-kaut-che-o-ke-maw, about the same
age; those are the two first Chiefs of the nation. The name of the
other is I-way-ma-taw. Their speaker, not a Chief, was Aus-kin-naw-
wau-wish, a pleasant, affectionate old man. He said:

"Father, I am happy to see you here to-day, and give you my hand,
as if given to our Great Father the President himself. The Sky is clear."

Pointing to the three Chiefs above named, he said, "These are our
three principal Chiefs, acknowledged to be such by the nation. They
bear the names, and have running in their veins, the blood, of our
former Chiefs.

Father, we are glad to see you. We welcome you here. We are
poor. The Great Spirit put us here in this world, as well as his other
children; and we were first found by the French.

Father, You see your children here before you, full of grief and
sorrow. We know not how to answer you. The moment we turned our
backs, this spring, a change took place; and our families and children
are all in trouble, in consequence of the conduct of some persons who
are not true Menominees.

Father, it is a clear day. We are happy in the opportunity to tell you
our complaints, and to explain to you our situation. We disapprove
of what has been done by the Agent, and of the conduct of those of
our nation, who treated with him, and sold our lands without our
consent."

After making some heavy complaints against the Agent, on
account of his rough treatment of them, and refusal to supply their
wants, when in distress, their speaker added:

"Father, notwithstanding our different color, the Great Spirit has
made us all. We hope that our talk today will go to our Great Father.

Father, the Great Spirit made everything. Formerly the white
people lived on the other side of the Great Water, and the red people
were thrown on this Great Island, and the game and the fish were
given them for their support.

Father, We are going to tell you what we think of the message you
bring us from our Great Father the President — or (as they described

him) 'he who governs the eighteen branches,' — meaning the eighteen states.

Father, It is a great happiness that we see you here. You have foolish men among you, who have education, and laws to regulate and govern you. We also have foolish men among us. How can we, who have no education or laws, govern them?"

The questions were here put to them, whether they would be willing to collect together in one place, large enough to accommodate each family with a farm; to cultivate the earth; have schools for their children, and live as the white people live? All this, they were told, might be done in consistency with their hunting and fishing, to a limited extent, and that their Great Father would aid and patronize them, in effecting these changes, so favorable to their happiness if they would give their consent, and make the proper efforts to bring them about.

They were informed that Mr. Williams, with a number of the Chiefs of the Six Nations, were on their way to Green Bay, to look out for a place of settlement for themselves, and such others of their tribes, as might be disposed to migrate and settle with them. Should they be pleased with the country, they were asked, will you sell, or give them lands on which they may settle?

Mau-cau-tau-bee, with apparent diffidence and modesty, then rose and said:

"Father, We don't know what to say, or what to do, in regard to the question you propose. We know that what you say is all good, and all true, and we take it as a great favor that you have come to see. Us. But we are but few here. The great part of our nation is elsewhere. If we were all together, we would give you a final answer.

Father, you see the few that are here of our nation. We cannot, therefore, give you a full and proper answer to your question. We can only speak for ourselves. But the Chiefs who are here, with myself, will endeavor to put in motion what our Great Father proposes. We hope to hear from our Great Father again on this subject. Our nation at present is scattered.

Father, In regard to the Delegates from the Six Nations, we

Menominee have no enemies. We are ready to give them our hand.
But in regard to a piece of land to give them, we know not what to say,
our Territory is so small.

Father, I listen always to what the white people say, but I do not
want to do as some of our foolish people have done. I do not want to
take on myself, or to have those with me of the disposition, to steal a
piece of land (*alluding to the sale of a large tract of their land, by a
minority of the nation, in opposition to the will of the majority.) but
if all our nation were together, we would know what to do.

Father, my conduct in life has not been irregular. We have listened
to the whites. In general what they have told us is the truth, or nearly
the truth; but in this place it is not the same thing. We have been led
into errors and confusion by the Agent, and by his means have been
scattered and divided. I have done."

Aus-kin-naw-wa-wish concluded saying

"Father, I look upon you the same as upon our Great Father the
President. The sky is clear. It is a happy day. The Traders here have
been our friends, have raised our children; and we wish, whatever
may happen in regard to our lands, that they may not be molested,
but remain quietly with us.

Father, The Chiefs, your children, whom you see before you, are
happy to see you, and hear you talk. They live in hope and belief, that
they shall receive the blessing which our Great Father proposes to
give us, if we comply with their wishes, which is our intention."

With another Menominee chief and three warriors, I afterward
had a short conversation. The name of the chief was *Sa-que-tock*, in
English, *very good natured*. His face and manners correspond very
well with his name. His village, of only thirty-six souls, is on Green
Bay, three miles below Fort Howard. Their food is fish, wild fowl, wild
rice and corn.[16]

We see here a recurring protest that not all the Menominee chiefs were
present to sign the Bowyer treaty, which they should have been according
to their customary decision-making process. The Menominee protested
that only a few signed the treaty, and moreover those who did sign were
manipulated by Bowyer and had no authority to cede Menominee lands.

As a result, the Menominee protests and discussions over who was authorized to sign treaties would be a point of controversy for years.

THE FIRST DELEGATION

The first delegation of New York Indians to arrive in Detroit included
members of the Oneida, Onondaga, St. Regis, and Seneca Nations.[17] The
Detroit Gazette chronicled their arrival on July 28, 1820:

> Rev. E. Williams, who has for several years past been officiating as a
> preacher for the Oneida Indians, in the State of New York arrived here
> in the steamboat Walk-in-the-water last Saturday. He is accompanied
> by some of the men of the tribe, who constitute a delegation to visit
> the Indians in this Territory for the purpose of ascertaining the
> prospect of success in the endeavor to Christianize them.
>
>   We learn that it is a further object with the delegation, to find a
> suitable tract of country within the Territory, to which the Oneida
> Indians, or a part of them will remove – for this purpose the country in
> the vicinity of Green Bay will be visited. No doubt can be entertained
> of the importance of this project. The influence which the example of
> Indians who are in a great measure civilized, will have over the habits
> of their more unfortunate brethren, will perhaps, have much more
> effect in weaning them from their savage modes of living, than all the
> theoretical lessons which can be given them by white men.[18]

When the New York Indian delegation was informed that the land they
were seeking was already earmarked for a different purpose in the Bowyer
treaty, they expressed their disappointment in a letter to Cass written from
Detroit on August 12, 1820:

> To his Excellency Lewis Cass
> Governor of the Michigan Territory
> Father,
> We the undersigned, deputies of the Oneida nation of Indians, being a
> branch of the Six Nations, have a few things to say to you.
>   Our Great Father, The President of the United States gave to the

Six Nations his consent that they should move to the west, if they could obtain lands from their brothers there. The Oneidas, have sent us to look out and procure a place for them from the Menominee Tribe in the neighborhood of Green Bay. Our Great Father the President, this thro Secretary of War, advised us to go there, and instructed his Agents thru this country to afford us all necessary facilities for that purpose.

Father, We have been in the vicinity of Detroit for some time past, not being able to immediately obtain a passage up the Lakes. While remaining, we have been informed on good authority that the lands at Green Bay, which we hope to obtain, have been purchased by the Great Father's Agent at that place. Whether this Agent has been authorized to make such a treaty, we do not as yet know. But we are disappointed because we cannot obtain from the Indians the land which we expected.

We think it altogether improper to procure at this time, we should excite jealousy of trouble among our brothers to the west.

We shall expect that you Father, and our Great Father the President of the United States, will remove these obstacles out of the way, that your children may get quiet possession of the land which they have been encouraged to expect.

Father, In your letter to a certain gentleman, you approved of our plan, and declared, that there are none of your citizens, in that country to oppose the measure that there will be no political prejudice to encounter, and no misrepresentations to correct.

It seems then, that you are disappointed too, and we hope that you will set these matters right, and deal fairly with your children.

Father, We wish peace — we wish to obtain a place to get our foot on peaceably, and to live in friendship with our brothers of the west, and our Great Father, the President.

Father, We now return to our nation & will declare to them what we have done.

We hope that it will be explained to us how these obstacles, have been thrown in the way, and if there lands, can be still procured, and if we can be assured that our Great Father wishes us to have them,

we expect to come back again & see these lands, which we wish to
purchase.

We hope, you, Father, will look into this matter, and, on your
return to Detroit, to be so good as to inform us by a letter, whether we
can still have the lands about the Green Bay.

With Sentiments of deepest respect, we are your Dutiful Children,

His

John & Brandt, —— mark

His

Cornelius & —— mark

His

Daniel & —— mark

His

John & —— mark

Detroit August 12th, 1820
Signed in the presence of Eleazer Williams
To His Excellency
    Lewis Cass[19]

The Oneida, after returning from Detroit to Oneida Castle, New
York, again wrote to Calhoun, this time on November 6, 1820. This let-
ter was signed by Cornelius Beard, John Anthony Brandt, and Daniel
Tegaiweiatiron.[20]

To His Excellency the Secretary at War
Honored and Respected Sir
We the undersigned an association of the Oneida Nation of Indians,
a branch of the Six Nations of the State of New York, in most humble
and respectful terms would beg leave to represent that, in accordance
with the wishes of our Nation and with the approbation of the
Government of the United States, in the season past in conjunction

with others of the Six Nations travelled into the territory of Michigan for the purpose of viewing the lands in the vicinity of Green Bay; that on our arrival at the city of Detroit to our exceeding regret we were informed by the then acting governor of Michigan and Maj. Gen. Macomb that previous to our arrival at that place the United States Agent at Green Bay had treated with the Menominie Indians for the purchase of those very lands which we have journeyed thus far to view and explore. This intelligence was also confirmed by the Rev. D. Morse whom we met at Detroit.

At this information, our astonishment could be equaled by nothing but our mortification knowing the general government to be our friends; our disappointment was the more aggravated and poignant.

Our instructions being directed solely to the lands in and about Green Bay and to no other place; and not wishing to confront the constitutes authorities — we were constrained, although with much chagrin and sorrow to terminate our mission.

We had a conference with many of the most respectable of Menominies, who expressed great dissatisfaction at the conduct of the United States Agent and their late treaty with the general government.

We, therefore, the undersigned do most humbly beseech and pray the Government might not ratify the said Treaty. The undersigned not willing to abandon the scheme, but contemplating a second tour the ensuing spring to that country and Mr. Williams not being able to satisfy us in many points as to the view of the General Government; would humbly ask that the Government would cause the said Six Nations to be represented at the City of Washington the coming winter; for the purpose of more fully and explicitly understanding the object of the General Government. The undersigned would most humbly ask and request a speedy answer to the above petition.

The undersigned would further represent that the Menominies were not only dissatisfied with the late treaty, but their neighbors the Winnebagoes and Chippeways were also dissatisfied, which would render a further prosecution of their journey wholly abortive.

Oneida Castle, Nov. 6, 1820

With sentiments of deepest respect we are your Excellency humble
servants,
Signed in the presences of Eleazer Williams
On behalf of the Deputies

    Cornelius X his mark Beard

    John Anthony X his mark Brandt

    Daniel X his mark Tegaweiateiron

P.S. Should your Excellency send any communication to us, please to
direct the same to Mr. Eleazer Williams of this place, or to his Hon.
Morris S. Miller of Utica.[21]

Cass wrote to Calhoun on November 11, 1820. Cass was in Green Bay
and learned from Bowyer that he had made a treaty for land forty miles
up the Fox River and twenty-five to thirty miles on each side of the Fox
River. Cass wrote: "I have reason to believe that the Six Nations from New
York would select a part of this Country for their residence, and the policy
of permitting them to do it, cannot be doubted."[22] This letter shows that
the intentions of the US government to resettle the New York Indians in
the area near Green Bay were well known. Cass knew that the New York
Indians reached Detroit only to learn that Bowyer had made the treaty.
"It is very desirable to place them in that Country," Cass told Calhoun, as
"Their habits & the strong pecuniary ties, which bind them to the United
States, would ensure their fidelity and they would act as a check upon the
Winnebagoes, the worst affected of any Indians upon our borders."[23] Cass
also suggested delaying approval of the Bowyer treaty as they might make
a better deal.

In February 1821, David A. Ogden, the land speculator, wrote to Calhoun regarding the Bowyer treaty. Ogden referred to the federal government's prior approval given to the New York Indians to acquire land near
Green Bay now at play in the Bowyer treaty. Ogden wrote, "If I was rightly
informed this plan was countenanced by the Government last year and
when Eleazar Williams, the Indian Catechist residing among the Oneidas,
applied to me to contribute towards the expedition."[24] Ogden also called
attention to the fact that the Stockbridge and Seneca were assured of land
near Green Bay, a reminder to Calhoun that the government made promises to the New York Indians for lands there.[25]

Calhoun wrote to Cass on April 4, 1821, to explain that the Bowyer treaty was not ratified. He explained that Monroe "did not think it necessary to lay before the Senate the treaty negotiated by (John) Bowyer with the Menominees."[26] This was because "the land that would be ceded under the treaty to the US remains, therefore, in the same status as if the treaty had never been negotiated. All Indians concerned should be notified. The Stockbridge of N.Y. are considering emigrating to the Green Bay area and intend to send a deputation to explore it this spring or summer."[27] In 1821, Calhoun then authorized delegates from the New York Indians to make a second trip to obtain land in Green Bay. Charles C. Trowbridge, a treaty negotiator assigned to accompany the New York Indians on their return trip to Green Bay, wrote that in 1821, "the New York Indians were encouraged to try again, and Mr. Williams . . . to accompany a delegation as Agent, but being under orders for other duty in the Indian Department, I did not accept."[28]

The events and letters of 1820 set the stage for the US government approving the second journey of the New York Indians to the Green Bay area to make a land treaty with the Menominee and Winnebago Nations.

3

THE TREATY OF 1821

Indian Nation to Indian Nation

In the spring of 1821, members of the Oneida Nation wrote letters to John C. Calhoun and President James Monroe asking for permission to make another trip to the Green Bay area to obtain land. Additionally, the Stockbridge wrote to Calhoun asking to travel to Green Bay. The journal of Charles C. Trowbridge and writings by A. G. Ellis provide information on the arrival of the New York Indian delegates and the treaty negotiations between the Menominee and Ho-Chunk Nations and the New York Indians.

As the 1821 treaty was made between Indian nations, the US military was present only to witness the proceedings. Included with the 1821 treaty is a receipt, signed by the Menominee, acknowledging payment made by the New York Indians for lands exchanged in the treaty. The treaty, between Menominee and Winnebago Nations and the delegates for the Oneida, Onondaga, Seneca, St. Regis, Stockbridge, and Munsee Nations, was signed on August 18, 1821, and approved by President Monroe on February 19, 1822.

EVENTS LEADING TO THE 1821 TREATY

The collusion among Williams, Calhoun, and the Ogden Land Company is evident in a letter sent from David A. Ogden to Calhoun on February 14, 1821. Ogden refers to the Bowyer treaty as including lands designated for the New York Indians. Ogden assumed that when Eleazer Williams requested funding from him that it meant Williams had governmental

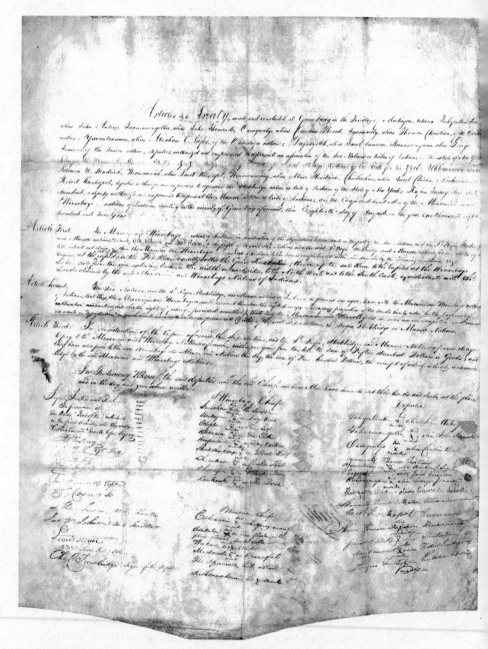

A page from the Treaty of Green Bay. Signed on August 18, 1821, this treaty was made Indian nation to Indian nation and was approved by President James Monroe on February 19, 1822.

WHI IMAGE ID 27037

approval. Ogden wrote, "The Stockbridge Tribe as well as the Senecas having separately received assurances of the grant of a seat to the west under former Administrations, they will no doubt claim the fulfillment of the pledge, and when circumstances shall more imperiously require their removal."[1] Ogden asked that the removal of the New York Indians continue and that he be informed when progress was made toward that end.

Oneidas Cornelius Beard, John Anthony Brandt, and Daniel Tegaweiat-iron wrote a letter to Calhoun on April 10, 1821, protesting the 1819 Bowyer treaty. The Oneida representatives requested permission to undertake another expedition to the Green Bay area to scout for and obtain land. Two days later, on April 12, 1821, a similar letter was sent to President Monroe.[2] The letter to Calhoun reads as follows:

Great Brother,

Having sent a memorial to Your Excellency, & receiving no answer as yet and hearing that our Great Father, the President has refused today the late Treaty of Col Bowyer with our Brothers the Menominee Indians, which was the cause of the failure of our last Spring expedition before the Senate for its ratification and thereby hoping that the Door for our proceeding to Green Bay was still open, we were induced [?] to write to Your Excellency — As the principle causes of the failure of our last year's expedition and mentioned in our memorials to Your Excellency of the 4th of November last we would refer Your Excellency to it and here omit the rehearsals [?] of them.

Great Brother — We are ready, and wishing to make another attempt — The "6 Nations" will also send delegations — the St. Regis tribe although they did not arrive in season, last year to accompany us, have this winter, sent a Delegation to our country, for the purpose of making arrangements for accompanying us this ensuing Spring.

Great Brother — The season is fast approaching when Your Children might go and they are in a state of suspense relative to this matter, we write this to Your Excellency, that we may know what to hope and whether it is the will of the Government that we should . . . and also whether the government is willing to afford us the same amount of subsistence as was held forth last season. The money furnished last season, was mostly all expended, but the powder of

Lead [?] was present & is now at Buffalo — We have written to our
Great Father, the President and hope an answer soon — It was thought
last fall expeditions that the Deputies would themselves communicate
to Your Excellency. The reason why our mission terminated at Detroit
and we find that the Rev. Mr. Williams has not written to Your
Excellency upon the subject, and the reason is because we choose to
do our own story [?], but now by our particular request he will send a
communication. — He is our Minister as well as our brother. He is an
Indian, as well as ourselves, and we chose him before any of our white
Brethren to lead us forward in this undertaking.

Great Brother, we would humbly pray & beseech Your Excellency,
that we may hear an answer to this, as soon as convenient. Will Your
Excellency be pleased to direct an answer to the Hon. M.S. Miller
of Utica who will we expect transmit the same to us. As also any
communication which Your Excellency may be pleased to send to
us . . . and location.

Brother, your very dutiful and obedient children.

Signed in the presences of Eleazer Williams, Missionary to the
Oneida Nation
Deputies.

Cornelius X his mark Beard

John X his mark Anthonis

Daniel X his mark Tegaweiatiron

Oneida Castle of 10th April 1821[3]

The letter written to Monroe reads as follows:

Great Father,

It is well known to You, that with your approbation and assistance,
we went on an expedition to the Westward, in search of, and for the
purpose of obtaining a country for ourselves & our children to dwell
in for future ages. We desire to thank you Great Father for the aid &
assistance, which you were pleased to give us last season. — As we
have sent memorials to the Secretary of War it is probably known
to you that in consequence of hearing at Detroit, that the very lands

which we have in view had been purchased by the US agent at Green
Bay. We were disappointed and after consulting with Gen. Macomb
& the honorable Mr. Woodbridge (the then acting Gov.) and finding
that our still proceeding would be confronting the Gen. Government,
we were induced to return to our canton, and thus our mission
terminated at Detroit and our object was left unaccomplished —
through not any neglect or activity [?] of ours, but for the interference
of the US Agent at Green Bay. — For further particulars we would
refer You Great Father, to our Memorial sent to the Secretary of War
of the 6th Nov. last.

Now Great Father being still anxious to make our . . . and hearing
that our Great Father had refused to lay the late treaty of the US agent
at Green Bay and the Menominee Indians before the Senate for its
ratification, we were encouraged yet to hope that the Door was still
open for us, we write this to ascertain our Great Father's mind upon
the subject — to know whether he is still willing that his Children
should go. — and whether he is willing to afford the same assistance
that was held forth last season. — As the season is fast approaching
when your children might go. They would in terms of humiliation
& respect pray and beseech You Great Father to grant, if possible,
your aid and assistance, and by all means to let us know what we may
depend upon as soon as convenient. — We hope that our Father will
consider the importance of this object — that is necessary the red men
of the west be provided with a country when they shall have no land
among their white brethren. — Will our Great Father be pleased to
send his answer to this to Judge [?] Miller of Utica.

Great Father, we are our Your most dutiful & obedient Children.

Signed in the presences of Eleazer Williams, Missionary to the
Oneida Nation

Deputies

Cornelius X his mark Beard
John X his mark Anthonie
Daniel X his mark Tegaweiatiron
Oneida Castle 10th April, 1821[4]

Calhoun responded on April 14, 1821, to the November 6, 1820, letter from Cornelius Beard, John Anthony Brandt, and Daniel Tegaweiatiron written from Oneida Castle to protest the Bowyer treaty (see Chapter 2). Calhoun wrote, "He regrets that their hope of obtaining land near Green Bay for emigration was dashed last year by the proposed treaty with the Menominees negotiated by [John Bowyer] without authorization. That treaty has not been submitted to the Senate for ratification, and the Six Nations can therefore obtain the land directly from the Menominees." He also "hopes that the St. Regis, Stockbridge, and others will join the Oneidas in another tour to the Green Bay area this year; rations and other similar accommodations will be provided again to those who make the tour of inspection. The Oneidas need not send a deputation to Washington."[5]

On June 4, 1821, Calhoun sent a letter to Williams confirming his instructions to the commissaries of US military posts at Detroit and Green Bay to pay Williams and his party with provisions for their trip to purchase land in the Green Bay area from the Menominee.[6]

Others wrote to Calhoun as well. From the Stockbridge Nation, Solomon U. Hendrick wrote to Calhoun expressing the Stockbridge nation's requests and concerns. He asked for another "fire place" for the Stockbridge people, which means he was asking for a permanent land base. Wrote Hendrick:

> Sir,
> I have been requested by my Chiefs and Head men to write few lines unto you, and to inform you that my Nation have agreed to send at least four of our men to go to Green Bay before this month will be expired with a view of, if possible, to procure or obtain another fire place in that country for our Nation, since we have failed in obtaining any part of the White River lands back again from the General Government.
> My colleague, Mr. Jackob Kunkapot and I together with a few others were appointed to undertake this intended expedition a little while after we return from Washington City but it has been impossible for us to get early an advance . . . by reason of the scarcity of money amongst us to repay the expenses of the delegates who were appointed to go to Green Bay.

We were informed of at Albany on our return from. . . . Of
government that the legislature of this State had made a law granting
our Nation one thousand dollars of the . . . of the money remaining
there belonging to the . . . session of land sold to the State. To the
finished law . . . had petitioned to the Legislature for the money to
defray the expenses of our said delegates to Green Bay.

After our arrival here, our tribe immediately held a council
where we delivered our report to them agreeable to our customs.
Our nations were dissatisfied with the treaty of the relinquishment
we had made for our claims of land in Washington to the United
States on the part [?] of our Nation! After what it states explaining [?]
to Nation and which our claims are viewed by our great Father, the
President and his great men . . . that the Munsees who are in this State
will consent also to relinquish their claims to this . . . after they . . .
heard us.

I have . . . here. The copy of the act passed the last session of
the Legislature last spring relative to the $1,000, wherein we were
extremely disappointed to find it had passed in such a manner
that we cannot obtain any part of it for this expedition unless our
whole tribe were actually to remove. It would be ridiculous in the
highest degree for our Nation to emigrate to other country before we
obtained a place to remain to which is not this . . . at present.

Perhaps it might be asked why we did not reserve any part of the
money . . . by us for this purpose! I answer we had such confident of
receiving the $1,000 from the State. That it induced our people to
divide the money amongst them and some was spent to repay the
debt the Nation has previously contracted. And . . . we are without
any funds to repay the said delegation to Green Bay.

My people are desirous to know that in the event of their borrowing
at least five or six hundred dollars in money from the Utica Bank,
whether the government would not be willing to replace the said . . . as
soon as we can obtain the claims of the relinquishment of the Munsees
who reside in this State provided their relinquishment is obtained
before two or three months from hence. This money to be deducted
from the money designated to be paid to us in the State Treaty.

They are likewise desiring to obtain some document or writing from the government to be carried by our delegates showing that we are going by or through the favorable consent and predilection of the United States.

You may recollect that you so advised us when we saw you last. You . . . us as making so that it can be we sent four of our people to Green Bay. This can or say . . . it provisions at every point belonging to the U States between here and Green Bay and during their continuance at the later . . . and likewise on their return back. And likewise you would write to Governor Cass of Detroit advising him to . . . all the facility in his power to enable said delegation to reach to the place of their destination with all possible expedition . . . providing there was any government vessels going up the lakes that they may take their passage . . . Our tribe is of the opinion that the Munsees in this State will probably wish to send one of their men to accompany our delegates. If this is the case it would be very desirable that they might also have the privilege of drawing provisions with them.

As I am well aware that you are continually . . . with business, I may perhaps weary your patience in reading these lines. But I hope after you shall have considered our Nations misfortune in losing a country which we once considered as our own, you will have the goodness to give them that attention which you would wish, I would do so provided we exchange our situations because it is of the highest importance for my tribe to hear from you soon to know your mind and the mind of our great father the President.

I may further add that the speed which was calculated to make to the Delawares beyond the Mississippi will be coming to the War Department as soon as practicable.

I regret to let you know that my people were not very well satisfied last spring because they did not receive the whole amount of their annuity annually delivered to them by our agent Capt. Parrish. As they had been as friendly to some members of Congress. That Congress had always appropriated money to defray the expenses of Indians whenever they had any business to transact with the government and they think that government ought to have allowed one hundred dollars (the amount kept back from our annuity) to

Jacob Kunkapot for his expenses while at the city of Washington one year ago last winter as he went on public business.

I earnestly pray you to send me an answer as soon as you possibly can — With great . . . I am very respectfully your most obedient servant. Solomon W. Hendricks[7]

Calhoun later wrote in a letter to Lewis Cass, the governor of Michigan Territory, to tell him the Stockbridge were going to Green Bay area and "that he knows the intended emigration of the Stockbridges and that it has the approval of the US."[8]

Weeks later, Cass wrote to Trowbridge with instructions to accompany the New York Indian delegation to Green Bay, telling Trowbridge, "The great object of the Six nations, is to procure from the Menominie, Winnebagoes and other Indians in the vicinity of Green Bay, permission to occupy such land as may be found advantageous." Additionally, Cass told Trowbridge, "As soon as you return, I will thank you to communicate to David Ogden, Esq. at Hamilton, St. Lawrence County, New York, the result of your mission. Your compensation will be paid by a draft upon Mr. Ogden, at the rate of two dollars per day."[9] Here again there is evidence of collusion that clearly shows the extent to which the Ogden Land Company was involved in the removal of the Six Nations to Green Bay.

The following day, Cass wrote a letter of introduction to John Biddle, an Indian agent at Green Bay, affirming he had appointed Trowbridge his personal secretary and instructing Biddle to cooperate with this effort.[10] Trowbridge wrote of his instructions from Cass:

W. Calhoun transmitted to Governor Cass in 1821, copies of the correspondence which had taken place on the subject, and requested him to select some person to accompany a delegation from the Six Nations to the Menomonees of Green Bay, which, you perceive, was then thought to be the place answering to the Presidents desire, for the isolation of the Red men of New York. The Governor honored me with the appointment . . . over the correspondence, gave me a letter of introduction to Major John Biddle, the Indian Agent at Green Bay, and another to myself. He referred to the correspondence as containing the view of the Government, for my guidance.[11]

In the letter that Cass wrote to Biddle, Cass also informed the Indian agent that "another effort will be made by the Six Nations to obtain a permanent site for their residence upon the Fox river." He wrote as well that "Mr. Trowbridge takes with him copies of all the necessary papers & instructions relating to this subject. By them you will perceive at once the situation of this business, and the interest, with which the Government regards its accomplishment."[12]

THE NEW YORK INDIANS ARRIVE IN GREEN BAY

The 1821 delegates (referred to as deputies on the treaty) of the Oneida, Stockbridge, Tuscarora, Seneca, and St. Regis were approved by the War Department to travel to Green Bay to inspect lands near Green Bay for a permanent home. The War Department sent orders to military posts along the way to give the travelers rations, and for the fort at Detroit to furnish a ship. In total, there were fourteen delegates, including three Stockbridge, four Oneida, one Onondaga, two Tuscarora, three Seneca, and one St. Regis.[13]

Ellis describes the French inhabitants of Green Bay, about four hundred people, as two classes. First were clerks in the North West Fur Company, who tended to be educated and married to Menominee women. The second group retired from the fur trade and lived more as farmers and also married Menominee women.[14] Therefore, the French had influence with the Menomonee in the negotiations, and they feared losing land and sources of income when treaties were made.

In September 1821, Trowbridge submitted a report to Cass that provides information on the actual events and negotiations leading to the 1821 treaty made between the Menominee and Ho-Chunk Nations and the Six Nations delegates:

> Sir,
>
> The deputation from the Six Nations and Stockbridge and Munsee nations of Indians having returned to this place. I have the honor to report to you the proceedings and the result of their mission to Green Bay.
>
> Soon after your departure from this place in July last, I learned

that Maj. Biddle, the Indian Agent at Green Bay (whose advice and assistance, I was instructed, would be afforded the deputies) was about to leave that place for the purpose of attending the treaty to be held at Chicago.

I communicated this information to the deputies on their arrival here, and at their request I addressed a letter to your Excellency at Chicago, requesting that such instruction as would be most likely to secure the object in view, might be immediately forwarded to me at Green Bay.

On our arrival at the place of our destination, we found the Agent absent, as was anticipated, and learned also to our very great mortification that his interpreter had accompanied him. Upon consultation it was thought advisable to proceed in our business without delay, although we were sensible that we should meet with many difficulties; and with this view we procured a cometions [accommodations] house in the vicinity of Fort Howard, where we were visited on the seventh of August by a Menomini Chief and a few of his warriors. We informed these men that we should be pleased to hold a council with such Menomini Chiefs as were at the place, and requested them to attend us, accompanied by these chiefs on the following day.

On the eighth a few of the Menomini Chiefs called at our house, and were soon followed by some Winnebagoes, who took seats with them in the council room, when the deputies addressed a short speech to the former, stating that they had an important communication to make to them if their principal Chiefs could be collected. This speech was the mistake interpreted to them as addressed to both nations, which fact we did not learn until they gave their answer, when it was too late to correct the error, as they all professed themselves gratified with the invitation, and engaged to send immediately for the Chiefs of both nations.

Knowing that an enmity existed between the two parties, and that the Winnebagoes had refused to listen to propositions for the purchase of their lands, we were not a little displeased at this mistake of our interpreter, but, as will appear to you, it eventuated in the accomplishment of our object.

On the sixteenth the Chiefs of the two nations arrived, and we immediately commenced business. The Deputies opened the object of their mission in a very handsome manner, taking care to set forth in a proper light, the advantages which would result to their brethren the Menominis and Winnebagos, from a cession as proposed and after delivering a belt of wampum according to the Indian custom, the opposite parties replied in very flattering terms, and begged leave to consult each other promising to give an answer on the following day.

On the [following day] the Menominies opened the council with a positive refusal to accept the proposals made to them, alleging as a reason the limited quantity of lands possessed by them, and the difficulty they therefore experienced in gaining a livelihood.

The Winnebagoes expressed a great deal of sorrow at this answer, and proposed to give their brethren of the east, the lands on the Fox river from the Grand Chute to the Winnebago Lake, a distance of four and half miles.

Perceiving that the Menominis were astonished at this reply, it was thought advisable to adjourn the council with a view to give them time for reflection.

On the following day, they met the deputies again, and having stated that their minds had changed, proposed to join the Winnebagoe in a cession of the lands from the foot of the Grand Kaccalin to the rapids at the Winnebago Lake.

Immediately the articles of the treaty were prepared, but before being finished the Menominis received a message from some person without the houses in consequence which some of the Chiefs left the room, and a bustle commenced among those who remained. The perceived cause of the confusion, and began seriously after the influence of the French inhabitants, some of whom had . . . themselves in opposition to our measures from the time of our arrival.

After some time had elapsed, the Chiefs who had left us returned and it was then difficult to procure a decisive answer to our questions "whether they would sign a grant, terms of which had been proposed by themselves alone"? After a good deal of hesitation between their own inclinations and that of their advisers, they told us, that their speaker had not expressed their true sentiments, but that their first determination on our proposition was unchanged and unchangeable. All hope of effecting a purchase of the Menomini were now at an end; for we felt sensible, as well from experiences as from information, that they were guided in everything by the advice and instruction of a few of the principal Frenchmen at the place who have ever opposed with zeal, the progress of settlement and improvement in their country.

Upon reflection it was thought advisable to make another attempt, and the council was declared adjourned until the morning of the nineteenth, at which time the Winnebagoes were invited to attend and sign the grant which they had first proposed. The Menomini were told, that if they should feel disposed to join the cession we should be pleased to see them also.

In the evening the two nations held a consultation at their encampment, and on the following morning they all assembled and signed the treaty, of which I have the honor to enclose you a copy, together with a sketch of a part of Fox River, exhibiting the breadth and course of the tract. [This map was not found with the report.]

The grant is not as wide as was wished for and expected by the deputies, but when it is considered that we were obliged to encounter serious obstacles, . . . and alone, it cannot be denied that the result has been favorable.

Some of the Deputies have visited the lands on and adjacent to the river, and are much pleased with the appearance of the soil, timber and local advantages. Indeed it is pronounced by the inhabitants to be the most value tract in that country.

The boundaries are expressed in the articles of the treaty and rather indefinite, but under the then existing circumstances it was difficult to make them less so. The grantors claim to the northwest as far as the Chippeway lands' sometimes they say three, and others, four, five, and six days march. On the southeast their claims extend to Lake Michigan. Should it be thought advisable, I have little doubt that a purchase may be affected, of the lands from the Rapids of the . . . four and a half miles above Fort Howard and near the upper extremity of the French settlement, to the Grand Kaccalin, a distance of thirteen and a half miles; which added to the present cession would make a breadth of upwards of thirty miles.

I cannot forbear expressing to your Excellency how highly I have
been gratified with the correct moral deportment and statesmen
like conduct of the deputies from the Six Nations, under the direction
of Mr. Williams, whose personal . . . in this business have been
very great.

With respect to the Deputation from the Stockbridge nation, I
cannot speak so favorably. Some of them, it is true, have genius and
energy, but they have been more addicted to intemperance than
becomes men on business of this importance; and I fear that some
part of their conduct has left an unfavorable impression on the minds
of the inhabitants at the Bay.

I am aware that I have been prolific in this report, but a desire to
give your Excellency a detailed statement of the facts attending the
mission, has been the cause, and I offer no other apology; not . . .
that when you shall take into consideration its imperfections, your
goodness will prompt you to excuse this under the belief that they do
not arise from a want of inclination to make it more satisfactory.
With the highest respect, I have the honor to be Your Excellency's
very humble and much obliged Servant,
Charles C. Trowbridge[15]

Ellis also submitted a report on the negotiations. He stated that French
and other Euro-American settlers quickly figured that Williams's plan was
"no less than a total subjugation of the whole country, and the establishment of an Indian government, of which he was to be the sole dictator."[16]
As a result, they made their opposition clear to the Menominee and Winnebago and advised them not to sign the 1821 treaty.

Ellis reports that several days were spent in discussions and a proposal
was made to cede a strip of land "five miles in width, running across the
Fox River at Little Chute as a center, and thence to the North-west and
South-east equi-distant with their claims or possessions."[17] He described
the vast territories of the Menominee and Winnebago and dismissed their
claim of being crowded. He said that there was much deliberation, hesitation, and discussion before the agreement was made and Trowbridge
wrote the treaty, which was signed on August 18, 1821.

THE TREATY OF 1821

The treaty of 1821 is presented here in its entirety:

TREATY OF GREEN BAY

Documents Relating to the Negotiation of an Unratified Treaty of August 18, 1821, between the THE MENOMINEE AND WINNEBAGO NATIONS AND THE DELEGATES FOR ONEIDA, ONONDAGA, SENECA, ST. REGIS, STOCKBRIDGE, AND MUNSEE INDIAN NATIONS

Articles of a Treaty made, and concluded at Green Bay, in the Territory of Michigan, between Tahyantanekea, alias John Antony, Tahnongotha, alias John Skenando, Onougwalgo, alias Cornelius Beard, Sganawaty, alias Thomas Christian, of the Oneida Nation. Yawenlanawen, alias Abraham C. Lafort of the Oneida nation; Dagaoyotek, alias Jacob Jameson, Hanawongwas, alias George Jameson, of the Seneca nation; Deputies, authorized, and empowered, to represent an association of the Six Nations, or Tribes of Indians of the State of New York; Eleazer Williams, alias Onwarenkaaki, a deputy authorized, and empowered, to represent the St. Regis Indians of the State of New York; Uhhaunowwaunmut, alias Solomon U. Hendrick, Wuhsaunuh, alias Jacob Konkapot, Wenowwommaug, alias Abner W. Henrick, Chicksaukon, alias Jacob Chicks, Naukawate, alias Robert Kunkapot, Deputies authorized, and empowered, to represent the Stockbridge Nation or Tribe of Indians of the State of New-York; Rufus Iwrkey, alias Hatkosakont, a Deputy authorized and empowered to represent the Munsee Nation, or Tribe of Indians; and the Chiefs, and Head Men of the Menominie and Winnebago Nations of Indians, residing in the vicinity of Green Bay aforesaid, this eighteenth day of August, in the year one thousand eight hundred and twenty one.

ARTICLE 1st. The Menominie and Winnebago Nations of Indians, in consideration of the stipulations herein made on the part of the Six Nations, and the St. Regis Stockbridge, and Munsee Nations, do hereby CEDE, Release, and QUIT CLAIM, to the people of the said Six Nations, and the said St. Regis, Stockbridge and Munsee Nations forever, all the right, title, interest and claim of them, the Menominie and Winnebago Nations of Indians, to the lands comprehended within, and described by the following boundaries, viz: Beginning at the foot of the rapids on the Fox River, usually called the Grand Kaccalin; thence up said River to the rapids at the Winnebago Lake; and from the River extending back, in this width, on each side to the North West and to the South East equidistant with the lands claimed by the said Menominie and Winnebago Nations of Indians.

ARTICLE 2d. The Six Nations, and the St. Regis, Stockbridge and Munsee Nations of Indians, do promise and agree to, and with the Menominie and Winnebago Nations of Indians, that they, the Menominies, and Winnebagoes, shall reserve to themselves the right of occupying a necessary proportion of the lands hereby ceded for the purposes of hunting, and also the right of fishing, provided nevertheless, that they, the Menominies, and Winnebagoes in such use, and occupation, shall commit no waste, or depredation on such lands as may be under improvement by either of the said Six Nations, St. Regis, Stockbridge or Munsee Nations.

ARTICLE 3d. In consideration of the cession aforesaid, the Six Nations, and the St. Regis, Stockbridge and Munsee Nations aforesaid, Do agree to pay to the Menominie and Winnebago Nations aforesaid, within one year from this date, the sum of fifteen hundred dollars in Goods; and they have also paid to the said Winnebago and Menominie Nations this day the sum of Five Hundred dollars, the receipt of which is hereby acknowledged by said Menominie and Winnebago Nations.

IN TESTIMONY whereof the said Deputies and the said Chiefs and Head Men have herunto set their hands and sales at the place and on the day and year above written.

In presence of

N. Pinckney, Col. 3d Reg. Inft.
Wm. Whistler, Capt. 3rd Reg. Inft.
J. Garland, Capt.
S. Cowan, Lt.
M. Irwin, U.S. Factor
Jno. Johnson, U.S. Factor
Lewis Rouse
J. B. C. Russell, Lieut. U.S. Army
Chs. C. Trowbridge, Agent
for the Deputation

Winnebago Chiefs.
Serachow his X mark or the Smoker
Skonkapow his X mark or Dogs Head
Ochopkaw his X mark or Four Legs
Karamanee his X mark or the Elk
Hompomoneek his X mark or Day Walker
Shonkshonksup his X mark or Black Wolf
Cheaukoo his X mark or Crooked Tail
Chausepk his X mark or Black Deer
Kauhawk his X mark the Dove

Menominie Chiefs.
Eskenanin his X mark or the Young Man
Osakataw his X mark or Pine shooter,
in the place of Tomas, son of Josette
Weekeus his X mark
The Spaniard
Kisheunakum
Muckometa his X mark or Bear's-foot

Deputies [for Six Nations, Stockbridge and Munsee Nations of Indians]
Tahyentaneken his X mark alias John Antony
Tahnonsongotha his X mark alias John Skenando
Onongwatgo his X mark alias Cornelius Beard

Sganawaty his X mark Thomas Christian
Yawenlanawen his X mark alias Abram C. Lafort
Dagayoht his X mark alias Jacob Jameson
Hanawongwas his X mark alias George Jameson
Eleazer Williams alias Onwarenkaaki
Solomon U. Hendrick, alias Uhhaunowwaunmut
Jacob Konkapot alias Wuhsaunuh
Abner W. Hendrick his X mark alias Wenowwommaug
Jacob Chicks his X mark alias Cheeksaucon
Naukauwaut his X mark alias Robert Konkapot
Rufus Turkey his X mark alias Katkosekort

Upon approving the treaty, President James Monroe wrote:

The written arrangement entered into between the Six Nations, the
St. Regis, Stockbridge and Munsee Nations of the one part, and the
Menominies and Winnebagoes of the other, is approved; with the
express understanding, that, the lands thereby conveyed to the Six
Nations, the St. Regis, Stockbridge and Munsee Nations are to be
held by them, in the same manner, as they were previously held, by
the Menominies and Winnebagoes.
James Monroe
February 9th, 1822

Attached to the 1821 treaty is a receipt that reads:

Received Green Bay, September 16th, one thousand, eight hundred
and twenty two, of the Stockbridge Deputies, nine hundred
dollars, of the Oneida deputies, four hundred dollars, and of the
Tuscarora deputy, two hundred dollars; all in goods, agreeable to the
stipulations of the third article of the within Treaty.
In presence of
J. Sergeant, Jr.
Henry Clark,
H. Browinng, Capt. 3rd Inft.
B. Watson, Maj. US Army,
Richard Printup.

Winnebago Chiefs.
> Serachow his X mark or the Smoker,
> Karamanee his X mark or the Elk,
> Shonkapaw his X mark or Dogshead,
> Ochopkaw his X mark or Four Legs,
> Shonkshonksup his X mark or Black Wolf,
> Aupommone his X mark or the Brave.

Menomini Chiefs.
> Ohguommonnekan his X mark or the Great Wave,
> The Spaniard his X mark,
> Ausketaw his X mark or Pine Shooter,
> Thaukaupomme his X mark or Scare-all,
> Thauwommin his X mark or Yellow Dog.[18]

The 1821 treaty was signed by Euro-American officials with the Indigenous names of the Winnebago and Menominee chiefs and deputies for the New York Indians who signed the treaty. Their names were written as they sounded and an X was put by their names by the Indigenous peoples gathered. Payment for the treaty was a promise of fifteen hundred dollars in goods payable within one year, and a receipt was signed by the Menominee and Winnebago acknowledging payment of five hundred dollars. On September 16, 1823, in Green Bay, Winnebago and Menominee chiefs signed for the following payments to fulfill the third article of the treaty:

$1,822 from the Stockbridge
$900 from the Oneida
$400 from the Tuskanan deputy $200 all in goods.[19]

BOUNDARIES ESTABLISHED IN THE 1821 TREATY

Included in the 1821 treaty are descriptions of the boundaries that the Menominee and Winnebago reserved "to themselves the right to occupy a necessary proportion of the lands hereby ceded." The boundaries described in the treaty and the reports from Trowbridge and Ellis are vague. There are no known surviving maps associated with the 1821 treaty, and several sources differ in how they describe the boundaries agreed upon in the treaty. There is an estimate of acreage in Docket 75 of the Indian Claims

Commission of 804,000 acres. A map referred to the 1821 treaty as attachment A in the 1842 *Memorial of Stockbridge Indians in Wisconsin, to the US Senate*. This document states that the 1821 treaty was "about thirty-two townships, or 737,280 acres."[20] Additionally, there is a "Map of the Fox River and the part of the Winnebago Lake as contained within the limits of the cession of 1821 by the Menominee and Winnebago Indians to the New York Tribes."[21] Furthermore, Ellis described the agreement for a strip of land, five miles in width, running from the Fox River at Little Chute as the center and then running northwest and southeast equidistantly. Ellis also described the lands of the Menomonee as reaching "from the mouth of Green Bay to the Milwaukee River, North and South, from Lake Michigan to the Mississippi, South-east and North-west" and stated that "Those of the Winnebagoes included all the remainder of what is now known as Southern Wisconsin, except the inconsiderable tract west of Sugar River, claimed by the Sauks and Foxes."[22] As we will see, there were significant consequences to these vague boundaries.

Submission and Approval of the 1821 Treaty

Cass wrote Calhoun on October 22, 1821, transmitting a copy of a treaty negotiated at Green Bay in which the Winnebago and the Menominee agreed to provide land for emigrants from the Six Nations, the Munsee, the Stockbridge, and the St. Regis Indians, and a copy of Trowbridge's report. Cass wrote, "The result of this negotiation I consider important to the parties and to the United States. If no improper influence be exerted, these Indians will gradually withdraw from New York, and establish themselves upon the land thus ceded. They will there form a barrier, which may be highly useful in the event any difficulties in that remote quarter."[23] Calhoun also wrote a letter to Solomon U. Hendrick of the Stockbridge Nation in which he expressed his, and Monroe's, approval of the 1821 treaty:

> I am much pleased that the Delegates from [the interlined] Mohiccan
> or Stockbridge nation have succeeded in their mission to the Indians
> in the neighborhood of Green Bay, to the satisfaction of the Nation.
> The treaty concluded by the Delegates with the Menominee &

Winnebagoes is approved by the President [James Monroe] which is
all the ratifications that is necessary as those Treaties only to which
the U(nited) States is a party require the addition of the sanction of
the Senate.[24]

Eleazer Williams wrote Calhoun in late 1821 to voice his opinion on
the 1821 treaty:

Most Excellent Sir, Your Excellency has doubtless ere this received a
communication from the Stockbridge Indians, stating the favorable
result of the last summer expedition of the Oneidas and other of the
Six Nations of Indians, to the westward.

On the 18th of August last, a Treaty was made and concluded,
between the Deputies from the Six Nations, & the Chiefs and Head
men of the Menomini and Winnebago nations of Indians living in
the vicinity of Green Bay, in which, the Six Nations obtained a small
territory for themselves & other Indians in the State of New York,
who may choose hereafter to emigrate thither.

I am particularly requested by the Chiefs of the First Christian
party of this nation, to entreat your Excellency to permit six or seven
of the Six Nations to visit the seat of Government this winter, in
order, that the Government may confirm the grant which they have
obtained from their western brethren. The President [James Madison]
engaged to do this, in a communication made to the . . . by Mr.
[William H.] Crawford [Secretary of War] in February 1816.[25]

In an interesting letter from Cass to Calhoun written in late December,
Cass transmitted his instructions to Trowbridge and to Biddle, writing,
"I find on examination that three original instruments were executed by
the parties to the arrangement & were retained by Mr. Eleazer Williams,
the Indian Missionary. One of these he intended to transmit to the War
Department & I have written to him requesting him to forward it."[26] The
"three original instruments" may have included the maps of lands ceded
in the 1821 treaty, as Williams was in possession of the original treaties
and maps, which he had been instructed to send to the War Department.

OPPOSITION TO THE TREATY BY THE SIX NATIONS

Opposition to the 1821 treaty began before it was ever signed. On August 8, 1821, ten days before the treaty was signed, The Oneida and Onondaga chiefs living in New York State wrote a letter to President Monroe. In the letter the chiefs complained that Williams was "contriving a plan to get us from our land and have us settle among the wild Indians of the west":

To his Excellency James Monroe Esquire, President of the United States of America.

Great Father,

By the permission of the Great Spirit the Chiefs of the Oneida & Onondaga Nations of Indians inhabiting the State, have met in great Council and have agreed to speak to their Father the President of the United States. And for that purpose have appointed three of their respectable and worthy young men to wit. Martin Denny and Alfonse Schuyler for Oneida and John Brown for Onondaga these delegates to go in person to see their Father the President and speak to him on behalf of their Brethren.

We have this made, rather than to write because sometimes our letters are not answered and at other times we are not understood and for our sentence [?] is different. But now shall send some of our tribes to deliver our letter with their own hands and if that is not enough they are authorized to have a Talk.

We think the President to be the greatest man in America. Everything is done by his consent. We think him to be both the friend and the Father of red men as well as white men.

Father, There is business going on without our consent or authority. We are alarmed at the reports abroad. The Reverend Mr. Eleazer Williams, our missionary, and his party are gone to Green Bay; and they report and give out that it is under the sanction of the Government, to obtain land from the Western Indians for us to remove unto. This matter is of so much interest and importance to us that we have determined on a mission to Washington. We know not what these things mean — our minds are turned at hearing them —

our minister is continuing a plan to get us from our land, and to have us settle among the wild Indians of the west, we don't know where. But we have no such idea. We have made up our minds to stay here and will not give it up. Our reservation is already diminished to a very small space; but we calculate to keep what we have got, and we think much of it; and intend it shall go down to generations after us.

We all speak to the President. He has said he would not hear anything that comes through the wilderness — if we have anything to say it must come strait . . .

Father, we beg of you not to notice the representation of Mr. Williams and his party. He has seduced away some of [our] young men but he is not authorized by our chiefs of Warriors. We think his actions be selfish motives. We have not sent him to obtain land for us; and we shall not send any one to do so; and we now send our delegates to inform our Father the President accordingly.

The land we inhabit has descended to us from our Forefathers through many generations. Our territory has been diminished by copious till it is now very small — and we hope that those who try from interested motives, to get us off will not be heard. We have always thought that our Father the President, and the Oneida Nation were friends — That he would take care of the red men inhabiting the lands under his Government; and that he would pity them when he saw them in trouble; and we hope he will proceed for our good.

We always aided the President when he called on us. We went to the late war at his request. We always said, if the President is in difficulty, and he bleeds; we bleed with him. We never refused him, but went where he called, and we stood by him till he told us we might sit down, and then our warriors set down and went to work for a living.

We have it in our mind that our Father will not despair nor neglect us, nor compel us to go from our old country. We hope he will protect us as our we shall . . . [see our] Children go to ruin.

We are making preparations to send a delegation next winter from the whole Six Nations together with the Agent, and we wish our Father the President to tell us through our present delegation at what time it would be acceptable to him to receive them. At that time the whole delegation shall come, they will <u>take the President by the hand</u> <u>and brighten the Chain of friendship</u> as it was when we first became <u>brethren.</u> We hope then to have a fair talk and a good understanding; and that all falsehood that either party have heard will be put aside.

The Nations have furnished this delegation, as they will that next winter, with money to bear their expenses to Washington; and we hope the President will furnish them for their expenses back.

We beg of our Father the President to treat these our young men civilly and fondly as they will be far from home and among strangers.

We shall submit these proceedings of ours to our good friend Capt. Parrish, Indian Agent for his approbation. And shall also notify the rest of the Six Nations of our doings and then our Young Men will carry this to Washington.

We devoutly put up our prayers to the Great Spirit that our Father the President may live long and happy in this world, and be blessed in the next; and now we say Farewell.

Dated at Oneida Castle, August 8, 1821.[27]

Just ten days later, on August 18, 1821, the board of the Hamilton Missionary Society sent a letter to Obadiah D. Brown stating that the Oneida and Onondaga, in New York State, were opposed to the treaty and had not authorized Williams and his companions to go to Green Bay to obtain land. They planned to send a communication and a delegation to Washington to oppose the project.[28]

When the delegation of New York Indians returned from their trip to Green Bay with the signed treaty, they met with opposition. Several Oneida councils were held and many disapproved of removal. Words were spoken, "condemning Mr. Williams' movements in the most severe terms, formally and solemnly repudiating the purchase at the West, and announcing, in the most earnest manner possible, their determination never to remove."[29] The Oneida council even censured the young men who were delegates on the journey. Ellis writes of the delegates that they

found much difficulty in giving satisfactory explanations. Movers in the opposition caused a written remonstrance against the whole proceedings to be circulated, which was largely signed, in which quite a number of the First Christian Party joined. This remonstrance was a free indictment of Mr. Williams, who was characterized as chief instigator to a scheme to rob the Oneidas of their homes, and make them a kind of wanderers and vagabonds of the earth.[30]

The Oneidas were now divided into two parties on the matter, one that supported removal and one that opposed it. The following letter, dated October 14, 1821, was submitted to President Monroe by the Oneida and Onondaga saying they wanted to remain on their lands in New York State:

To our Father the President of the United States
Father,
     We have today received information of your communication sent from the Secretary of War to the Hamilton Baptist Missionary Society and we are much pleased with the interest you have expressed in our welfare, and we rejoice that you have expressed in our welfare, and rejoice that you . . . to protect us.
     We feel happy in receiving the communication you sent us, both Nations [the Oneida and Onondaga] being convened in council at this time to rejoice together.
     Father, We are very happy that you took into consideration our communication which was made last summer by our delegates, and that you are willing to protect us from our enemies.
     We assure you, Father, its our will and determination to stay where we are, and we feel strong while we find you our friend.
     Father, We rejoice to hear that you will protect us, by which we believe you love us, and will do us good. We want to inform our Father the President that we wish him not to take any notion of any communication that may be sent to him in relation to this matter and that he would give sanction to nothing without first being satisfied that the head chiefs and the Nation in general are agreed in it. There is much intrigue used against us, and the President may be deceived; with the hope he will be cautious.
     Father
     If Mr. Eleazer Williams, our Missionary, makes any

communication to you with respect to us, you may be sure that we are not found in it. He has a few young men around him, who are general agreement in his plans; but we consider them as boys, they have never done anything for the Nation as we place no confidence in them.
We have written to the bishop to take Mr. Williams away as we are unwilling any longer to have him our Missionary.

Father

When we get ready to emigrate we shall not apply to you by writing; you may expect to see the Chiefs in person, and until you are applied to in this way, you may conclude we are contented where we are.

Farewell

Onondaga chiefs
Ante his X mark Sreyour [?]
Samuel his X mark Parker
Captain his X mark George [?]
John his X mark Kirke toate [?]
John his X mark Brown
John his X mark Oasedasa

Oneida chiefs and warriors
Peter his X mark Summer
Captain his X mark Petter
Jacob his X mark Oto tot sant [?]
Anthony his X mark Te wa gwa cah loch [?]
Abram his X mark Wat sat ah
Wm his X mark Cornelius
Hendrick his X mark Scuyler
Nicolas his X mark Cah rah com to [?]
Jacob his X mark Anthony

The following list of names are attached to this document:
Matinas his X mark White
Adam his X mark Leon on da we
Jacob his X mark Doxtater

Thomas his X mark Webster
Anthony his X mark Otoeguiah
John his X mark Swamp
John his X mark Cornelius
Hendrick [?] his X mark Smith
John his X mark Smith
John his X mark Johnson
Moses his X mark Otsogweh
Thomas his X mark Summer
William his X mark Leuglh [?]
Martin Dinney[31]

Peter Summer and other Oneida Indians, "in Council at the new school house, Oneida Castle," wrote to President Monroe in January 1822. They informed "Monroe that they have dismissed the Rev. Eleazer Williams as their missionary," noting "The majority of the Six Nations are opposed to William's plan to move the Indians to Green Bay. The Stockbridge Indians are willing to emigrate. All Indians of the Six Nations were pleased when they hear the letter from the Secretary of War; the letter indicated that the government feels an interest in the welfare of the Indians."[32]

THE FRENCH PROTEST

French settlers had acquired lands in Green Bay and were opposed to Menominee treaties because they feared they would lose their land. The French included two groups: the first were fur traders, and the second supported themselves as farmers and hunters. Both groups had intermarried with the Menominee, which gave them access to land.[33]

Cass informed the delegation from the Six Nations that the French living in the Green Bay area were "hostile to their intentions."[34] The French settlers had influence with the Menominee and interfered in treaty negotiations. Their interference was so strong that it was apparent that treaty decisions were being made by the French. The New York Indian delegates asked the Menominee and Winnebago to make their decisions themselves without French aid.[35]

The French made several unsubstantiated claims in their protest to the treaty. They said that Williams wrote the 1821 treaty; however, Ellis states that Trowbridge wrote the treaty.[36] In a November 1823 petition, the French argue that Williams wrote the 1821 treaty to suit his own purposes, and that the Menominee and Winnebago who signed were not authorized to do so.[37] The French petition states that no one from the army was present to witness this treaty, but there are army signatures on the 1821 treaty.[38]

THE ONEIDA PROTEST ELEAZER WILLIAMS

The Oneida wrote a letter to Bishop John H. Hobart on November 12, 1821, to express their displeasure with Williams and to assert their sovereign right to select whom they wanted as a minister:

> To our Father, the Bishop John H. Hobart: — Father, we have received your communication dated at Utica, and have taken the advice you therein gave us. We have awaited the return of Mr. Williams, but he gave us no satisfaction. We are satisfied that he is engaged in the service of a speculating company, who have for their object the routing of Indians from their plantation. We are able to prove that a letter has been seen from the Cashier of the Bank of Geneva purporting to be an answer of one sent to him by Mr. Williams in which an application had been made to draw $250 in the name of a certain company which we forbear to name at this time, stating that the company would comply with his request only on condition of his removing the Indians.
>
> Father, we have no disposition to complain unreasonably, we wish to do right, and we want to be treated honorably by others, and especially by our minister. We have lost our confidence in him, we are afraid he is not honest.
>
> We had left in the hands of Judge Miller and Nathan Williams, after building our meeting house, 254 dollars, out of which we have been furnished with a bell for our meeting house at 154 dollars including transportation, and $10 for hanging it. The rest of the money Mr. Williams by some means or other, has obtained without our approbation, and renders no account of it. We had designed that money for building our Missionary house; but Mr. Williams

pretended that there was no money left and we have had to pay $200 out of our annuities for that building, but we have since ascertained how the business stands.

Father, Mr. Williams, is taking every measure to deceive us, to bring us to the necessity of leaving the land of our nativity. He has sent a message to Buffalo, to state to the Indians there, that the Oneida tribe, is preparing to go to Green Bay, when we have no such intention. There are a few individuals among us, and very few, who are agreed with his plan, we are determined not to be ruled by a man of so much intrigue.

Father, we are not a little astonished at the conduct of the man, you have sent us for a teacher. We had no expectation that he would or could use the Oneida Nation, as he has done; but we think we have found him out and all his plans. He is not contented in the place where you sent him, but he wants to rule, and have the command of the whole Six Nations.

Father, we wish you to take away this man and give us one that is a true minister of the gospel. We don't want a man that is a speculator for a minister; we want a man that will attend to the duties of his holy office, and look to the good of our souls, and be content in his station. We have no design of renouncing our religion. We are established in the faith, but we want a good minister to go before us.

We have many pious old people among us whose feelings are much wounded with the conduct of Mr. Williams, they never knew a minister conduct as he has done before.

Father, we are sorry to find these things have a bad effect in the minds of the Indians of other tribes, and prejudices them against receiving the gospel. They say that they are better off without it than we are with it — while we are all confusion among us, they remain in peace.

Father, we consider ourselves an independent nation, and when we get ready to emigrate we will take measures to secure a country where WE think best. We don't want a man to come from another tribe to persuade and compel us to go where he says is best, we wish to choose for ourselves, we have the right, and no man shall take it from us, and we consider it an insult for any man to attempt such a thing. We think we have used Mr. Williams in every respect well. We have furnished him with Grain, hay, and wood, besides presents in meat, &c ever since he has lived here. He has also drawn his share in our annuities every year, and we have given him 150 acres of land valued at 1500 dollars; and besides all this, he receives annually seventy dollars, which is the rent of lands we have left out in Westmoreland, which were appropriated by the nation for the support of the Mission at this place.

The Oneida Nation has always stood like a great tree, firmly rooted — and with great branches, which is not to be removed — and has always been considered so by the general government.

Mr. Williams has complained much that he could not live unless we should give him more salary, that the Bishop gave him but little, but we think if — he had been a true Christian, he would have been contented. Mr. Williams told us before he started his journey, that the Bishop had directed him to go, and that there he would go, if he had to go through a lake of fire. Mr. Williams has always told the nation that they were not worthy to speak to the Bishop, but we have presumed to address him as a friend and a father; we could come to a close by stating that the chiefs of both parties are assembled, and unite in this request to you for aid in this time of trial. We hope you will give us a gracious hearing, and relieve your obedient children from this burden of grief of which we complain.
Farewell.
Antony Ostregerate
Thomas Swamp
Hendrick Smith
John Thompson
Moses Schuyler
Moses Ostregerate
Thomas Summer
William Schuyler
Martin Dinney
Peter Summer
Captain Peter
Jacob Otot Sait

Anth'y Tawaguacahlockgua
Abm. Wat-sa-tak
Wm. Cornelius
Hendrick Schuyler
Nicholas Cah-vate-coon-ter
Jacob Anthony
Mrtinus White
Adam Scanadwah
Jacob Doxtader
Thomas Webster
Signed in the presence of Robert Powell
Oneida Castle, Nov. 12, 1821.[39]

The 1821 treaty is so significant because it was made and signed between the sovereign Indigenous nations of Menominee, Ho-Chunk,
Stockbridge, Oneida, and Munsee. This treaty was approved by President
Monroe and not submitted to Congress because treaties made between
Indian nations do not require congressional approval. As Calhoun wrote
in late 1822, "The treaty concluded by the Delegates with the Menominees
& Winnebagoes is approved by the President which is all the ratifications
that is necessary as those Treaties only to which the United States is a party
require the addition of the sanction of the Senate."[40] Protests were made
by the Six Nations and the French, and the removal of Eleazer Williams
was requested by the Oneida. However, the lands designated for the New
York Indians in the 1821 treaty were too small to accommodate all of the
Six Nations, and a request was made to return the land and petition the
Menominee for a much larger tract.

4

THE TREATIES OF
1822, 1824, AND 1825

Indian Nation to Indian Nation

In 1822, the New York Indians wrote to Secretary of War John C. Calhoun requesting more land from the Menominee Nation. The New York Indians felt the land designated to them in the 1821 treaty was not large enough to support the number of New York Indians who planned to emigrate. This request was approved by Calhoun, and a second trip was made by New York Indian delegates to make a treaty with the Menominee.

The continued interaction between Indigenous nations was evident in the 1824 Indian nation–to–Indian nation treaty in which provisions for land were made by the Stockbridge, First Christian Party of the Oneida, St. Regis, Munsee, and Tuscarora with the Brothertown, who had not participated in the 1821 and 1822 treaties but who were part of the removal policy of the United States. These Indian nation–to–Indian nation treaties are significant because all future treaties were made with New York State or the United States.

Documents in the Eleazer Williams papers and the Solomon U. Hendrick letters, as well as reports from John Sergeant Jr. and A.G. Ellis, indicate that ancient diplomatic protocols between Indian nations were followed during treaty negotiations. Words and phrases such as *polish the chain of friendship, using wampum,* and *brothers* indicate the continued usage of diplomatic protocols, as these diplomatic terms were used in the Two Row Wampum Treaty with the Dutch in 1613.

THE ONEIDA REQUEST MORE LAND

On January 25, 1822, Cornelius Beard, representing the First Christian Party of the Oneida, wrote to Calhoun. Beard requested approval for another trip to the Green Bay area to extend the lands obtained in the 1821 treaty because the original lands offered were too far from Green Bay. This letter was signed in the presence of Eleazer Williams.

Sir,

On the 18th day of August 1821 by a treaty made between the Six Nations, the St. Regis, & Stockbridge & Munsee Nations of Indians of New York of the one part, and the Menomine and Winnebago Indians in the vicinity of Green Bay of their part, a certain tract of land was ceded to the former for the consideration of two thousand dollars, which treaty has been duly ratified by the President. This land was obtained with a view of removing to the purchase, but a part of the Six Nations are dissatisfied that the land does not extend more than 18 miles of the Bay.

Our particular object in addressing you at this time is to solicit from our father, the President, permission to make another effort to meet with the said Indians near Green Bay so as to obtain an extension of the grant . . . toward the said Bay, to within four miles of the United States fort in the Bay which was acceded to by the President on a former occasion.

We have further to solicit information whether the above mentioned additional tract should be ceded to us, together with the . . . [large section illegible]) already ceded, and any part of the Six Nations of Indians should still object thereto and refuses to pay their proportion of the purchase money whether the remaining Six Nations who may make the payment may . . . such treaty be deemed . . . of the whole purchase.

And inasmuch as we find it present and necessary to employ a fit and proper agent who may protect and urge our rights and wishes in treating on the subject. And having great confidence he the agent

who for the last thirteen years has been employed by the State of New
York, whether we may employ such agent to go with us to Green Bay
and whether a stipulation may not be contained in such treaty to
remunerate and pay such agent of lands which may be ceded to us.

And in addition to this we would further add that the French
residing on the land are anxious to identify their interests with the
Six Nations, St. Regis, Stockbridge and Munsee Nations of Indians,
and their children are half breeds and . . . savage may participate in
the advantages of instruction in husbandry and literature that will be
imparted in the ceded territory.

I apprehend the majority of the other Tribes would prefer the
young gentleman who Gov. Cass had authorized the season past to
accompany the deputies, would again go with us, as they are under
great obligations to that young man, he having rendered great
assistance at the late treaty.
With great consideration
I have the honor to be your
Obt. Servant

In presence of
Eleazer Williams
Albany 25th January 1822
Cornelius his X mark Beard
In behalf of the first Christian Party of the Oneida Nation of Indians[1]

Calhoun responded to Beard in a letter dated February 13, 1822, in
which he returned a copy of the 1821 treaty that was approved and signed
by President James Monroe. Calhoun authorized a second trip to the Green
Bay area to obtain more land.[2] The letter reads:

I have received your communication of the 5th Instant and return
herewith the original treaty concluded at Green Bay between the
Deputies from the Stockbridge and other tribes of the Six Nations
and the Menomeenees and Winnebagoes, endorsed by the President
approved.

I regret that any portion of the Six Nations is dissatisfied with

THE TREATIES OF 1822, 1824, AND 1825

the treaty, but as one of the causes of dissatisfaction appears to be the distance of the Country ceded thereby from Green Bay, and may be obviated by procuring an extension of the Cession as proposed, the permission which is solicited for another deputation from the Stockbridge and other tribes of the Six Nations, to visit the Country again for that purpose, is granted.

The country the Six Nations have or may acquire from the Menomeenees & Winnebageos, will be held by them in the same manner as the Indians who previously owned it. The Deputies that may be appointed to make the arrangement (not exceeding six in number) will be provided with letters similar to those given to them last year and orders will be given for them to furnished with one ration each while on their journey and engaged in effecting the object of their visit. . . .

Governor [Lewis] Cass has been instructed to give the Indians who may emigrate from the Stockbridge or other tribes of the Six Nations every facility in his power, in fixing themselves upon the lands they have acquired of the Menomeeness and Winnebagoes; but no additional expense can be incurred. He will also be instructed to make the representation to the Menomeemees and Winnebagoes which you suggest relative to their civilization. No doubt is entertained but the example of their new and more civilized Neighbours will, in time, have the happy effect of introducing among them the same degree of improvement.

In relation to the degree of title which the respective tribes forming the Six Nations may have in the lands which have been or may be ceded to them by the Menomeenees & Winnebagoes, it is a subject in which the Government cannot interfere. The claim of each tribe it is believed can be more satisfactorily settled among themselves by their head men.[3]

Another letter was sent to Calhoun, this one in March 1822, that expressed the Oneida's desire to make another treaty with the Menominee and Winnebago. The Oneida chiefs of the First Christian Party wrote to Calhoun "relating to their treaty with the Menominees and Winnebagoes & wish to make another treaty." They wrote:

To our Great & Most Excellent Brother, The Secretary of War
We the chiefs of the first Christian party of the Oneida Nation, desire
through the medium of this paper to express to You our most sincere
& humble thanks for the very kind aid and assistance which You
have been pleased to render us in effecting our late Treaty with our
western brothers, the Menominies & Winnebagoes.

But while doing this we beg leave to state to our kind Brother, that
although many of our brothers of the Six Nations, are unpleased with
the treaty, Yet some of them object as a reason for not paying a certain
sum agreeable to the third article thereof, that the country ceded
thereby is at too great a distance from the mouth of the Fox River.

Great Brother, to obviate the above objections and obtain other
important information relative to our mission, we wish humbly to
submit for Your consideration the following . . .

1st could not we be permitted to extend our territory toward the
mouth of the River by making a second treaty?

2nd Will the French in that vicinity now connected with the
Indians by marriage, be allowed with their improvements to join
with, and become Indian claimers & . . . with ourselves?

3rd Will not the Government of the United States be pleased to
take firm measures to prevent the sale or disposal in any manner,
spirituous liquors within the limits of our territories?

4th To what extent may we expect the general Government to
and in their support of missionaries & . . . for our benefit then by
instructing us in agricultures, arts, sciences, and letters?

We hope if permitted to make the second expedition, that we will
again be provided rations etc — and as soon as of our agent & others
wish to accompany us to take a view of the country, we wish to know
what no. of rations may be granted?

Reports are in circulation, that if we ratify this Treaty, we shall
immediately be obliged by the Gen. Government to remove there,
in a Genl. Body — we wish to know if this be so? — and as may result,
may we answer how attached to the Government seal.

Great Brother, as these questions are of the utmost importance to
Your Brethren, we hope that our most excellent Brother will favor us
with an answer as soon as convenient. — We remain with the most

sincere regard Your — . . . Humble Brethren —
Signed in presence of
A.G. Ellis
Eleazer Williams
Missionary to the Oneida Indians.

Anthony his X mark Arongowa
John his X mark Brandt
Hendrick his X mark Powlis
John his X mark August
John his X mark Scanandoa
Neddy his X mark Aterigust
Cornelius his X mark Brant
Thomas his X mark Scanandoa
Peter his X mark August
John his X mark Cornelius
John his X mark Peters

Oneida council fire
14th March 1822[4]

In a June 14, 1822, letter from Calhoun, Reverend John Sergeant Jr. answered portions of the March 14 letter, saying if the Stockbridge and Six Nations moved to Green Bay, "the friendship and protection of the government will go with them; the United States will do all that it can do to promote their prosperity and happiness." Calhoun mentioned preventing the use of alcohol as well as the animosity of French settlers near Green Bay to New York Indians moving there, and he advised that "arrangements must be left entirely to the Indians." Eleazer Williams was scheduled to go on the trip.[5]

COLLUSION BETWEEN ELEAZER WILLIAMS AND THE OGDEN LAND COMPANY

The Oneida Council at Oneida Castle in New York State clearly understood the plan of Eleazer Williams and the relationship between the Ogden Land

Company and Williams. They said as much in a letter to President Monroe written in January 1822:

> Dear Father,
> We your red children of the Oneida Nation once more address you, on the subject of our Temporal [?] concerns. We hope our Father the President will give one more pertinent hearing; the first & second party Uniting in this address.
> Father
> Mr. Williams has essentially injured the Six Nations & produced great uneasiness among us. We have been at much trouble and expense to defeat him in his fraudulent designs. We have found leave to defeat him and we are wholly dissatisfied him as a communicator of the Gospel, and he is no longer considered as having to do with any of our concerns.
> We assure the President that a very large majority of this Tribe and of the six Nations in council are opposed to Mr. Williams plans of taking us off to Green Bay, where he says he has provided a plan for us. We have had no agency in selecting that place of retreat, nor are we disposed to accept it from the hand of a foreigner, who is so liberal of his services (Mr. Williams descends from the St. Regis Tribe) Mr. Williams has no right here. If he has found in his own estimation a desirable land, he is welcome to go and enjoy it, in company with the Stockbridge Tribe with whom he obtained it, we can spare his persons and services without inconvenience.
> Father,
> We expect that Mr. Williams and our Indians from this Tribe in company with him, will visit you before many days, but they are not authorized to do no business in our name, and we hope the President will give no hearing on business which concerns us.
> There are a few individuals of this tribe who are bribed to his interest that are united with him. But the whole scheme is set forth by a combination of speculators under the name the "Ogden Company" who have for this object the routing of the Indians from their plantations [?]. And Mr. W. is the tool of this company.
> Father,

The sentiments herein contained are not only the sentiments of the Chiefs but the views and feelings of the . . . The President is assured that the Indian that companions Mr. W. is bribed into his service.

Father,

We shall rest assured that you will pay no regard to Mr. Williams during his visit with you as it was positively affirmed that the Great Council of the Six Nation recently held at Onondaga, that he had never been authorized by any of them to act in their behalf. At the council above referred to we held our council in the house while Mr. Williams and his bribed party held their interviews . . . the . . . of the fewer consequently he was ignorant of our resolutions.

Father,

The Stockbridge Tribe has no connection with us. They have found a people to the west that agree with them in their language and they can go and live with them in peace.

But our forefathers have ever been at variance with that people, and we find that the stand we took in favor of this country during the last war has received their former hostile feelings towards us. This was declared to be the fact at the Great Council above mentioned.

Father,

You have a long time been . . . us to keep and cultivate our lands, and now at this time we are considerably and advanced in the art of cultivation & beside all this there is an establishment making by a religious society to instruct our young men in some of the most useful Mechanical arts accompanied also with a school which promises great usefulness to the rising generations among us, and if we leave this place all this will be exhausted for the privilege of hunting and fishing.

Father,

We have found out that Captain Parrish is the plan to remove us. He thoroughly advised the Indians at a Council held at Buffalo last fall to go, and advised (as the most judicious course) to send a thousand dollars of the property we receive in clothing from the U. State to the western Indians to pay for that land.

Father,

The whole six nations were much pleased when they heard the letter read which was sent from the secretary of war. By which we learn the claims of the Government toward us and their interest in our welfare.

We hope for our father's health when he shall read this letter, as we your red children are enjoying the same blessing from the Great Spirit, we subscribe ourselves, ever yours.

Peter his X mark Summers

Wm. his X mark Th hon eventimonjo [?]

Abrams his X mark Ah west satah [?]

Jacob his X mark Anthony

Thomas his X mark Scanandoah

Anthony his X mark White

Jacob his X mark Doxtater

Peter his X mark Braid

Henry his X mark Schuyler

Wm. his X mark Cornelius

Nicolas his X mark Cah ra coon tu

Captain his X mark Peter

Captain his X mark Peter Jr.

Adam his X mark Scanandoah

John his X mark Thompson

Baptist his X mark Skenanda

Moses his X mark Schuyler

Peter his X mark Doxtater

George his X mark . . .

Sheffles [?] his X mark Schuyler

Abram his X mark Schuyler

Peter his X mark Webster

Abrams his X mark Webster

Martin Denny

Baptist Denny

John Denny

Signed in Presence Robert Powell, of Ashna Lawton

Done in Council at the new school house, Oneida Castle January 22, 1822[6]

On March 2, 1822, Ogden wrote to Christopher Vandeventer. In the letter, he revealed his ongoing attempts to be informed of and involved in the removal of the Stockbridge and other New York Indians. Ogden had been informed that the New York state legislature enacted a law granting the Stockbridge Indians four thousand to five thousand dollars "to enable them to remove upon their late purchase on Fox River the ensuing Spring." Ogden noted, "I was however informed that the Six Nations could not come to any Decision as to their Removal to these Lands. The Pagan Party, at the Head of which is Red Jacket, being opposed while the Christian Party were in favor of the measure." The two factions agreed "to submit the subject to the decision of the President of the United States," James Monroe.

Ogden asked Vandeventer to obtain permission from Calhoun for Ogden to be informed about "the substance of the Communication made to the War Department, by the Six Nations, through their Agent Mr. [Jasper] Parrish," and whether Monroe had reached a decision.[7] Ogden continued his involvement in Indian removal by writing to Calhoun again, asking this time about the 1821 treaty between the New York Indians and the Menominee and Winnebago, and wondering if removal will require "any immediate necessity for the relinquishment of their present seats."

In June 1822, Parrish was told by the chiefs of the Six Nations that they will "have nothing to do with the Green Bay purchase of land." He noted that if "the Stockbridge tribe with a few individuals of the Six Nations should think proper to receive, ratify and pay for the land purchased at Green Bay, they may do so, with their private money." The chiefs of the Six Nations had well stated that "no part of their national annuity should be applied to make any part of the payments."[8] Parrish wrote to Calhoun again on October 21, 1822, to state he had attended a council meeting of the Six Nations held in Buffalo on October 18, in which the Six Nations made it clear that "They are . . . wishing to come to an understanding with government respecting the Green Bay purchase, being at present much divided in opinion upon that subject."[9]

Meanwhile, the First Christian Party of Oneidas wrote to Calhoun on July 4, 1822, regarding their annuity payment, which they wanted to use to purchase lands in Green Bay. They informed Calhoun that the Oneida were divided into two parties.

Great Brother,

We the Chiefs and Warriors of the first Christian party of the Oneida Nation, beg leave to remind your Excellency that we wrote to you last winter, requesting you to permit us to receive our gratuity (heretofore paid in goods) in money. That the money might be forwarded to Jasper Parish, agent, for the purpose of aiding us in the payment of the late Green Bay purchase of lands — and we are happy to say, that You now complied with our request.

But, Great Brother, we beg You to remember that there are recognized by the Legislature of this State, two parties of this Nation, of one of which, we are now the head men. We understand by Mr. Parish that your Excellency's instruction to him in relation to the whole nation as one, wherefore he does not feel authorized to divide to us our share of the gratuity as the other party of the nation oppose this most desirable object.

Our present purpose is therefore, most Excellent Brother, to beg of Your Excellency to instruct the Agent to divide to us our portion of the money that we may be enabled to meet our engagements with our western Brethren.

If our Great Brother should be pleased to gratify our wishes, we hope he will inform Mr. agent immediately, as the time is already arrived when we should set away.

We remain Your affectionate Brethren,

Peter his X mark Neddy

. . . his X mark Ninham

George his X mark Doxtater

Thomas his X mark Scanandoa

Nedy his X mark Atriquet

Peter his X mark August

John his X mark Antone

Cornelius his X mark Beard

Henry his X mark Powlis

John his X mark Scanandoa

David his X mark Bread

Cornelius his X mark John

John his X mark Williams[10]

Parrish wrote to Calhoun August 2, 1822, regarding the division of annuities among the Six Nations. Referring to the chiefs of the Six Nations, Parrish wrote, "I made application to them to Agree to divide the $4,500 by populations of the villages, as stated the Oneida have two parties and the annuity will be divided among the two parties." The 1794 Canandaigua Treaty between the Six Nations and the United States promised $4,500 annuity to the Six Nations to be paid annually forever.[11]

The Tuscarora Nation expressed its interest to the Stockbridge Nation by sending a delegate to the 1822 treaty negotiations. The Tuscarora wrote:

Brothers,
   We having the opportunity to send another few lines to you — respecting our wishes — We wish you would assist our young man in his transactions if should be required — When interview the Western Indians.
   Brother, We wish you would relate the proceedings what takes place between us and the western Indians respecting the treaty — We wish you would write down on a paper and send it by our person — that we may have satisfaction of the business.
   Brother, We respectfully represent our salutations to you and return thanks for your favourable addresses received.
   From your friends & Brothers from the Chiefs of Tuscarora Tribe of Indians
Jacob Cauretauwacaugh his X mark
Nicholas Cusik
Geroge Printup his x mark
James Johnson his x mark
John Tose his x mark[12]

THE TREATY OF 1822

Diplomatic Procedures

There were ancient protocols for meeting among Indigenous nations long before Europeans arrived. It is insightful to read that these ancient protocols were understood and utilized by settler colonists and the US government in the 1700s and 1800s.[13] All treaty meetings were held using

the governmental protocols of Native nations well into the 1850s. Haudenosaunee nations (Six Nations) had a governmental process of meeting
in clans before the larger meeting was held so that the chiefs knew and
expressed the wishes of the people.

Before a treaty was discussed, an invitation was extended to those nations that would participate. It was generally good manners to feed and
provide lodging for those attending. The council fire was kindled, and the
meeting was opened by giving thanks for everyone's healthy and ability to
be present. There was a greeting ceremony of shaking hands to greet all
the attendees and express gratitude for each other's presence. The greet-
ings may have included polishing the chain of friendship, establishing the
relationship as brothers, father to children, grandfather to grandchildren,
or other family relationships.

As the council began, one person would speak at a time, presenting the
purpose of the meeting, expressing information on the issue, and giving

Daniel Bread, leader of the First Christian
Party of Oneidas, was a central political
and cultural figure among the Oneida for
decades. WHI IMAGE ID 2550

Stockbridge political leader John W
Quinney represented the Stockbridge
during treaty negotiations throughout
the 1820s and 1830s. WHI IMAGE ID 49

their perspectives or requests from the other side. A string or belt of wampum would be given to confirm the words of the speaker. The other side would then discuss and respond, one person speaking for each side, giving their information, perspectives, and decisions on the issue. A string or belt of wampum would be presented to confirm their words. This process would go back and forth during the negotiations until an agreement was made or the meeting adjourned for the day.

On September 16, 1822, A. G. Ellis reported events of the first day, the invitation to the Indigenous nations, the seating protocol, and the diplomatic protocol for opening the meeting. Ellis wrote:

> This day much has been done. The chiefs & warriors of both nations gave in [by sticks] the no [number] of . . . people, and also that they were ready to wait upon the deputies. Accordingly, about 12 o'clock the council fire was kindled in front of the house, (at the residence of Col. Bowyer) a large circled . . . Deputy — man the door — the Menominee on the right — Winnebago on the left, and the gentlemen officers of the garrison and citizens opposite the deputy. A pile of tobacco was placed in the mid as each lit his pipe and after ceremony of shaking hands. Mr. Solomon U. Hendricks opened the council by holding forth a string of wampum, and on hearing, through the medium of Mr. Prickert, public interpreter, the following speech — to the chief and warriors of Menominee & Winnebago Nations.[14]

From this description it is evident that Indigenous protocols were followed. Ellis states that those attending this treaty were five thousand combined Menominee and Winnebago, New York Indians, French, people of mixed ancestry, and Americans.[15] Ellis later wrote that three thousand to four thousand Indians attended, and he described a dance with two thousand people. John Sergeant Jr. reported about eight hundred people attending, which is quite a difference from Ellis.

Ellis recorded speeches by Solomon Hendrick (Stockbridge) and Dogs Head (Winnebago) at the opening of the meeting in which the issues were stated. They are included here.

Speech from Solomon U. Hendrick (Stockbridge)

Children:

I am thankful that the Great Spirit has allowed so many of us to assemble around this council fire, to shake hands together, and smoke a pipe of peace & friendship. I have followed the path which was opened the last season, and was happy to find it clear of obstructions and hope it will thus continue so. The chain of friendship which was presented last season by the Stockbridge, Six Nations, St. Regis & Munsee Nations is again renewed by now, and I hope it will be kept bright till . . . generations. You . . . conduct that your last season conveyed to us a piece of your land, to kindle our fire upon. We have now come to take possession of it and sit down among you. Our Great Father, the President of the US, has been informed of the last season transaction between us and was well pleased to find his new children so kind to each other. It is his wish that we may settle here among you, and this time to promote each others welfare. Your Great Father, the President, was also much pleased to find that you acknowledged him as your father, and that you considered yourselves under the government of the US At the time you conveyed to us the land, we presented you with some goods and promised you some more, which we have bro't and deliver accordingly, Kind children, I now salute you, the chiefs, you young men, women & children, in which our brethren the Oneida's, St. Regis & Tuscarora's join and deliver these words (presenting the wampum) in the name & behalf of the Stockbridge, Oneida, St. Regis & Tuscarora Nations.[16]

Speech from Dogs Head (Winnebago)

I feel very thankful to the Great Spirit, that we are all assembled to shake hands together, and smoke a pipe of peace & friendship.

You my Grand fathers the Abanaqwis [?] and my Brothers the Oneida and also my friends, and I call the Americans my Father.

No one of us are against your coming here — We take you my Grand Father, my Brothers the Oneidas and my Father the Americans

by the hand at the same time, and are pleased to see you all, and in
this all our Chiefs, Young Men, Women & children agree — all are
extremely happy to see you —

Now my friends I will tell to you what my chiefs think — at the
time the Americans & British fought, I sent forward and shook hands
& my American Father wished then to purchase some our lands. But
I thought it . . . and was not . . . pleased and I now see that the Great
Spirit is taking pity upon us and about to do something for us, by
sending you here — You told us last season, that our Grand Father
the President — of the United States, desires you to settle among us,
and that if we were willing You would do so; to this we consented,
and looked for you some days ago, and I began to despair, and fear
that you had only flattered us with a lie, and would never come here
now; But how do I now rejoice to find you here as you told us, I rejoice
that you have "followed the path by which you came last season, and
that it is not stopped up." I also rejoice that my G. Father, my Fathers
& Brothers are all assembled together behold this wampum is now
in my hand before you, also to this I . . . as the chain of friendship
betwixt us.

. . . our chiefs would not then agree to it. — For said they if we sell
them our lands — where shall we go? —

The Great Spirit made the lands & put us upon them, and taught us
the manner of gaining our subsistence and to fear him — But in all, he
never taught us that he made lands twice — therefore we would not
sell it for fear of offending him — But notwithstanding, I see that our
Great Father the President has taken pity upon us, — and has in his . . .
instructed you to come us — & when I took you by the hand, I beheld
to my surprise that you not only spoke of him but actually appeared
like him — in manner, customs and. . . . Wherefore my Grandfather &
Brethren it pleased me, and I was tempted, and persuaded not to sell
but grant to you a piece of our land, that you might sit down among
us, in hope that we might in time. . . . You . . . example. — Now my
friends I hope you will take . . . of what has been given you and may
. . . always remain . . . & in peace. —

But I hope you will not at present ask of us more. — You are now
. . . the same . . . with us, although having a partition betwext us —

But should you ask now and get farther into the lands of our Territory then . . . be nothing betwext us and we should be altogether which we are yet strangers — and as we do not yet understand each other, and our . . . sometimes foolish, difficulties might ensure, and our peace & friendship be disturbed. — But when we shall better acquainted, and understand each other . . . then we may mix with. . . . I speak then to you because you are civilized, you have the . . . knowledge and understanding of the white people. — You do not make fools & beasts of yourselves with strong drink — but we, and our young men, when they have opportunities, make themselves beasts & fools with it — therefore do I fear, should you be to much among us that we might be unhappy —

Now I wish to address myself to my Father, the Americans — Fathers — I wish you to inform our Great Father the President of the U. States, that this land this is all his — We give it to him, and he has conquered from his enemies — The land is valuable — You may use the timber, and cultivate it to great advantage, raise all things which the white people wish — and I hope that this will make you charitable to give something to us every year to satisfy our hunger, and cover our nakedness. —

Furthermore — when my Fathers, the Americans came here to establish the fort, they saw that our Great Father the President would pay us something for the lands — But how is it that we have received nothing? Have we been deceived by him? no — I believe not — I do not believe he ever knew of the promise which his men made to us — but I hope you will soon tell him, and doubt not but he will pay us. — I hope you will carry this my talk to him — let him know all that I have thus far saw.

I would not forget to mention one thing particularly to you — When you first came among us, you were not a little fond of our women — not infrequently following them & enticing them with a bottle of whiskey!! Some of our young men were offended — although themselves injured, and were . . . on the point of . . . you — I would not have you think that I mention this in anger for you see I join in a hearty laughs and we are pleased to see any of our women bring forth a white child! — I would also mention to you, my friendship for the poor French men who are connected with us, and wish to have you take pity upon them; though some of them have become quite . . , and wish how . . . . speak to such a man as myself, . . . I wish you to pity them & treat them as Brothers. —

Fathers you have an influence with our Great Father the President of the US — and we have a request to make to you & to him — We wish to have our former blacksmith, who was this spring removed again given to us — He is a good man & our Brother & can do our work better than any other. —

Finally my Brethren one & all let us treat one another kindly & him & peace, let us become together a great nation, that shall . . . the earth — let us be similar in our . . .[17]

Solomon U. Hendrick Report on the 1822 Treaty

Solomon U. Hendrick (Stockbridge) also presented a report on his version of the events as they happened in the negotiations of the 1822 treaty:

We arrived at Green Bay on the 1st day of Sept. where messengers were immediately sent on to different encampments or towns of the Menominies & Winnebagoes to notify them of our arrival.

In a few days after the Indians from the two Nations began to arrive & collect near where we had our quarters, accompanied by their Chiefs & Head Warriors. On the 16th September a council was held with the Chiefs & Warriors of the two nations, when a short talk was delivered to them renewing the covenant of our friendship and the agreement we had made with them last year.

I had the gratification to find by their reply that they were all satisfied with the Treaty. "No one, as they say, is against it." They were much pleased to see a number [of] families from our Tribe had come, with a view to live near them. The goods were then delivered to them & the amount each Nation paid receipted on the back of the Treaty.

A few days after a council was again held with the Menominies with a view to endeavor to have an extension made to the cession of last year, and I have now the satisfaction to inform you that the Deputies succeeded in obtaining from the Menominies the cession

of all the lands owned by them situated from the lower line of the
Territory ceded to us last year including all islands in the Bay. The
Treaty was signed on the 23rd day of Sept. and I was requested
by my Chiefs to carry the same to our father the President for his
approbation and ratification and which I have honor to present
to the Hnble the Secy of War, Together, with a letter from John
Sergeant Jr. Esq. originally directed to his Excellency Lew Cass
who was absent having, as I understood, started for the seat of
Government four days before our arrival at Detroit. I. e. Deputies
from the Oneida, Tuscarora, St Regis, Munsee & Stockbridge Tribe
of Indians. (N.Y.)[18]

John Sergeant Jr. Report

The US government appointed to negotiate this treaty, John Sergeant Jr.,
recorded his view of the 1822 treaty in the follow way:

Sir, — with respect to the commission with which your Excellency
was pleased to honour me, I beg leave to submit the following report.

I left Detroit on the 19th, in company with the New-York Indians,
and arrived at Green Bay on the 1st September. Messengers were
immediately dispatched to the different lodges of the Menominies
and Winnebago Indians, who returned and collected of both tribes
about 800 people, old and young. They assembled on the 16th
September, and received from the New-York Indians the amount of
goods stipulated in the third article of the treaty made last year. The
Winnebagoes then returned to their homes. The Menominies were
then invited to treat with the New-York Indians for an extension of
the purchase made last year.

They were particularly informed, through their interpreter, that
the purchase, if made, would be approbated by the government of
the United States; and that I, as a commissioner under government,
was directed to make the statement to them. The French and other
inhabitants in this place, who were interested in the subject, also
received the same notice.

The Menominies, after deliberating on the subject, met on the 23d
day of September, and as far as I could learn, without a dissenting

voice agreed to the proposal made by the New-York Indians, which were put in form of a treaty, which treaty is herewith transmitted to your Excellency, reference being had to the same, all particulars will more fully appear.

I have been credibly informed, that some of the French people at this place have taken much pains to create a party among the Menominies, to frustrate the designs of government and the New-York in the aforesaid purchase. They have been entirely unsuccessful in their attempts; and I have the pleasure further to state that the Menominies appear to be much pleased with the bargain and their new neighbors.

The subject of any former purchase having been made by the French, British, or American Government has been particularly inquired into & that no transfer has ever been made to either, except a piece of land immediately in the vicinity of Fort Howard which the Indians acknowledge though it has never been reduced to writing. All of which is respectfully submitted by, dear Sire,

Your Excellency's most obedient servant,

John Sergeant, Jun.[19]

THE TREATY OF SEPTEMBER 23, 1822

The treaty of 1822 is presented here in its entirety:

Articles of a Treaty (no other official title) Muheconuk or Stockbridge nation or tribe of Indians, First Christian party of the Oneida nation, Tuscarora nation or tribe of Indians, Eleazer Williams, a deputy authorized to represent the St. Regis nation or tribe of Indians (Mohawk), Munsee nation, with the Chiefs and head men of the Menominie nation. Approved by President James Monroe, March 13, 1823

Articles of a Treaty

Made and concluded at Green Bay, in the territory of Michigan, between

Uhhaunowwaunmut, alias Solomon U. Hendrick, Waunnacon,
alias John W. Quinney, Wenowwommaug, alias Abner W. Hendrick,
and Owwohthommaug, alias Sampson, deputies authorized and
empowered to represent the Mucheconnuk or Stockbridge nation or
tribe of Indians, of the state of New York;
Keniegowa, alias John August, Tekarihonentee, alias Neddy Atsiguet,
deputized, authorized, and empowered to represent the first
Christian party of the Oneida nation of Indians, in the state of
New York;
Sagowitha, alias Jonathan Printup, a deputy authorized, and
empowered to represent the Tuscarora nation or tribe of Indians, in
the state of New York;
Onwerenhicaki, alias Eleazor Williams, a deputy authorized and
empowered to represent the St. Regis nation or tribe of Indians, in the
state of New York;
Waulauque Koh, alias Last Night, a deputy from the Munsee nation;
and the chiefs and head men of the Menominie nation of Indians,
residing in the vicinity of Green Bay aforesaid, this twenty-third day
of September, in the year of our Lord one thousand eight hundred
and twenty-two.

ARTICLE I The Menominie nation of Indians, in consideration of
the stipulations herein made on the part of the Muhheconnuk or
Stockbridge, and the first Christian party of the Oneida, and the
Tuscarora, and the St. Regis, and Munsee nations, do hereby cede,
release and quit claim to them, the people of the said Stockbridge,
Oneida, Tuscarora, St. Regis and Munsee nations, for ever, all the
right, title, interest, and claim of them, the Menominie nation
of Indians, to all the lands and islands comprehended within and
described by the following boundaries, viz, beginning at the foot of
the rapids on Fox river, usually called the grand Kaccalin; thence
south east (or on the lower line of the lands last season ceded by the
Menominie and Winnebago nations of Indians to the Six Nations,
St. Regis, Stockbridge, and Munsee nations,) to or equidistant with
the Manawahkiah river, emptying into lake Michigan; thence on an
easterly course to and down said river to its mouth; then northerly,

on the borders of Lake Michigan, to and across the mouth of Green
Bay, so as to include all the islands of the Grand Traverse; thence
from the mouth of Green Bay aforesaid, a north westerly course to
a place on the north-west shore of Lake Michigan, generally known
and distinguished by the name of Weyohquatonk by the Indians,
and Bay-de-noque by the French; thence a westerly course on the
height of land separating the waters running into Lake Superior and
those running into Lake Michigan, to the head of the Menominie
river; thence continuing nearly the same course, until it strikes the
north-eastern boundary line of the lands ceded as aforesaid by the
Menominie and Winnebago nations to the Six Nations, St. Regis,
Stockbridge, and Munsee nations of Indians, in eighteen hundred
and twenty-one; thence southerly to the place of beginning.

ARTICLE II. The Stockbridge, Oneida, Tuscarora, St. Regis, and
Munsee nations aforesaid, do promise and agree to and with the
said Menominies, that they, the said Menominies, shall have the
free permission and privilege of occupying and residing upon the
lands herein ceded in common with them the Stockbridge, Oneida,
Tuscarora, St. Regis, and Munsee nations; provided, nevertheless,
that they, the Menominie nation, shall not in any manner infringe
upon any settlements, or improvements whatever, which may be in
any manner made by said Stockbridge, Oneida, Tuscarora, St. Regis,
and Munsee nations.

ARTICLE III. The Stockbridge, Oneida, Tuscarora, St. Regis, and
Munsee nations, do further promise and agree to and with the said
Menominies, that according to their request, all the French and other
inhabitants who have just and lawful claims to, and are now settled
and living upon any lands herein ceded, shall remain unmolested
by them the said Stockbridge, Oneida, Tuscarora, St. Regis, and
Munsees. It is also expressly understood by the Stockbridge, Oneida,
Tuscarora, St. Regis, and Munsee nations, that the Menominies
do not herein cede to them, the Stockbridge, Oneida, Tuscarora,
St. Regis, and Munsee nations, any lands in the vicinity of Fort
Howard, or near the mouth of Fox river; the title of which may have
been heretofore extinguished by the American government.

ARTICLE IV. In consideration of the cession herein made by

the Menominies, the Stockbridge and Munsee nations of Indians aforesaid have, by the hands of their deputies, paid to the chiefs and head men of the Menominie nation, this day, the sum of one thousand dollars in goods, in full of all demands in this treaty on their part, the receipt whereof is hereby acknowledged by the Menominie nation. And the Oneida, Tuscarora, and St. Regis nations of Indians, do promise and agree to and with the Menominie nation, to pay to them, the Menominies, the sum of one thousand dollars in one year from the date hereof, and also one thousand dollars in two years from the date hereof — the whole to be paid in goods; the which respective sums are to be a full and complete recompense and compensation for the lands hereby ceded, released and quit claimed to the Stockbridge, Oneida, Tuscarora, St. Regis, and Munsee nations.

In testimony whereof, the said deputies and the said chiefs and head men, have hereunto set their hands and seals, at the place and on the day and year above written.

Witness, John Sergeant, jun., Agent on the part of the government of the United States.

Menominee Chiefs
Ohgummonnekurr X or Great Wave,
The Spaniard X
Pohmonikoht X
Saghkittoht X The Pheasant,
Wyhnisaught X Yellow Dog,
Pyaughkeenagh X The Tower,
Wyghtchunequagh X The Rubber,
Wypuhkauchywen X End of the Rapids,
Chishawinohmitch X South Bag,
Theykaughong X Scare-all.

Deputies
Uhhaunowwaunmut, alias Solomon U. Hendrick,
Waunnaucon, alias John W. Quinney,
Wenowwommaug, alias Abner W. Hendrick,
Owwohthommaug, alias Sampson,
Waulauquekoh + alias Last Night,

Keniakowa + John August,
Tegarihontia + alias Needy Atsiguet,
Sagowisha + alias Jonathan Printup,
Eleazer Williams.
Signed, sealed and delivered, in presence of
N. Pinckney, Col. 3d Reg. Infantry,
J. Bliss, Capt. 3d Infantry,
B. Babren, Major US army,
J. Nelson, Capt. US army,
Thomas C. Legate, Capt. US Artillery,
Henry H. Loring, Lieut.
Benj. Walker, Lieut. US army,
S. Cowan, Lieut. Infantry,
George Wright, US army.

President's Approval
The foregoing instrument is approved, so far as it conveys to the
Stockbridge, Oneida, Tuscarora, St. Regis, and Munsee tribes or
nations of Indians, that portion of the country therein described
which lies between Sturgeon Bay, Green Bay, Fox river, that part of
the former purchase made by said tribes or nations of Indians of the
Menominie and Winnebago Indians, on the 8th August, 1821, which
lies south of Fox river, and a line drawn from the south-western
extremity of said purchase to the head of Sturgeon-Bay, and no
further: that quantity being deemed sufficient for the use of the first
before mentioned tribes and nations of Indians. It is to be understood,
however, that the lands, to the cession which to the tribes or nations
aforesaid the government has assented, are to be held by them in
the same manner as they were held by the Menominies, previous to
concluding and signing the aforegoing instrument; and that the title
which they have acquired is not to interfere, in any manner whatever,
with the lands previously acquired or occupied by the government of
the United States, or its citizens.
Given under my hand, at the city of Washington, this 13th day of
March, in the year of our Lord, 1823.
JAMES MONROE[20]

In the *Memorial of the Stockbridge Nation of Indians of Wisconsin, 1842*, the authors identify the boundaries of the 1822 treaty as letter B, which is not attached, containing "thirty townships or 691,200 acres, making, with the former tract 1,428,480 acres."[21] There are several estimations of the acreage all the way up to eight million acres. Please note that the actual boundaries approved by President Monroe were much less than those described in the original treaty. He only granted what he thought was suitable for agriculture. The president's approval of the 1822 treaty was partial in that it did not include all of the larger land area as described in the treaty, though Monroe felt he had approved sufficient acreage to meet the needs of the New York Indians. The president allowed the Six Nations and the Stockbridge only six hundred thousand acres, which caused discontent because it greatly reduced the millions of acres of land described in the 1822 treaty. Even Eleazer Williams pushed for approval of the entire area as specified in the 1822 treaty:

> The friendly part of the Six Nations obtained this Extension of the Territory treated for in 1821 with a view of pleasing the opposition party as they complained that the Country was too small and lying too far from the Bay and mouth of the River. The consequence is that the Six Nations refuse to fulfill their Engagements with the Menominee as they suppose the payment cannot be justly due unless they receive the whole of the Land treated for.[22]

New York Indians and Six Nations Express Opposition

In December 1822, members of the Stockbridge and Six Nations who had emigrated to Green Bay wrote a letter to Monroe complaining about the French and expressing their dissatisfaction with the 1822 treaty:

> Great Father — The undersigned being of such of the Stockbridge & Six Nations, as have by our Great Father's permission removed from the state of New York, are after having with the advice and approbation of the General Government, made Treaties with our Brethren here, for a tract of their county, made a settlement on the same, hearing that some parties . . . leading ones of the French settled

here, are ill disposed towards us, and that they have represented things unfavorable to our last Treaty, beg leave also to suggest a few hints on the subject.

Great Father—We understand they are dissatisfied with the Treaty of this season, and intend if possible to induce our Great Father not to ratify it, tho we know what they have, or could say to him against it—and we humbly conceive they have no just cause of complaint, as a provision is made in the Treaty (of which our Great Father is doubtless ere this aware) for their peaceful remainder upon the land, as long as they shall see fit.

Furthermore, supposing them somewhat interested in the affair, we, before the council was held, consulted them upon the subject, inviting them to attend the Treaty, and suggest anything they might think proper, and even if they desired, to join us in the purchase of the lands, and become equal claimers and sharers with ourselves, to which proposition they expressed . . . much pleasure, and promptly agreed to attend.

But Great Father, we were much surprised to find that although they were faithfully notified of the time, and politely invited, yet not one of them appeared, but kept back, and as we have since learned, exerted themselves to their utmost to dissuade the Menominies from attending, enticing them with whisky and presents. —But nevertheless, Great Father, and notwithstanding what they may have said to the contrary, we are well assured by the Acting Indian Agent here—the public interpreter, and others who know, that the nation was unusually well represented: and Great Father, if facts be evidence, we have that which appear that no dissatisfaction is to [be] found in the Menominies; for they treat us as Brothers, —agree to follow our examples in agriculture, and seem fondly to anticipate the day when they shall have become like one of us—shall have learned each others languages, and appreciate as members of the same family.

Great Father—We are credibly informed that now there are but a few (three or four) of these French people, direct a few with our Treaty, which are the leading characters. —We also learn, that these men expect soon to have their improvements confirmed to them by our Great Father. —Tho lower class also expect the same; but it appears they are almost universally tributary to the leading men, and that these poor peoples land are very generally mortgaged to the more abler class already. — In case the lands be confirmed, these few will have only to foreclose the mortgages, and deprive these poor of their lands. — their only means of subsistence. The consequence will be, they send their children will immediately be thrown upon us, for removal from how here they cannot. — It is not that we object to receiving them so much as the injustice of oppression — which we feel . . . will be practiced. — The root of the objection then on the part of these few characters, against our Treaty affairs appears to be this; that our last treaty includes the lands about the mouth of the Fox River, (not however without a provision for them would . . . If it should be confirmed) it would prevent them from monopolizing the whole country around which they now do, were easily buildings mills cutting off the valuable timber, ec. —

The Menominies have complained that they do not perfectly understand the manner in which their Great Father is to give their lands to the French as they have never sold them to any purchase but merely loaned them to the French as they had married one of their women — They requested us to speak this to our Great Father which we promised. —

Great Father, we understand furthermore that some have put in claims which cannot in truth be lawfully substantiated — instances are on our Great Fathers public field! — With these remarks however we leave the subject.

Great Father we have not made these words in haste, but after mature deliberations. We hold no enmity whatever against our Brothers, the French but wish to live in peace and friendship with all our Brethren. But hearing that they had designs against us, we felt our solemn duty bound to speak to our Great Father, and hope he will become well acquainted with his children the French before he suffers his heart to be turned by their tongues against his red children of the Stockbridge & Six Nations.

Great Father — In taking our leave we wish you health, long life & happiness & subscribe ourselves your dutiful children.

To James Monroe

Martinus Schenendoah

Jacob Konkapot

John

Robt

Jonas Konkapot

Jonas Lcharter [?]

Simon Metoxen

Johncann [?] Metoxen

Joseph Quinney

Andrew Miller

John Quinney

William Toucee[23]

Statements made by the United States in a later treaty signed in 1827 show that the US clearly understood the Menominee belief that the nation had negotiated with the New York Indians for a piece of land to "sit down upon" only. The Menominee offering land to "sit down upon" meant to share the land.

John W. Quinney, who is identified in the documents as Oneida but is actually Stockbridge, spoke to negotiators at the 1827 treaty, explaining his understandings of the treaty made with the Menominee in 1822:

> Big Wave (Menominee), with a wampum in his hand, then said to us, "We are happy to receive you as brothers. You may share the land with us. We think you may be of service to us in helping to cultivate it. We will permit you to be joint owners with us, of all of it." The Menominees said that the land described in the second treaty was theirs.[24]

Furthermore, in the 1827 Treaty at Butte Des Morts, Cass made it clear that the United States understood that the Menominee and New York Indians were *sharing* the land: "A number of your brothers from New York have been crowded out by the white people & have come to this country. The Menominies have given them a seat to sit down upon, on the Fox River."[25]

At the 1827 treaty negotiations, Four Legs (Winnebago) made a speech that revealed a similar understanding of the 1822 treaty:

When they first came, they asked for a small piece of land, sufficient
for them put their children on, that they might live. They said,
"Menominees, Our Brothers! We hope you will give us what we ask.
We ask you to lend and not to sell us, a small piece of land. Do this, in
charity to our impoverished situation."

What harm can it do to grant their request, since they only want to
borrow the land, and not to buy it. It was not a sale, nor a gift, but it
was a loan.

When you the Eastlanders came, we lent you a piece of land and its
boundary was marked on a tree by one of your own chiefs, showing
that it extended from the "little Shoot, to where you are now settled."
The tree has fallen but the stump and the mark are there now.

My Brothers! You said, as we had lent you the land, you were glad,
and that you would then return to your own country and when you
came back here again, you would pay us for the use of it. This is all.[26]

The journal continues:

[Big Wave (Menominee),] with a wampum in his hand, then said to us,
"We are happy to receive you as brothers. You may share the land with
us. We think you may be of service to us in helping to cultivate it. We
will permit you to be joint owners with us of all of it." The Menominees
said that the land described in the second Treaty was theirs. Our
ancient Covenant renewed in 1821 has been always preserved.[27]

OGDEN LAND COMPANY CONTINUES ITS INVOLVEMENT

Calhoun wrote a letter to Ogden and B. W. Rogers on August 21, 1823. In it,
he wrote that the government "is desirous of giving every encouragement
it can, consistently to the removal of the Indians from New York." The
president, in sanctioning only part of the 1822 treaty, believed "that the
quantity of land confirmed under the late agreement would be sufficient
for that purpose. Anything beyond that must be a matter of arrangement
between the Indians themselves." However, Calhoun went on to say he
would submit Ogden's proposal to the president for the lands between the

Fox and Menominee Rivers.[28] Ogden had proposed different boundaries and wanted the New York Indians to relinquish the 1821 treaty boundaries. Calhoun agreed and submitted Ogden's request. Ogden continued to hold the preemption rights to purchase Six Nations lands in New York State, so he favored the larger boundaries as revised by him. Calhoun later told Ogden and Rogers in October 1823 that Monroe

> does not mean to interfere at all with the title acquired by the Six Nations of the Menominee and Winnebagoes . . . Before, therefore, the President gives his approbation as proposed, he deems it proper that the Six Nations should absolve the government from the sanction which it has already given, so as to leave all the lands embraced by the arrangement referred to subject to it operations as it originally stood between the Indians without the interference of the government.
>
> Anything beyond what may be embraced by the sanction of the government must, as I have before stated to you, be entirely a matter of arrangement between the Indians themselves; to which although the government cannot give its express sanction, it has not the least objection, and the Six Nation will be permitted peaceably to occupy and use the country as acquired.[29]

Calhoun sent another letter, this time on October 27, 1823, to the chiefs and head men of the Onondaga, Seneca, Tuscarora, Oneida, and Stockbridge, the "tribes or nations of Indians residing in" New York. Calhoun acknowledged that the "Green Bay treaty held last season [the 1822 treaty] with your brothers the Menomonee and Winnebago has been formally confirmed by your great father, the President." He stated the president approved implementation of the treaty "conducted with the Menomonee and has not now the least objection to the arrangements that have been entered into between you and the Menominees in its fullest extent." However, he explained that the president reduced the amount of lands proposed in the treaty to the amount he thought was sufficient for agriculture. Calhoun went on to describe changes in the boundaries, stating the underlying assumption that the new boundaries

will be confirmed to you by the proposed changes in that part of
the land embraced by your new arrangement with the Menominees
which lies between the Menominee River and the former grant of
1821 extending on the east of Green Bay and the Fox river, and to the
west to a line to be drawn from the high . . . between Lake Michigan
and Superior to the southern line of the former grant just mentioned
containing by estimation near two millions of acres. Before, however,
the President give his approbation in the manner . . . he deems it
proper that you should absolve the government [of the lands in the
1821 treaty].

This requirement meant the New York Indians would have to relinquish the lands along the Fox River that they had settled in order to obtain
approval of the 1822 treaty. These messages from Calhoun seem like doublespeak, as first we learn President Monroe has sanctioned only part of
the lands described in the 1822 treaty, but then Calhoun states he doesn't
want to interfere in the agreements between the Menominee and the New
York Indians for all the land described in the 1822 treaty, though the president's partial sanction of the lands does in fact amount to interference.
Calhoun then assures the New York Indians that they "will continue to
receive the same protection and friendship from the government as they
did while they resided in New York" and their relationship with the government will continue as before.[30]

On October 31, 1823, Calhoun sent a letter to Ogden stating the president would not approve Ogden's proposed revisions unless there was evidence that the Indians agreed. Thus, Ogden's attempts to secure more land
for himself ultimately failed.[31]

INDIAN NATION–TO–INDIAN NATION TREATIES, 1824 AND 1825

Around 1824 it became clear to the Native nations that a new treaty would
be needed to provide land to the Brothertown, who were not party to the
1821 and 1822 treaties. Two versions of the Brothertown treaty are found in
the records. The first treaty was between the Muhheconnuk or Stockbridge
Nation, the St. Regis Nation, the First Christian Party of the Oneida, the
Tuscarora Nation, and the Munsee Tribe of Indians, on the one hand,

and the Brothertown Nation, on the other hand. This treaty was dated June 16, 1824. The second treaty, dated January 8, 1825, is a version of this same treaty but with more precise boundaries for the land ceded. I have included both copies for comparison, as there are more signatures on the second treaty.[32]

Both versions of the treaty describe $950 in goods to be paid to the Menominee for lands that were ceded to the New York Indians in the 1822 treaty. The $950 was part of the amount agreed upon in the 1822 treaty.

The preamble to the 1825 version lists the names of the Brothertown who negotiated this treaty, while the 1824 treaty does not mention names. The signatures on the two documents include many of the same names from each nation, but some signatures on the 1824 treaty are not on the 1825 treaty and vice versa. The 1824 treaty is signed with Thos. Dean as the only witness, but the 1825 treaty includes a number of superintendents and Indian agents in addition to Thos. Dean. The second version of the treaty includes signatures by the St. Regis chiefs at Hogansburgh, where the Mohawk live in upstate New York, signed on January 27, 1825, and by the chiefs of the Tuscarora Nation on August 29, 1825. These dates show this treaty was being discussed among these nations for well over a year.

The 1824 treaty refers to both the 1821 treaty and the 1822 treaty. The 1825 treaty focuses on just the 1822 treaty. The boundaries for the land to be ceded to the Brothertown are described vaguely in the 1824 treaty as twelve miles wide and twenty miles long, while in the 1825 treaty the boundaries are clearly defined.

There is no evidence that these Indian nation–to–Indian nation treaties were ever submitted to Congress or the president for ratification. The fact that these nations were providing land for another Indian nation in a time of political strife with the United States shows a solidarity with one another and the importance of making treaties. After the American Revolution, the Oneida provided land for both the Stockbridge and Brothertown in New York State. In the 1825 treaty they specified that "They, the said Stockbridge, Oneida, St. Regis, Tuscarora Tribes or Nations reserving to each tribe for themselves respectively a tract of land, as large as the one herein ceded to the Brothertown Indians." This statement in the treaty shows the New York Indians, although clumped together by the US for treaties, continued to be separate and distinct nations. The writers of these

documents refer to each nation as a "Tribe or Nation of Indians," which is
how they negotiated treaties.

First Version, June 16, 1824

Whereas the Six Nations of Indians so called residing in the State
of New York and the Stockbridge tribe or nation, St. Regis tribe or
nation and the Munsee tribe or nation of Indians all residing the
State of New York did on the eighteenth day of August in the year
one thousand eight hundred and twenty one hold a treaty with and
purchase of the Menomonee tribe or Nation of Indians and the
Winnebago tribe or nation of Indians in the Territory of Michigan a
tract of country in the vicinity of Green Bay and the Winnebago Lake
in the Territory of Michigan, and whereas the Stockbridge tribe or
nation of Indians and the First Christian Party of the Oneida tribe or
Nation of Indians and the Tuscarora tribe or Nation and the St. Regis
tribe or nation and the Munsee tribe or Nation all of the State of
New York did by a treaty on the twenty third day of September in
the Year one Thousand Eight hundred and twenty two purchase of
the Menominee tribe or Nation of Indians in the territory Michigan
a tract of land in the vicinity of Green Bay and Lake Michigan and
adjoining the first mentioned tract as designated by the said treaty,
and

   whereas the Brothertown Indians residing at Brothertown in the
County of Oneida and State of New York . . . Six Nations and St. Regis,
Stockbridge, Tuscarora and Munsee nations or tribe of Indians
aforesaid — for and in consideration of the sum of nine hundred
& fifty dollars to be paid by the said Brothertown Indians in goods
to the Menominee tribe or Nations at Green Bay (it being a part of
the amount for the purchase of said land as in stipulated in the said
treaty) that they, the said Six Nations the St. Regis, the First Christian
party of the Oneida Nation, the Stockbridge tribe or Nation, the
Tuscarora tribe or nation of Indians and the Munsee Tribe or Nation
aforesaid . . . covenant & agree . . . as soon as the said payment of nine
hundred and fifty dollars is made as before mentioned. That they will
jointly or severally make and execute a full and absolute conveyance

to the Brothertown Indians . . . equal proportion of the said land or country so purchased.

And whereas the Brothertown Indians have requested to have a part of the said land set off for their own particular separate use occupation and benefit.

Now it is . . . covenants and agreed by the said Six Nations, the Stockbridge Tribe or Nation, the St. Regis Tribe or nation, the First Christian party of the Oneida Tribe or Nations, the Tuscarora tribe or nation, the Munsee Tribe or Nation that they will jointly or severally make and execute full and absolute conveyance in the most amplest manner to the said Brothertown Indians and their posterity forever of all their right title interest or claim of whatsoever kind or nation to a certain party of the said lands so purchased of the Winnebago or Menominee tribe or nations aforesaid to be situated on Fox river or Green Bay as the Brothertown Indians by their agent or delegates may choose to select said piece or parcel of land shall be about twelve miles wide and twenty miles long provided never the less that if the said Brothertown Indians should make a location on the Fox River the said land shall not extend in width on the waters of the said river so far as to exclude the other Tribes or Nations of Indians before mentioned from having an equal proportion of the land bordering on the said River and in that case it shall extend back in length what it may be diminished in breadth.

In . . . where of the Chiefs head men and warriors of the before mentioned tribes or Nations have hereunto set their hands & affixed their seals this 16th day of June 1824.

In the presence of:

Thos. Dean Witness to the signature of the

Peace makers and head men of the Stockbridge Nation

Hendrick Aupaumant

S. U. Hendricks

John W. Quinney

Abrams his X mark Maenan . . .

Jacob his X mark Littleman

Sampson Marquis

Jon his X mark Littleman

John Littleman
Solomon Hendrick

Oneida chiefs
　Neddy Attiquet his X mark
　Paul Powles his X mark
　Antone his X mark Asaregowa
　Henry Powlis his X mark
　Daniel Bread his X mark
　Cornelius Beard his X mark
　Henry Christian his X mark
　Tho Neddy his X mark
　Marti . . . Dana . . . tasfe [?] his X mark

Tuscorara chiefs
　Sach . . . his X mark
　Nicholas Cusik
　George S . . . his X mark

By the foregoing nine Oneida Chiefs in presence of A.G. Ellis this
18th June, 1824
J Dean [signature]
Signed by the within named Tuscarora Chiefs this the 7th day of July
1824 in the presence of Thomas Dean, William Dick, George Samson
Next entry

　Know all men by these present that we the undersigned being the
chiefs and principal men of the Stockbridge Tribe of Indians have
settled on Fox River in the Territory of Michigan that is consideration
of the payment of nine hundred and fifty dollars to Menominee Tribe
or nation agreeable to the stipulations of the forgoing agreement
we hereby certify that we in general council assembled have agreed
with the deputies appointed by the Brothertown Indians that the
Brothertown Indians take a piece of land on Fox River bounded as
follows, beginning on the south east side of Fox River at the upper
part of a small Bay above the foot of the Grand Kaklin or rapids in
the said river near a sugar maple from the mouth of a small brook

running into the said river and running from there a south east course twenty nine miles and twenty one chains then a north east course eight miles hence a north west course thirty miles and fifty nine chains to the Fox River and thence up the said river to the place of beginning for them the said Brothertown Indians to have this as described piece or parcel of land released and ceded and quite claim unto them the said Brothertown Indians and their posterity forever for their . . . of the foregoing agreements the said piece or parcel of land . . . not been chosen or selected or occupied by any one of the before mentioned Nations or tribes or their deputies. Given under our hands at Green Bay this 18th day of September in the year of our Lord 1824.

In the presence of J. Dean agent for the Brothertown Indians
Chiefs and principle men: Stockbridge

Robert Konkapot his X mark
Austin Brother Calvin Quinney
Benjam Palmer his X mark
John Quinney
James Joshua his X mark
Baptist Powlas his X mark, Agent for the Oneida Indians[33]

Second Version, January 8, 1825

Although our brethren the Brothertown Indians, were not included in the original Treaties made by us, the said several tribes of N. York Indians, with the Winnebago and Menominie Indians; yet, by an agreement of ours, the said several tribes of N. York Indians, with the Brothertown Indians, they, the Brothertown Indians have become very deeply interested in the purchases, and the sure tenure of these lands, as the following articles of the said agreement will show.

(Copy)

ARTICLES of an agreement or Treaty made between the Muhheconnuk or Stockbridge Tribe or Nation, and the St. Regis Tribe or Nation, and the first Christian party of the Oneida tribe or Nation, and the Tuscarora Tribe or Nation, and the Munsee Tribe or Nation of Indians, all residing in the State of New York, of the

first part; and William Dick, George Sampson, Paul Dick, George
Scipio, Daniel Dick, and David Towcey, Deputies appointed and
authorized by the Brothertown Tribe or Nation of Indians, residing in
Brothertown, in the county of Oneida and state aforesaid, of the other
part, Witnesseth: —

ARTICLE 1st. That the parties of the first part for and in
consideration of the payment of nine hundred and fifty dollars paid
to the Menominie Tribe or Nation of Indians, residing at, Green
Bay and on the Fox River, in the Territory of Michigan, by the said
William Dick, George Sampson, Paul Dick, George Scipio, Daniel
Dick, and David Towcey, deputies appointed as aforesaid, the which
payment is hereby confessed and acknowledged by the parties of the
first part, said nine hundred and fifty dollars being in part payment
of the amount of purchase money, due from the said Oneida, St. Regis
and Tuscarora Tribes or Nations of Indians before mentioned, to
the Menominie Tribe or Nation aforesaid, for lands sold by the said
Menominie Tribe or Nation, to the said Stockbridge, first Christian
party of Oneida, the St. Regis, Tuscarora, and Munsee Tribes, lying
in the vicinity of Green Bay and the Fox River, in the Territory of
Michigan, agreeable to the conveyance, stipulation, covenant and
agreement made in a treaty entered into by the said Stockbridge,
Oneida, Tuscarora, St. Regis, Munsee Tribes or Nations, by their
deputies authorized for that purpose, and the Chiefs and Head Men
of the Menominie Tribe or Nation before mentioned. Dated the
twenty-third day of September, in the year of our Lord one thousand
eight hundred and twenty two.

ARTICLE 2nd That in consideration of the payment above
mentioned, the Muhheconnuk or Stockbridge, the Oneida, the
St. Regis, the Tuscarora and Munsee tribes or nations aforesaid, do
CEDE, CONVEY, and forever QUIT-CLAIM unto the Brothertown
Indians aforesaid, in the most full and absolute manner, all their
right, title, interest and claim, in and to that certain piece or parcel of
land, situated and lying on Fox River, in the Territory of Michigan,
and bounded as follows: Beginning on the south-east side of Fox
River aforesaid, two miles down the River below a Maple tree and an
Elm tree, both marked, near the mouth of a small stream or brook

running into the said River at the upper part of a small bay or cove above the foot of the Grand Kockalin or rapids in said River, and running from said place of beginning a south-east course thirty miles, thence North-east eight miles, thence North-west thirty miles to the Fox River aforesaid, thence up the said River to the place of beginning. TO HAVE and to HOLD the above described piece or parcel to the said Brothertown Indians and their posterity forever.

ARTICLE 3rd. The said Muhheconnuk or Stockbridge, the Oneida, St. Regis, Tuscarora and Munsee Tribes or Nations aforesaid for the consideration above mentioned, do further cede, convey, and quit claim to the said Brothertown Indians, and their posterity forever, an equal undivided part of all the country ceded to them, the said Muhheconnuk or Stockbridge, the Oneida, St. Regis, Tuscarora and Munsee Tribes or Nations, by the said Menominie Tribe or Nation, agreeable to the above mentioned Treaty of the twenty-third of September eighteen hundred and twenty two. — They the said Stockbridge, Oneida, St Regis, Tuscarora Tribes or Nations reserving to each tribe for themselves respectively a tract of land, as large as the one herein ceded to the Brothertown Indians, as described in the second article of this Indenture, in any part of the country before mentioned except that ceded and described to the Brothertown Indians, as above mentioned.

In testimony whereof the said Deputies, Chiefs and Head Men of the aforesaid Tribes or Nations of Indians, have hereunto set their hands and seals at New Stockbridge, this eighth day of January in the year of our Lord one thousand eight hundred and twenty-five.
Signed, sealed & delivered in presence of
Joseph Stebbins,
Sam'l L. Hubbard,
Superintendents of the Brothertown and Stockbridge Indians

Alpheus Colbourn,T. Dean, Agent for the Brothertown Indians,
The above signature of the Stockbridge and Oneida chiefs
Oneida chiefs
  Daniel Bread,
  Paul X Powles,

Antonio X Big Knife,
Neddy X Attsequette,
Cornelius X Beard,
Antonio X John,
Daniel X Peter,
Martin Denny

Stockbridge chiefs
Hendrick Aupaumut,
John Metoxen,
Solomon U. Hendrick,
John W. Quinney,
Jacob P. Seth,
Abraham X Maumauntuthecon,
Thomas Tautaukeem Hendrick,
Maunomaug alias John Baldwin X,
Jacob X Littleman

Signed and sealed by the St. Regis Chiefs at Hogansburgh,
27th January, 1825
Lonyhotiiataharongwenthin, X
Thomas Thorgwenegen
Mitchel Thareha, X
Peter Konasagenrat, X
Saro Shakohawitha, X
Roren Hononsawenra, X
Peter horoniatagon, X

Signature of the chiefs and head men of the Tuscarora Nation, the
29th day of August, 1825
Sacharisa, X
Nicholas Cusick
Jacob Caurealawako, X
George Printup, X
Isaac Johnson, X

James Patason, X
Jacob X
John Beach, X
Joseph Stebbins,
Sam'l L. Hubbard,
Superintendents of the Brothertown and Stockbridge Indians

Alpheus Colbourn,
T. Dean, Agent for the Brothertown Indians,
The above signature of the Stockbridge and Oneida Chiefs

W.L. Gray, Int. for the said Chiefs of the St. Regis Indians

Wm. Hogan, witness to the acknowledgement by
Lewis Mitchel,
Peter Charles & Lewis Cook and
White Peter, Chiefs of the St. Regis Indians,
Lemuel Warren,
T. Dean, Agent for the Brothertown Indians

Witness to the signing and sealing of the Tuscarora chiefs
T. Dean, Agent for the Brothertown Indians,
William T. Alvis, Interpreter[34]

Indigenous nations made treaties in 1822, 1824, and 1825 among themselves for land in what is now Wisconsin. Their treaties are very formal and clear that they are providing for each other. Because these treaties were made Indian nation to Indian nation, there was much controversy later when the United States sought to obtain the same lands, and the validity of the treaties among Indian nations was questioned.

5

PROTESTING THE
1821 AND 1822 TREATIES

Information on when the New York Indians actually moved to Wisconsin is scarce. Constant controversy plagued their movements, and when they did settle, there would be more treaties that put their land in jeopardy. On August 2, 1822, Jasper Parrish wrote to John C. Calhoun asking that the disbursement of the $4,500 annual annuity for the Six Nations from the 1794 Canandaigua Treaty be based on Indian village populations. Parrish wrote, "The Oneida have two parties and the annuity will be divided among the two parties." He added that "the delegation from the Stockbridge and the Oneida tribes passed through this place to Green Bay."[1]

The earliest settlement that can be identified comes from a map showing Stockbridge settlement of an area called Statesburgh. This map is very faint and difficult to read. It says,

> Map of the Fox River and the part of the Winnebago Lake as contained within the limits of the cession of 1821 by the Menominee and Winnebago Indians to the New York Tribes.
> The vermillion lines represent the breadth of the cession.
> The Stockbridge Indians commenced the settlement of the Grand Kaccalin, in the month of November 1822 — and by the number of buildings, now on the map, is represented by both its situation & present extent (March 1832).
> At a general council held by the males of the Stockbridge and Munsee Tribes Jan. 1826.

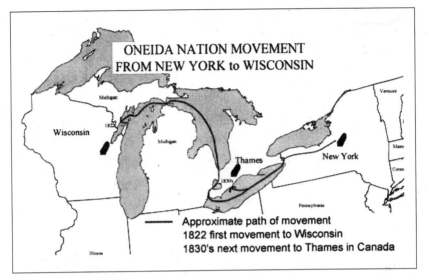

Oneida Nation movement from New York to Wisconsin
ONEIDA NATION GLIS DEPARTMENT

Resolved that as a mark of our grateful acknowledgement for the aid afforded the New York Indians in the purchase of lands in this Country by the Government of the UNITED STATES that, that portion whereon the Stockbridge & Munsee Tribes are located, i.e., on the South East side of Fox River & between Grand Kaccalin & Winnebago Lake be named STATESBURGH and that by this name it shall hereafter be called in all public documents or whereinsoever it be named.

The population of these Tribes is about 700 of whom a little more than one half is settled on the tract—the surface of the Country is generally level & the climate healthy.[2]

After signing the treaty made on September 23, 1822, A. G. Ellis wrote, "The negotiations concluded, the Menomonees having retired, the New York Indians began to look out for winter quarters. There were but a few of either party that had come as emigrants; those of the Stockbridges located at Grand Kaukalin; the few Oneida chose the Little Kaukalin. Many of the deputies returned to New York."[3] Ellis went on to state that an "immigrant party of about 50 Stockbridge arrived and settled at the Grand Kaklin on the east side of the Fox River."[4] Ellis claims as well that John

Metoxen (Stockbridge) and families moved to the Green Bay area in 1822.[5] This makes sense given that the Stockbridge agreement for lands in White River, Indiana, never materialized as planned, as the Stockbridge were encouraged by President James Monroe to join with the other New York Indians and be part of the 1821 and 1822 treaties. The United States government lumped the nations together as the New York Indians. But the tribes settled on their own lands as separate nations.

More New York Indians arrived to Wisconsin in 1823. Ellis commented that in 1823 "another tribe, which had joined the Mo-he-kun-nucks (Stockbridge) in the purchase, to-wit, the Munsee [and] a small party of the Brothertown reached Green Bay the following year, and located at Little Kaklin, on the east side of the river."[6] He also noted, "In 1823 a small party of Oneida moved to WI and a 2nd party of Stockbridge. The Oneida, led by Neddy Atsiguet, settled on the Little Kaklin until 1825, when they removed to Duck Creek."[7]

The New York Indians continued to move west in 1824. Ellis wrote that in that year, "a small party of the Brothertown reached Green Bay . . . and located at Little Kaklin, on the east side of the river."[8] Together, the Stockbridge, Munsee, and Brothertown migrated in small groups over many years from New York State to lands near Green Bay. These lands, however, were never totally secure, as the Menominee and Winnebago understood the land to be held in common, while the New York Indians believed they had purchased the lands in the 1821 and 1822 treaties.

PROTESTING THE TREATIES

Protests of the 1821 and 1822 treaties came from several directions. The Menominee clearly stated that the persons who signed these treaties were not designated by the Menominee Nation. The Menominee thought they agreed to share the land with the New York Indians and that they had not sold the land. Ellis noted as much, writing, "The Menominees, for a trifling consideration, ceded to the New York Indians a right in common to the whole of their lands."[9] After Monroe approved the treaty, the New York Indians were, as Ellis observed, "thereby recognized as joint owners with the Menominee of all of their immense territories comprising nearly half of the State of Wisconsin."[10] Moreover, the French residents of Green

Bay protested as well, as many were afraid that they would lose their lands if treaties were made. Finally, when the Oneida returned from Wisconsin to their homelands in New York State, some of the Six Nations were not supportive of the treaties, as they did not wish to leave New York and settle in the Green Bay area.

Protests started in late 1822, with the Menominee writing a letter of protest in 1824, and continued through the signing of treaties in 1825, 1827, 1831, and 1832. In these treaties, the land bases of the Menominee, Ho-Chunk, Oneida, Stockbridge-Munsee, and Brothertown Nations were established, but their land bases were changed in later treaties.

Protests from the Six Nations and the French

In June 1822, Parrish wrote to Calhoun, telling him that he had been made aware that the chiefs of the Six Nations were protesting the 1821 treaty. Parrish claimed that he had been informed by the chiefs of the Six Nations that they would "have nothing to do with the Green Bay purchase of land." If, Parrish continued, "the Stockbridge tribe with a few individuals of the Six Nations should think proper to receive, ratify, and pay for the land purchased at Green Bay, they may do so, with their private money," but he said the chiefs of the Six Nations had stated that "no part of their national annuity should be applied to make any part of the payments."[11]

The French inhabitants at Green Bay wrote to Congress in September 1822 objecting to the Menominee making treaties with the New York Indians. They claimed that Eleazer Williams wrote the 1822 treaty between the Stockbridge and the Menominee and Winnebago, and alleged that the people involved were not authorized to sign it. Furthermore, the French inhabitants said the Menominee and Winnebago rejected the treaty because they didn't have an interpreter. However, the French inhabitants claimed the treaty was signed by "some miserable outcasts of the Menomini," and witnessed by military people "who were not present." The inhabitants of Green Bay protested the legality of the treaty, believing it to be fraudulent and fearing their lands would be taken by this treaty.[12]

Despite assertions from the French that Eleazer Williams wrote the 1822 treaty, this is not true. The authorized agent for and author of the 1821 treaty was Charles C. Trowbridge, and for the 1822 treaty it was John Sergeant.

At some point in or around 1823, the Stockbridge, Oneida, St. Regis (Mohawk), and Brothertown Nations wrote a memorial to Monroe. The memorial is dated July 5, 1822, but the date must be incorrect, as both the 1821 and 1822 treaties are cited. The Stockbridge, Oneida, St. Regis, and Brothertown authors of the memorial saw themselves as addressing the president on a nation-to-nation basis.

The letter reads as follows:

To his excellency James Monroe, President of the United States
    of America
Father,
    We the Chiefs and headmen of the Muhheconnuck or Stockbridge, Oneida, St. Regis and Brothertown tribes or Nations of Indians residing in the State of New York would beg leave to address a few words unto you at this time, on a subject which we consider to be of great importance not only to the welfare and interests of our present respective Tribes, but also to the posterity of our tribes, and we hope you will give that attention of our present communication as the subject deserves.
    Father, You are well aware that our respective tribes or nations have for several years past turned their attention towards the setting sun where they hoped that at some future period they would concentrate themselves in order to promote each other's welfare and the welfare of those of their western Brethren who may be near them.
    Father, In pursuance of these intention of ours and children some deputies were sent by our Nations to Green Bay, Michigan Territory by and through the consent and permission of general government who, you are well aware & proceeded in obtaining portion of the country claimed by the Menominee and Winnebagoes which cession was made in the form of a treaty and which treaty has met the approbation and ratification our father the President. But as the lands therein conveyed were situated so far up the Fox River from the Bay another permission was solicited from the general government for an extension of lands to the first cession which was according granted.
    The last treaty had been with Menominee by the . . . send on agreeably to the last permission have been also communicated to our

father the President which our father did not think proper to give
his special sanction by ratify the treaty but in part.[13] When this was
known to the tribes involved with the last purchase. They addressed a
memorial to the honorable the Secretary of War to be communicated
to our father the President and an answer was received in reply to our
Memorial.

Father, we may . . . assure you that the answer received was in
some measure satisfactory, and in some degree silenced our minds
and feelings, but as we could not possibly be willing to absolve the
government of its former sanction by a relinquishment of the lands
thereby confirmed to us have induced us again to petition our father
the President to confirm those lands to us comprehended in the . . .
letter "from the Secretary of War without relinquishing the lands in
the ratification of the President the last treaty."

Father, We would address many reasons and conversations
which would perhaps induce our father to be willing to grant us our
requests, but forbear to enc . . . things on papers as we have a special
agent who will transmit to the seat of general government and will
inform you of everything which you may forbear to have relative to
our affairs at Green Bay.

One great conversation which we will mention which . . . I think
will have some insight with our fathers to reconsider the proposed
validation of the first ratification to the last treaty as mentioned in
the letter received of some time ago . . . ratifying those lands already
confirmed . . . to us by the Secretary of War in the following. Thus, in
negotiating with the Menominees for the lands comprehended in the
last treaty, it was not seem proper to insert the names of all the tribes
residing in the State of New York . . . of those who were represented
at the last treaty inasmuch as some of them had refused to ratify the
former treaty, or to pay their proportion of the goods agreed to be
paid to the Menominee and Winnebagos agreeable to the 3rd article
of the treaty of 1821. But it was our intention that whenever any the
other tribes were desirous hereafter to become sharers with us to
some of the lands, we were willing to give them that privilege by
paying a certain stipulated sum as may be agreed upon by the nations
interested in the last purchase. Agreeably to this . . . invitation [?] . . .

it was ascertained that those tribes who were to pay the balance of
the goods stipulated to be paid to the Menominees . . . probably . . .
in paying this proportion of the goods, and our brothers remnants
of seven different tribes formerly from the Eastern States, called the
Brothertown of Indians were promised to have a share of the country
with us, in consideration of their paying the sum of nine hundred and
fifty dollars, worth of goods to the Menominees, which they have
accordingly fulfilled.

As by the documents transmitted to you may more fully appear.
We hope the agreements made between our respective tribes, therein
will meet the approbation of our father the President.

It is expected also that the rest of the 6 nations residing in New
York may gradually be induced to become sharers with us. And at no
distant period will probably be willing to emigrate to the West with
the rest, in this case, a larger extent of country will be requested for
their accommodation.

We may now request some assurance by Government that all here
who may choose to change their residence and continue to receive
the same protection and friendship from the government as they
had whilst they lived in New York, and that their . . . removal will
in no wise change the relation in which may previously stood to the
government.

We may now assure you father, that we need the protection so
often provided especially as a part of the New York Indians have
already emigrated to Green Bay from the Stockbridge tribe, who have
established themselves in the Fox River, about 20 miles up river from
its entrance into the Bay.

We have received information from that country to us by men of
undoubted veracity, that the French and other white settlers residing
in the vicinity of Green Bay have been endeavoring to persuade
the Menominees to have animosities against the New York Indians
. . . with their utmost influence to present stories taking the goods
brought to them by the Brothertown Indians. You will be informed
more particularly of the shameful conduct of some of these men
that because of this, if required; and we earnestly ask and pray that

our father, the President with his great councillers would use and order such measures to be taken as will effectively root out and put an end to this growing evil by ordering the officers stationed at this post particularly the I. agent to use his influence to suppress any such proceedings for the future and preventable wicked, designing and intriguing white men from raising or causing any dissensions or animosity amongst the Menomoniee or Winnebagoes against any of the N. York Indians.

Father, We had fondly hoped that in the event of our emigrating and concentrating our respective tribes away by themselves at our place where they would not be surrounded by their White brethren again. They might have a better prospect to promote that peace and harmony which ought to exist among all Nations.

But if the whites at Green Bay are permitted to continue the practice of making or creating disturbances among the Menominee & Winnebagoes with our Indians, all our hopes and expectations in seating ourselves in peace and safety at Green Bay will be blasted.

We . . . hope the powerful arm of government will prevent all these apprehensions, and if there is no law at present which will apply to this we hope and pray that Congress will have the good . . . To enact such . . . and officially laws or will affect our protection and our posterity who may be after us.

Father, We have understood that some of the principal Menomonee Chiefs has . . . that they had many Chiefs in their nations. Some of them have been created as such by the British contrary to the customs of their nation. And they were reasons that government would institute an inquiry by some of the officers in order to ascertain the real Chiefs and that those made as such by the British officer may be disbanded. We would not have mentioned this if . . . Indians think by complying with . . . of some of these Chiefs it might have a tendency keep peace among themselves, and may in time put an end to this visiting the territories belonging to the British and be more firmly attached to the government of the United States.

Father, we pray you to have the goodness to give an answer as soon as you conveniently can.

Stockbridge chiefs
   Hendrick Aupaument
   John Metoxen
   Solomon U. Hendrick
   John W. Quinney
   Thomas . . . Hendrick
   Sampson Marquis
   Jacob his X mark Smith
   John M. B . . .
   Solomon Q. Hendrick
   Cornelius Aaron

Oneida chiefs
   Daniel Bread
   Thomas Christian
   Jacob Williams
   Stuart his X mark Powles
   Anthony his X mark Ohahteen [?]
   Neddy his X mark . . .
   Harry his X mark Powles
   Henry his X mark Smith, Jr.
   Thomas his X mark . . .
   Thomas his X mark Powles

Brothertown chiefs &
   Randal Abner
   Benjamin G. Fowler
   Thomas Dick
   John Janson
   . . . Dick
   Rhadolphes [?] Fowler
   Daniel Dick
   Joseph T . . .
   John Coyhis

Jacob Folwer

Abram Sh . . .

Elary [?] Dick

. . . CSA . . . les

John B. . . .

St. Regis chiefs

   Levy . . .

   Mitchell X Cook

   Thomas Williams

   Peter X onasokenot [?]

   Charles X Cook

   Larson X . . .

   . . . for the . . . chiefs

   Memuel Warren

   Witness to the signatures of the St. Regis Chiefs.[14]

In 1825, Thomas L. McKenney, the superintendent of Indian Affairs, wrote to James Barbour, the secretary of war in President John Quincy Adams's cabinet. McKenney enclosed a copy of his letter to the Indian agent at Green Bay, Major Henry B. Brevoort. On French settlers causing trouble, McKenney wrote:

Sir, It has been represented to the Secretary of War that the French Settlers in the neighborhood of Green Bay have very improperly interfered to prevent the carrying into effect the arrangements made between the Menomenees, Winnebagoes, and the New York Indians (& which have been sanctioned by the Government) for a portion of the Territory of the former for the latter to settle on; & that they have also endeavoured to excite the Indians in that vicinity, to hostility against the New York Indians, with a view of deterring them from settling on the lands which they have acquired under those arrangements.

The conduct of these settlers from the representation which has been made of it, is highly reprehensible & cannot be suffered by the Government with impunity. I am, accordingly, directed by the

Secretary of War to instruct you, forthwith to take strong measure
to suppress effectually, such improper & dangerous interference &
to prevent the evil consequences which it is calculated to produce,
by rigidly enforcing against all who may be found, or known
to be engaged in it the provision of the law of Intercourse. The
commanding Office of the Post is order to co-operate with you shou'd
it be necessary, in carrying these instructions into effect. A copy of
the order is enclosed.

It is very important to preserve peace between the Indians at Green
Bay & the New York Indians who may join them the arrangements
between them to this effect having been made with the Sanction of
the Government, gives them a peculiar claim to protection against
the arts of designing & intermeddling white men.

I am Very Respy &c&c Thos L. McKenney[15]

Several months later, McKenney wrote to Lewis Cass, the governor of
Michigan Territory. On April 16, 1825, McKenney informed Cass that the
petition about complaints regarding the behavior of the settlers in Green
Bay had been dealt with by the War Department. McKenney enclosed what
he called a "petition to the President from certain Indians who have removed from New York to Green Bay." He added, "The application for an
extension of the sanction of the government to the Conventional arrangement between the New York Indians and the Menomonie and Winnebago,
had some time since been submitted to the Department, but nothing final
has been done with it."[16]

Protests from the Ogden Land Company
In a letter from Williams to land speculator Thomas L. Ogden dated May
15, 1823, Williams acknowledged that former President Monroe received
the 1822 treaty and approved it, but only in part, as he reduced the amount
of land acquired by the Six Nations and Stockbridge to just six hundred
thousand acres. "The Reduction of the Tract which was treated for has,"
wrote Williams,

I find been the cause of much discontent with both Menominees
and Six Nations. The friendly part of the Six Nations obtained this

Extension of the Territory treated for in 1821 with a view of pleasing the opposition party as they complained that the Country too small and lying too far from the Bay and mouth of the River.[17]

Williams wrote further that the Six Nations refused to make payment to the Menominee until they could obtain an agreement on the entire tract of land defined in the 1822 treaty:

> Another great Evil arising out of it is that the Menominee charge the Six Nations with having deceived them respecting the unlimited permission which they pretended they had to treat with them as the Six Nations exhibited their Instruction to the Menominee before making the Treaty. This, say the Menominee, was a base deception for their Great Father the President does not allow them to set down upon the whole though the fact was the Six Nations had actually *unlimited permission*.[18]

Williams wrote that the Six Nations "rejoiced" that they now had land, but the "United States may purchase any share of it they should wish and at any time." This statement leaves a lot of doubt over the cession and the boundaries.[19]

On August 14, 1823, Thomas L. Ogden, B. W. Rogers, and Colonel Robert Troup sent a letter to Calhoun. They signed the letter "for themselves & (as) Trustees for the Association." They enclosed the May 15 letter from Williams to Ogden and acknowledged that the approval of only part of the treaty had caused concern. Their "principal object" was to remind the secretary of war that President James Madison had approved for the Six Nations to "effect an arrangement with their Western Brethren for the acquisition of a permanent Seat."[20] There was a written document "delivered to a delegation of the Six Nations, by Mr. [George] Graham, then Acting Secretary of War, & as we have been informed by Mr. David A. Ogden, an exemplified Copy of it was afterwards deposited by him in the War Office, on occasion of some communication from him regarding their removal."[21]

Ogden had talked with Ellis concerning the amount of land ceded in the 1822 treaty, which the Six Nations agreed upon, as being between the Fox and Menominee Rivers. He asked the president to confirm the "new cession as to the Territory lying between the Menominee River & the former grant of 1821, extending on the East to Green Bay & Fox River & on the west to a Line to be drawn from the high Lands between Lake Michigan & Superior to the Southern line of the former grant, they would be Satisfied."[22] Ogden, Rogers, and Troup also wrote:

> We beg leave most respectfully to add that in consequence of the suspicions and Jealousies which have been excited among some of the Tribes in this State it is important that the Sanction of the President to the late Treaty, so far as he may think proper to sanction it, be communicated to the Six Nations in the most formal & authentic Shape and by some document which the Sub-Agent (Jasper Parrish) may be directed to deposit with them.

They concluded by acknowledging that there were two parties in the tribes, and they asked for the protection of the Great Father and payment of annuities "at Green Bay, should they remove thither." They further acknowledged the Christian Party, which supported the government's views, noting that there was opposition to those views.[23]

Calhoun's response to Ogden and Rogers came just a few weeks later, on August 21, 1823. He approved of and encouraged the removal "of the Indians from New York" and approved the lands near Green Bay for their settlement, stating that the president approved the amount of land rhe thought would be sufficient for the Six Nations. He added, "Anything beyond that must be a matter of arrangement between the Indians themselves." Calhoun also wrote that he would submit the Ogden proposition to the president regarding land between the Fox and Menominee Rivers.[24]

Protests from the Menominee

The Menominee submitted a formal protest regarding the 1821 and 1822 treaties with the New York Indians to Calhoun on June 16, 1824. They wrote:

> To the Secretary of War June 16, 1824
>   The Memorial and petition of the undersigned chiefs and principal

men of the Menomine nation of Indians, residing with the Michigan
Territory, represents:

That when the New York Indians, or Nautoways, first came to this
country they asked the Menomonies to sell to them a small piece of
their lands. That the Menomines replied to them, they had no land
to sell; that their country was already too small for their numbers,
and that they were themselves compelled to hunt upon other Indians'
lands. That, notwithstanding this answer, the Nautoways held a
treaty with some of the men of the Menominie nation, at which
none of the principal chiefs attended, and purchased, or pretended
to purchase, a part of the Menomonies' country, the boundaries of
which they knew nothing about. That the only men of this nation who
have any right to the country claimed by the nation, which extends
from Lake Michigan to the upper part of the Wisconsin River, now
sign this paper; not one of who was present at that treaty; and that
soon as their backs were turned, some of their men, who had no right
to dispose of the land, held the treaty; and whatever consideration
was then paid, or has since been paid, they know not, having received
no portion of the same. And as an evidence of the fact, that they knew
nothing of that treaty, not one of the old inhabitants of this place was
called upon, as is usual, to attend at the making of the same: and they
are not accustomed to transact so important a business as this would
have been, without asking their advice.

They state the same facts, or objections, to the second, or last
treaty which is said to have been held; and their object now is, to, and
they do, protest against any further settlements being made upon
their lands, by the Nautoways. If any more should come here, what
shall we do with our wives and children, whom we can now scarcely
support? We beg of our great father to prevent any more of them
from coming to this country. With the Winnebagoes we are united
by kindred, yet it is with great difficulty that we live upon terms of
friendship even with them. We are satisfied with the settlement made
here by the whites, *but we cannot admit any nation of Indians to settle in
the country.*

Green Bay, June 16, 1824

Menominies

OASH-KOSH, the Brave	X
JOSEPH CORRON, son of Thomas	X
KETS-KAN-NO-NIEN,	X
PE-WAY-TINENT,	X
SAY-KEE-TOAK,	X
AMABLE CARRON,	X
MUK-KAY-TAY-WET,	X

This speech, memorial, or petition, made and signed in our presence:

H.B. Brevoort, Agent of Indian Affairs

James Duane Doty, one of the Judges of the Territory of Michigan

Jq. Porlier

John Lawe

Robert Irwin

J.H. Lockwood

Geo. Johnston

Act. Grignon

Lamt. Fily

Lewis Rouse

Enene. Childs

Paul Grignon

L. Grignon[25]

Support for the Menominee

This section presents statements of support for the Menominee made by Paul Grignon, Pierre Grignon, Henry Brevoort, Lewis Rouse, and residents of Green Bay who confirm they were at the August 1821 treaty and knew the head men of the Menominee. They state those who made the treaty were "with several men of little consideration in the nation."[26] They also document that the brother of one of the head chiefs attended the council and said "he was sent by the head chiefs of the nation to say, they had no land for sale; that they could not spare their lands, for their lands were already so small they there were obliged to go on the lands of neighboring tribes to hunt."[27]

A report from the Twenty-Second Congress includes the Menominee protest of 1824, the supporting statements of the events surrounding the 1821 and 1822 treaties, and statements from Paul Grignon, Lewis Rouse, Pierre Grignon, Henry Brevoort, and the US inhabitants of the township of Green Bay, who support the Menominee position that the treaties were not legal.[28]

Paul Grignon, June 16, 1824

Paul Grignon wrote that he was present at the 1821 treaty and was well acquainted with the Menominee chiefs, saying the head chiefs were not present at the signing of the treaty. He said the brother of a chief came to the treaty stating he was sent by the "chiefs of the nation to say that they had no land to sell."[29]

Lewis Rouse, June 16, 1824

Rouse was present at the 1821 Treaty and confirmed that the head chiefs were not there, but he did write, "but that the council was with men of some consideration in the nation." He interpreted French into English and vice versa.[30]

Pierre Grignon, June 17, 1824

Pierre Grignon was present at the 1821 treaty and confirmed the head chiefs were not there. However, he explained

> that the interpreter did not explain to the Indians who were present at this council that the agreement which they entered into was to sell their lands to the New York Indians, but that it was a permission to them to hunt on and cultivate a small piece of land like themselves; and that the council was held with men of little consideration in the nation, who, at the time stated, they had not the authority to make any final arrangements.[31]

Henry Brevoort, September 21, 1824

Brevoort was the Indian agent who met with the Menominee to hear their statements on the treaty. He said the principal chiefs would not accept the New York Indians' payment in goods, but that "inconsiderable men" did accept the goods the next day. When the Menominee tried to meet with the men, Brevoort would not meet with them, saying they should write down their speech. He admonished the Menomoniee to follow the proper procedure to meet with the Indian agent.[32]

CONTINUED FRENCH INTERFERENCE

On September 21, 1824, the inhabitants of Green Bay wrote to the president expressing their views. They wrote "that the principal chiefs of the Menominee nation of Indians are opposed to the settlement of the New York Indians upon their lands."[33] They also wrote, "That the said chiefs were told by the said agent and others, that it was useless to oppose said settlement of the New York Indians; that the Government was determined to establish it here."[34] At this point, these inhabitants of Green Bay gathered with some of the chiefs at the fence surrounding the home of Brevoort, whereupon they were handed a note informing them that no citizen can "dare call Indians together."[35]

Just six months later, McKenney noted that the French at Green Bay had "very improperly interfered to prevent the carrying into effect the arrangements made between the Menominees, Winnebagoes, and the New York Indians (and which have been sanctioned by the government)."[36] The French had caused hostility against the New York Indians to prevent them from settling on the lands from the treaties of 1821 and 1822.

McKenney asked that "strong measures" be taken "to suppress effectually, such improper and dangerous interference."[37] McKenney wrote Barbour on March 8, 1825, stating that he was enclosing a letter from him to the Indian agent at Green Bay and requesting military assistance to deal with the French settlers and to enforce laws, regulations, and trade with Indians.

The leaders of the Stockbridge Nation complained to Rev. Jedidiah Morse, a geographer and theologian sympathetic to Indians, about the French in a letter dated November 6, 1824. They wrote:

> Rev. Sir
> Having known you to be an acceptable friend to Indians, and to have had a respect to the interests of our nation while in New York, we beg leave to solicit your attention to a subject, interesting [?] our

Austin E. Quinney, an elected Stockbridge chief, led his nation
during their move from New York State to Wisconsin.
WHI IMAGE ID 1923

peace in this our new settlement. It appears that the commissioners
for examining the claims of the French & others to lands in this
neighborhood, have reported favorably on a claim of one Paul
Ducharme a French man to a piece of land on that which is confirmed
to us by the President of the US, and only about ¾ mile . . . (on the
same side of the river) where we have commenced our settlement. In
the first place we have abundant proof that this is not a lawful claim
as it was never cultivated by the French according to the statutes, but
only sometimes encamped upon by fishermen for a few days in the
spring season. The Menominee's however, have long continued to
raise corn upon the spot, and now complain that the government is
about to give away their corn fields to the French.

Jane Quinney, the wife of Austin E. Quinney, and their daughter, Harriet B. Quinney
WHI IMAGE ID 2882

But our principal complaint arises from evils which having grown out of a Frenchmen's already having gained a possession of a piece directly opposite to our settlement on the other side of the river by former confirmations. He constantly annoys us in the most serious manner, by sending to our people spiritous liquor the great . . . & destruction from which we had hoped to have escaped by leaving its immediate vicinity — But as his is one but one shop of the kind, & being separated from us by the river, we should hope could we prevent others from coming in, not to suffer this evil to our nation; for they could not obtain it without going 20 miles, which is too great a distance to be travelled very frequently. — But should this piece be confirmed, to the claimant we can easily fore see that it would soon be the station for a grog shop & a house of death to Indians. — We have therefore to pray of you Rev. Father, to take measures to have the subject properly represented in Congress the ensuing winter (at which session it is expected the French claims at this place will be brought for confirmation), and to endeavor to get some members enlisted in our cause, to prevent the confirmation of an unjust claim (by one who has never taken the oath of allegiance to the US) to our lands, & which is done would undoubtedly prove seriously injurious to your red children.

On behalf of the Stockbridge Nation
Jacob Cheekthanions [?]
Austin Quinney
Benjamin [his X mark] Palmer
John N. Chicks
Brotherwe [?] Calvin
Genius Ninham
Henry [his X mark] Beard — Oneidas[38]

Brothertown Lands in 1825

Thomas Dean, the Indian agent to the Brothertown Nation, wrote to Calhoun in February 1825 about "the arrangement between the Stockbridge & other tribes and the Brothertown Indians for lands at Green Bay."[39] Dean addressed issues regarding the Brothertown and their purchase of land at Green Bay. He explained that Parrish, who had been the Brothertown agent in New York, said "that he had no authority to act in the affairs. I believe that the Brothertown Indians have been exclusively under the protection of the Government of the State of New York."[40] He said when the Brothertown paid for land at Green Bay, he thought they should have consulted Cass.

Cass told Dean that the Brothertown should make a direct application with the president to confirm the treaty. The president advised there were provisions made "for the accommodation of those visiting the seat of Government on the Affairs of their respective Tribes and it would be attended to." Cass asked the government not to give the Brothertown more land than in the treaty and what is necessary. He provided information on the lands, saying "a great proportion of it is unfit for cultivation,"[41] and the Brothertown "are justly entitled to their proportion of the country ceded to the New York Indians by the Menominee Indians."[42]

The Stockbridge, Menominee, Six Nations, and French settlers protested, expressing their disagreement with the 1821 and 1822 treaties. All of this uncertainty and controversy was evident when the United States made treaties, in 1825 and 1827, with the Menominee and other Indigenous nations to establish new political boundaries for the Indigenous nations of Wisconsin and for the New York Indians.

6

THE TREATIES OF
1825 AND 1827

Indian Nation to United States

The United States made treaties in 1825 and 1827 that impacted the land boundaries of both the Menominee and the New York Indians. In 1825, the United States entered into a treaty with the Chippewa, Sac and Fox, Menominee, Ioway, Sioux, Winnebago, and a portion of the Ottawa, Chippewa, and Potawatomie tribes at Prairie du Chien.

At this time, Euro-American settlers were arriving in greater numbers to farm and harvest pine forests in Wisconsin, and miners were seeking valuable lead deposits. The settlers were encroaching on Indian lands, but boundaries between Native nations, and between Native nations and the United States, were unclear. One reason for this is that Native nations generally shared the land and knew whose territory they were in when hunting.

The treaty of 1825 was made to establish the land boundaries of these Native nations, as establishing clearly defined boundaries would make it easier for the United States to make treaties with Native nations. General William Clark, of the Lewis and Clark expedition, and Lewis Cass, the governor of Michigan Territory, were designated as commissioners for the United States to make the 1825 treaty. The purpose of this treaty, according to Clark and Cass, was to end wars between the Native nations involved, affirm a lasting peace, and establish working political borders. The preamble to the 1825 treaty states:

In order, therefore, to promote peace among these tribes, and to
establish boundaries among them and the other tribes who live in
their vicinity, and thereby to remove all cause of future difficulty,
the United States have invited [the tribes listed above] . . . to assemble
together, and in a spirit of mutual conciliation to accomplish these
objects.[1]

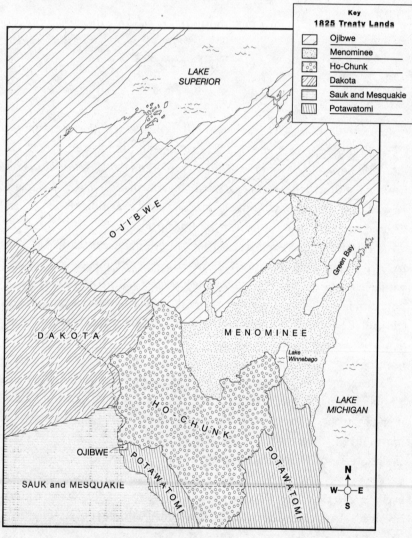

Wisconsin Indian treaty lands in 1825
AMELIA JANES, MIDWEST EDUCATIONAL GRAPHICS

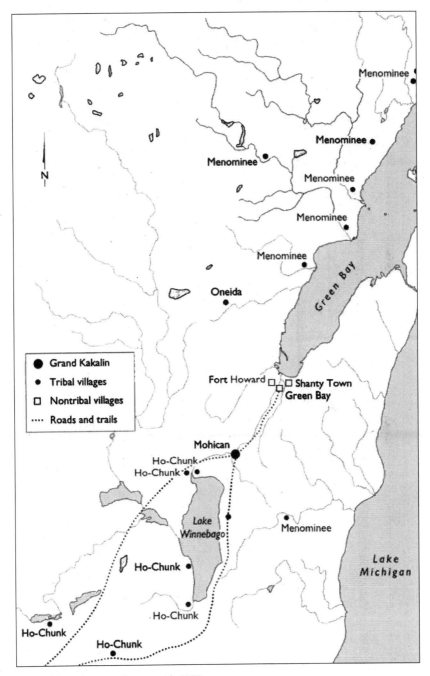

The Mohicans' new environment in 1825
© 2005 STOCKBRIDGE-MUNSEE COMMUNITY, REPRINTED BY PERMISSION OF THE PUBLISHER

Terms for the boundaries for the Menominee and New York Indians were described in Article 8:

> The representatives of the Menominies not being sufficiently acquainted with their proper boundaries, to settle the same definitively, and some uncertainty existing in consequence of the cession made by that tribe upon Fox River and Green Bay, to the New York Indians, it is agreed between the said Menominie tribe, and the Sioux, Chippewas, Winnebagoes, Ottawa, Chippewa and Potawatomie Indians of the Illinois, that the claim of the Menominies to any portion of the land within the boundaries allotted to either of the said tribes, shall not be barred by any stipulation herein; but the same shall remain as valid as if the treaty had not been concluded. It is, however, understood that the general claim of the Menominies is bounded on the north by the Chippewa country, on the east by Green Bay and lake Michigan extending as far south as Millawaukee river, and the West they claim to Black River.[2]

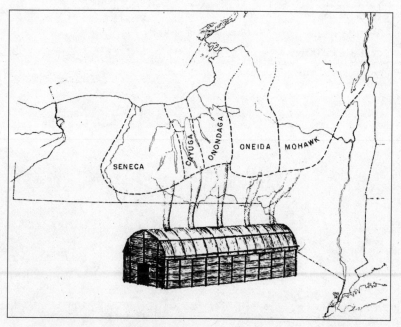

Lands of the Iroquois and the Poosepatuck and Shinnecock of Long Island
ILLUSTRATION BY GWEN GILLETTE, COURTESY NEW YORK STATE MUSEUM, ALBANY, NY

Article 8 acknowledged that the Menominee had made a "cession" of land to the New York Indians, and provided broad parameters of Menominee lands. The New York Indians were not included as participants in this treaty.

A page from the Treaty of Prairie du Chien. Signed on August 19, 1825, the Treaty of Prairie du Chien established land boundaries between several Indian nations.
WHI IMAGE ID 44423

O-wan-ich-koh, Little Elk, a Ho-Chunk chief, sketched by J. O. Lewis at the Treaty of Prairie du Chien in 1825
WHI IMAGE ID 26882

Wadt-he-doo-kaana, a Ho-Chunk chief, sketched by J. O. Lewis at the Treaty of Prairie du Chien in 1825
WHI IMAGE ID 26934

Waa-kaun-see-kaa, the Rattle-Snake, a Ho-Chunk chief, sketched by J. O. Lewis at the Treaty of Prairie du Chien in 1825
WHI IMAGE ID 26965

O-che-na-shink-kaa, the Man that Stands and Strikes, a Ho-Chunk chief, sketched by J. O. Lewis at the Treaty of Prairie du Chien in 1825

WHI IMAGE ID 26878

Wa-kaun, the Snake, a Ho-Chunk chief, sketched by J. O. Lewis at the Treaty of Prairie du Chien in 1825

WHI IMAGE ID 4795

Article 11 of the 1825 treaty also concerns Menominee land claims. According to Article 11, "The United States agree, whenever the President may think it necessary and proper, to convene such of the tribes, wither separately or together, as are interested in the line left unsettled herein, and to recommend to them an amicable and final adjustment of their respective claims, so that the work, now happily begun, may be consummated."[3]

Land boundaries for the Menominee were not firmly established in the 1825 treaty due to the controversy over the treaties of 1821 and 1822 conducted with the New York Indians, or what the treaty authors noted were "some uncertainty existing in consequence of the cession made by that tribe upon Fox River and Green Bay, to the New York Indians."[4] The wording in the treaty meant the US government acknowledged the 1821 and 1822 Menominee and New York Indian treaties, and Article 11 of the 1825 treaty endorsed another council/treaty negotiation on this issue.

Treaty of 1827 with the Chippewa, Menominee, and Winnebago (Treaty of Butte des Morts)

On March 27, 1827, Secretary of War James Barbour sent a letter to Cass and Thomas L. McKenney, the superintendent of Indian Affairs, appointing them to be treaty commissioners and requesting them to convene another council meeting. Article 11 of the 1825 treaty directed that this meeting be held to continue the settlement of boundaries. Barbour appropriated twelve thousand dollars to cover all the expenses for the council meeting, and McKenney kept a journal of the proceedings.

Barbour further acknowledged the New York Indians and their right to land in Wisconsin when he wrote of:

> two memorials both of the 17th January having been received by the President of the United States, from the Brothertown Indians, of Oneida County in the State of New York, setting forth, among other things, that they have purchased a certain tract of land on Fox River eight miles wide and thirty miles long; and that they have in other respects an interest with other tribes of Indians of the state of New York in the Country in the vicinity of Green Bay, and to which Country they have a prospect of removing; and as the Indians of whom it is represented they purchased said country will doubtless form part of the General Council.

Barbour approved the Brothertown attending the council, and he told the commissioners that the citizens of Green Bay were opposed to the purchase. A footnote stated that the two memorials from the Brothertown were not attached.[5] Additionally, Barbour's letter specifically referred to a *purchase* of land by the Brothertown and other New York Indians, even though the issue had not yet been settled, and Articles 2 and 3 of the 1827 treaty addressed this issue.

Many nations were in attendance. Members of the Chippewa, Menominee, Winnebago, Ottawa, Seneca, Oneida, Stockbridge, and Brothertown were all gathered. McKenney's reports mentioned that as many as one thousand Chippewa, Menominee, and Winnebago attended the council.[6]

MA_KO_ME_TA_ or BEAR'S OIL;

A Menomonie Chief.

Menominee Chief Ma-ko-me-ta, Bear's Oil,
sketched by J. O. Lewis at the Treaty of Butte
des Morts in 1827
WHI IMAGE ID 4791

Article 2 of the 1827 treaty stated the key issues to be addressed in the
negotiations:

Much difficulty having arisen from negotiations between the
Menomonie and Winnebago tribes and the various tribes and
portions of tribes of Indian of the State of New York, and the claims
of the respective parties being much contested, as well with relation
to the tenure and boundaries of two tracts, claimed by the New
York Indians, west of Lake Michigan, as to the authority of the
persons who signed the agreement on the part of the Menomonies,
and the whole subject having been fully examined as the Council
this day concluded, and the allegations, proofs, and statements,
of the respective parties having been entered upon the Journal of
Commissioners, so that the same can be decided by the President of
the United States; it is agreed by the Menomonies and Winebagoes,
that so, far as respects their interest in the premises, the whole matter

shall be referred to the President of the United States, whose decision
shall be final. And the President is authorized, on their parts, to
establish such boundaries between them and the New York Indians as
he may consider equitable and just.[7]

McKenney recorded the negotiations that preceded the signing of the
1827 treaty. His journal includes speeches made by representatives from
Indigenous nations, and many are included here in their entirety.[8]

When the council began, the parties followed Indigenous protocol.
Someone lighted the council fire, and the attending Indian nations smoked
the pipe of peace. Then Cass explained that the first purpose of the treaty
was to settle the boundary lines between the Menominee and the Chippewa, which had been left unclear in the 1825 treaty. Cass then spoke to the
second purpose of the 1827 treaty. "A number of your Brothers from New
York have been crowded out by the white people," Cass told the council,
"& have come to this country. The Menomonies have given them a seat
to sit down upon, on the Fox River."[9] This statement indicates that Cass
understood the Menominee position—that they were willing to share land
with the New York Indians. As a representative of the United States government, he wanted to define boundaries between the New York Indians, the
French settlers, and the Menominee. At first, Cass told the Menominee he
wanted some of the old chiefs to meet and decide the boundary line, but,
he warned, "If they cannot agree, we shall agree for them."[10]

Cass and others in the US government did not understand the legal
procedures of the Menominee people. When huge decisions were to be
made, the chiefs from each clan and village attended a meeting and they
made their decisions together following Menominee Nation protocols.
Certain chiefs were designated by the people of the Menominee Nation to
negotiate and sign treaties. Government officials did not want to wait for
all the chiefs and people to gather for discussion and decision making, so
the Menominee governmental and diplomatic procedures were ignored.
The US government knew that a large number of people attending a treaty-
making council meant that the government had to spend more money to
feed the attendees.

Moreover, though Cass saw that the Menominee did not have one
principal chief, he stated that the president, or the "Great Father," had

given Cass a directive "to appoint a principal Chief for the Menominees."
McKenney followed suit and told the Menominee that the president "wants
one mouth, . . . & one pair of ears . . . & a pair of eyes." McKenney also
claimed that he was instructed by the president to select one Menominee
Chief and put a "medal around his neck, & a robe over his shoulders, & give
him a flag. . . . his heart must hold only good American blood."[11]

The third purpose of the treaty was to clarify jurisdiction in criminal matters, which is often found in Indian treaties. McKenney told the
Menominee not to kill any white people and said that they should tell the
Great Father when white people do wrong, and the Great Father would
deal with them. He urged the Menominee not to get involved.[12]

As promised, Cass appointed a principal chief for the Menominee when
the treaty negotiations convened on August 7, 1827. Cass, like many government officials, chose to ignore the Menominee system of government
in order to deal with an individual instead of a group. In turn, the Menominee replied to Cass, "We told you yesterday, we would make a chief for
you. We have selected two from among you & now give them presents, &
this medal & this robe. You (pointing to a Menominee man) are now the
great Menomine Chief."[13]

Next, Cass discussed the boundary lines between the Menominee and
the New York Indians. The agent for the New York Indians, Thomas Dean,
submitted six documents to substantiate the claims of the New York Indians to land in Wisconsin. The list of documents the New York Indians
submitted is included in McKenney's journal, but copies of the actual
documents are not.[14] Dean also mentions that another source of important information would be the report of Charles C. Trowbridge, who had
negotiated the 1821 treaty. Dean included the Trowbridge report for the
government's consideration.[15]

According to McKenney, two chiefs were appointed by the Menominee
to speak on their behalf during the opening day of the treaty council. The
second chief spoke first, addressing the council as follows:

My Father.
   I & my nation recommend ourselves to the care of the Great Spirit.
We were all made by one Being. We offer you this pipe as a mark of
friendship. Everything we say shall be the truth. I am not ashamed

to stand before you as a Chief for I have been one from a child. As was
my father before me. I thank the Great Sprit that he has given me
an opportunity to stand before you this day, that I may speak what I
think. I recommend myself & my nation to the mercy of our father.
We have felt until now as if we were in a steel trap, but hope now to be
delivered from it. We put ourselves in the hand of our great Father.
It is for these reasons we are thankful. We have long wished for a
conference with you.[16]

The first chief followed the second and said:

My Father.
    From the time that the stranger Indians first came here, we have
no knowledge of having ever ceded any part of our country to them.
When I hear of their arrival, I sent my brother to them to say, that we
could not sell any part of our land, because it was so small. I did not
go myself. I was sick.[17]

The second chief then spoke again:

My Father. This is the answer the Menomonie nation makes to all the
treaties which have been read here.[18]

Since part of the issue was whether or not the Menominee and Winnebago who signed the 1821 and 1822 treaties were actually chiefs, the
commissioners then asked the Menominee and Winnebago for a list of the
names of who signed the treaty, designating who was a chief, who was not
a chief, and who was a war chief.[19]
    The 1821 treaty provides lists of the Menominee and Winnebago who
signed it and includes a list of the Menominee who signed the receipt
for cash payments. There are signatures on the receipt for payment of
five Menominee, and the names are different from those who signed the
treaty. The 1822 treaty was signed by six Menominee, three chiefs and three
war chiefs, and they were not the same chiefs that signed the 1821 treaty.
    The following Menominee and Winnebago signed the 1821 treaty:

Menominee
    Eskenanin, not a chief
    Asakutaw, not a chief
    Weekaw, chief
    Muchaonetaw, war chief
    Spaniard, war chief
    Kiskunakum, war chief

Winnebago
    Serachon (Smoker), chief
    Skoukapaw (Dogs Head), chief
    Ochoskaw (Four Legs), chief
    Keeramane (Elk), chief
    Hompemonick (Dog Walker), war chief
    Cheankoo (Crooked Tail), war chief
    Chausepk (Blackdeer), war chief
    Kaukauk (Dove), war chief

The Menominee who signed the receipt acknowledging payment for the 1821 treaty were as follows:

Great Wave, chief (denied signing)
Asakukaw (Spaniard), chief
Ocquonckaw (Pine shooter), chief
Iskakaw (Score all), chief
Skawwonnim, war chief (died by 1827)

The following Menominee signed the 1822 treaty:

Oquonmonikon, chief
Lahmonikopt, chief
Saghkettat, chief
Wiknisaught, war chief
Lyweekeenaugh, war chief
Wyhtchanighaugh, war chief[20]

Ho-Chunk Chief O'-check-ka, Four Legs, sketched by J. O. Lewis
at the Treaty of Butte des Morts in 1827
WHI IMAGE ID 26879

The next day, August 8, McKenney noted in his journal that the council
turned to the business concerning the Menominee and claims made by
the New York Indians to lands in Wisconsin. An unidentified Menominee
chief then addressed the council, arguing that the Menominee did not
understand the New York Indians' intentions or agree to a land purchase:

Father,

　　You shall hear from me, what has passed between the New York
Indians and my Nation, and you shall hear the truth. Father: When
they arrived in this Country, I was too sick to meet them, but I sent
my brother to the Bay to take them by the hand.

They told us on their arrival that they had not come here for land, that they had enough in their own country, that they had come only to take us by the hand. We understood their object be, not to purchase land, but to procure the grant of a small piece to sit down upon, that they might live with us like brothers. We never comprehended either that they wished, or that they had, purchased any part of our territory. This is the absolute truth. Mr. Rouse, who is here, interpreted for my brother when I sent him with the message. This is all we have to say.[21]

Four Legs (Winnebago) then shared with the council how he interpreted the New York Indians' intentions:

My Father,

I will tell you what has passed between our brothers from the East and us. I will tell you the truth. What I say, I say before the Great Spirit, who is the Father of Life, as well in the heaven above us, as on the Earth upon which we stand.

They said, 'Our Brothers!, It was at the request of our Great Father that we have come here to meet you. We are here on your lands. Our Brothers! Winnebagos and Menominees! We are poor. We ask you to take pity on us. We are not masters of our own land, neither of the waters within it nor of the trees upon it. We ask of you therefore, the charity to let us sit down upon your land here.

Father, When they first came, they asked for a small piece of land, sufficient for them to put their children on, that they might live. They and the Menominees were assembled at the first visit, and that Menomine Chief who has spoken to you was hesitating for two days so much that he did not know what answer to make.

They said, "Menominees, Our Brothers! We hope you will give us what we ask. We ask you to lend and not to sell us, a small piece of land. Do this, in charity to our impoverished situation."

Father: It was long before the Menominee would consent but we, the Winnebagos, interposed and said, What harm can it do to grant their request, since they only want to borrow the land, and not to buy it. It was not a sale, nor a gift, but it was a loan. We had too little ourselves to be willing to sell it. The New York Indians told us, that we should not request the loan, nor the charity we had yielded them. If they had sugar camps, our children should occupy them in common.

When you the Eastlanders came, we lent you a piece of land and its boundary was marked on a tree by one of your own chiefs, showing that it extended from the "little Shoot, to where you are now settled." The tree has fallen but the stump and the mark are there now.

There must have been some bad faith in this matter, as the tree, and the Chief who marked it, are both dead.

The Interpreter, Mr. Rouse, is standing here now, who stood between us then. We said to you, there is the tree and you are not move one inch beyond it. This is what was said to you.

My Brothers! You said, as we had lent you the land, you were glad, and that you would then return to your own country and when you came back here again, you would pay us for the use of it. This is all.[22]

Residents from Green Bay were also present at the council. Many were French and most had attended the 1821 treaty negotiations. McKenney wrote that after Four Legs finished:

Mr. Rouse was called, who stated, that the Menominees understood that the land was to be used in common by the Three Nations. He did not understand it to be a sale. Mr. Williams, (a half breed of the Oneida Tribe) expressed this belief also, to Mr. Rouse. Mr. Grignon was present, who can state his impressions of the subject.[23]

The commissioners then called Mr. Grignon,

who stated that the interpreters employed at the Treaty, did not interpret correctly either to or from the Menominees and Winnebagos. The land intended to be transferred from them to the New York Indians, he understood, was that comprehended between the Little Rapids and the Kakalin. It was interpreted to the Menominees. It was not a sale, but a loan. The New York Indians asked as a matter of charity, that the Menominees and Winnebago should let them have a small piece of land, promising to recompense them for it, when they would return from their own country. Mr. Paul Grignon being called, said that the New York Indians did not ask to purchase land. They only requested that they might live among the Menominees. Mr. Doty stated, that the principal men never received one farthing of the purchase money, and that such a fact could not be proved.[24]

When the proceedings convened the next day, the commissioners moved to the issue of establishing boundaries between the Menominee, Chippewa, and Winnebago. Four Legs spoke again on behalf of the Winnebago, expressing a longstanding tradition of communal land use for hunting:

> My Father! Since the Great Spirit first placed us upon this earth, the Menomonies our brothers, the Chippeways, & ourselves, have always hunted together peaceably. We hope still to do so.
>
> The Father of Life, made the Earth for the Indian to roam upon — that the Chippeways & Menomonies & Winebagos might wander wherever they pleased. Since the time that we can first remember, the fires of the Chippeways & Menomonies & Winebagos have been one fire. We have always held each other by the hand. We appeal to the ancient traders to say whether they have not at all time hunted upon our land, & whether they have not found us hunting together as brothers. And we hope, that we, the Menomonies, Chippeways & Winebagoes will continue to live together like three brothers, as we have hitherto lived.
>
> We do not need any line.[25]

Cornelius Baird [Beard], whom McKenney misidentified as Seneca, spoke to the commissioners next, offering an Oneida perspective on the acquisition of lands in Wisconsin by the New York Indians.

> Father,
> You are here in the midst of us. You are authorized by our great Father, the President, to settle the misunderstanding which exist among his children who are here assembled. All that will be said will go to our Great Father from you. We offer our thanks to the Great

Spirit that he has thus far continued us in health, now Father
listen.

We came from the East. We had a place there. It extended to the
shores of the salt waters. At that time, we knew you not. There,
while we were walking on the Sea shores, we discovered you. We
thought at first, you were ghost for you seemed bloodless. You asked
for small place to sit down on. Your words were good. From that
time our hands have been joined with yours. You made yourselves
a shelter. You began to grow and spread, and the Indians began to
melt. My forefathers saw the consequences of your coming. They
made a league with the ancestors of these Indians here, that when
we should not have land enough ourselves, we should come and sit
down with them. The time has come when we have not enough to live
on and our Great Father has sanctioned our coming here to live with
our brothers. When he gave us permission to remove, I made up my
pack, and on my way hither I saw you, my Father, at our place. You
sent a young man [Trowbridge] with us, when you told us to obey as
our Father, and that what he did, you would approve. On our arrival,
the terms of our contract were discussed with our Brothers, the
Menominees and Winnebagos. Our Treaty was made by the young
man who was placed here as our Father. We did not expect then that
we should now be charged with doing this in a secret manner. All was
done by that young man, who employed two interpreters, who stood
between us and our Brothers. If this was fraud, he could not have been
the only one guilty. But there were others who could testify to the
fairness of the transaction. There were many who were putting word
into the ears of our Menominee Brothers. The Agent said that they
were interfering, though they had nothing to do with it and ought
not to interrupt us. This was the way the matters was conducted at the
Bay. Even when we came back, the Menominees were told that if they
did not accept the presents it would destroy the whole Treaty. This
interference has existed from the beginning and the same disposition
is even now exhibited before you.

Therefore, we do not blame our brothers, the Menomineees for
what they have said, as they have been taught to believe that all our
bargains with them were made in darkness and in mist. But we do

not consider our bargain a fraud, because we have our Father with us when it was made.

There is but one place when this opposition has come. We have long known it as well as we know it now, for our brothers the Menominees and Winnebagos have always informed us of it. It came from a man who was considered a Father to them and who always wanted them to join the English Government. And it is owing to his influence that some of them are now attached to that Government. Our brothers here said that their French Father always told them, that the American Government was bad, but the English Government was good for them. When therefore these advisors profess to be Americans, their words come from the lips and not from the heart.

We see two flags flying here. We know but one as that to which we yield honor and obedience. A few days since the Americans had a quarrel and we were there seen under that flag. What we say is from the heart. At that times when they shed their blood, we mingled ours with it, and it is not only the heights of Niagara or the Shores of Ontario, that can testify that our hearts were American hearts. The effect of introducing a foreign flag, is shown in an instance which occurred in my Nation where two flags were taken into one house (St. Regis) and it cost the loss of three lives.

Father, we were glad to hear you say that you had come here to build a strong fence, and that if any strange animal got over it, your arms were long and strong enough to pull it back. We expect as we have joined our hands with the Menominees and Winebagos, you will put down this interference in our business. We do not charge the French alone with opposing us. We charge a man also, who was sent here to administer justice.

We deny that there has been any fraud, for we came here in the path in which our Father directed us to walk. What that man said yesterday, is not only extraordinary but dreadful. What! Does he not only try to make white men of us, but descends himself to the level of an Indian!

Our Father has always wanted us to adopt his habits, but as long as Indian blood runs in our veins, we shall always be Indians.

We have been told, that there was a man appointed by the

Menominees and Winnebagos to defeat our contract with them.
We have no objection and are ready to meet him. I have done.[26]

In response, the commissioners asked the Menominee signers of the
second treaty if "they did not agree that the New York Indians should have
the land and they [the Menominee] should live with them common?"[27]
Great Wave answered for the Menominee:

Father,

The New York Indians came to us in great distress and we listened
to them. They said, "We are pushed out of our own Country and
have come here to take you by the hand." We answered, since it is our
Great Fathers pleasure, we are glad to have you with us. We are few, &
possibly our Country may be large enough for us all to sit down upon!
They [New York Indians] said, "We are glad we have been sent here.
We have been assisted much by our Great Father. We are looked upon
as Americans ourselves. We call the Great Spirit to witness that we
will not injure you in any way. All we want is a small piece of ground
to sow. We are surprised to see you in so bad a condition and not
more industrious."

We thought our Great Father wanted farmers here and that
they would show us and make us more comfortable. This is what
we understood, and we appeal for the truth of it, to Rickett the
interpreter, who was there. They said they would plough our fields
and give us cattle and show us how to cultivate the ground.[28]

Great Wave was then asked several questions by the commissioners.
McKenney recorded this exchange:

Mr. Dean asked the "Wave": Have not the New York Indians done as
   they agreed?
Great Wave: "They Ploughed three little fields and ½."
Commissioners: Did you sign this paper?
Great Wave: We signed it without knowing the contents.
Commissioners: Describe the country you agreed to let the New York
   Indians have.

Great Wave: That between the "Little Shoot" and the "Kakalin."
Commissioners: Was this for the New York Indians alone or for both
    of you?
Great Wave: It was to be held in common.

Following this, the second Menominee chief explained to the commissioners the difficulties the tribe encountered during treaty negotiations in 1821 and 1822:

Father, the Great Spirit sees me here before you and hears me speak
the truth. I speak for my Chief, who is young. He is the head Chief of
the Nation. We are like you. You have Many officers about you, but
you are the Greatest. So with us. You appoint your officers, we ours.
When the Chief heard what had been done, he wished to send to his
Great Father and tell him what was in our hearts, but he could not.
We had not even recourse to the whites at the Bay. We had to consult
among ourselves. We asked Judge Doty to aid us, because he was a
man who knew the law. What I say, I say before all the nation, who
can stop me if I lie.[29]

The Stockbridge delegate, John W. Quinney, who McKenney records incorrectly as Oneida, was next to speak. Among other things, Quinney attempted to clear any misunderstandings between the New York Indians and the Menominee:

Father, we have put confidence in you. We believe you can
discriminate between right and wrong. I was one of the five delegates
who came here to extend our purchase (1822). We proposed to our
brothers that we should take more land as we had not enough. We
offered them $3000 in merchandise, if they would let us go further
down towards the Bay. There sits a Menominee who said he was
willing to sell but had not determined how much he was disposed to
part with. We thought as far as the Little Rapids would answer. Big
Wave, with a wampum in his hand, then said to us, "We are happy to
receive you as brothers. You may share the land with us. We think you
may be of service to us in helping to cultivate it. We will permit you

to be joint owners with us of all of it." The Menominees said that the land described in the second Treaty was theirs.

Our ancient Covenant renewed in 1821 has been always preserved. We labor under disadvantages because we do not understand each other. Something has grown up now to disturb our mutual relations, but we depend on what you said the other day, that you came here to learn the truth. We hope you will hear it.

It was our wish that the Menominees should sit down and cultivate the ground and profit by our example. We wished also, that at this place, all our Eastern brethren should concentrate. We saw that we were losing ground in mental improvement by the too frequent use of ardent spirits. Since we have been here, we have done better. We are fully persuaded that it is best for the Indians to be by themselves.[30]

At this point in his journal, McKenney recorded some responses given by the Americans at the council. He wrote, "Mr. Doty, for the people of Green Bay, said that they were innocent of all that had been charged against them, denying altogether the truth of everything that had been said, implicating their conduct." He also wrote, "Mr. Rouse denies that he was an interpreter, and adds, that if he had been, he would have told Mr. Trowbridge at the time, that the transaction was unfair." Finally, McKenney noted, "Mr. Schoolcraft being called upon stated, that Capt. Smith had told him that he (Smith) was at Fort Howard when the 2nd Treaty was concluded, and refused to sign it because he thought the transaction partial and that the Menominee were not properly represented."[31]

Four Legs then spoke:

Father, I take you and your friend by the hand. Listen! Long since, I heard you were coming from our Great Father to meet us.

You have forbidden us to tell a lie. But yet this has not prevented that there should be bad mouths here from which bad words come. You, Brother of mine! I do not know how you can speak so bad to our Great Father, I, a Winnebago, am afraid to speak so loud to him. Father. All we care for is to hear your words and we will obey them. I love my Chiefs who are here, my women and children, and we want to live yet a little longer. I hope the Great Father of Life will have pity

on me and my Nation. I think of what was said yesterday, that my
brothers, Chippewas, the Menominees, the New York Indians and all
would live together in peace.

I wish this business was finished. We want to know your intentions.
We are afraid of you. We want the time to come when we may say this
matter is settled. I have not two mouths. What I said at first to your
officer who came here, I say now.[32]

Two days later, on August 11, 1827, the new treaty had been read and
interpreted to and signed by representatives from the Indian nations present at the council.[33]

Four Legs again spoke, this time urging the government officials in
front of him to enforce their laws and hold to their promises:

Father, I have not much to say. You have always told us to be still,
to raise our children, provide for our families & not be afraid of
your men. But I am afraid of your young men at the mines. There
are a great many Americans on our land, working it without our
permissions, & I want to tell our Great Father to stop it—to reach out
his long arm & draw them back.

Father. You know we have a great many young men in our nation
& I cannot take care of them. They will do wrong. You know as well
as I do that your people, knowing how to read & write, yet do wrong,
how much more are they to be wondered at, than we, who are poor
& ignorant. What is a Chief among us? They are little better than the
rest of the nation. They have no power or authority with the others
except in Council, & but very little influence. We had a father at the
Prairie once, who was good to us & taught us to act like the white
people, but now he is dead & we are all scattered like a flock without
its leader.

Father. What you have told us shall be done if it is my power. This
is the last time I shall see you. I have said all.[34]

An unidentified chief then spoke, asking, like Four Legs, for the commissioners to abide by the terms of the treaty:

Father. You are sitting here before the Great Spirit & us. You took pity
on us & I hope our people will listen to what you have told them.

You gave us some flints. We want you to give us some powder. We
have no way to support our families, but by hunting. We hope you
will give us some.[35]

When Four Legs had finished, one of the commissioners addressed the
issue of redress for the murder of an unknown person on Lake Pepin by the
Chippewa. He stated that the Chippewa must give up the guilty men or the
United States would stop the traders from entering Chippewa lands. The
commissioner sent a string of wampum to the Chippewa Nation to carry
his message about turning over the guilty men, a sign that the commissioners understood and implemented the diplomatic protocols of Native
nations when it suited their interests.

The New York Indians then turned to the Chippewa delegates and addressed them as their grandchildren. They also presented the Chippewa a
wampum belt to renew an ancient understanding between their nations:

Grandchildren,

I address you by the name which the Covenant of Friendship made
between our forefathers, established, and which is used by us, their
offspring to this day.

I thank the Great Spirit, that he has permitted us to meet around
the Council Fire our Great Father has kindled, and to smoke together,
the pipe of peace with him.

We are glad that we can take you by the hand this day and renew
our Covenant of Friendship. Our fire is now nearer yours, and we
hope to be able to manifest our good feeling for you oftener than
we have heretofore done. Do not listen to any bad birds that may
be flying about, and trying to injure those feelings. We shall try to
preserve them bright to the latest generation.[36]

In turn, the Chippewa confirmed the Covenant of Friendship:

Brothers, The Great Spirit made us all. We have no wish but to live
as friends, since you desire it. We are glad that you bear in mind the

Covenant made by our fathers, though the time has been so long that few among us remember it. Whenever we meet any of you here after we shall know that we are friends.[37]

Shortly after the Treaty of Butte des Morts had been signed by all parties, Cass and McKenney sent copies of the 1821, 1822, and 1827 treaties to Secretary of War Barbour. They assured Barbour that a boundary line with the Chippewa had been established. Regarding the New York Indians' issue with the Menominee and the Winnebago, McKenney stated:

It has been agreed, as the clear understanding of both parties that the Menominees were to remain joint owners with the New York Indians of all the land ceded to the latter. This understanding is not however expressed in the Treaties.

It is contended by the Menominees, that the persons who signed the papers on their part were not authorized to do so.

We believe from an examination of the various facts, that the Menominee Tribe was not sufficiently represented on those occasions. . . . It is also contended by the Menominee, and we think with justice, that the terms and extent of the cession were not understood by their people. . . . Besides the cessions extend beyond the acknowledged limits of the Menominee Country, north to the Chippewas and south to the Manitowoc and Milwaukee Indians. And it will be perceived that there is some difference respecting the boundary upon the Fox River, of the Second cession.[38]

The commissioners went on to state that they did not think the New York Indians needed all that land described in the treaties. They reasoned that if the New York Indians were in possession of such vast acreage, they might slip back into "savagery," when the goal was to make all Native peoples into assimilated agriculturists. The commissioners distributed $15,682 in presents for the treaty and claimed that everyone in attendance understood "that the sale is at their own risk," because the president and Senate had to ratify the treaty.[39]

Article 3 of the 1827 treaty defined the boundaries of the Menominee lands and stated the following regarding the New York Indians:

Provided, that if the President of the United States should be of
opinion that the boundaries thus established interfere with any just
claims of the New York Indians, the President may then change the
said boundaries in any manner he may think proper.[40]

Without a doubt, the 1827 treaty acknowledged the claims of the New
York Indians, although it did not specify the actual boundaries established
in the 1821 and 1822 treaties between the Menominee and Winnebago and
the New York Indians. The questions regarding the legality of the 1821 and
1822 treaties continued to be discussed in later treaty negotiations. This
1827 treaty was signed by the Chippewa, Menominee, and Winnebago
Nations, and there are no signatures of the New York Indians on it. Thus,
this treaty did not settle the controversy. Article 2 of the 1827 treaty referred the final decision on land for the New York Indians to the president
of the United States.

7

PETITIONS BY THE
NEW YORK INDIANS

The Oneida, Stockbridge and Munsee, Tuscarora, and Brothertown Nations made several appeals to the US government regarding the 1821, 1822, and 1827 treaties and their uncertainty of their possession of the lands outlined in those treaties. In the 1827 treaty, the US government defined Menominee land boundaries that included the same lands that were identified in the 1821 and 1822 treaties as being set aside for the New York Indians. The first appeal is thirty-two pages long and includes a summary of the history of events from 1810 to 1829. The petition was signed by the Stockbridge and Munsee at Green Bay on November 13, 1828, and by the Oneida in New York on December 18, 1828. The petition also included signatures for Tuscarora and Brothertown signees. The second petition was signed by John Metoxen and Austin Quinney (Stockbridge), who signed as representatives of the New York Indians. They protested the sale of alcohol and asked that a law be passed to prevent its sale in the future. They also proposed boundaries for land for New York Indians that would be acceptable.

PETITION OF 1828

The following excerpt is from the petition written to the US Senate in 1828:

Fathers,
We your children being chiefs and principal men of the several

Indian Tribes hereunto subscribed, would request your Hon. Body to
hear us a few words.

As the settlements of the white people were crowding upon ours
in the State of N. York, where we all heretofore resided and where
many of our people still reside, and as they were greatly annoyed by
the venders of ardent spirits among them, and by other evils under
which they were fast diminishing, they clearly saw the necessity of
seeking a new fire-place, where they would be more secluded from
the influence of wicked white people, and less exposed to many
temptations. After some delays and disappointment our Great Father
the President of the United States, gave us permission to make a
Treaty with our Brethren in the Northwest part of the Territory of
Michigan, to purchase lands, where we might enjoy the advantages
we desired. We accordingly made a Treaty [1821] with our Brethren
the Menominie and Winnebago Tribes of Indians, to purchase a tract
of land lying on both sides of Fox River, from the outlet of Winnebago
Lake to the foot of the Grand Kaccalin. This Treaty was approved by
the President of the US, and [next two lines are crossed out; a stain on
the paper makes it unreadable]. The Treaty did not contain sufficient
land for a convenient settlement of the several Tribes concerned in
it, a second permission was obtained of the President of the US to
make a second Treaty [1822] to purchase land, and we purchased of
the Menominie Indians a large tract of land lying on both sides of
Fox River, and Green Bay, to be occupied in common with us, they
having a right to settle thereon, wherever it should be agreeable, not
interfering with our settlements. Of this purchase, that part lying
on the South East side of Fox River and Green Bay as far as Sturgeon
Bay, was approved by the President of the US, that being deemed by
him sufficient for the Tribes concerned in the Treaties. But we were
at the same time informed by the Hon. the Secretary at War, that we
might settle on any part of the land purchased with perfect safety.
Here, Fathers, we hoped to enjoy a safe retreat for ourselves and
children, and that to remote generations, we and they should remain
undisturbed in the possession of this distant country.

But how great was our surprise and sorrow, when at the late Treaty
held by his Excellency Gov. L. Cass and Col. Thos. L. McKenny, at the

Little Butte des Morts [in 1827], our lands were purchased by them as Commissioners of the US and thus our hopes of security in this last refuge destroyed. If Treaties thus made by us with the approbation of public authority, and confirmed by the same, are to be thus disregarded and trampled on, on what can we rely, or where shall we ever rest?

This purchase of our lands was made, not only without our consent and contrary to our most earnest wishes, but also without even consulting us at all! We were not allowed a hearing nor even asked whether we would consent to sell or not. It has indeed been said to us, that this Treaty does not affect our claims, but leaves them still good. But if our right to the land we have purchased is considered good, why is it purchased again from other, and nothing said to us? And if any right could be thus obtained to the land which we occupied in common with the Menominies, surely it could not be to that part which lies within the first Treaty, in which there [is] no such condition We are not unwilling that our white Brethren should have some land in this region, but we entreat you not to suffer our lands to be thus forcibly taken from us contrary to solemn Treaty and without our consent. If this Treaty, to purchase our land from us without our consent, and against our wishes, should be confirmed, it will serve wholly to discourage the emigration of our people from the East. Indeed the attempts which have been making to obtain such a Treaty have hindered many from coming to this country who would have been here before now, if no such attempts had been made. It would be unreasonable for them to leave their country and their homes, when they could, have no security that they should remain undisturbed in the country they had purchased. Fathers, we wish that this Treaty may not be confirmed, but that Commissioners might be appointed, and sent to Green Bay next spring, to meet Delegates from all the Tribes of Indians in the State of N. York, concerned in the purchase of land in that country, fully authorized to assist them in fixing the boundaries of their several locations, on principles of Justice and Equity, and to confirm these locations to them and their descendants forever, but without their possessing the right of selling them to white people, without the appropriation of all the Tribes concerned.

This measure if adopted would give our people that security in the possession of their lands, which need, and would encourage the scattered remnants of our Tribes to remove to that country, in the hope of enjoying for themselves and their children a permanent residence. Fathers, we have no more to say. We put confidence in your clemency and Justice to hear us, and trust you will not suffer us to be deprived of that country which we have fairly and honorably obtained and which we wish to inhabit, and leave for a possession to our children.

We remain with sentiment of the highest respect your friends and children.

Oneida Tribe
John X Anthony
Thomas X Powlas
Henry X Jonrdan [?]
National X Agigwet War Chief
Daniel Bread W.C.
Henry X Powlas First Chief
Paul X Powlas C.
Anthony X Anthony C.
Peach tree X Christian C.
Nicolas X Wheelock W. C.
John X August W. C.
Joseph X Me W. C.
Thomas X Neddy
John X Cornelius
William X Anthony
George X Hill
Coopers X Hill
William X Bread
Anthony X. John War Chief
William X Cornelius W C.
William X Day
Moses X Cornelius
Jacob X Cornelius

For & in behalf of the rest.
Oneida, N.Y. 18th Dec., 1828

Stockbridge & Munsee Tribes
  John Metoxen
  Robert X Konkapot
  Chief. Jacob Chicks
  Jacob X Littleman
  Austin Quinney
  Cornelius X Doxtador
  John N. Chicks
  John W. Quinney
  Thomas X Simon
  Joseph M. Quinnukkaut
  John X Hunt
  Capt. Porter

For and in behalf of the rest.
Green Bay, Michigan Territory,
13th Nov., 1828

Tuscarora Tribe
  Sacharisa X
  George X Printup
  John X Fox

Brothertown Tribe
  B.G. Fowler
  Eliphalet Marthers
  William Dick
  John Johnson
  Asa Dick
  James Niles[1]

The petitioners also expressed "their reasons for objecting to the ratification of the Treaty made by US Commissioners at the Butte de Morts in

1827."[2] The petition then provided a review of the history of the continuing pressure by the US government for the New York Indians to remove to the West. Indeed, the petition stated, "As early as 1810 the Council of Six Nations was 'encouraged' by 'Officers of Government' that they might be provided a 'permanent resting place' for their people."[3]

Years earlier, in 1815, the sachems and chiefs of the Six Nations sent a memorial to the War Department asking questions relating to the outcome of emigrating to the West. The memorial reads:

> The Sachems and Chiefs of the Six Nations are however aware of the impropriety of forming any definitive resolutions on a measure so materially affecting the future condition or welfare of their people without the advice and approbation of the government of the US that has so long cherished and protected them, and to which they are closely united by the brightest chain of peace and friendship
>
> The object of this memorial is therefore to enquire.
>
> First, whether the government will consent to our leaving our present habitations, and removing into the neighborhood of our western Brethren?
>
> Secondly, whether if we should obtain either by gift or purchase, from our western friends, a seat on their lands, the government will acknowledge our title in the same manner as it now acknowledges it in those from whom we may receive it?
>
> And thirdly, whether our removal will be considered as changing in any manner the relations now subsisting between our Tribes and the Government, or whether they will be permitted to continue the same; and existing treaties still remain in force, and annuities paid as heretofore?
>
> After the strong and repeated proofs given by the Six Nations of their friendship and attachment to the US, the Sachems and Chiefs feel assured that their wish of removing to a more distant part of the country will not be attributed to any dissatisfaction towards their white brethren. And they are persuaded that no political consequences injurious to the US will result from such removal. On the contrary they cannot but hope that the representation they will be able to make to their western brethren of the friendly

position of the people toward the natives under their protection, and of the honor and good faith always observed by the Government in its dealing with us, will greatly tend to render their friendship permanent and their fidelity secure.[4]

The Secretary of War, William H. Crawford, replied on February 16, 1816. He began his reply by addressing them as "Brothers of the Six Nations" and said the president had approved all their requests. He also asked them to "define the limits of the seats which you are about to obtain from your brethren in the west, and furnish the government with metes and bounds so that in treaties to be held hereafter with other tribes, your lands may not be granted away by them."

This is relevant to the petition written in 1828, because the petitioners reminded the government of this history. They also noted that in 1819, Rev. Jedidiah Morse, who supported and encouraged the removal of the New York Indians, was funded by the War Department to take a journey to Green Bay to judge the suitability of the land for the New York Indians. He reported the lands near Green Bay were a suitable place for the New York Indians to settle.[5]

The following winter, Eleazer Williams went to Washington, DC. There he held conferences with the president, James Monroe, and his secretary of war, John C. Calhoun, to discuss the expediency of Williams being sent to the Green Bay area by the US government, and to request funds for his journey. His goal was to explore the country around the waters of Green Bay and the Fox River, with a view to select a suitable site for the Six Nations and, if possible, to make a treaty with the Wisconsin tribes who owned the land on which the government hoped to relocate the New York Indians.

On February 20, 1820, Calhoun wrote to Williams approving expenses for ten people to go on the journey. He provided three hundred dollars, a blanket for each person, rifle powder, lead, a copy of Morse's Geography and his gazetteer, and orders for rations to be furnished by military posts along the route to Green Bay. Calhoun, writing to Lewis Cass, the governor of Michigan Territory, and General Alexander Macomb, the commanding general of the US Army, assured both that this journey "has the approbation of the President."[6]

In the summer of 1820, Williams and his party set out on their trip to the Green Bay area. When they reached Detroit, however, they were told that the lands they wanted to procure had been sold in a treaty with the Menominee by John Bowyer. The delegation turned around and went back to New York to protest the treaty to the secretary of war and ask that the Bowyer treaty not be approved. Calhoun was inclined to agree with their request, and the Bowyer treaty was never sent to the Senate for ratification (see Chapter 2).

With the aforementioned history, the petition written in 1828 additionally cites the 1821 journey made by the New York Indians, including the Stockbridge and Munsee, to Green Bay (see Chapter 3). The Stockbridge and Munsee had been promised land on the White River in Indiana, but upon their arrival they were told the land was no longer available to them, as it had been exchanged in an earlier treaty.[7]

The complete 1821 treaty between the Menominee and Winnebago and the New York Indians is included with the petition. The petitioners noted that Monroe signed his approval of this treaty on February 9, 1823. The receipts for $950 paid by the Stockbridge and $200 paid by the Tuscarora to the Menominee are attached to this treaty.

Moreover, the petitioners noted that the New York Indians had requested more land, as the land in the 1821 treaty was too small to accommodate all of the Six Nations. The response to this request was addressed on February 13, 1822, in a letter from Calhoun to Solomon U. Hendrick, a deputy from the Stockbridge Nation. Calhoun wrote that he had received

> your communication of the 5th inst. And return herewith the original Treaty concluded at Green Bay, between the Deputies from the Stockbridge and other Tribes of the Six Nations and the Menominies, and Winnebagoes endorsed by the President approved. I regret that any portion of the Six Nations is dissatisfied with the Treaty, but as one of the causes of dissatisfaction appears to be the distance of the country cede thereby from Green Bay.

On May 8, 1822, Calhoun approved another journey to the Green Bay area to negotiate for more land.[8] Calhoun also sent a letter to Cass appointing the missionary John Sergeant to negotiate for the United States in another treaty in 1822. Calhoun told Cass, "The object in procuring this cession, is not only to provide a Tract of country sufficient for the residence of these Indians, but also to exclude from it, and from its vicinity any white settlements." Calhoun also stressed the need to advance these Indians in "education, habits, and association and the annuities which are due to them to secure their friendship and fidelity to the United States." He stated the connection with getting land was also to prevent "the introduction of that bane of Indian improvement ARDENT SPRIRITS." He advised that the lands acquired should be "as far down the Fox River as possible."⁹

The full transcript of the 1822 treaty between the New York Indians and the Menominee includes a receipt for $950 paid to the Menominee, as well as President Monroe's approval of the treaty on March 13, 1823. But Monroe approved only the land that he thought sufficient for the New York Indians' needs, which was less land than stated in the treaty. Of course, the New York Indians expressed dissatisfaction with the partial approval of the 1822 treaty, and it was made clear that only the president had to sign these treaties because the treaties were between Indian nations and did not require congressional approval. The interference by the French was included in the report of John Sergeant, who wrote:

The Menominies, without a dissenting voice agreed to the proposals of the New York Indians. I have been credibly informed that some of the French people at this place have taken much pains to create a party among the Menominies to frustrate the designs of Government, and the New York Indians, in the aforesaid purchase, and have been entirely unsuccessful in their attempts, and I have the pleasure further to state that the Menominies appear to be much pleased with the bargain, and their new neighbors.¹⁰

All of this is important to understand, as the 1828 petition continues with this statement from the Six Nations:

From the foregoing documents, it must appear to every candid person. That We, the Six Nations, Stockbridge and others had fairly and honorably acquired, a title to our lands, specified in the Treaties, at least so far as ratified by the President: — and that the government was pledged in the most unqualified manner, to sustain us in our new possessions. The many promises and engagements of the Government, only a part of which are here adduced; we believe to have been duly authorized, and that the good faith of the Nation was most sincerely and solemnly pledged to us. It is true, that some of our friends suggested the propriety of bringing these Treaties before the Senate of the US for its concurrence, but the following extract of a letter from the Secretary of War, to Solomon U. Hendrick, "Dated, Department of War 22nd Nov. 1821," deterred us from so doing.[11]

We therefore know of no further assurance or transaction necessary, either on the part of the Government, or our Brethren at Green Bay, to make our title to those lands valid; to have it acknowledged to be in us, "the same as the Government acknowledges the title of all friendly Indian Tribes." And we thought abundant care had been taken "to furnish the Government with its metes and bounds, so that in Treaties it should hold thereafter with other Tribes, our land might not be granted away by them;" especially as the Agents, appointed to superintend the negotiation on the part of the US, were instructed to assist in defining and making the lines or our new possessions.

What we now complain of, as most unheard of injustice is, that an attempt has been made to deprive us of a great portion of these very lands without consulting or even inviting us to the Treaty — we refer to the Treaty of August 1827. It is with reluctance we refer to this Treaty, but we feel constrained to notice some of the proceedings are from the minutes taken down at the time by a gentleman who attended this Treaty.

The Treaty was then made in some private conferences, by which the Menominie Nation ceded to the US all that tract or parcel of land commencing near Grassy point, at the Head of Green Bay, and extending six miles wide, on each side of Fox River, and up the same to the upper part of the Grand Kaccalin, a distance of about 26 miles; which will include the settlement of the Oneida Indians, on the west side of Fox River, and a part of the settlement of the Stockbridge Indians, this being on the east side of the River, also including the location of the Brothertown Indians. We appeal to reason, equity and humanity; to the magnanimity of the Great American people if we may not in justice complain of these proceedings.[12]

We now, therefore, pray the Chief Council of the Nation, to listen patiently to our petition, to consider the solemn promises that have been so repeatedly made to us: — the great expense which both the Government and we have been at, to accomplish the object of concentrating our scattered Tribes, thus far; — we hope it will not be forgotten, that we were induced to make choice of this country by government in order that its benevolent views towards us, by way of instruction in religion, arts &c. might, more effectually reach us, and the our Great Father the President thought in 1822, "that it would be better for the respective Tribes of the Six Nations & c. to dispose of their land, in the state of New York, and to remove to the land which had been ceded to them by the Menominies and Winnebagoes, because they could there, concentrate their now scattered population, and being removed to a distance from the white settlements, they would be more SECURE AGAINST THE EFFECTS OF VIOLENCE AND INJUSTICE, and the efforts of the Government to improve their condition, would be rendered less difficult and expensive" all of which must fail of its intended effect, if we be compelled to remove.[13] We pray them to consider how often we have been chased from our possessions upon professions of friendship, and how effectually the confidence of their faithful friends the Indians in the Nation's promises, must be destroyed, if this measure be not arrested. — We pray not only to have this Treaty set aside, but to have a law passed, setting off the lands granted and ratified to us in our treaties with the Menominies and Winnebagoes, for our and their benefit forever — and so established to the various tribes interested in them, that it may not be lawful for the United States or any other authority to purchase them from us while Indians are Indians. Then shall we feel assured that the professions of Government were made in sober earnest; that in all this business of several years, it has not been mocking us with illusions to beguile us of our scanty possessions in New York but has, like an affectionate parent, sought the best good of its dutiful children. Then shall we see a rational consistency in its spending large sums annually for the civilization of Indians, which

is only sporting with their misery, if they are every few years to be
driven back to the savage wilds. We leave our cause, to us of the most
vital importance, in the hands of wisdom, and integrity; believing
that abundance of both are to be found in the Chief Council of the
American Nation, asking only for that clemency and justice which a
fair representation our claims must demand.[14]

PETITION OF 1829

Another petition was sent by the New York Indians to Congress in
December 1829.[15] In it the Stockbridge and Oneida addressed interference
in the treaties by both Americans and French "trespassers," asked for a law
to prevent alcohol being sold in their lands, and described the lands they
were requesting. It appears here in its entirety:

Fathers,
The Chiefs and Warriors of the several Tribes hereunto subscribed
formerly from the State of New York but now resident at Green Bay
in Michigan Territory respectfully showeth:
That it is well known to your Honorable Body that those called
New York Indians by the permission of the General Government
purchased a tract of land at Green Bay from Menominees and
Winnebagoes in two Treaties in 1821 and 1822 which were also
sanctioned by the same.
That accordingly we, comprising a small proportion of the
aforementioned Tribes, emigrated hither in the anticipation of
finding a permanent peace, of which we were long deprived in the
places where we resided. It also pleased our Brethren to see us come
and take possession of the Country they had ceded to us, and as
we considered our title to the same government acquired in good
faith. So it greatly revived our dropping hearts, and all our powers
by which we were enabled to adopt more freely and put in practice
experimentally the good ways of the civilized people, in which we
are pleased to say we have been greatly benefitted. We also hoped to
be materially advantage to our Brethren in this Country by setting
forth to them examples of this kind and by maintaining and keeping

a pacific and friendly intercourse with them to be instrumental of
preserving a continued peace between them and the United States.
But we regret extremely to say that we have been much troubled by a
few Americans who have come into this distant country for no other
purpose (as appeared to us) than to spy out the Land and speculate
of poor Indians. We do not hesitate to say that to this description of
men, we attribute all the difficulties with which we have met since
we came to this Country. That by their intriguing machinations
they greatly injured the peace and good understanding which
subsisted between the New York Indians and the Menominees and
Winnebagoes by insinuating to them that we the New York Indians
have cheated them of their Country, which led some of them to a
denial of our purchases of lands aforesaid, and we believe did also
deceive the Honorable Commissioners of the United States as led
them to treat with the Menominees and Winnebagoes in the year
1827, for those very lands we had previously purchased and owned,
not that they (the aforesaid Americans) cared anything for the
Indians but that they might get the lands afterwards to themselves.
That they have also, as we have been credibly informed in connection
with several unprincipled Frenchmen at Green Bay made out several
claims to lands (within our said purchases) in the vicinity of green
Bay, in many cases where they have occupied as sugar camps or
mowed wild grapes for one or two seasons; and that under these
circumstances, in the view of the US Laws they are trespassers,
and the Hon. Judge Doty had volunteered his services to get them
confirmed in the present session of Congress, for a liberal share of all
the lands he may so obtain. We are led to believe this, as he has ever
manifested much zeal in counteracting the views of Government in
regard to the establishment of the New York Indians in this Quarter.

    We are constrained to mention further that we are destructively
annoyed by the unlicenced practices of citizens (in this vicinity) of
selling to us ardent spirits, and in taking from our ignorant and poor
people, in exchange therefor, the very necessaries of life. The last
mentioned evil, is in our view, one of enormous magnitude, and
if not checked by some interposition of Government will forever
preclude of our arriving to an honorable degree of advancement in

civilization and the Mechanick Arts to which we laudably aspire. The influence in favor of these iniquitous practices, is so overwhelming, that the authority who should ever be vigilant to suppress these evils, are so overawed that no notice is taken of the most flagrant violations of Law and Equity: And as various expediencies have often been proposed by good men for the suppression of this evil, but have as often been abandoned as being useless. We have thought of one expedient, by which we would abide, if it would meet the views of your Honorable Body to have a Law passed punishing both the seller and buyer of ardent spirits in summary way by flogging. We think that a measure of this kind, if put in force would arrest the progress of said evil. We think in this way both parties would soon agree to desist. These evils, in connection with others, together with the unsettled limits of our Country tend greatly to retard the industry of our people here and check the emigration hither of those from the East. That it is not only the wish of your memorialists hereunto subscribed but it is also the wish and prayer of the several thousands of your red children to the East residing within or near the latitude of this Country, that Congress would be pleased to establish this Country for their permanent abiding place to them and their heirs forever, so that they need not be disturbed for ages and ages to come; that besides the vast sacrifices your memorialists have made in purchasing and opening settlements so they feel confident that your Honorable Body are not sensible to the fidelity and attachment they have manifested towards the US, for whenever they were called upon by government to aid, in the support of its rights and liberties they have never refused a prompt compliance. That our bones mingled with yours upon the Battle grounds of our Country are witnesses of the truth to this day. This is indeed the very Country which we were encouraged to hope should be our secure resting place. But how has it grieved our hearts for thus few years past to be constantly in jeopardy concerning our residence.

Our faith however, to the integrity, magnanimity, justice and goodness of the US Government towards the aborigines of the Country continues steadfast and unshaken and we have the utmost confidence that the Government only need information respecting us in order to do us justice and give us every necessary assistance to promote our welfare and happiness. And since objections have been made against the extent of our purchases aforementioned, in the manner we have stated (i.e. through the insinuation of evil designing men) and if it should appear in the opinion of your Honorable Body that our interests and future happiness require that we should give up some portion of our lands we had acquired as above stated.

We thereupon ask leave to designate to your Honorable Body the smallest extent of Territory with which we can be satisfied and which may suffice for the maintenance of us and subsequent heirs (viz.). Beginning at the outlet of Winnebago Lake and on the upper or Southwesterly boundary line of our first purchase, Twenty five miles on each side of Fox River and extending in length down Fox River and Green Bay to Sturgeon Bay, excepting only all the land the Indian title of which has heretofore been extinguished by the Government with the same. We would then relinquish all our claims of the remainder of the lands to the original proprietors. It is a consideration that deserve to be noticed here that a considerable portion of the above described Territory is low and swampy and unfit for cultivation. We wish also to be distinctly understood that although we are firmly impressed with the justice and fairness of our claims to all the lands we have purchased yet for the sake of permanent peace only we would consent to the sacrifice above mentioned.

Father, this is all we have to say. We have been particular to acquaint you with some of our principal troubles and wants; as you are wise and able to help us. We pray the great spirit may assist you in your deliberations for the red children to do them good. We subscribe ourselves your dutiful friends and children.

Done in General Council held at Green Bay, Michigan Territory, Dec. 4th, 1829.

John Metoxen Austin Quinney[16]
   Madincy [?] his X mark King
   Anthony his X mark Naddy
   Anoist his X mark Naddy
   Jacob Cheekthon

Robert Konkapot
Cornelius Doxtator
Andrew Miller
Joseph M. Quinnuckbaut [?]
Elisha Konkapot
John Moses
Hendrick Aupaument
John W. Quinney

For & in behalf of the Stockbridge Tribe
##
Capt. Porter his X mark
In behalf of the Munsee Tribe
##
Oneidas
Henry his X mark Pawles
John his X mark Anthony
Naddy his X mark Tagareontye
Daniel Bread X mark
William Johnson
Thomas Neddy his x mark
George his X mark Hill
Williams his X mark Anthony
John his X mark Lowe
Peter his X mark Naddy
David his X mark Peter
Lewis his X mark Denny
Henry his x mark Smith

In these petitions, we see that the French had continued to interfere with the treaties of 1821 and 1822. A crucial statement was made by the New York Indians, saying the French sought to "deceive the Honorable Commissioners of the United States as led them to treat with the Menominees and Winnebagoes in the year 1827, for those very lands we had previously purchased and owned." Another request was that a law be passed to punish by flogging the seller and buyer of ardent spirits. They reminded the government that New York Indians fought for the United States in the Revolutionary War. What they wanted was to establish lands permanently for them and to propose boundaries of the land that would be sufficient.

The 1829 petition was submitted to the Senate, where it was considered by the Committee on Indian Affairs. On May 13, 1830, the Senate sent the petition to the president, Andrew Jackson, for further consideration. President Jackson referred the petition to the secretary of war, John H. Eaten, and then it went to Thomas L. McKenney, the superintendent of Indian Affairs. When McKenney replied to Eaton, he wrote that the

purchases purported to have been made in 1821 and 1822, by the New York Indians of certain tracts of Country, of the Winnebago and Menomonie Indians, were subjects of enquiry, and as a matter in dispute by Commissioners in 1827, and that after a full hearing, in open Council, all the parties being present or represented, the Commissioners saw no possible way of reconciling the difference of opinion, as to the nature and extent of those alleged purchases, except to obtain as they did, in the Treaty of the Butte Des Morts, of the Winnebago and Menomonie Indians their agreement to grant any district of Country, which, upon a full examination of the subject, the President of the United States might esteem it proper to cause to be laid off for the accommodation of the aforesaid New York Indians. But a ratification of the alleged purchases of 1821 and 1822, as prayed for by the petitioners, it is not believed to be possible.[17]

McKenney further stated that he believed the land ceded in the 1821 and 1822 treaties was not the Menomonie and Winnebagos land to sell, and the "money purported to have been paid for these domains, was too trifling to be considered in light of anything like an equivalent." He continued, saying the "consideration money given, was received only as an offering for the permission to be allowed to sit down among those who owned it." In his letter to Eaton, McKenney asked Congress to "enable" the president to appoint commissioners to settle the controversy.[18]

These documents captured the feelings, thoughts, and beliefs of the New York Indians that they were entitled to lands near Green Bay they had obtained in the 1821 treaty with the Menominee and Winnebago, and

the 1822 treaty with the Menominee, and their disbelief that their lands
had been sold in the 1827 treaty between the Menominee and the United
States government. The New York Indians expressed their abhorrence of
the sale of alcohol to their people and requested a law be passed to punish
the sellers and consumers of alcohol. They clearly expressed the history of
the events that transpired through 1829 and requested the president send
commissioners to settle the dispute.

8

ATTEMPTING TO RESOLVE
THE CONTROVERSY

*I believe the Menomonie tribe of Indians have been most shamefully
deceived both by the agents of the New York Indians and by their own
agents and advisers. I believe the New York Indians have been duped
and deceived by their own agents, and I am sorry to say the Government
appears to have participated in the deception.*

—OFFICE OF THE INDIAN AGENT, S. C. STAMBAUGH
TO PRESIDENT ANDREW JACKSON, SEPTEMBER 8, 1830

The above statement was made just a week after the end of the August
24, 1830, to September 1, 1830, council meeting between three US
commissioners and the Menominee, Winnebago, Stockbridge, and Oneida
Nations.

The United States had not yet settled the issue of land for the New York
Indians in the 1827 treaty with the Chippewa, Menominee, and Winnebago
Nations. The second article of the 1827 treaty included language referring
the final decision on lands for the New York Indians directly to the president of the United States, Andrew Jackson. President Jackson was a staunch
supporter of the Indian Removal Act of 1830 that made it lawful to move
all eastern Indians west of the Mississippi to what was then called Indian
Territory. This removal policy had been in effect for the New York Indians
long before Congress passed the 1830 act.

In 1829, the New York Indians sent petitions directly to Jackson asking him to make the decision as stated in the 1827 treaty. A year later, these petitions resulted in Jackson sending three commissioners to Green Bay in 1830 to try to resolve the issues of the removal of New York Indians to the Green Bay area and to establish boundaries for those lands designated in treaties.

The journal of the commissioners sent by the United States provides documentation of extensive negotiations with the three commissioners. This journal also includes the voices of the Menominee, Winnebago, Oneida, and Stockbridge Nations. John Quinney (Stockbridge) presented an eloquent, extensive, and philosophical document to the commissioners from the Oneida, Stockbridge-Munsee, and Brothertown Nations, which outlined the New York Indians' reasoning on the issues of treaties not being recognized as valid and what lands were to be designated for them. Throughout the council meeting, possible boundaries were submitted by the commissioners, the Menominee, and the New York Indians, but no agreement was reached.

The president sent the 1829 petitions from the New York Indians to his secretary of war, John Eaton, who then forwarded the petitions to Thomas L. McKenney, the superintendent of Indian Affairs. On May 18, 1830, McKenney responded to Eaton outlining the complex history of events and treaties leading up to 1830, and to request that commissioners be assigned to resolve the issues:

> Sir, On the Order of the Hon: The Senate of the United States, of the
> 13th Inst discharging the Committee on Indian Affairs, from the
> further consideration of the petition of the Chiefs and Warriors of
> those tribes of Indians that have emigrated from New York to Green
> Bay and referring the same to the President of the United States by
> whom it is referred to the Secretary of War, and by him, to this Office,
> I have the honor to report, that the purchases purported to have been
> made in 1821 and 1822, by the New York Indians of certain tracts of
> Country, of the Winnebago and Menomonie Indians, were subjects
> of enquiry, and as a matter in dispute by Commissioners in 1827,
> and that after a full hearing, in open Council, all the parties being
> present or represented, the Commissioners saw no possible way of

reconciling the difference of opinion, as to the nature and extent of those alleged purchases, except to obtain as they did, in the [1827] Treaty of the Butte Des Morts, of the Winnebago and Menomonie Indians their agreement to grant any district of Country, which, upon a full examination of the subject, the President of the United States might esteem it proper to cause to be laid off for the accommodation of the aforesaid New York Indians. But a ratification of the alleged purchases of 1821 and 1822, as prayed for by the petitioners, it is not believed to be possible to make without a violation of the plainest principles of right, and propriety, — of right, because immense territories of the Country purporting to have been sold by the Winnebago and Menomonie Indians, were not theirs to sell; and of propriety, because the consideration money purported to have been paid for these domains, was too trifling to be considered in the light of any thing like an equivalent. But further — a confirmation of these purchases would inevitably lead to the destruction of the New York Indians by the Winnebagoes and Menomonies, who deny that they ever sold the Country; and assert that the consideration money given, was received only as an offering for the permission to be allowed to sit down among those who owned it.

It was to settle this controversy, upon the one hand, and secure a Country for the New York Indians on the other, that the provision referred to in the Treaty of the Butte Des Morts was made; and it is to carry this intention into effect that an appropriation has been asked of Congress to enable the President, by Commissioners, to be appointed for that purpose.

I know nothing of the private wrongs complained of by the petitioners — but suppose it likely enough that like all Indians who border white settlements, as the petitioners do those at Green Bay, that they do suffer from the introduction among them of ardent spirits. I know nothing of the agency attributed to Judge Doty in regard to the lands.

As to the proposition made by the Petitioners for twenty five miles on each side of Fox River, beginning at the outlet of Winnebago Lake this will be for the consideration of the Commissioners, to whom the

President may entrust the duty of laying off for them a Country in pursuance of the terms of the Treaty aforesaid.

I will just add in conclusion that the Journal of the Commissioners who negotiated the Treaty of the Butte Des Mort is full on the points touching the Controversy arising out of the purchases of 1821 and 1822, and to that the Secretary of War is respectfully referred. Thos L. McKenney.[1]

THE ISSUES

The United States selected three commissioners to go to Green Bay with instructions to resolve the disputes over lands between the Menominee and the New York Indians. The discussions included several perspectives on the validity of the 1821 and 1822 treaties. The New York Indians believed that treaties signed by the president of the United States were valid documents. Those opposed to the 1821 and 1822 treaties raised the issue that these treaties did not go to Congress for approval, but the New York Indians were told by the president that congressional approval was not required because the treaties were made Indian nation to Indian nation.

In the August 11, 1827, Treaty of Butte des Morts between the United States and the Chippewa, Menominee, and Winnebago Nations, the United States established boundaries between Indian nations as it had in the 1825 treaty. In this treaty, the United States tried to purchase the same lands designated for the New York Indians in the 1821 and 1822 treaties, which astonished the New York Indians. Article 2 of the 1827 treaty stated that such issues would be left to the president to resolve.

Instructions to the Three Commissioners
On June 7, 1830, President Jackson appointed James McCall, General Erastus Root, and J. T. Mason as the commissioners who were to travel to Green Bay to settle the boundaries of land for the New York Indians.[2]

Two days later, on June 9, 1830, Eaton gave instructions to the commissioners. He refers to Article 2 of the 1827 treaty, writing:

Butte de Morts, on Fox River, Territory of Michigan, between Lewis Cass and Thomas L. McKenney, commissioners on the part of the

United States, and the Chippewa, and Menomonie and Winnebago tribes of Indians, provides that a reference of a difficulty as set forth in said article, between the Menomonie and Winnebago, and the New York Indians, shall be referred to the President of the United States, whose decision in regard to it shall be final.

The difficulty referred to, consists in disputes between the two parties named, respecting the alleged purchase and sale of lands in the years of 1821 and 1822. The New York Indians claim to have made bona fide purchases and the Menomonies and Winnebagoes deny it, alleging their intention to have been only to grant permission to their brothers in New York to sit down among them.

The Menomonies and Winnebagoes, in the second article of the treaty aforesaid, having given the right to the President to decide upon this controversy, and the right also to establish such boundaries between them and the New York Indians, as he may consider equitable and just; and the President esteeming it proper to waive any decision upon the question of the validity of those compacts of 1821 and 1822, has determined to accommodate the New York Indians, under the privilege given to him to do so, by locating a country, and establishing such boundaries between the parties, as may be equitable and just. That you may know the country purported to have been bought in 1821 and 1822, I enclose, herewith, extracts from the articles of agreement made at those periods, which define the alleged cessions.

The controversy hitherto existing between those Indians, as to what was, or what was not, purchased and sold in 1821 and 1822, may be assumed settled in the treaty aforesaid, and in the authority vested in the President by the Menomonies and Winnebagoes, to act as umpire in establishing boundaries between them.[3]

Eaton then instructed the commissioners to submit maps or drawings of the land selected for his approval:

Two principal objects will present themselves to you, and these you will keep steadily in view.

First, the providing a country and a home for New York Indians that shall be acceptable to them in extent, and soil, and wood, and water, &c

Second, in consulting the views, and feelings, and condition of the Menomonies and Winnebagoes, who have generously given the permission to do so. It will be important that you harmonize these interests.

Eaton referred to those Indians as being in the "hunter" state, meaning the Menominee and Winnebago "require large tracts of country; whilst tribes whose condition is essentially agricultural, (and this is the condition of the New York Indians) require a less extensive domain." He cautioned as well that not having enough land for the New York Indians ran the risk of them reverting to the hunter state and "would undo all that instruction and necessity combined have accomplished, to lift them from the hunter to the agricultural state."

Eaton advised that there were about 2,420 Indians in New York State who claimed approximately 131,640 acres, but these numbers should not be used to determine the quantity of land required. What was important was providing land sufficient in quantity to keep the New York Indians as agricultural people who would not "give up their present state of improvements, and return again to the roaming and hunter state. This is particularly to be guarded against." Eaton also wrote, "It is, however of the highest importance that both parties should acquiesce, so far as that may be possible, in the boundaries that may be established between them."[4]

Eaton appropriated five thousand dollars for the entire trip, including salaries, expenses, and, if necessary, the distribution of goods "equally among the Menomonie and Winnebago Indians. Part of those expenses can include five Menominee and Winnebago, and three New York Indians to examine lands that are in the treaties, at the rate of one dollar and fifty cents per day." Eaton stressed the importance of harmony in this endeavor to prevent the New York Indians from feeling strife and deciding not to emigrate. It was important, wrote Eaton, to "preserve good and kind feelings amongst all the parties. The New York Indians are a weak and feeble tribe, peaceably disposed, and incapable to contend in war with the powerful tribes on the lakes. It would be cruelty in the government to send them to a new home, where they would be under any feelings of dissatisfaction, and be subjected to danger."[5]

The Commissioners Arrive in Green Bay
Eaton assigned the commissioners four objectives for their trip:

1. To send for the chiefs of the Menominee and Winnebago to ascertain their views in relation to the section of country to be designated for the New York Indians, with a view to harmonize the feelings of all.

2. To notify the chiefs to assemble at Green Bay in two weeks, it being the shortest period in which they could be collected according to the information received.

3. To invite the New York Indians to attend the council with the Winnebago and Menominee.

4. To use the time before the assembling of the Indians to examine the country on both sides of the Fox River and to visit the settlements of the New York Indians.[6]

Mr. Conner, who served as the interpreter for the Menominee and Winnebago chiefs, was told to carry out these notifications, as the commissioners wrote that "Runners were dispatched, with the wampum and tobacco to the Countries of the Winnebagoes and Menominees and messages to the New York Indians, inviting them to assemble at that place on the 24th instant. The intermediate time was employed in exploring and surveying the country."[7] This action confirms that the commissioners understood the Indigenous diplomatic protocol of sending runners with wampum and tobacco to invite Indigenous nations to meetings. In the meantime, the commissioners were to survey the territory in those two weeks, with A. G. Ellis working as the surveyor.

On August 16, at the outlet of Lake Winnebago, the commissioners met with Chief Four Legs of the Winnebago. He wanted another chief, named Duck, to serve as the interpreter. Four Legs said:

Father, when the Wabanakies [New York Indians] came to this country, I was the first to take them by the hand. They asked us for land to sit down upon — to cultivate and raise something to feed their children. They gave us some presents — not enough to clothe us; and we gave them permission to sit down and cultivate the land as we did; **but did not sell it.** At first, few came; but since that they are coming yearly, as though they would claim the whole country in spite of us. We granted them permission to settle upon the land they now inhabit, and as far up as the Little Chute. But the chief is now dead, and the tree fallen where he marked the limits. If they say we did more than this, they tell lies; and we appeal to God, who made the day-light, for the truth of what we say. You will hear from all the chiefs in council, and they will declare to you the same.[8]

The following day, the commissioners met with the Stockbridge. They explained the purpose of the upcoming meeting on August 24 and invited the Stockbridge to attend. John Metoxen, the principal chief, said:

Brothers, listen to a few words from me at this time. I thank the Great spirit for preservation, and for this opportunity given us to meet with you this day at this place.

We (present) are also pleased to hear that our great father, the President of the United States, has not forgotten us, but has sent you to pay us a visit. We rejoice to hear you say that he has a regard for our interests, as we will find in those papers you handed to us for our perusal.

I have nothing to communicate in particular at present, only wishing that the chain of covenant friendship, established between your forefathers and mine, may always be kept bright by us. I have spoken principally to express to you our satisfaction and pleasure to see and shake hands with you. We shall acquaint ourselves with those papers, and I hope by the time when we shall meet with you, agreeably to your appointment, our minds will be settled to communicate to you such things as we shall find necessary. This is all at present.[9]

Days later, on August 20, 1830, the commissioners met some of the Oneida chiefs at Eleazer Williams's home. The commissioners explained their mission as established by the president, who had sent them "to fix a boundary for your lands, that you may be free from interruption." Williams was full of reassurances that the president would be "altogether kind and parental towards you."[10]

On August 21, 1830, the chiefs of the New York Indians listed three points regarding the upcoming meeting with the three commissioners. They wrote to the commissioners:

> The Chiefs of the New York Indians to the Honorable the Commissions
> of the President of the United States, now at Green Bay, —
> Respectfully make known;
> That they are happy to hear of the errand on which the Honorable
> Commissioners have come, — & to congratulate them on their safe
> arrival. —
> The Chiefs of the New York Indians hereby acknowledge the
> official notification of the Commissioners — calling them to a
> united Council, to be composed of the Honorable Commissioners,
> the Winnebagoes, the Menominies & the New York Indians, for the
> purpose of settling certain questions known to be at issues between
> these New York Indians & the other Tribes above named, which
> council the Commissioners have appointed to be opened on Tuesday,
> the 24th Inst at or near Green Bay. —
> The Chiefs of the New York Indians beg leave to make the
> following preliminary requests:
> First — That the place of holding the Council, may be without the
> settlement of Green Bay.
> Secondly — That no one but the parties concerned and the
> Honorable the Commissioners may be admitted to witness the
> deliberations of the Council:
> Thirdly — That the doings of the Council shall be sacredly kept
> from all persons without, — until the deliberations are concluded.
> The Honorable Commissioners will be able to appreciate the
> motives of these requests, when they are informed, that the Chiefs
> are fully certified of the interested & meddling interference of
> the white Citizens of Green Bay, in the affairs of the Indians; — &
> moreover, that the Chiefs have . . . to be fully convinced, that little
> or nothing can be effected in the contemplated negotiations of this
> Council toward the adjustment of existing difference, & for the

attainment of the objects of this Commission, unless the influence of
the white citizens of Green Bay can be entirely excluded.

Confiding in the . . . Of the Honorable Commissioners, and in their
earnest desire to fulfill the purposes of their Commissions, the Chiefs
of the New York Indians, flatter themselves that the Commissioners
will see & feel the reason — in behalf of these requests — & that they,
the Commissioners, in view of these reasons, will institute and
sustain effectual measures for the sessions & deliberations of the
contemplated Council to be held in strict & rigid conclaves, until they
are concluded — so that those without cannot be made acquainted
with what is passing within. —
Most respectfully submitted,
John T. Mason
Erastus Root
James McCall
J. W. Quinney
A. Miller
Daniel his X mark Bread
John his X mark Anthony
Henry his X mark Powlis
Neddy his X mark Arttsequette[11]

On August 23, the commissioners replied. They wrote that the meetings could be either public or private with the Oneida and Stockbridge,
and they advised that having secret meetings with the Winnebago and
Menominee would be "impracticable." Changing the place of the meeting
was not possible because the Indians had already set up camp. As to the
influence and interference by citizens of Green Bay, the commissioners
hoped this was not true, but if it happened, they would have "a duty to
counteract it." And as to the request for the meeting to be private, the
commissioners said they must listen to citizens and Indians.[12]

To this, Daniel Bread replied:

Gentlemen,

We have received your answer to our request & have nothing to
reply, except, that from an expression of yours on the subject of

"holding secret conferences," we have apprehended you may be
mistaken our intentions. We are perfectly willing, that all the world
should know at the time, provided, the improper influence from a
particular quarter might be excluded, so as to have the Indians free to
act for themselves —
Yours, Gentlemen, with high consideration of esteem & respect —
Daniel Bread, Per order of the Chiefs of the New York Indians
John T. Mason
Erastus Root
James Mc Call[13]

Concerns about interpreters were often expressed and became a major
point in later negotiations on whether what was written in the treaty accurately reflected the decisions by the Indigenous nations. John W. Quinney
and Daniel Bread told the commissioners as much in a letter sent to them
on August 25:

Gentlemen,
    We, the Chiefs of the New York Indians having been informed
that an interpreter has been recommended to you from Green Bay
to communicate between the Commissioners & the Menominees,
instead of Mr. Conner — beg leave to say: that, since the objections
to Mr. Conner are not of a moral character, but only because he
does not speak the Menominee . . . the Chiefs of the Menominee
Nation can speak Chippewa, which Mr. Conner can understand &
speaks also; & since Mr. Conner is your own Interpreter, coming
from abroad & disinterested; & since Mr. Conner has heretofore been
accepted & officiated in the same capacity, for the same parties, in
public negotiations without objections; — & since so far as we know
Mr. Conner possesses the mutual confidence of all concerned for his
fidelity; Therefore the Chiefs of the New York Indians beg leave to
request that Mr. Conner may remain the standing interpreter for the
current negotiations.
    The Chiefs of the New York Indians desire to . . . their obligations
to the Commissioners for the offer for an interpreter to communicate
between themselves and the Menominiees this afternoon — I say that

for the same occasions, which have originated this letter, they have
no occasions to make use of him.

The Chiefs of the New York Indians do not consider that the
obstacle in the way of conferences with the Menominees this
morning, was for want of our interpreters, but the interference of
the Citizens of Green Bay. And the Chiefs of the N. York Indians,
beg leave to call the attention of the Commissioners to their kind
assurances, in their letter to us of the 23 inst. "that should they
discover exceptionable cause by any one on that subject it will be their
duty to counteract it."
By the Order of the Chiefs of the New York Indians, Daniel Bread,
J. W. Quinney[14]

The commissioners stated that Conner was to carry out the above orders. In the meantime, the commissioners were to survey the territory in
those two weeks, with Ellis as the surveyor.

The Council Meeting

The commissioners' journal provides an account of the events as they happened at this historic meeting. It begins with a list the chiefs attending on
August 24, 1830, which included St. Regis, Brothertown, Oneida, Stockbridge, Munsee, Winnebago, and Menominee:

St. Regis:	Eleazer Williams
Brothertown Indians:	William Dick
	R. Fowler
	John Johnson
Oneida Indians:	John Anthony
	Daniel Bread
	Henry Powlas
	Cornelius Stevens
	Neddy Autlequette

Stockbridge Indians:	John Metoxen	
	John W. Quinney	
	R. Kunkpot	
	Jacob Chicks	
	Andrew Miller	
Munsees:	James Hunt	
Winnebagoes:	Hoo-tshoop	or Four Legs
	Shounk-tshunk-siap	or Black Wolf
	Whe-ank-kaw	or Big Duck
	Monk-ka-kaw	
Principal Menomonie Chiefs:	OsKaush	or The Brave
	Josette	Josette Carron
	Paw-we-gon-ma	The Grand Soldier
	Kaush-kaw-no-nawe	The Bear's Grease
	Pe-wit-net	The Rain
	Waw-lose	The Hare or Rabbit
	Mau-hus-se-ause	do
	Miha-naun-posh	The Wave
	Tchi-kau-mha-ki-chin	The Little Chief
	Txhe-naun-paw-ma	One whom all looks upon

Evidence that the group followed an Indigenous protocol for opening meetings is expressed in the journal, as the commissioners noted that a pipe was passed from the commissioners to the chiefs of the different tribes. Then General Root spoke for the government:

Brothers, Your red Brethren the New York Indians came to your Country some years ago, and you took them by the hand and told them they might have a home among you. You sold them land to live on, and they paid you money and goods for it. They believed that you were satisfied, and they have brought their wives and children from a great distance and have built houses and have put the lands in corn and settled on them as their own.

Root used very paternalistic language, which is often found in treaty negotiations. However, he does address the chiefs as brothers, though that action does not reflect equality. Root then made a statement that he wanted included in the journal, one that actually acknowledged the boundaries established in the 1821 treaty between Indigenous nations:

> By the Treaty of Green Bay concluded between the New York Indians on the one part, and the Winnebago and Menomonie Nation of Indians on the other part, on the 18th August 1821, the latter ceded to the former all their rights to the interest and claims of the following lands viz
>
> Beginning at the Foot of the Rapid of the Fox River, usually called the Grand Kakalin, thence up said River to the Rapids at Winnebago Lake, and from the River extending back in this width on each side, to the Northwest and to the Northeast equi-distant with the lands claimed by the said Menomine and Winnebago Nations of Indians.[15]

Root continued, recounting the reserved right to hunt and fish, acknowledging that Indians had reserved "to themselves the right of occupying a necessary proportion of the Lands ceded" for these activities. He included provisions from the 1821 treaty, which amounted to two thousand dollars in total with five hundred dollars to be paid on the same day the treaty was signed. "The purchase was made in conformity to the will of the government of the United States," Root noted, "and afterward received its entire approbation."[16]

He continues by citing the New York Indians' 1822 request for more land, as the 1821 portion was not large enough for all of the Six Nations, which the government agreed was true. Additionally, the treaty of 1822 between the New York Indians and the Menominee was for three thousand dollars, "the whole of which," according to Root,

has been paid, ceded, released and quit claimed to the New York
Indians to be held by them in common with the Menomines a very
large tract of land extending Southwesterly to the tract ceded to them
in 1821, by the Winnebago and Menominie Nations of Indians, and to
the Mil-wau-kie: — eastwardly to Lake Michigan, Northeastwardly to
the mouth of Green Bay, including the Islands of the Grand Traverse
and the Bay de Nock — northerly to the sources of the Great River
Menominie at the height of land between the waters of Lake Superior
and there running into Lake Michigan, and westerly to the tract
ceded by the treaty of 1821.[17]

This tract of land "covered at least 4 or 5 million of acres." Root goes
on to describe sharing of the "tract in common," saying, "In short that all
should enjoy their own improvements, and that the lands not improved,
should be owned by the whole community of all parties." These comments
show the government clearly understood what was meant by land shared
"in common."

Nevertheless, misunderstandings—Root doesn't say by whom—led to
Article 2 of the 1827 Treaty at Butte de Morts, which left the final decision
on land boundaries to the discretion of the president. In response, President Jackson sent the commissioners to settle the "difficulty among his red
children," with Root asking the Menominee to advise what they thought
the land boundaries should be for the New York Indians.[18]

The next day, the issue of proper interpreters was again raised. The
Menominee chief Os-Kaush stated the Menominee could not understand
or speak the Chippewa language, which the interpreter, Mr. Conner,
spoke. The meeting was adjourned to take time of find another interpreter.
At 3 p.m. the council reconvened with Mr. Grignon as interpreter for the
Menominee. Mr. Conner was to be assisted by Mrs. Frome to interpret
from Winnebago into French.

The main speakers for the Indigenous nations were persons well
respected and dignified, who were selected by their people to represent their nations. Os-Kaush, or the Brave (Menominee) addressed the
commissioners:

We believe that we know what you were sent here for, but we want a copy of your instructions that we may make you a reply. I speak for myself and also for the whole nation. The New York Indians are men of learning, they have a person to assist them. We ask the same privilege. This all we have to say at present.

Four Legs, the Winnebago Chief, confirmed the request made by Os-Kaush the Menominee speaker. The commissioners noted,

That he wished also a copy of the same instructions — that we do not know who may live or who may die, and he wished to contend for his rights as well as those of the Menomines, that he thought one person would suffice for both. As they were entirely ignorant of reading and writing, they want some individual to defend their rights, and they will abide the result, but do not know who the Commissioners will appoint.[19]

The commissioners advised the Winnebago and Menominee chiefs that they could choose someone to assist them who understood how to read and write English. Os-Kaush replied, "We do not wish to say that Old Traders are not good men, but we will select one of your own rank — one who lives in a Brick House — One who tries criminal cases — Mr. Doty." Thoo-tshopp, a chief of the Winnebago, was the next speaker. He replied "that he respected the Chief on his left as his Brother — that they had no previous talk together, but happened to be both of one opinion, that it was for want of learning that he had requested that Judge Doty might defend them — that it was all he had to say today, and was ready at all times to hear the Commissions as patiently as had done today." Finally, Josette, a Menominee chief, stood and addressed the commissioners, saying, "We the people of the Red Skins wish to know of you the Commissioners, what the New York Indians want to do. We repeat (I speak by myself the voice of the men, women and children) we want to know what the New York Indians want."

Questions were asked to help clarify the intent and purpose of the New York Indians and the commissioners. Os-Kaush said,

For a long time I have heard murmurings of business done without our knowledge & previous to the Treaty at the Butte des Morts. All the papers I have any knowledge of signing was at that Treaty. We there acknowledged to have agreed to give the New York Indians from the Grand Cascade to the 'little Chute' one days march for a man and his family back each way. This is all we have to say until we hear from the New York Indians.

Os-Kaush and Four Legs then described their understandings of the land designated for the New York Indians. Said Four Legs,

Fathers — My voice is with the Menomonies, and can say nothing different. Eight years ago, I had a conversation with the New York Indians and gave a cession from the Grand Kakalin to the Little Chute. It is evident to all who were at the Treaty at the Little Buttes, that I did sign the Treaty and gave them from the Grand Kakalin to the Little Chute, and one days march (fifteen miles) in the year. . . . I have said this to the New York Indians, and my Father, it is all I have to say, and I want to hear what the New York Indians have to say. What I did was in public; if they want to take more land than this, they wish to get it by fraud and corruption. None of our Chiefs ever consented to more. But is their turn to speak.

These opening statements were made to clarify and define what the Menominee and Winnebago understood to be the issue. The New York Indians clarified that they would put their statements in writing. Peter Augustin then said, "What the New York Indians have to say shall be in writing. But as it is lengthy and will take some time to interpret it, we wish copies furnished to the Menomines and Winnebagos for them to peruse at their leisure—to which the Menomines assent." John Metoxen, a Stock-bridge chief, then expressed their relationship as brothers, proclaiming, "I thank the Great Spirit for allowing us this day wherein we may hear each other. It is becoming Brethren to speak to each other in a friendly way. Now we shall begin to hear one another."

On August 27, Quinney presented an extensive document on behalf of the Six Nations, St. Regis, Stockbridge, Munsee, and Brothertown Nations, arguing for the settlement of this dispute on the grounds that "evidence in support of those claims is three-fold: Presumptive, circumstantial & documentary." Quinney provided a sophisticated discussion on the doctrine of discovery and the precepts of Western civilization. *Presumptive* means "supposed presumptions made about civilized and barbarous peoples." He asked if it is presumed the New York Indians would leave their climate in New York State in exchange "for an insecure abode in this inhospitable region." *Circumstantial* refers to the circumstances surrounding the treaties. *Documentary* refers to the content and making of treaties. The 1827 treaty at Butte des Morts was an astonishment and a grievance because the same lands they bought in the 1821 and 1822 treaties were being sold to the United States.

Said Quinney:

The Chiefs of the New York Indians, now resident near & about Green Bay, including New York Indians, now resident near & about Green Bay, including those of the six Nations, and of the St. Regis, Stockbridge, Munsee and Brothertown Nations, who have removed from the State of New York,

To the Honorable Commissioners from the President of the United States, in mutual Council assembled at Green Bay, respectfully show: —

Brothers: We have received your communications, accompanied with a copy of your powers and instructions from our Father, The President of the United States — with which we desire to say we are much satisfied — as also with your own kind expressions of a willingness to hear us patiently & cordially in all the matters we may have to communicate.

Brothers, We thank you for this kindness, and we thank our Great Father the President, that he has been pleased to hear our talk sent to him at a former time, & commission such trust-worthy servants as we believe you to be, to hold a council with us in his name & on his behalf — relating to our misunderstandings here with our brethren the Winnebagoes & Menominees.

And we thank the Great & good Spirit, our God & Father in

heavens, as also yours — that he has been pleased to hear our prayers, and put it in the heart of our Father the President to give this needful attention to our wants. And it is now our earnest desire, that wisdom, Justice, and mutual kindness may be given to us from on high — to you the Commissioners — to us and to our brethren the Winnebagoes & Menominee, the original parties in the present differences — that our deliberations may be conducted with a mutual good will & decorum — be brought to a just & satisfactory issue — & that our Father the President & the supreme authorities of the United States may confirm to us & to our children a territorial inheritance which shall not hereafter be disturbed.

Brothers, you say to us in your introductory communications: — "Your interests are deeply concerned in these deliberations, & we are desirous to hear you in candour & plainness. On our part we are prepared to do you full justice — to enter into your wants & sympathies with entire sincerity — & to exhibit the feelings of your father, the President which are altogether kind & parental towards you."

This, Brothers, is very good. And we are encouraged by these assurances to repose great confidence, both in you & in the President. And we will now proceed to lay before your — & through you, before our Father the President some of our thoughts.

First, Brothers, we speak what is well known — that the customary negotiations between Indians Nations themselves, & between them & white people, have heretofore & generally been such, as to leave little, or no documentary evidence of their nature & terms, except the brief record, contained in the short & very comprehensive articles of a Treaty. And sometimes very important items of agreement are wanting even in this general and often undefined evidence. Indians are accustomed to depend on good faith, & on the conscious recourse of the heart, with some slight external memorials, of those impressions, set up by mutual agreement.

Whenever therefore, for any reasons of interest, or of will, then is a wiliness in party to an agreement to forget its minute & important items, parliamentary & judicial evidence is very difficult to attainment.

We presume this, brothers, that you may anticipate the difficulty which exists, and the right which ought reasonably to be awarded to

us in lieu of documentary evidence in making out the argument of
our cause.

The questions to be discussed at this Council, and understood by
us — are — the nature and extent of the territorial claims of the New
York Indians — first, in relation to their brethren the Winnebago &
Menominees — & next in relation to the Government & jurisdiction
of the United States, — it being understood, that the claims here
spoken of have respect to certain land on Fox River in the Territory of
Michigan.

The evidence in support of those claims is three fold: Presumptive,
circumstantial & documentary.

First, Brothers, we would make a remark or two, expressive of
our opinion, as to the nature of our claims: — first in relation to our
brethren the Winnebagoes & Menomionees

The Treaty between us & them of the 18th August, 1821 will
show — that the Menominee and Winnebago Nations "ceded released,
& quit claimed" to us "forever all" their "right, title, interest, — claims"
in the territory defined in that treaty — "Reserving to themselves the
right to occupying a necessary proportion of the lands thereby ceded
for the purpose of hunting, and also the right fishing"— stipulating
on their part — that "in such use & occupation, they would commit
no waste, or depredation on our improvements." It will be seen,
therefore, that here is a conveyance of an entire & exclusive right
in the territory, with the reservation of the privileges and on the
conditions specified. And this conveyance was made for certain
valuable consideration — a part of which were specified in the third
article, and others of a moral & confidential nature.

The Treaty of 23 of Sept. 1822, between us & the Menomonee
Nation also "ceded, releases, & quit claims" to us "forever all" their
"right, title, interest and claim", in the territory defined by said
Treaty. And we, on our part, have "promised & agreed to & with
the Menominee Nation — that they shall have the free permission
& privilege of occupying & residing upon the lands, thus ceded, in
common with us; — provided nevertheless, that they shall not in any
manner infringe upon any of our settlements & improvements." And
this conveyance was also made for like valuable considerations with

the former — part pecuniary — and part moral & confidential. Such
are the terms of the two Treaties: — both vesting in us the exclusive
territorial right, so far as we & they are concerned, & so far as the
title vested in them; — the first Treaty reserving to the Winnebagoes
& Menominee the right of hunting & fishing, on the conditions
specified; — & the second Treaty reserving to the Menominee, who
were the only other party concerned, the right of a joint occupancy &
use with us, on the conditions therein specified.

The nature of our claim, therefore, in relation to our brethren the
Winnebagoes & Menomonees, we think sufficiently obvious by the
terms of negotiation — it being understood, that the territory defined
in the first Treaty is separate from & bordering upon the Territory
defined in the second — The Winnebagoes & Menominee being a joint
part in the first, and Menominees being a joint party in the first, and
the Menominee a party alone in the last.

Next, as to the nature of our claims, in relation to the United
States. We are aware, that certain learned & expounders of the laws
of Nation, so called, have expressed an opinion on this subject, from
which, in duty to ourselves & to the world, we feel bound to dissent,
and against which, so far as it has received the sanction of authority,
we are equally bound to enter our solemn protest We are a simple
people. And we can never consent to surrender the principles of
natural conscience & of natural justice to any form of law — national,
conventional, or whatever — which are merely convenient to parties
interested — & by them originated & declared for interested purposes.
In other words, we declare & maintain a primeval & unqualified
title to vest in any Nation or tribe of men — be they more or less
civilized, or more or less barbarous — who are found in the exclusive
occupancy of any territory, for any purposes, whatever, Convenient &
agreeable to themselves — a territorial title transferable only at their
will & by their act — to be alienated only by their free & sovereign
consent, — and that no adventitious difference in the fact or degree of
civilization thereby invest its subject with a prior or superior claim of
this description.

This is our doctrine. And although in our case, we should be
unable, in a conflict of opinion, to maintain it against the physical

force of the great & powerful Nation, into whose power we have
providentially fallen — yet knowing their magnanimity, we do not
hesitate to declare it. — And moreover, we believe & predict, that
this doctrine will yet become the public opinion of the world, & it
legitimate results awarded to all concerned.

However, therefore, we ourselves may be treated, we claim, as in
duty we are bound to claim — that the Indian title in all territories
by them heretofore occupied & claimed, & which have not been
transferred by their own voluntary acts, & in an equitable manner
is as full & perfect, as that of any other people for all political, civil,
& municipal purposes, — & for all the rights of private property &
all other personal prerogatives of individuals — whether they have
claims & used those rights, or not; — except so far, as territorial
jurisdiction, or any other original rights have been voluntarily
surrendered by negotiations to any other Government for its
protection & for other privileges.

This, of course, is a mere declaration of our opinion — & connected
& identified; as we are with the people & government of the United
Sates by a long series of negotiation, & by a gradual surrender of our
original rights, this doctrine can have no other practical influence
with us than to enable us to define the nature of our territorial
claims, taking into consideration what we have surrendered. We
are satisfied with our Condition, provided we can be secured in our
rightful territorial possessions.

The doctrine — that certain accidental and undefined superiorities
of our Nation, themselves being judge of those superiorities, over
another Nation, thereby invest the former with the right of ejecting
the latter from their territory — a territory occupied & used by
them alone from time immemorial, simply because the former,
in their wandering enterprise have happened to come in sight of
this territory — this doctrine, we say, if it were not for the first
time divulged & in it naked form, would doubtless be regarded as
singular & startling. Yet, this is declared to be the law of Nations by
prescription — making out the right of discovery — so called.

Can this law of nation be analyzed, — and its component elements made palpable? — It seems to us to be something like this: — The right of appropriation & jurisdiction over all the territories of barbarous Nations vests in civilized Nation, by the simple fact of this difference in their conditions. And that civilized Nation, which may happen to make the first discovery of any & of whatever portions of the territory of barbarous Nations, is thereby entitled to those territories, by general Consent. —

Now, it is a known & acknowledged fact that Nations once civilized have become barbarous & Nations once barbarous, have become civilized. May we ask, there, for the lines, which divided between the two? — This previous question, it will be seen — is very necessary to be settled. — First — that a civilized Nation may know when & where it is entitled to its right of discovery; — next — that barbarous may know, when they are bound to submit to such claims. And also in that fluctuation of human things, which depresses civilized nation to the condition of barbarism & elevates barbarous to the prerogatives of civilization — That the latter may know where they are entitled to make reprisal on the former. Does this line consist in any measured degree of intellectual & moral improvement — of advancement in literature, science, and art. — of. . . . In the science of government, — of actual incorporation under Statues & ordinances, recorded in visible forms — as also of submission to the faith of Christianity? — And if so, — what is that measure, or degree? — We ourselves, our brethren, and all the world are interested in the decision of this question.

The New York Indians, now resident at Green Bay, profess to be civilized. And we have been so far complimented by those whom we are disposed to regard, as disinterested & competent observers, as to be allowed to be more civilized, to observe better regulations in society, to have better manners, more virtue & more religion of the Christian name, that some white citizens, who now occupy large territories in the new settlements of the United States. Now, the question is, — whether those citizens are reduced to a condition of barbarism, & we entitled to make reprisal on them, in consideration of our former deprivation by the same law? — If the question arise —

who, in this case, are the first discovered? It is easy to see, that the Indians were not only the discoverers, but the original holder, so far as the present parties are concerned.

Under these observations we submit our opinion of the <u>Nature</u> of our territorial claim in relation to the United States, — taking into consideration that we have voluntarily surrendered our original right of territorial jurisdiction to a certain extent & sundry other prerogatives of independent Nations, for protection & other valuable helps, which we have received & continue to enjoy. We consider & acknowledge ourselves as children, the Government of the United States our protecting & fostering parent.

As to the extent of our territorial claims, ["on Fox River in the Territory Michigan" is crossed out] they are as nearly defined in the Treaties of 1821 & 1822, already referred to, as is at present in our power. It only remains for them to be reduced to actual survey by the metes & bounds therein fixed, & by the settlement of the claims of our brethren, with whom we have negotiated in relation to the United States.

We now come to the <u>evidence</u> in <u>support</u> of our claims, we have stated to be <u>three–fold</u>: <u>Presumptive</u>, <u>Circumstantial</u> & <u>Documentary</u>

Presumptive Evidence

We acknowledge, in the first place, that, at first sight, — it was to be presumed, our brethren the Winnebagoes & Menominees would not cede to us those portions of their territory, defined in the Treaties between us & them, without valuable considerations, in their view equivalent. On the other hand — was it to be presumed, that the New York Indians would abandon a good & sure territorial inheritance, in a comparatively mild climate, located in the bosom of a civilized people, whose influence had already civilized us, given us the useful arts of life, & instructed us & our children in common learning, & in the Christian religion, & put us in a career of improvement, which bid fair to us with the common progress of civilization among our white neighbors; — & appreciating so highly as all our people do, these advantages, & these privileges, & wishing to avail ourselves of all their benefits; — was it to be presumed, that we would abandon such a certain inheritance —

for an uncertain — that we would remove from lands so fertile, & from a climate so mild, to this cold & sterile region; — that we would sacrifice such privileges, cherishing them dear as existing for the great disadvantages of our circumstance here? And that too, without an indemnification — without something prospectively equivalent? — Was it to be presumed, that we would exchange territory for a less exclusive & less true title? — Was it to be presumed, that we were willing to return to the savage state & to the hunters life? — On the contrary, it is not known & settled, that all our dependence & hopes are fixed upon the intellectual & moral improvement, upon the regulations and arts of civilized life, & upon the privileges of the Christian religion? When our attention was first directed to Green Bay, & when we commenced negotiation with our brethren here, the territory was theirs. And we disclosed to them distinctly our purposes & plans to have a fixed habitation — a territory which we could call our own — to cultivate the arts and refinements of civilized communities. — And it was then altogether in their power to refuse us an admission & a place among them. We came also under the patronage & instructions of the General government, with official letters of introduction, & commendation from under their hand — those documents declaring our purpose & explaining our views. We received the strongest & most solemn assurances from our friends in the State of New York, private & public, & from the General Government, that we should be assisted in every possible manner & protected in the accomplishment of our designs.

It is possible, indeed, that some of our brethren did not fully understand our views. But it is not true, that all convenient methods were not used to make them understand. We had no motives to be wily, or to employ insidious measures. For our own people, as a body, did not wish to come here, — & would willingly have been prevented. But we were compelled by extraneous influences — by the interest & policy of white men, both in the Government & out of the Government. And it was to gratify them, and not our people that we came.

And now, brothers, . . . — let the candid — let the world Judge, from the probabilities & presumptions of the case — whether we would have left our inheritance in the State of New York for an insecure abode in this inhospitable region? —

What we denominate circumstantial evidence in support of our claims, are first, the moral & confidential considerations, named by the Winnebagoes and Menomonees, during the negotiation, but not reduced to record; & next, the current and well known remarks upon the Treaties, after they were concluded.

The Menomonees distinctly stated at the time of negotiation in 1822, as reasons not only they were willing, but desirous to have us come among them, in terms equivalent to the Following: —

"You, brothers, know the ways of the white people better than we do. You know they always want more land — that when a white man puts his fingers upon our lands, he had long nails, & they go deep, and it is hard to get them out. You have had sad experiences that this is true. You have told us, the white people have got your lands. And you have come to seek an asylum among us. For which we are glad, that you thought of us. Now, brothers, it is for this reason we have agreed, at your request, to let you have more lands, according as you asked the other day. —And so brothers, you will help us keep off the white man."

We then told the Menominees, that in order for us effectually to keep of the white men, they must give us a title. To which they agreed as it is expressed & bounded in the Treaty.

The territory first proposed by us to purchases, — that is, at the opening of this negotiation — was an extension of the former purchase down Fox river to rapids des peres — making in all about 700,000 acres. And this is the territory for which we proposed to have paid, the sum being $5,000. The more extended boundaries actually defined in the Treaty were fixed, at the voluntary instance of the Menominie, for the confidential considerations above named in consequence of which a tenancy in common was agreed upon between the parties, as specified in the Treaty.

The other portion of the circumstantial evidence consists in the current complaints of the French people, & in the consequent remarks of the Menominees, soon after the Treaty of 1822. The latter reported those complaints, notwithstanding, expressed their own satisfaction at what they had done. And the common understanding of the terms of the Treaty accorded substantially with the facts.

All this we regard as testimony of a character deserving great weight, & would probably be conclusive with disinterested minds.

For the documentary evidence, brothers, we have only to refer to the Treaties themselves.

We are aware, the Menominee Nation are said not to have been fairly represented in the negotiations between us & them — to which we think it sufficient to reply: — that when this question was under a sort of judicial process before the Commissioners of 1827 [several lines crossed out] it was there proved, that all the men who signed the Treaties with us, were Chiefs & principal men of the Nation, except two, whose claims as such were contested between themselves, rather than challenged by others. Of course one of these was doubtless entitled to the office.

Besides, the authority for the Council was the highest — possible — directly from the Government; — the Menomonee Nation were duly notified, as is customary in such cases; — all attended, who were pleased so to do. & we have no reason to suppose there was any dissatisfaction, at the time, as a reason why any did not come, and, the accordance of those, who were present, to our proposals, was cheerful. And all the dissatisfactions which have since arisen have proceeded from disturbing causes without — & but for the introduction & operations of those causes, we might till now have been in perfect harmony both with the Menominees & Winnebagoes.

We have a few remarks, brothers, to make on the Treaty of Butte des morts of Aug. 11, 1827. Negotiated by Lewis Cass and T.L Mckenny, as Commissioners on the part of the United States. And here brothers, we must not only declare ourselves aggrieved, but we are obliged to confess our astonishment. We are astonished that such an irregularity should be authorized by the President of the United States & aggrieved that such a violent aggression should be made on our rights. We should be glad to be certified whether Commission for this was ever authorized by the President. For it has seemed to us incredible; and if so, we should still be glad to whether it was not done in ignorance of our Treaties as authorized and approved by his

Presidency; — in as much as the Treaty of 1827 disregarded entirely the former Treaties, — & negotiated for the United States, parts, & the most valuable parts of the same territories, which we had purchased, and which was in the first place authorized and afterwards approved by the President of the United States. And no Congressional — no official act whatever of the Government had ever in any form, challenged, or questioned the validity of our purchase. What right, then, brothers, we demand, had even the President of the United States to disregard & even nullify the official & solemn acts of his predecessor?

That decorum & common respect, which our public officer owes to the official & confirmed acts of another, ought surely to have arrested this proceedings, at least, till the validity of the Treaties of 1821 & 1822, if questioned, had been determined by the proper authorities. — It will not surely be maintained that these Treaties were void, because they were not ratified by the Senate of the United States — for this rule applies only where the Government is a party.

Mr. Calhoun, Secretary of War, expressly says to us in an official communication:

"Your Treaty with the Menomines & Winnebagoes is approved by the President — which is all the ratification which is necessary, as those Treaties only, to which the United States are a party, require the addition of the sanction of the Senate."

And even admitting, that the President & the Secretary of War were erroneous in this opinion, & irregular in this act — (which we cannot suppose), — still, when, we had been so notified by the official organs of Government, & rested upon it, — Should another President our, father, take such advantage of us, his children, as to appoint a special Commission to take away our lands — land obtained & sanctioned by such authority? — And then, again how could the Senate of the United States ratify such a Treaty? We have found upon inquiry, that this ratification was hurried and forced through the Senate by that same influence which had organized and conducted the Treaty at the very close of the session of 1827, when we charitably suppose they were fatigued and impatient, and morally incapable to give a due attention to so important a transaction.

By some means, however, thro the kindness of Providence, it seems, they got a glimpse of our previous negotiations, respecting the same territories & have inserted for us this saving clause: "Provided, that the said Treaty shall not impair or effect any right or claim, which the New York Indians, or any of them have to the lands, or any of the lands, mentioned in the said Treaty." One of two things is doubtless true in law: — either the Treaties of 1821 & 1822, or the transactions of 1827 are invalid. The first cannot be so, even admitting the truth of all the objections, which are alleged against them. Because they are formal covenants between the parties named in the, duly & thoroughly executed — authorized & approved by the President of the United States.

And even though there were sufficient reasons, why they should not remain in force, then their validity as seems to us, cannot be disturbed by anything, but a decision of the proper court of adjudication, or by a special act of Congress. Consequently, the Treaty of 1827 negotiating for the same premises, was not only irregular, but is null & void — and that too notwithstanding its formal ratification — null & void, we mean so far as its negotiations interfere with those of 1821 & 1822. — The more we have examined this matter, the more have we been afraid of some moral wrong, unknown to Government, lurking under the premises, on which these transaction have been founded. We find, that this Treaty had not been authorized by Congress as, or if we mistake not, is customary in such cases; — & that no appropriations had been made for the object. What occasion for such urgency? A great stretch of power, & a fearful responsibility, we apprehend must have been assumed somewhere, & shall we add, what we would be most happy not to be obliged to feel, assumed for the purpose of wresting from us violently our sole inheritance.

Thanks to the Great & good Spirit for his over ruling providence, which has subverted these designs, & still left us a gleam of hope, that our cause, in its true and proper light will yet come before our Father the President & before the supreme authorities of the Nation.

And thanks to you, Brothers, for the errand on which you have come, & for your kind assurances of a willingness to hear us, & fairly to represent our case.

We have a word to say upon your letter of instructions. It is this: If our Father, the President has supposed — (as our constructions of his letter have led us to fear he has) that we have made an unconditional and final submission, so as to bar us from all appeal — we beg leave to say — that we have not intended to be so understood — And this, — not at all to express a want of confidence, but only to correct an error, if such an impression has been received.

If a satisfactory compromise can now be effected, it will give us the greatest pleasure to unite in a joint submission to the decision of the President, as final.

Brothers, we take this opportunity to express our utmost confidence in our father & in you his Commissioners — & our hope, that by your advice, influence, & mediations, we may yet be able to come to such compromise with our brethren the Menominees & Winnebagoes, as to unite with them in a joint submission of our agreement for the approval of the President.

We would not, brother forfeit your good opinion, nor. . . . The judgement of a candid and generous public, by showing our unwillingness to make sacrifices for the sake of peace. And we assure you that any overture for compromise, approved by you, & likely to be accorded to, through your mediations by our brethren the Menominees & Winnebagoes; from whatever quarter they may come — unless in our opinion they impose upon us a flagrant injustice, and disappoint our most reasonable hopes. — Shall claim our most serious consideration. We have great confidence in your ability to effect such an arrangement. We are unwilling to remain longer under such a cloud, to see our families & our people dejected under the doubtfulness of their prospect, their courage subdued, & their former confidence in the repeated & solemn assurances of protection & patronage from the Government almost annihilated.

Give us, brothers, a home, & we will bless you — & our children will bless you, & we will pray God to bless you. You have told us, brothers, in your letters, — that "our interests are deeply concerned in these deliberations." — which indeed we feel. You have sent us a copy of your letter of instructions from our father the President, & told us "to read it well, & think well on what he has said, & to be prepared to give an expression of our feelings & opinions fully made up"—We have endeavored to do so, confiding in your candour & generosity of feeling, that you will not regard us as wanting in deference to our superiors, for a free & manly expression of our sentiments.

You have declared yourselves "disposed to do us full justice, & to enter into our wants and sympathies with entire sincerity"—which, brothers, permit us to say, has greatly endeared you to our hearts. You have also assured us, that "the feelings of our Father, the President, are altogether kind and parental towards us." Brothers, we accept this assurance with implicit confidence, & with grateful affection.

Brothers, may the Great & Good Spirit preside over all our deliberations, & give to all concerned a mutual good feeling towards each other. — kindness, an impartiality, & a wisdom that shall guide this Council to the most desirable results.

Brothers, We have no more to say at present.[20]

The next day, the council reconvened. Daniel Bread rose and said:

Our Brethren, the Menomonies and Winnebagoe asked us yesterday what we wanted: To which we have only to reply; that we want peace and good will, and we present the following overture for that purpose.

The New York Indians, as a proof of their sincerity in their declaration of yesterday of a willingness to make sacrifice, for the sake of peace, and to come to an amicable adjustment of the differences, between them and their brethren the Menomonies and Winnebagoes, do hereby consent and covenant, to be satisfied with the territory defined as following.

Assuming as a base, the upper or South west line of as defined in the Treaty 1821 crossing Lake Winnebago at the Rapids, or outlet of its waters; bounded on the northeast or lower side by a line crossing Fox River at the Rapids des Peres (or lower rapids) running parallel with the southwest or upper line, as at above described, until it intersect, on the northwest, a line drawn at right angles with this, and the upper boundary and passing then a point, distant thirty mile from the foot of the Grand Kackalin, this distance being measured on a line from the foot of said falls [?] parallel to the upper and lower boundaries, as above described. On the Northwest bounded by the line last described, thirty miles, from the foot of the Grand Kackalin, and at right angles with the upper and lower boundaries: — on the Southeast bounded by a line drawn parallel with the general course of the River, between the upper and lower boundaries, and fifteen miles distant from the said general course, and as much farther as the Menomonies & Winnebaboes have claimed. It being understood that the upper and lower boundaries, are to run either way from the River, till they intersect the Northwest and Southeast boundaries above described.

It being also understood, that of the settlement of the Oneida on Duck Creek, shall be without these boundaries, a piece shall be added so as to include that settlement built upon the point making the fork of the two streams between which, the settlement now lies, by the following rule.

Bounded by parallel lines at right angles, with the Northeast boundary five miles asunder, and equidistant from the forks, or point above namely running till they intersect another line, parallel to the Northeast boundary in a direct line down Duck Creek, from the fork or point above named. The Northeast Boundary from Duck Creek settlement is, in any case, to fall three miles below the fork herein named.[21]

The commissioners directed Conner to take the proposal to the Menominees and Winnebagoes for discussion. The commissioners asked if the Menominees would approve all of the above lands, or only part of the requested lands. He advised the interpreter to tell the Menominee and Winnebagoes to send their young men, women, and children home, and he would only allow two more days of provisions. He wanted only the chiefs to stay.

Following this, Kaush Kaw ne re en, Bears Grease, a Menominee chief, spoke for his nation:

Father, We do not doubt but you are sent by the President, and we came to see you. Father, you know our lands are small. We do not know why our Great Father sends, you here. Our Father, the President well knows that we occupy the smallest section of land of any Indians in the Country. It appears the President has sent the New York Indians to take a section of the small country we inhabit. I speak, but I represent the whole Nation, and our friends the Winnebagoes, are of one opinion. Father—as our recollection is short, we cannot speak long. We will sit down, and let the Winnebagoes speak; after they have spoken, we will rise again, and let you know how much land we are willing to let the New York Indians have.

Four Legs was next to speak:

We are not ignorant of your business. We know you are sent by our Great Father to arrange this business: — We know that we have but little ground and we are surprised that the President of the United States should send so many people to occupy the small space we own. We know well, that we cannot object to the old cession, but we can go no farther; The Menomine and I have agreed what to set off to the New York Indians.

Josette Carron, a Menominee chief, spoke next:

Father,
    You that are sent by the President of the United States, and you all, that are here present know well, that there is but one Supreme Being, that is able to put us on the land we now occupy.
    Father; — When we have said one thing, we do not want to say another, in order to entrap ourselves — I extend my hand towards the President, as though he was near at hand. We grant
    Commencing at a small island above the Grand Kackalin from thence running up to the Little Butte des Morts, on the Northwest side of the River, and running back two days journey for a man and his family, (about 30 miles).

To this Four Legs added:

Father,
    We acknowledge you are sent by our Great Father, and that is all
the land we can grant the New York Indians.

Then Shounk-Whunk-siap, Black Wolf, a Winnebago chief, took his
opportunity to speak:

Father,
    God knows, we have but this small country to live in. But we are
willing to give the land above mentioned to the New York Indians; I
speak before my God and this company, that our young men women
and children, as well as the Menomines, are willing to cede that much
land to the New York Indians.

Afterward, Four Legs spoke again:

Fathers,
    It must be well understood to be but two days journey back, for
a man & his family. That the New York Indians must move onto the
lands now granted. We reserved the benefits of the River — said that
the reason, they gave them so far back, was that they might have the
privilege of the Bank of the River.

Finally, Menominee Chief Josette Carron spoke again:

Fathers,
    All the Winnebago have said we accede to, and as we have nothing
more to say we sit down.[22]

General Root then asked them about the Oneida living on Duck Creek,
to which the chiefs replied "that they must move onto the lands just given."
    The commissioners spent the following day examining Ellis's map pro-
posing possible boundaries for the New York Indians. Statements related
to the proposed boundaries were different and caused many discussions

trying to resolve those proposed boundaries. The New York Indians replied to the boundaries proposed, as the discussion went back and forth
throughout this council meeting. Ultimately, the chiefs of the New York
Indians proposed the following boundaries, which they presented to the
commissioners:

> The New York Indians, having received intimation, by private, and
> bonafide conversations, with the Commissioners, that it might
> be of service for them to make another concession still, wish it to
> be distinctly understood, that it is only with the hope of a final
> adjustment of differences now, and with extreme reluctance that
> their chiefs in council, have agreed; that they will relinquish ten miles
> from the Northwest side of the tract defined in their last overture,
> on the Southwest Side of Fox River; they will relinquish the tract cut
> off by a line drawn from the lower extremity of Black Bird Island in
> a Southeasterly direction, parallel with the lower boundary, as last
> described; provided that their tract on the Northwest side of the
> River, be so extended as to embrace all the land falling within the
> following boundaries, to wit;
> The extension of the Northwest boundary as herein fixed,
> northeasterly, in a direct line till it inter sect another line, drawn
> from the mouth of Duck Creek, parallel with the former upper &
> lower boundaries; thence along said line to the mouth of Duck Creek;
> thence from the mouth of Duck Creek along the margin of Green Bay,
> to the claims already confirmed as defined on the maps drawn by Mr.
> Ellis for the Commissioners; at this time; and thence following the
> rear of those claims, as defined on said Map, till it strikes Fox River;
> it being understood that this offer is not hereafter in any case to be
> construed to the disadvantage of the former claims, of the New York
> Indians, provided the result aimed at in this overture, shall not be
> accomplished.
> By order of the Chiefs of the New York Indians
> M. H. Augustine

A reply to the previous day's proposal for boundaries was made on
August 31 to the New York Indians. Mason proposed it, but Root and

McCall objected. The commissioners stressed that the amount of land for the New York Indians should be based on the fact that they "are to be considered as an agricultural people, and lands is to allotted them according to fixed and reasonable agricultural limits." The commissioners proposed to establish separate pieces of land for the different tribes and requested population numbers of the New York Indians by the heads of families, women, and children settled near Green Bay.[23]

On the afternoon of August 31, the commissioner again met with the chiefs of the Winnebago, Menominee, and New York Indians in council. General Root addressed them. He acknowledged that "a bad soldier" "has stabbed one of the Menomonees" and assured them the perpetrator was in prison and would be punished. He commended the Menominee for not killing the soldier. He continued by stating that "at one time the Menomonees and Winnebagoes owned all the country; but have since sold a part to the New York Indians; they let their New York Brethren come in to own a share with them. Where the Menomonees and Winnebagos had wigwams and cornfields, the New York Indians were not to disturb them." He then reviewed the 1827 treaty, claiming, "The Menomonees sold to the United States, a strip of land on each side of Fox River. At the time they agreed that their Great Father, the President, might set off a portion of land to the New York Indians." The commissioners, he explained, were sent to fulfill that direction for the president and to have peace among all the parties. "As they have not agreed among themselves, the Commissioners have concluded to set off as we will show them on the map; and we hope after they have examined it, that all parties will agree to the division."[24]

To this, Bears Grease replied:

Fathers,

I hope you will hear what I have to say in representing the other Chiefs. It is not unknown to you that the Indians in this Country are depending upon their rice harvest; We have already told you how much land we are willing to give to the New York Indians — we will not give an inch more. We think we have been very considerate to give so much but it was to please our Great Father. The wild rice is preparing on us. We all go tomorrow. When we heard that our Great Father wanted to see us, we left our canoes on the Stocks and now we have no canoes to get our rice with. Father, — We cannot complain; you have fed us well with pork & flour, but we have no broth with it. — this is all we have to say.

Four Legs added:

Fathers,

If you will hear, I will speak. I will not do any more than the Menomonees have done. We all agreed to give that much, and no more. I cannot deviate from the Menomonees, what they say, I agree to. The Menomonees have said truth about the rice — if we neglect it we shall starve.

We are willing to let the New York Indians have the land we mentioned but no more. They must not cross the lines. If they take what is offered, well; if not, no more will be given. As the President has sent you, you may go back and tell him what I say.

The next day, September 1, John Metoxen, principal chief, added his thoughts to the council:

Brothers & Friends, — Listen to a few words I have to say. — You of the Menomonee & Winnebago Nations; I am glad to see you together today: — I thank the Great Spirit also, for giving us light that we may see each other. I am glad also, that we have seen each other in peace, before the Commissioners, whom our Great Father the President has sent to arrange our affairs, for the interests of all. Now Brothers, I am glad of one thing, that our covenant friendship is still good, and I hope it will remain so. But Brothers, with respect to one thing, with reference to our Brothers, the Commissioners, I regret I am not satisfied with it. Brothers, I should have been very happy if this business had been settled between us, brother Indians, and the Commissioners; But I see it cannot be. But Brethren, I still wish that the Covenant friendship, which we entered into some years since, may continue. Brother, I take this opportunity to shew you the custom of my forefathers; that when they make an arrangement, they always keep their word. And I am determined to do the same. Now

Brothers, I hope our Great President will take our concerns into his own hands, and he will do what is best. — Brothers, under this, I hope we shall always meet in friendship; For my part, it should be so with me. I have no more to say.

When Metoxen had finished, Bears Grease again addressed the commissioners:

You heard yesterday what we had to say. — it was in behalf of all — you will hear no more from us. — Fathers — It is now ten days since we have been together in council; We are of one mind. We have not two mouths. We have always said but one thing.[25]

James Doty, speaking on behalf of the Menominee Nation, then took a turn to address the council at length:

The Counsel of the Menomonee and Winnebago Nations of Indians, at the request of the said Nations, and by the permission of the Commissioners of the United States, reply to the Speeches of the Commissioners, and of the New York Indians, for, and on behalf of the said Nations, as follows:

The Commissioners, and the New York Indians assert, in their opening speeches, that those Indians have bought this country of these Nations and paid them for it in money, and in goods. — This assertion, these Nations shewed the Commissioners in 1827, at the Butte des Morts, was false; and it is equally so now. In support of this they ask leave to refer to the testimony recorded on the Journal of these Commissioners. They then said (and so did the Persons with whom it is asserted these purchases were made; as also the New York Indians then present, who did not understand the English Language) that at neither of the Treaties of 1821 & 1822, were the Chiefs of those nations present; nor did the person then there, pretend to act for them, or for their nations, and they signed without the knowledge of either. — that the "metes and bound" described in those Treaties, were not made known to those individuals. — but their permission was asked and they gave it, for the New York Indians to sit down upon, and cultivate the lands, from the foot of the Grand Kackalin, to the foot of the Little Chute. And it is apparent, that this was clearly the understanding of the New York Indians; for they first settled upon this very spot; — and until lately, have and find themselves within those limits. But with this broad denial of any right of the New York Indians, as acquired from these Nations to the country from Lake Michigan to the Wisconsin River and the highlands of Lake Superior, they decline entering into any further discussion upon those Treaties, as the President has declared in his instruction to his Commissioners, "that he esteems it proper to waive any decision upon the question of the validity of the compact of 1821 and 1822."[26]

The President also says he *"has determined to accommodate the New York Indians, under the privilege given him to do so, by locating a Country and establishing such boundaries between the parties as may be equitable & just."* It was for this purpose that the Commission was instituted, and not to ascertain rights, under any previous compact with the Menomonees, and Winnebagoes.

The first demand now made by the New York Indians, of a country to be set apart for them to inhabit as agriculturists, and not as hunters is estimated to be at least 140 [?] miles long, and 75 in widths, and to contain at least . . . 20,000 acres, which, at the sum, which they, insist they paid in goods will be at the rate of one half mill per acres and of 2,800 acres for every soul, which it is even conjectured will remove the State of New York.

Treating this demand as altogether ridiculous these Nation have inquired in Council, of the New York Indians, whether they could not consent to make a more reasonable request, then of the whole Menomonee country. To this they have replied; — that to evince their disposition to preserve peace by making a great sacrifice, they will be satisfied with a tract which is traversed by Fox River, with a perpendicular breadth of 27 miles, and extending to the north west 30 miles, and to the South east 15 miles and as much further in that direction, as the possession of the Menomonees extends. The least quantity which is contained in those limits is 777,800 acres; for which they say they have paid, as above stated the sum of $3,950.00 in goods, which is equal to five mills per acre and 324 acres to every soul.

To this it is replied by these Nations, that this tract is larger then they can separate from their hunting grounds in this part of their Territory: — that it embraces many of their encamping grounds, villages, rivers, rice beds, and cornfields; — that it is more than the New York Indians can cultivate; that they do not require it therefore to make themselves comfortable, while the Menomonees and Winnebagos do, for their territory is already so small, that many packs of Beaver, are they now compelled to pay annually to the Indians west of the Mississippi for leave to hunt only two months of the year on their grounds. And that this privilege has already cost them more than the sum which the New York Indians have paid for the whole of this country.

"But" say these Nations, "Since our Great Father the President has commanded us to receive these men and give them a home, we consent to yield to them for this reason, the only portion of our country, which we wish to part with for, no consideration. We should not seem ourselves poor, if we were as well . . . , however, as are our Brothers from New York. — and we think from their appearance, they must have sold their land for a good price. — If the whites have long nails, when they put their hands upon our country our Brothers nails appear to be a good deal longer."

The Country we now offer them, and if the cost of this, they must give up all claim to every other part of the country, (Since they are dissatisfied with what we gave them at the Butte des Morts in 1827) is from the heel of the Rapids of the Grand Kackalin, to the Little Butte des Morts, bordering on the west side of Fox River, and bounded by lines running west from these places to encampments, or thirty miles.

This tract contains more than 166,000 acres, which, if it be admitted that the New York Indians have truly paid the sum claimed to have been paid by them, will then cost them at the rate of two cents and eight mills per acre, and may be divided sixty acres to every soul.

It is neither equitable nor just that, as agriculturists, they should require more land for this consideration. If they were to be provided for as hunters, it is admitted that a different principle would

govern. — In a negotiation for the purpose of transferring them from
one country to another, they estimate the value of a country by the
quality of its soil, and the number and power of it, water courses,
rather than by the game which roams over it, or by its wild fruits, or
by the fish which may be taken in its waters.

All who are acquainted with the history of the Menomonees are
aware that they have been compelled to seek new hunting grounds
west of the Mississippi. It is manifest they cannot, without yielding
themselves up to starvation, surrender any part of their own country
to another tribe, for the purposes of hunting its' game. The New York
Indians are not here, in the view of the Government, in the double
capacity of husbandmen, and of hunting — It has claimed them in
New York as a civilized people. And it has never intended to change
their character, and return to the hunter state.

Let the Commissioners look at their parties, as they now stand
before them, and can they say they are equal? Let them turn to their
speeches which are recorded and do they not perceive, on the one
side, a learned cunning, even too acute perhaps for it own purposes,
which attempts to render the line obscure between civilization and
barbarism, and then demand, to be informed whether this party
or their neighbors are on the right side: — which in one paragraph
claims the protection of the Government as barbarians, and again
in another, that they have advanced so far in the path of civilization
as to have overtaken the white man; — which claims that they came
here as agriculturists, and speedily on their arrival, became entitled
to all the rights of a savage people. — made bargains as civilized men,
and asked their confirmation as untutored Indians: — and which, in
addition to all this, discourses most ingeniously of doctrinal matters,
and questions of natural law, upon the traditions, it is presumed, of
the Iroquois tribe.

It appears to be doubtful, whether the number of Indians
which it is now stated will remove from New York, is not greatly
overestimated. It is not deemed just that these hunting grounds
should be given up to a body of men who may never take possession
of them; and it certainly is not, if they should be allowed to pass into
the hands of a few civilized Indians undivided; for it seems, they are

to be owned by those <u>who remove</u> from the State of New York. If they are the property of tribes, which do not emigrate, this proceeding is unjust, because unnecessary for their welfare.

The proposal however of the Menomonees and Winnebagoes is rejected by the New York Indians; and there upon, the Commissioners demand of them, if the will accept of a tract, on the east side of Fox River, bounded in front by said River, and extending from the Little Kackalin to the mouth of Plum Creek for the <u>Brothertown Indians</u> amounting to 20,000 acres: of another tract at the Grand Kackalin, now occupied by the Stockbridge Indians, amounting to 6,000 acres; of another tract, bounded by the River from a point, opposite the mouth of Plum Creek, to the Little Butte des Morts; — thence 16 or 17 miles north west; thence to a point on the United States line, . . . of the mouth of Duck Creek; thence to the said mouth — thence on a line to pass the Oneida Settlement on Duck Creek, leaving it to the north, until it intersects the United States line of . . . thence along that line to the point west of the mouth of Plum Creek, and thence to the mouth of said creek; — the last described tract, to contain 250,000 acres.

To this the New York Delegates reply that they will not. And the Menomonees and Winnebagoes say they will not give one inch more than what they have already offered. The quantity offered is more than enough to supply all the New York Indians who are here and after they have settled the whole of this tract, if there are any more who are unprovided for, perhaps enough can be found for them. The United States can give it if the nations cannot. If the whites have been unjust to those tribes in New York, as <u>they</u> say, this is by no means a reason why the United States in its attempt to repair this injustice, should, with it strong arm, take from the tribes in this country their possessions without right and without renumeration.
Signed J.D. Doty, Green Bay Sept 1, 1830[27]

Near the end of the proceedings, Four Legs spoke to the commissioners:

Fathers,

It has been with great satisfaction that I have heard the

Commissioners. — But I have lost one of my young men at Winnebago Lake, and am sad. Why should I answer all the questions that are asked me? The Great Spirit is not now making the Earth. When he did, he made the Indians on it. I told you on the other side of the River what I had to say. When the New York Indians first came to this country, I did not sell my land; — I lent it to them. They said "we do not want much of your country but a little to sit down upon." Finally I agreed they might have a small quantity of land to plant corn and get a living upon. — The goods that were received at the Butte des Morts, were not enough to make each one a breech clout. The goods I considered <u>given</u> by our Great Father the President, not by the New York Indians. It is for this reason I have not answered all the questions. We were promised other things, by way of thanks, but never received them. We cannot grant any more land — any more than we did the other day.

When Four Legs had finished, the commissioners had the interpreter, Mr. Conner, inform those gathered that the meeting had ended.

On September 2, 1830, the chiefs of the New York Indians replied to Doty's statements, writing:

The Chiefs of the New York Indians to the Honorable Commissioners, beg leave to reply to the communication of Judge Doty, of the 1st Inst. On behalf of the Menominee & Winnebago Nations: —

First — as to the assertion — that the declaration of the Honorable Commissioners & of the New York Indians of a <u>sale</u> of land & <u>payment</u> there for, as negotiated between the parties now at issue — "is false." Whatever might have been the intention of the Commissioners in assuming this ground, the New York Indians rest solely upon the terms of the Treaties & the receipts passed in acknowledgement of the considerations; which they have supposed sufficient, at least, to justify the calling of the transactions "sale" & c. [The word *false* has been crossed out and *sale* written above it.] Whether the sale was <u>fair</u> seemed to be the question at issue. And it was hardly to be expected, in common courtesy, that giving these transactions their own <u>legal & proper</u> denomination without assuming the question of their equity, would subject the Commissioners, or the New York Indians, to so harsh a charge, as that of falsehood. To support this charge, reference is made "to the testimony recorded in the Journal of the Commissioners" of the 1827. It is not in our power to quote that Journal.

The utmost possible, however, it can be supposed to prove, could not annihilate the fact, but only affect the character of the sale in equity. And we have before to the same transactions in proof of the equity of the purchase. The notes, preserved by us of the testimony referred to, and also by a disinterested person, who happened to be present at the Treaty of 1827, — which notes we presume cannot differ essentially from the official documents of the Commissioners — go to establish on that is essential to . . . especially when the character & relations of that . . . are understood & appreciated. —

Since the learned Counsel, opposed to us, has accused [?] us of falsehood, we suppose it fair to refer to a document presented & read by himself in 1827, as part of the testimony which he now refers to — & which document is said to have been formed by himself — himself a witness to its veracity. — This Document is a memorial of certain Menominee Chiefs to the President of the United States, dated June 16th, 1824. And it asserts "not one of whom (the Chiefs signing this memorial) was present at that Treaty;" — that is, the Treaty of 1822. Whereas one of these Chiefs — viz Say hee took, signed that Treaty. Now, we allow, this might have been a mistake. But it was a very strange & very unnecessary one. Another of the same Chiefs, viz Keh Hani no nien, signed the Treaty of 1821.

This document, got up in 1824, as a Memorial to the President, under all its advantages & pains, may, we suppose fairly be considered, as embodying the substance of the testimony referred to. Only seven of all the Menominee Chiefs, it seems, could be persuaded to subscribe it — two whom were subscribed to the Treaties of 1821 & 1822 — (one to the former & one to the latter); — another of the seven — Oush-kosh, — was a mere boy at the time of those Treaties. And besides, when these very Chiefs came to be informed of the true nature & intent of that Memorial, they sent word to Detroit to have it arrested — & at their instance it was arrested — but after a year or two forwarded without their consent.

It is Singular, indeed, that because certain men have been <u>created</u> Chiefs & made <u>Principal,</u> since 1821 & 1822, & consequently, could not have been the highest authorities in those Treaties — it should thence be asserted the <u>none</u> of the Chiefs & principal men were concerned in those negotiations — The New York Indians are willing to abide by the proofs in the case, — when fairly addressed. It not their design here to go into the argument. They have only to request, that the confidence of <u>assertion</u> may not be taken for evidence.

As the moral & confidential considerations, involved in the negotiation of 1821 & 1822 have been necessarily drawn out in this controversy, it is due to the New York Indians in the present State of the argument, & especially to meet the . . . of the communication now under review — on the <u>price per acre</u> paid by us for a territory 140 miles by 75 — to make some remarks.

The additional territory desired & asked for by us in 1822, including what was negotiated in 1821, embraced precisely, or nearly the same with that which was comprehended in our first overture to the Honorable Commissioners — covering a country about 45 miles by 26. At the voluntary instance of the Menominees themselves, & for the moral & confidential considerations already referred to, we <u>accepted</u> the larger territory in trust, — to be tenanted & used in common. We did not desire it. We have never asserted a <u>purchase</u> of this wide territory, except confidentially, & for the sacred considerations specified. Had we been limited to our own request, we should have taken the land only on the terms of the first Treaty — independent of the right of tenancy in common. And we ourselves have become embarrassed in our claims, for the sake of doing a favor to our brethren the Menominees.

Considering, therefore, the actual limits supposed to be involved in the <u>purchase</u> — considering the time when the negotiations were held, & the value then attached to these lands, there is no evidence, that the price stipulated & discharged by us, was not a fair one between these parties. And if the value of this territory has since risen in a supposititous [?] market, it is altogether unfair to turn upon us, and say — we have over reached [?] the Menominees. Why not bring the same charge against the United States, for the many wide territories they have acquired of Indian Nations for even smaller considerations, & which have since become highly valuable: — Ten miles square — or a hundred square miles on Connecticut river in Massachusetts taking Northampton for center — was once sold by Indians to the whites for 20 shillings sterling — & has been gravely defended by moralists as a fair bargain — the full value of the land at the time. And are we to be ejected for our purchase at this time by a showing — that this land is now worth more than what we gave for it. —

As to the invidious remarks of the learned Counsel respecting our better dress & manners — & the superiorities of our condition in sundry respects — our . . . — earning &c — we do not think it becoming to make a grave reply. The argument of our cause lies in its own merits — in naked facts — & on these we are willing to rest it before the Commissioners — before our Father the President — before the Nation & before the world.

By order of the Chiefs of the New York Indians

Green Bay, Sept. 1830

P. N. H. Augustine (interpreter for Oneida)

N.B. The statement made by Judge Doty — of $3,950 paid by the New York Indians for their lands should have been $5000.[28]

Since the Menominee were not satisfied with the decisions made by the three commissioners, they immediately asked for approval of a journey to Washington to meet with the secretary of war and the president. The Menominee chiefs were accustomed to dealing with the United States on a nation-to-nation basis, thus their dissatisfaction with the commissioners went to the next logical step—to meet with the president. In turn, the United States requested that Indian nations obtain approval from the Indian agent before going to Washington, which they requested in the following document:

Application by the Menomonie Indians to visit their Great Father, the President of the United States.

Grizzle Bear, Josette, the Sun, and their bands, called on the United States' Indian agent this day, with their bands, and, in the presence of Robert Irwin, esq., Mr. Jackson of New York, and General Mason, Grizzle Bear said,

"Father, you see us all here to bid your farewell; our people are all pleased with the hope of going to their great father. Our people have all great love for you, and place confidence in you; they say they can now see before them, and think they will be happy. Father, we all wish you alone to go with us to Washington and take care of our interests there."

Josette said — "Father, we did not for a long time know who to look to or ask for advice. Our people are now all happy when they see you. We ask you, one and all, to urge our request to go to see great father; and there are many who say now that they will go with us, but we want to go with you."

The above speeches were made in presence of Mr. Irwin, postmaster, Mr. Jackson, Mr. Mason, and Mr. Prickett, United States' interpreter.

DANIEL JACKSON.[29]

Just three days after this request, the Indian agent at Green Bay, S. C. Stambaugh, wrote a long letter to President Jackson. Stambaugh began by endorsing the request of the Menominee to meet with the president to resolve the dispute with the New York Indians. He provided an in-depth overview of the complex circumstances surrounding the 1821 and 1822 treaties and asked how many people he could bring with him and receive coverage of expenses.

Stambaugh referred to the approval of the 1822 treaty when he wrote,

Mr. Calhoun sanctions this confirmation in a letter to the chiefs and head-men of the New York Indians, dated October 27, 1823. By these article of a treaty, the Menomonies and Winnebagoes cede to the New York Indians (including a cession made by the same parties the year previous) about six million, seven hundred and twenty thousand acres of land, covering an extent of about one hundred and forty miles in length, and about seventy-five miles in breadth, embracing all the best land, water privileges, &c, &c, in the country.

Stambaugh then referred to the 1824 and 1825 treaties made between the Stockbridge, St. Regis, Tuscarora, Oneida, and Munsee with the Brothertown for land. The Brothertown paid $950 to the Menominee. He includes discussion of the 1825 Prairie du Chien and 1827 Butte de Morts treaties, saying the confusion from the 1827 treaty was when the commissioners "purchased of the two former tribes (Menomonie and Winnebago) a tract of land on the Fox river, surrounding the settlement of Green Bay, and covering an extent, as I have ascertained, of about twenty-six miles in length, and six miles in width, on each side of the Fox river." But in the final version of the treaty, the issue is referred to the president to make a decision. Stambaugh wrote as well, "I believe the Menomonie tribe of Indians have been most shamefully deceived both by the agents of the New York Indians and by their own agents and advisers. I believe the New York Indians have been duped and deceived by their own agents, and I am sorry to say the Government appears to have participated in the deception." Additionally, Stambaugh felt the US government had not received the correct information to make a decision and that the three commissioners were not successful in defining the boundaries in a way that satisfied all the parties. He said he had talked with the principal chiefs of Menomonie and they

> expressed a desire to sell a portion of their land to their great father;
> they say they are the only tribe in the country who are not receiving
> annuities, and that they thought the reason of it was, because their
> great father, the President, did not love them . . . they were all hungry
> and almost naked when they came here; and I found myself almost
> destitute of *means* to alleviate their miserable condition.

As the council adjourned, Stambaugh held a talk on September 1 with about four hundred Indians, including "all their chiefs, except Josette Carron." In attendance were Mason, McCall, Conner, and a Mr. Hunt. Root refused to attend. Stambaugh stated he took down every word as interpreted to him in the presence of the commissioners. Their complaints included that they gave land to "some of their kindred," and this land was now being sold to pay off their debts. The issue stated that they had not received annuities for the land held in common with the Winnebagoes that was ceded in the 1825 Prairie du Chien treaty. Finally, Stambaugh claimed that the Menominee Nation wanted a line drawn "between their country and the Winnebagoes," and he concluded that all the issues could be resolved if the Menominee chiefs, including Bears Grease, Josette, and Os-Kaush, were allowed to visit Washington.[30]

Doty wrote to the commissioners on September 10. He said he had discovered the meaning of the terms "'moral and confidential and sacred considerations' which were 'alleged'" to have been made in 1822 by the New York Indians. His opinion was that the 1822 statement was to have the New York Indians protect the Menominee from the government taking all the Menominee lands. The New York Indians would be their guardians and trustees and make this area entirely Indian Country. The statement included removing the white settlers. Doty also stated that this is why President Monroe "set aside the treaty of Bowyer, by which this country was ceded to the United States, and for which the Indians duly received payment."[31] The Bowyer treaty was never ratified, and payment was not made. In fact, the president approved of the New York Indians going again to the Green Bay area to negotiate for land.

The report of A. G. Ellis, who was sent to assess the lands, was submitted on September 24, well after the council meeting concluded. He described the land near Duck Creek as good for growing corn, as the Oneida had shown. He mentioned the Oneida living at Duck Creek, and his overall assessment was of good lands, enormous forests, game, and plenty of fish.[32]

On September 21, the commissioners proposed boundaries for lands at Green Bay to accommodate the New York Indians. Their proposition included 275,000 acres on the east side of Fox River and another 6,000 acres, which already included land for the Brothertown of 20,000 acres.

GOING TO WASHINGTON

Yet the issue of land for the New York Indians remained unresolved. In Washington, Quinney presented a statement to the president on behalf of the Stockbridge and Munsee, and the Brothertown also submitted a statement. On December 14, 1830, Quinney presented the following memorial:

GREAT FATHER: Your red children of the Stockbridge and Munsee tribes, who have emigrated from the State of New York to Green Bay, send through me their salutations to you and your wise men, who are sitting around the great council fire to deliberate upon the welfare of your nation, and have entrusted me to make known to you their wishes and their wants. We thank the Great Spirit, who has given us a father, who always attends to the cries of his red children.

Difficulties and doubts have arisen in the minds of our people, in regard to their true situation, which we wish to have settled this winter. We desire to understand our situation fully, and to know what we have to depend upon. It was hoped when the late commissions arrived at Green Bay, that all things would have been finally adjusted, and an allotment of lands made suitable to our wishes and sufficient for agricultural purposes. This, father, so far as our interests are concerned, has not been done.

In the application now made it is intended to set forth the claims and wants of the tribes which I represent, without any connexion with our brethren of the Six Nations; and it may be necessary to explain the origin of our association with them in the negotiations of 1821 and 1822.

Many years ago the Miami and Maumee and other tribes granted to the Stockbridge, Munsee, and Delaware tribes, a large tract of country on White river, in the now Indiana State, whither the Delawares and a portion of our tribes immediately removed, and our people remained there until the late war, when they were obliged to return to the State of New York.

At the restoration of peace we contemplated a reunion of our people upon White river, and a portion of the Stockbridge tribe accordingly fitted out in the year 1818 to go on in advance of the rest; be ere they arrived at the place of their destination, the Delawares alone had sold to the United States, at the treaty of St. Mary's, (Ohio) all the lands which were owned jointly and equally by themselves and their brethren, the Stockbridge and Munsee tribes.

In 1819, the Stockbridge made an application to the Government for redress; in 1820, they renewed their application; and, in 1821, they and the Munsee tribe agreed to relinquish their claim upon the White river to the United States; provided that, besides the payment of three thousand dollars, they should be in assisted in procuring a country somewhere to the westward, and which was to be confirmed to them and their posterity forever.

About this time the Six Nations, and other residents in the State of New York, under the auspices of the United States Government, were deeply engaged in securing a country some where to the westward for their future residence; and the Stockbridge and Munsee tribes having now the same object in view, co-operated with them, and sent a deputation to Green Bay, the same year, supported and protected by an agent from the Government, specially deputed for that purpose. Thus, father, has arisen a connexion, which we have no other objection to, save that we are anxious to urge our stronger claims particularly and alone.

Of the consideration paid to the Winnebagoes and Menomonies for the sale of their lands in 1821 and '22, we contributed the one half; and we think it nothing but proper and fair, that whatever may be your opinion as to quantity, the New York Indians, as a whole, are entitled to, we should receive that proportion rightfully to be expected from the pledges of the Government at the sale of the White river tract, and from the amount of our contributions in the negotiations with our brethren of west.

In the report of the late commission we are set down for six thousand acres, at the Grand Kakalin of Fox river; and were told that if this was insufficient for our wants, a portion of our brethren might cross the river and reside on the tract there allotted to the Oneida and other tribes. To this arrangement we have to oppose the strongest objection; our father is well aware of the inconvenience and injury a separation of this sort would produce; besides which we are now settled on the east side of the river, and have already made, at great expense and hard labor, extensive improvements in clearing land, building houses, mill, &c, &c.

We ask, therefore, father to have allotted to us, the Stockbridge and Munsee tribes, all that portion of land, being a part of the tract the New York Indians proposed to accept of the United States' commissioners in a final adjustment of their claims, comprehended in the following boundaries, viz:

Beginning at the southern boundary line of the purchase, in 1821, from the Winnebagoes and Menomonies; thence, running down the Fox river to the upper or southern line of the cession, made by the New York Indians to the Brothertown Indians in 1825; thence, running east with said line to a point fifteen miles from the river; then, south to the upper or southern boundary line of the purchase of 1821 aforesaid; from thence, northwest along said last mention line to the place of beginning, on Fox river.

We wish moreover to know if the decision of our great father, in the case, will be final, and prevent all further difficulties, and by what tenure we are to hold these lands; this question involves all that is dear and valuable to us. We hope, therefore, that you will inform us certainly and fully.

Father, we wish a home: give us that home: let it be free from intrusion, violence, and the interests of strangers, and we shall be content. We will bless you and teach our children to bless you, and the Good Spirit will bless you.

Father, we understand a question has been made by interested white men, in regard to the validity of our treaty with the Menomonies, in 1822. It is not necessary for us here to enter into a vindication of our proceedings, and to establish the engagements of each party in that transaction as being fair and for ever binding; the ratification by our great father, President Monroe, saves us this. But we wish to lay fast hold of your good opinion, and for this purpose desire that you will ascertain yourself of all circumstances connected with that transaction. To avoid difficulty with our western brethren, we and our confederates, the Six Nations, proposed to the commissioners to relinquish all the rest, provided a small part, (which was then defined) was secured to us forever. The same overture is still made and your concurrence most ardently desired.

Great father, may you live long and rule this nation in peace and happiness.

John W. Quinney,

For and in behalf of the Chiefs and Head-men of the Stockbridge and Munsee tribes.

To his Excellency the President of the United States[33]

Just a few weeks later, the Brothertown submitted their statements:

The petition of the undersigned respectfully showeth, that your
petitioners are of the tribes of Indians called the Mohegan, Montouck,
Stonington, Narragansett, Pequots of Groton, and Nahantic Indians,
who were formerly called the New England Indians; and that we,
the said Indians and our fathers, having procured of our brother, the
Oneida Indians, in the year 1774, a tract of land, then a wilderness,
in the now county of Oneida, and State of New York, where your
petitioners have since resided, by the name of the Brothertown
Indians; that your petitioners immediately after were surrounded by a
dense population of white people; and although agriculture has been
the exclusive pursuit of your petitioners for some generations past,
yet have they experienced many inconveniences, arising from the
smallness of the territory.

They were again induced to turn their attention to the wilderness,
to procure a residence amongst their brethren to the West. In the
year 1809, your petitioners sent a delegation to the Delawares and
Miamies, in the then Territory of Indiana, who agreed for a tract of
land on White river; and in the 1817, they sent another delegation
to the said nations, to renew the covenant by which the Delawares
had conveyed to your memorialists a part of their country on White
river, in the most solemn manner, agreeably to the ancient customs
among Indians. But before your memorialists could remove on to
their newly acquired lands, the Government of the United States
purchased the whole country of the Miamie and Delaware tribes
of Indians; by which purchase, your petitioners lost their country,
and all they had expended in acquiring it; and in the year 1824, the
Stockbridge Indians, and Oneida and other tribes, of the State of New
York, invited your petitioners to join with them, and purchase land
at Green Bay; and having seen the treaties between their brethren,
the New York Indians, and the Winnebago and Menomonie tribes, of
the years 1821 and 1822, for a tract of land at Green Bay, and that the
President had approved and ratified the same, your petitions accepted
the invitations, provided their brethren the Menomonies, would

consent to our purchasing a piece of land of the New York Indians.
And at a council held in September, 1824, by the Menomonies and a
delegation of your petitioners, the Menomonie tribe kindly invited
the Brothertown Indians to come and settle in their country; that the
path was clear, and there was not a bush in their way; and that they
were willing they should purchase the land of the New York Indians,
as had been proposed. And no obstacle appearing, your petitioners
purchased a piece of land, eight miles wide, on Fox river, and thirty
miles long; for which, they paid nine hundred and fifty dollars to
the Menomonies, besides the expense of conveying the goods to
Green Bay, and furnishing provisions to the Menomonie tribe, while
collected to receive the goods, &c., which amounted to four hundred
and fifty or five hundred dollars more.

Your petitioners believed that all parties were mutually satisfied
with the arrangement, and your petitioners were making preparations
to remove to the wilderness of Green Bay, and settle on the lands
they had purchased; but, in the year 1827, Governor Cass and Colonel
Thomas L. McKenney, commissioners on the part of the United States,
made a treaty with the Chippewa, Winnebago, and Menomonie
tribes of Indians, at the Butte de Morts; and the commissioners took a
cession from the Menomonie tribe Indians, of a tract of country about
six miles wide, on each side of the Fox river, from the Grand Kackalin,
or rapids, to its mouth, which included the most valuable part of the
land purchased by your petitioners. But your petitioners were happy
to learn that the President, in his approval of the said treaty, reserved
to the New York Indians all the rights and claims they, or either of
them, had to the lands mentioned in said treaty, as expressed by the
resolution of the honorable the Senate of the United States, on the 19th
February, 1829.

In the same treaty, our brethren, the Menomonies, referred all
their claims to the decision of the President of the United States;
and inasmuch as the Menomonies held a right in common with the
New York Indians in the purchase of 1822, it was desirable to have a
division of the lands, agreeably to the just rights of the parties. To
obtain such division, the New York Indians petitioned the President
to appoint commissioners to make partition of the lands between the

Menomonie and New York Indians, and to assist the New York Indians in dividing their lands among themselves, and for establishing such metes and bounds between them as could be agreed on by the parties.

In compliance with the said petition, the President did appoint the honorable E. Root, James McCall, and John T. Mason, esqrs., commissioners, to make partition of the lands between the New York Indians and the Menomonies. The said commissioners met at Green Bay in August last, and held several councils with our brethren, the Menomonies, and such of our brethren of the State of New York, as were at Green Bay. Our brethren, the Menomines were apparently under the influences of the French, and other inhabitants settled at Green Bay; insomuch, that they would not consent to any reasonable compromise relative to the division of said lands, which they had sold and received their pay for. And it appears that the honorable commissioners thought proper to set apart a tract of land for your petitioners.

Beginning on the east side of Fox river, at the corner made by Thomas Dean, near the foot of the rapids called the Little Kackalin; thence, up Fox river to the mouth of Plum creek, five miles, and extending back this width, south forty-five degrees, east far enough to make twenty thousand acres, being a part of the land which your petitioners purchased and paid for, as above-mentioned.

Your petitioners are not disposed to complain of any unkindness on the part of the honorable commissioners; on the contrary, they avail themselves of this opportunity to assure the President of the high respect they entertain for the honorable gentlemen; but your petitioners cannot do justice to their own feelings, without stating to the President, that they believe that the honorable commissioners were parsimonious in setting of so small a piece of land to your petitioners, inasmuch as it would be but about one-eighth part of what they purchased, and something less than fifty acres to each person.

And were we to estimate the various sums expended by your petitioners in procuring the land, it would amount to about fifty cents per acre, which is nearly as high as the United States sell their land after it has been surveyed, if that part of the twenty thousand acres which is not fit for cultivation be deducted. Therefore, your petitioners pray that the President would be pleased to confirm an extension of said location.

By beginning at the place mentioned by the commissioners, and extending up Fox river eight miles; then, back this width south forty-five degrees, east twelve miles, or so far as to contain sixty-one thousand four hundred, and forty acres; and would be a little less than one hundred and fifty-three acres to each person. And, if that part of it which is unfit for cultivation was excluded, it would be about one hundred acres of tillable land to each person, which your petitioners do not believe is an extravagant quantity for an agriculturalist. Your petitioners take the liberty to mention, that they never anticipated or intended the purchase of a large tract of country for the purpose of hunting, but they purchased the land for themselves and their posterity, for agricultural purpose. That has been the principal pursuit of ourselves and our ancestor for nearly one hundred and fifty years.

Your memorialists believe that the possession of one hundred and fifty or two hundred acres of land for each individual, would rather increase the agricultural enterprise of your memorialist than diminish it. Your petitioners rely on the justice and magnanimity of the Government of the United States, with a full confidence that the President will deal with his red children with parental kindness, and deal justice to them, as their circumstances and equity require.

Your memorialist would further mention, that it would be very desirable to be informed of the pleasure of the President respecting their lands at Green Bay as soon as consistent, inasmuch as your petitioners anticipate having their land surveyed into lots for each individual, as soon as it is ascertained what quantity of land they are permitted to hold. It would be very desirable to your petitioners to have the land which may be set off to them, confirmed to them by an act of Congress, that your petitioners may have a title in fee simple to their lands.

And your petitioners, as in duty bound, will ever pray.
Peace-makers and head-men

RANDALL ABNER,

ELIPHALET MARTHETERS,

WILLIAM DICK,

ASA DICK,

THOMAS DICK,

B.G. FOWLER,

GEORGE CROSBY

JAMES NILES, HIS X MARK

JOSEPH PALMER,

JOHN JOHNSON,

JACOB FOWLER,

JESSE CORRECOMB,

NEWTON MOSSUCK,

JOHN ONION,

AARON POQUINANTRY,

THOMAS COMMUCK,

THOMAS WIATT,

CHARLES SEKETER,

DANIEL WIATT,

DANIEL DICK,

NATHAN PAUL,

CALVIN SCIPIO,

JACOB SINNARD,

SOLOMON PAUL,

WM. CROPLEY

SIMON ADAM

DAVID JOHNSON,

LATHROP DICK,

RODOLPHUS FOWLER,

WM. JOHNSON,

SETH MATHERS,

THEOPHILUS FOWLER,

DAVID SAWSER,

ISSAC WAUBEY

SAML. SKESUCK, JR.

JAMES FOULD

JOHN DICK

SAML. SCIPIO,

ISAAC SCIPIO,

SAML. JAMES
GEORGE SCIPIO
CHARLES ANTHONY.[34]

Despite days of negotiations and submission of a number of proposed boundaries by the commissioners, the Menominee, and the New York Indians, an agreement was not reached. This lack of agreement would result in both the Menominee and the New York Indians going to Washington in 1831 to meet directly with the president to reach a solution. The journey to Washington eventually led to the Menominee treaties of 1831 and 1832 with the United States, which provide a possible solution for land for the New York Indians.

9

1831 TREATY WITH
THE MENOMINEE

Indian Nation to the United States

The issue of land for the New York Indians was not resolved by the three United States commissioners during the 1830 council meeting. As a result, the New York Indians and the Menominee went to Washington in January of 1831 to meet with President Andrew Jackson to resolve the issues on a direct nation-to-nation basis. Memorials to the president were submitted on January 20, 1831. In February 1831, President Jackson authorized the secretary of war, John H. Eaton, and Samuel C. Stambaugh, an Indian agent at Green Bay, to make a treaty with the Menominee that included lands in the amount of five hundred thousand acres for the New York Indians. On February 8, 1831, the treaty, sometimes known as the Treaty of Washington or Stambaugh's Treaty, was made with the Menominee, but when the treaty went to the Senate, it was amended to also provide specific lands for the Stockbridge and Brothertown Nations. The treaty was not approved in that Senate session, so another agreement was made on March 16 with the Menominee.

In July 1831, Stambaugh was sent to obtain approval from the Menominee for the amended treaty and submitted a report with extensive discussions where we hear the voices of the Menominee and New York Indians.

In December 1831, the New York Indians went to Washington to object to this treaty because the five hundred thousand acres did not include adequate agricultural lands. The New York Indians proposed a land exchange with the Menominee, but the Menominee did not agree. George

Bryan Porter, the governor of Michigan Territory, was assigned to meet in council with the New York Indians and the Menominee to resolve the issue. Additionally, the Seneca Nation rejected the continued pressure to remove from New York.

In January 1831, Big Kettle, a representative of the Seneca Nation, wrote to Jackson to express that the Seneca did not wish to leave New York State to settle in Wisconsin:

> TO THE PRESIDENT: We have the honor to say a word to the chief magistrate of the United States. We have come as delegates from the Seneca Nation vested with a legal power to make an inquiry concerning our annuity. We wish to make known to our father, that our chiefs did not give or grant authority to us to take a part of the Green Bay question. They have concurringly rejected this sort of policy. They have made expressed and decisive determination not to remove from their land to another country, believing as they do, that their great father, the President, is constitutionally bound to afford them a protection, according to the letter of our treaties; these treaties, made with much deliberation, ratified by the President in Washington, with the consent of the Senate of the United States. These treaties become public laws of the land: these public laws now stand unrepealed. No State has a right to abrogate and repeal these laws, unless or until both contracting parties give consent, or in the case of violation a treaty.
>
> Rome herself went to the school of a despot; there she learned to give a 'cunning interpretation and breaking treaties.' We presume such institution as this cannot exist within our father's dominion, because he possesses a great knowledge and enlarged understanding; that he will arrest the proceeding of injustice and oppression.
> BIG KETTLE, his X mark
> SENECA WHITE, his X mark
> THOMSON S. HARRIS.[1]

The New York Indians chose representatives to be delegates to Washington, DC, to meet with Congress and President Jackson to voice their proposal of boundaries for the individual New York Indian nations to lands designated for them in the Green Bay area. Among the delegates were John W. Quinney from the Stockbridge and Munsee tribes, David Toucee from the Brothertown tribe, Eleazer Williams from the St. Regis tribe, and Daniel Bread from the Oneida Nation. These delegates presented a letter to President Jackson on January 20, 1831, to explain their position on lands for the New York Indians in Green Bay:

The Memorial of the undersigned delegated from the Oneida, Brothertown, St. Regis, Stockbridge and Munsee Tribe of Indians, respectfully showeth:

That they have received instructions and powers from the Tribes they respectively represent, to repair to the seat of government and make such arrangements and dispositions of their claims to lands at Green Bay, in the Territory of Michigan, with the Executive and Congress of the United States, as to them, the said delegates may seem proper and right.

Your memorialist, in the proposition which they now jointly and unanimously make to your excellency, have abridged their claims to the lowest amount of lands they have estimated to be necessary for the agricultural purposes of their Tribes. To this they have been inducted by their desire to show the government that their purposes in the Treaties of 1821 and 1822 were not those of speculation and extortion; and for the further purpose to preview a good understanding with their brethren, the Menominees.

It will be unnecessary for your memorialists at this time to enter into arguments to show the fairness and binding effect of their treaties with their brethren, the Menominees, or to vindicate their proceedings, throughout this controversy, from many aspersions which have been or may be thrown upon them by individuals personally interested against them. Your memorialists consider that the question of right ought not, and cannot now be agitated for any purpose of destroying their original claims, or of refusing the good will and sanction of the Executive to their present overture.

Your memorialists, however anxious to relieve your mind of any impression unfavorable to their interest, and to maintain the friendly correspondence hitherto enjoyed by them with the government of the United States, have accompanied this memorial with a statement of all the material facts connected with negotiations originated by the direction of the United States under the superintendent of an agent specially deputed for that purpose, and finally, made for ever binding by ratification of President Monroe.

Your memorialists think it necessary to advert to the fact, that, in the treaties of 1821 and '22, it was originally the intention of the tribes they represent, and the policy of this Government, to relieve the State of New York of its entire Indians population, and to provide for the Six Nations, and their confederates, a home in the vicinity of Green Bay, which should belong to them and their posterity forever. In pursuance of this intention, and for the purpose of securing a retreat for our brethren (who are not represented in this negotiation) when their emigration may become necessary, we have concluded to designate that portion of our lands which they can occupy whenever they may choose to dispose of their present possessions and remove.

Your memorialists believe that this course must meet the approbation of the government and will be justified by the speedy removal of all the immigrants of tribes in the State of New York.

Your memorialist therefore, for and in behalf of the Tribes they represent, and with the intent of securing to their brethren (who have not a voice in this transaction) a portion sufficient for their wants, do propose to accept, (as a final settlement of their claims) and they do pray the concurrences and sanctions of your excellency to the following routes and boundaries to wit;

commencing on the east side of Fox river, at a corner made by Thos. Dean, near the foot of the rapids, called the Little Kakalin of Fox River;

thence S.E. 12 miles; thence S.W. 21 miles; thence N.W. 13 miles to Fox River;

thence continuing across Fox River along the said last mentioned line, to a point 30 miles from the river;

thence N.E. 35 miles;

thence S.E 30 miles (more or less) to the mouth of Duck Creek;

thence nearly on the last mentioned S.E. line to the mouth of Fox River, two miles, be the same more or less;

thence S.W. along the Fox River to a point perpendicularly
distant 12 miles from its mouth, be the same more or
less, and opposite to the corner
first above-mentioned as made by Thomas Dean;
thence S.E. across Fox River to the place of beginning.

Your memorialists, in this specification of boundaries, from their
own imperfect, knowledge of the bearing and relations which
different land marks of the country have to each other, have perhaps
given your Excellency but a very vague idea of the extent and
particular location of the tract they desire and claim. By a reference,
however, to the map which accompanies this communication, it will
be seen that they desire to include upon the east side of Fox River, in
round number 161,000 acres, and on the west side 697,000, making
the sum total of 858,000 acres for the whole body of the New York
Indian Tribes. It is believed, from the most accurate census which
has been taken of those Tribes, that their whole members maybe
computed at 5,549; so that throwing aside fractional difference, the
lands called for as above, will be in the proportion of 150 acres to each
individual. From this, subtracting the number of acres which never
can be used or improved there will remain about 120 acres per head of
soil fit for the purposes of agriculture.

Your memorialists have taken into consideration the subject of
a community of property in these lands, and they unanimously
conclude upon reasons of propriety and necessity, that to each tribe
there should be a specific allotment, which shall be treated and
disposed of as such Tribe may deem proper, without the consent or
interference of any other nation or interest. It must be apparent to
the slightest reflection, that the diversity of interest and pursuit —
the extreme difference in language, custom, improvement, and
institutions of every kind of the individual tribes, one from another —
will render any attempt at amalgamation hopeless and destructive.
It would, indeed, place us in circumstances infinitely worse than
our present situation, surrounded as we are by a pressure of white
population, which is continually urging us from existence. It will be
in vain that your Excellency shall have interfered for the settlement
of our difficulties with the Menominees, and asserted the right of the

New York Indians to lands at Green Bay, if we shall be left to the more
fearful consequences of jarring and disunion amongst ourselves.

For these reasons we have unanimously settled the metes and
bounds of particular tracts for each tribe now represented (reserving
a proper portion for the use of such of our brother as may come after
us) to wit:

> commencing on the East Side of Fox River, at a corner made by
> Thomas Dean, near the foot of the rapids called Little Kaklin,
> and extending up Fox River 8 miles; thence back this width
> south 45 (degrees), east 12 miles, or so far as to contain 61,440
> acres; this division for the Brothertown Indians. From which,
> excluding that part which is unfit for cultivation, there would
> be about 100 acres per head of tillable land.

By extending the two lines of the Brothertown tract just mentioned,
which are parallel with the river to the upper or the southern line of
the purchase of 1821, by the New York Indians from the Menominees
and Winnebagoes, and including all lands on the river, the tract
is defined which we have allotted to the Stockbridge and Munsee
Tribes, who reside together, and whose interest cannot be separated;
and having subtracted the useless from the improvable land, there
will be formed to be about 110 acres per head.

The tract for the Oneidas and St. Regis Tribes is located on the
west side of the Fox River, between the mouth of Duck Creek, and a
point one mile above the mouth of Apple Creek, excluding therefrom
the lands occupied by the United States garrison, all private land
claims confirmed, and a piece at the Little Kaklin, understood to be
rightfully owned and claimed by M.H. Williams, wife of the Rev.
E. Williams; then assuming the distance between the two aforementioned points, as a base, or perpendicular, going back at right
angles from the given course of Fox River, on this width, so far as to
include 240,250 acres of land. The division of this tract between the
Oneida and St Regis Indians, to be in the following manner;

> Beginning at the upper line of private land claims confirmed
> No. 29, on the west side of Fox River, near the Rapids
> Des Peres;

thence N.W. on said line to the S.W. corner of said land claim,
No. 29;

thence up Fox River parallel with its course. 4½ miles;

thence back N.W. parallel with the upper and lower boundaries
of the Oneida and St Regis locations, to

the N.W. boundary of the same. The upper division

to be for the St. Regis Indians.

Your memorialists would further state, that these amicable
arrangements are made at this time with the view of having the
concurrence and sanction of your excellency, and such further
ratification as in your wisdom may be deemed necessary to bar all
future contest and difficulties.

Your memorialists would suggest the propriety of your
Excellency's immediately presenting all the arrangements and
overtures here in contained, (should they meet your approbation)
to Congress, for its confirmation, at this session, in order that the
business may be finally adjusted beyond all controversy, and we once
more be permitted to abide in the assurance that a home is provided
for us and our children, this the kind mediation of the Government of
this free and happy Union.

Your memorialists are fully sensible, that in a great measure your
Excellency has now at your disposal their destinies for happiness or
misery, and deeply impressed with the conviction of the integrity and
fairness of your Excellency's purposes.

They, as in duty bound, will every pray etc.etc

John W. Quinney

Delegate from the Stockbridge and Munsee Tribes

David Toucee

Delegate from the Brothertown Tribe

Eleazer Williams

Delegate from the St. Regis Tribe

Daniel Bread

Delegate from the Oneida Nation.

Test: S.W. Beall

City of Washington January 20th, 1831[2]

Two weeks later, on February 1, 1831, Jackson authorized Eaton and Stambaugh to make a treaty with the Menominee. Jackson wrote:

> You are specially authorized and directed to enter into some amicable arrangement with the Menomonie tribe of Indians, now at the city of Washington, for a settlement of their dispute with the New York Indians, and to obtain from them such cessions of country as may appear just and reasonable, and also such portions of their country as they may be disposed to cede to the United States. Given under my hand.
>   ANDREW JACKSON[3]

This treaty was conducted in Washington, DC, with eleven Menominee chiefs and head men signing the document. In this treaty, the boundaries of Menominee lands are defined, and the boundaries of their cession of 2.5 million acres were defined, with 500,000 acres designated for the New York Indians. The United States and the Menominee Nation did not allow the New York Indians to be involved in the 1831 treaty. The signatures on the treaty do not include any New York Indians.

In the first article, the Menominee declare they are friends and allies of the United States:

> Under whose parental care and protection they desire to continue; and although always protesting that they are under no obligation to recognize any claim of the New York Indians to any portion of their country; that they neither sold nor received any value, for the land claimed by these tribe; yet, at the solicitation of their Great Father, the President of the United States, and as an evidence of their love and veneration for him, they agree that such part of the lands described, being within the following boundaries as he may direct, may be set apart as a home to the several tribe of the New York Indians, who may remove to, and settle upon the same, within three years from the date of this agreement, viz:
>> Beginning on the west side of Fox river, near the 'Little Kackalin,' at a point known as the 'Old Mill Dam"; thence northwest forty miles, thence northeast to the Oconto Creek, falling into Green Bay; thence down said Oconto creek to Green

Territory ceded by the Menominee in the Treaty of 1831
ORIGINALLY PUBLISHED IN *FAITH IN PAPER: THE ETHNOHISTORY AND LITIGATION OF UPPER GREAT LAKES INDIAN TREATIES* BY CHARLES CLELAND, COPYRIGHT 2011 UNIVERSITY OF MICHIGAN PRESS

Bay; thence up and along Green Bay and Fox River to the place of beginning.

The treaty defines boundaries for military purposes, timber and firewood resources, and land for public highways. The treaty designates five hundred thousand acres for the New York Indians, at the rate of one hundred acres per person for those New York Indians actually settled on the land:

The country hereby ceded to the United Sates, for the benefit of the New York Indians, contains by estimation about five hundred

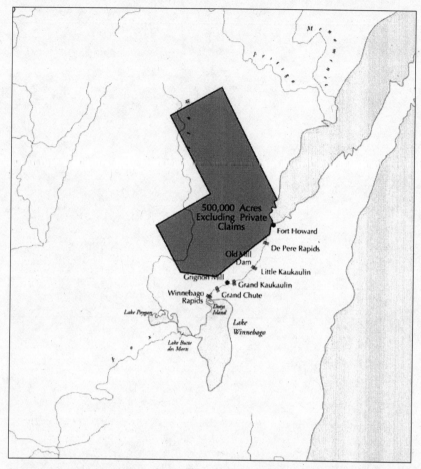

Approximate location of the land cession for New York Indians in the final version of the 1831 treaty

ORIGINALLY PUBLISHED IN *FAITH IN PAPER: THE ETHNOHISTORY AND LITIGATION OF UPPER GREAT LAKES INDIAN TREATIES* BY CHARLES CLELAND, COPYRIGHT 2011 UNIVERSITY OF MICHIGAN PRESS

thousand acres, and includes all their improvements on the west side of Fox river. As it is intended for a home for the several tribes of the New York Indians, who may be residing upon the lands at the expiration of three years from this date, and for none others, the President of the United States is hereby empowered to apportion the lands among the actual occupants at that time, so as not to assign to any tribe a greater number of acres than may be equal to one hundred for each soul actually settled upon the lands, and if, at the time such apportionment, any lands shall remain unoccupied by any tribe of

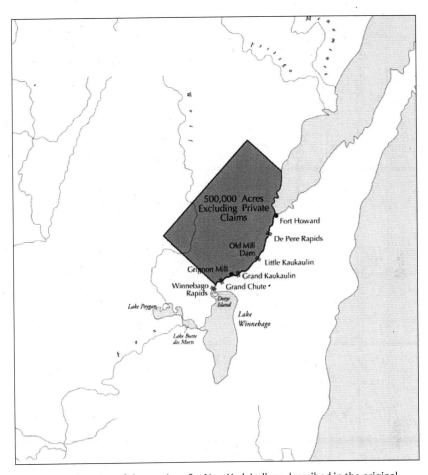

Approximate location of the cessions for New York Indians described in the original
version of the treaty of 1831
ORIGINALLY PUBLISHED IN *FAITH IN PAPER: THE ETHNOHISTORY AND LITIGATION OF UPPER GREAT
LAKES INDIAN TREATIES* BY CHARLES CLELAND, COPYRIGHT 2011 UNIVERSITY OF MICHIGAN PRESS

the New York Indians, such portions as would have belonged to said
Indians, had it been occupied, shall revert to the United States.[4]

Article 2 states that for the cession of land to the New York Indians, the
United States will pay the Menominee twenty thousand dollars, with five
thousand dollars to be paid in August 1831. The remaining would be paid
at the rate of five thousand dollars per year, "which sums shall be applied
to the use of the Menomonees, after such manner as the President of the
United States may direct." Thus, the president retained control of monies

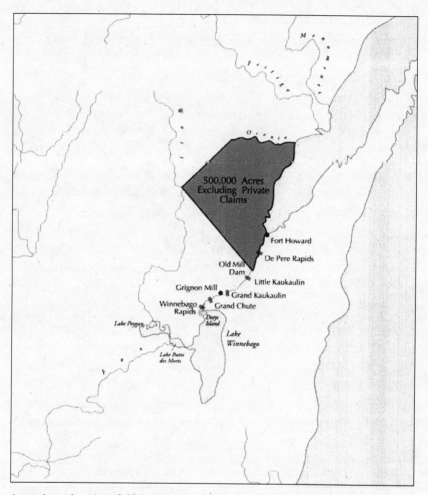

Approximate location of the land cession for New York Indians proposed as a US Senate amendment to the 1831 treaty

ORIGINALLY PUBLISHED IN *FAITH IN PAPER: THE ETHNOHISTORY AND LITIGATION OF UPPER GREAT LAKES INDIAN TREATIES* BY CHARLES CLELAND, COPYRIGHT 2011 UNIVERSITY OF MICHIGAN PRESS

for the Menominee, which looks like an annuity but keeps control of the funds in the hands of the government.

Article 3 describes the boundaries of this cession. Whether the figure included the five hundred thousand acres for the New York Indians is not clear. Article 4 defines a tract of land the Menominee reserved for their future homes. The United States was determined to make the Menominee into farmers, so the government designated funding for farmers, teachers, building houses, household articles, horses, cows, hogs, sheep, and farming utensils, clothing, flour, interpreters, blacksmith shops, and schools.

The United States designated six thousand dollars to build, on the Fox River, a grist mill and saw mill for the benefit of the Menominee, at annual pay of six hundred dollars. If the grist and saw mills produced more than the Menominee needed, the rest could be sold and the money would go to the Green Bay Indian agency.

In Article 6, it is stated that the Menominee "shall be at liberty to hunt and fish on the lands they have now ceded to the United States, on east side of Fox River and Green Bay until the land is surveyed and offered for sale by the President."

Finally, the chiefs and warriors of the Menominee "solemnly pledge themselves to preserve peace and harmony between their people" and the US. If they did not keep this pledge and allied with others, they would forfeit the protection of the United States and all annuities would stop. Therefore, the Menominee had great confidence in "their great father, the President of the United States" to fulfill the terms of this treaty.

The Menominee chiefs requested that the land designated for the New York Indians be submitted to the New York Indians for their approval and, if they refused to accept the lands set aside, they would be removed from Menominee lands. If they agreed, "the Menomonee tribe as dutiful children of the great father the President, will take them by the hand as brothers, and settle down with them in peace and friendship."

The treaty was signed on February 8, 1831, by Eaton and Stambaugh for the United States. The Menominee signatures included the following representatives:

Kaush-kau-no-naïve, grizzly bear, his X mark
A-ya-mah-taw, fish spawn, his X mark
Ko-ma-ni-kin, big wave, his X mark
Ko-ma-ni-kee-no-shah, little wave, his X mark
O-ho-pa-shah, little whoop, his X mark
Ah-ke-na-pa-weh, earth standing, his X mark
Shaw-wan-noh, the south, his X mark
Mash-ke-wet, his X mark
Pah-she-nah-sheu, his X mark
Chi-mi-na-na-quet, great cloud, his X mark

A-na-quet-to-a-peh, setting in a cloud, his X mark
Sha-ka-cho-ka-mo, great chief, his X mark

The witnesses were R. A. Forsyth, C. A. Grignon, and the list of interpreters:

A.G. Ellis,
Richard Pricket, United States Interpreter, his x mark
William Wilkins of Pennsylvania, Samuel Swartwout, of N. York
John T. Mason, Michigan
Rh. M. Johnson, Kentucky

Just a few weeks later, on February 17, the Senate made changes to the treaty, and it was approved with the amendments.

The revisions to the first article changed the removal within three years to leaving it to the president to "prescribe the time for the removal and settlement of the New York Indians upon the lands." The president could "apportion" the land among the New York Indians, and if they didn't settle all the land, it "shall be, and remain the property of the United States." The second change reinforced the change to the removal time frame being left up to the president, and further loss of land to the United States if the land wasn't settled.

After the signatures, there is a note:

Note. — this treaty was ratified with the following Proviso contained in the Resolution of the Senate: Amendment

Provided, That for the purpose of establishing the rights of the New York Indians, on a permanent and just footing, the said treaty shall be ratified with the express understanding that two townships of land on the east side of Winnebago lake equal to forty-six thousand and eight acres shall be laid of (to commence at some point to be agreed on,) for the use of the Stockbridge and Munsee tribes; and that the improvements made on the lands now in the possession of the said tribes on the east side of the Fox river, which said lands are to be relinquished, shall, after being valued by a commissioner to be appointed by the President of the United States, be paid for by the Government;

Provided, however, that the valuation of such improvements shall not exceed the sum of twenty-five thousand dollars; and that there shall be one township of land, adjoining the foregoing, equal to twenty-three thousand and forty acres, laid off and granted for the use of the Brothertown Indians who are to be paid, by the Government the sum of one thousand six hundred dollars for the improvements on the lands now in their possession, on the east side of Fox River, and which lands are to be relinquished by said Indians:

Also, that a new line shall be run, parallel to the southwestern boundary line, or course of the tract of five hundred thousand acres described in the first article of this treaty, and set apart for the New York Indians, to commence at a point on the west side of the Fox river, and one mile above the Grand Shute on Fox River, and at a sufficient distance from the said boundary line as established by the said first article, as shall comprehend the additional quantity of two hundred thousand acres of land, on and along the west side of Fox river, without including any of the confirmed private land claims on the Fox river, and which two huindred thousand acres shall be part of the five hundred thousand acres intended to be set apart for the Six Nations of the New York Indians and the St. Regis tribe; and that an equal quantity to that which is added on the southwestern side shall be taken off from the northeastern side of the said tract, described in that article, on the Oconto Creek, to be determined by a Commissioner, to be appointed by the President of the United States; so that the whole number of acres to the Six Nations, and St. Regis tribe of Indians, shall not exceed the quantity originally stipulated by the treaty.

On March 16, the Menominee were informed in an agreement with Eaton and Stambaugh that the treaty "by which certain portions of their lands on Fox River and Green Bay were ceded to the United States," wasn't acted upon in the Senate session, but would be on the agenda for the next Senate session. When the Menominee delegation to Washington returned home, they were to receive presents worth five thousand dollars. An interpreter's house and blacksmith shop at Green Bay for the benefit of the Menominee was funded at eight hundred dollars. For medical aid, two hundred dollars per year was allotted to begin in 1831. Six thousand dollars was to be paid to the Menominee as a result of the government's "failure in fully accomplishing an arrangement which would have settled the long existing disputes between the Menomonies and New York Indians." This six thousand dollars was to be taken out of funds stipulated in the treaty.

The Menominee asked the president to inform the Winnebago that none of the land ceded in 1827 treaty at Butte des Morts belonged to the Winnebago and they stressed as well that it was

> important for the safe transaction of business with the agents of the United States, that the Menomonie nation should have an interpreter who can understand and speak their language." This interpreter would be in addition to the current US interpreter who speaks the Chippewa language only.

The signatures on the March 16, 1831, treaty included Eaton and Stambaugh and several Menominee representatives:

Kaush-kau-nau-nein, Grizzle Bear, his X mark	
Aya-ma tau,	X
O ho-pa-shak, Small Whoop	X
Koma-ni-kin, Big Wave	X
Koma-ni-kin-no-sa, Small Wave	X
Ah-ke-ne-pa-weh, Standing Earth	X
Mash-ke-wet	X
Shau-aunno, South	X
Che-mi-na-no-gwet, Cloud	X
Pa sha nah sheuh	X
Che-ea-cho-ke-mah, the Chief	X[5]

Several months later, the Brothertown, Stockbridge-Munsee, and Oneida wrote to the governor of New York expressing their views on the history of their right to land for the New York Indians and their opposition to the treaty made between the Menominee Nation and the United States.

They expressed their frustration throughout the history of these treaties and their feeling the US government was not supporting them. They asked the governor to investigate the issues and take the information to their senators in Congress. They wrote:

We the undersigned are delegates from several of the New York Tribes of Indians and desire to say a few words to your Excellency in reference to the present crisis of our affairs. Being in circumstances of distress and passing through the state of New York on our way home a proper oration is offered to make known our situation and to ask your advice and assistance. We have never heretofore appealed to your government in vain, we have lived long under its protection and enjoyed the happiness which its regulations afforded and we feel assured and elevated in the hope that our present application will be heard.

We are returning from a visit to Washington which was undertaken with the approbation of the Stambaugh Indian Agent at Green Bay, in the view of settling our difficulties with the Menominees. After the ineffectual, and unsatisfactory decision of the commissioner appointed by the President during the last year, it was thought expedient that a delegation from both of the contending parties should accompany him to the seat of Government there to discuss and settle the question of boundary, the merits of this question and the origin of our claims to lands in the vicinity of Green Bay. Your Excellency must be well acquainted with, but that you may understand every circumstance belonging to the subject and be fully ascertained of the correctness of our conduct and that you may perceive the propriety of our appeal to the State of New York at the present time. We have accompanied this communication with an exposition of the whole case. Showing the authority which supported us in our negotiation with the Western Indians, the views and policy of Genl. Government in our removal.

The inducements which were offered the opposition of individuals at Green Bay, the prompt interference of the War department in our behalf. The ratification of our contracts the subsequent intrigues of certain persons which operating on the ignorance and cupidity of the Menominees, produced a feeling of jealousy and distrust which has

never been allayed and which has originated the present difficulty.
The attack upon our rights by the commissioners of 1827, the refusal
of the Senate to assist in impairing those rights, and the proceedings
of the commissioners appointed the last year by the President to settle
the controversy. We do not err in saying that no step has even been
taken in any of our negotiations in opposition to the views earnest
wishes of the Government. We could have no notion in relinquishing
our pleasant situation in the State of New York, in changing a certain
inheritance in lands which we were bound by every tie of interest and
feeling for an uncertain possession in the cold region of the North West
unless we had been induced by the strongest assurances of support and
by our desire to relieve the State of New York of its Indian population.

We felt the importance of this measure for our own preservation
and were convinced of its necessity be representation of Agents both
in and out of the Government. We were reminded of our dreadful
situation surrounded by a pressure of the White population which was
continually encroaching upon our possessions and bringing with it
vices and evils which corrupted our young men and were urging us as
a people from existence. That our lands were valuable, situated in the
heart of New York and were needed for the settlement and growth of
the State.

That we had made extensive purchases from the Western Tribes
which had been sanctioned by proper authority, that our emigration
was a favorite policy with the Executive, that the territory we had
bought unquestionably belonged to us and our children, and that faith
of the Government was pledged to support us there in. These offers
were generous, our former dealing had not led us to expect duplicity
and we concluded that there was no sufficient reason to prevent
removal. A part of our Tribes accordingly emigrated and others are
now disposing of their lands with the same object in view — thereby
everything that is dear and valuable to them. We will not believe
that being brought by such means into circumstances of peril and
difficulty, Your Excellency will now desert us when assistance is most
necessary. Your Excellency after this development of the causes which
led us to emigrate to Green Bay will hardly credit the information that
attempts are now making to eject us entirely from the country, that

we are charged with deceit and double dealing in the acquisition of the land and that impelled by motives of speculation and, extortion we were anxious to build our own fortunes upon the ruin of Menominees, the charges are not only current among individuals personally interested against us but we have just reason to believe that they are attended to and believed by the present Secretary of War.

It is affirmed in the first place that in our treaties with the Menominees they did not understand what we required, and what they gave, and secondly that no consideration was ever paid for the lands conveyed. In reply we state that we acted under the direction of an Agent deputed by the Government of the United States to superintend the negotiation. That the object on our part was fully understood by him, that he used his influence to ascertain who were the chiefs of the Menominee Nation and to collect them together, that the best interpreters in the county were sworn and employed to explain properly what was the object of the mission and that after the proposals were made and the treaty completed no explanation were sought or complaints of misunderstanding heard.

We say over that in the Treaty of 1822, it was not contemplated by the New York Indians to purchase further down the Fox River or a greater width of country that from the Northern line of the purchase of 1821 to the Rapides des Peres and that when the Menominees were informed of our wishes in this respect they desired us to extend the limits and to take a conveyance of a tenancy in common with them to nearly their whole country North East of the first purchase alleging as a reason, that they feared the White people that to use their own strong language, the knives of the pale men were sharp and their nails were long and when fastened upon the lands of the Indian they went deep and held fast. They feared their own ability, to keep them off and wished us, who were better able to cope with them, to have an interest in the soil and thus prevent any frauds which might there after be practiced.

We produced further their treaties signed by respectable witnesses and their receipts for the payment of the purchase money. We show all the evidence which can be given in cases of this kind and far greater and more conclusive than can be produced to substantiate many of the contracts between the United States and different Indian Tribes, but it is said that the smallness of the consideration furnished grounds for belief that there was fraud in the transaction, we deny the fact that if the price was not a full and sufficient consideration for the interest conveyed, it was nevertheless not so trifling as to warrant any such presumption. We paid a sum that the US authority themselves having the immediate control and direction of the bargain considered a proper compensation. It was more than double the price paid from the Treasury of the Union for the same extent of the Indian's lands in some of the rich and fertile regions of the South. But should this presumption be held conclusive against us, we call upon the Government to discharge their long account for lands bought of our tribes in different States and for which we have as yet received no satisfaction, we will then be enabled and cheerfully willing to pay to the "poor savages of the west the full value of his acres even ten times told."

The country around Green Bay in 1822 was not in demand, the project of the Huron territory not thought of a supposititious market had not then been raised the growing importance and value of the lands. The Menominees were not then heard to complain their hard bargain nor would they now but for intrigues which operate on their cupidity and induce them to measure the most bare and detestable. It has been said of us that we desired the ruin of the Menominees that our plans were laid for purposes of speculation, and that we have worked upon their simplicity for our advantage and their destruction, this is ungenerous and untrue. On this subject we have begged the most critical scrutiny. We have published a detailed statement of the whole transaction showing that our conduct was induced and guided by the agency of the Government and if any error or sin has been committed we are not to be held accountable. It was not originally our intention or desire to emigrate, we resisted until overcome by the superior address of White men who promised us what has never been fulfilled. We were to have peace and protection. A territory was to be set off for the exclusive occupancy of the remnants of Tribes in the State of New York free from the destroying influence and intrusion of strangers, instead of finding a fulfillment of these engagements, we are left exposed to the arts calumnies of designing white men charged with fraud and extortion, and measures are taken to drive us from the country. These difficulties have not originated, nor have they been protracted and embittered by any pertinacious conduct on our part. There have been frequent opportunities when the Government might and should have investigated the subject and produced a settlement.

When our lands were wrongfully bought by the commissioners of 1827, the President and Senate in their constitutional action on that treaty might have ascertained and defined the rights of all parties, this was not done but the subject left more perplexed by the conditional ratification of the acts of the Commissioners thus prolonging the controversy and inviting a renewal of the attacks and calumnies which for years had depressed and harassed us. Commissioners were appointed the last year by the President to adjust the matter with certain instructions prohibited them from concluding upon any principle of Equity or Justice. The treaties under which our rights arise were . . . from their consideration. A boundary was to be fixed and lands allotted to us not from any right by purchase, but from the generous permission of the Menominees given in a written reference of their cause to the President. These commissioners were to decide upon fact and reasons wholly foreign from the subject, if your Excellency will examine this part of the subject it will be found the US and not the Menominees were chiefly interested. If our treaties are really fraudulent and inefficiencies we are not willing to receive anything from the charity of the Menominees. We are not disposed to receive a title to their lands upon any other principal than of fair purchase and right, but we ask who is now competent to decide upon the character of these contracts. President Monroe has ratified them solemnly and the Senate has recognized them at different times is it true that the present Executive can be a tribunal of appeal from the acting of a power every way equal to itself and can the fairness of our purchases be questioned at this day.

How easily and readily would the contest have ended, if treaties had constituted the basis of the negotiations of the last year, or if the Commissioners had been empowered to investigate and decide upon their merits. So firmly, however, were they convinced of their efficacy, that Gen. Root and Judge McCall felt constrained to express their opinions and entered into agreement to show their legal and binding effect.

In our late visit to Washington, the whole subject was before the department of war, our treaties and the reports of the Comm. substantiating they were there. The Menominees had submitted to the decision of the President and were present to subscribe any arrangement which might have made, but nothing was done satisfactorily and in the spirit of proper mediation after we had relinquished three fourth of our claim and agreed to receive 876,000 acres, in final satisfaction for the accommodation of all the remnants of tribes in the State of New York. It was required that we should submit unconditionally to the decision of the Secretary of War. This we refused to do and respectfully stated our reasons, at this stage all communication ceased and in a few days a treaty between the Menominees and the US was announced in which were not consulted nor our claims recognized. We are not accurately informed of all the provisions of this treaty but we have good reasons to believe that 200,000 acres are conveyed to the US for consideration of 90,000 dollars and that the Menominees although always denying our rights for the love and veneration they entertain toward their Great Father consent to give us 500,000 acres for the consideration of $20,000 to be paid them by the United States. This treaty has gone before the Senate for its ratification at its next session.

We have remonstrated and endeavored to show its illegal unjust and oppressive features. This cession is loaded with conditions alike odious, degrading and insecure with which no diligence or perseverance belonging to an Indian could possibly comply and in its operation must produce our entire expulsion from the country. We refer your Excellency to an extract from this Treaty herewith transmitted for your inspection. We are told that some of the terms are modified in our favor but to what extent we have no knowledge. The Secretary of War has repeatedly declared that the Government did not need this land. That he was anxious we should have a home and our just claims be satisfied, why then does he become instrumental in defeating our title by accepting a second conveyance to the benefit of the United States of the lands which had previously

been conveyed to us under the direction of a former administration.
Why does he thus volunteer in the work of our destruction? It needed
but a word to the Menominees to produce a final settlement, they
did not act in this late treaty from the suggestions of their own free
will and pleasure, nor had they on leaving their homes the slightest
instruction from their tribes or intention of their own to dispose
of their Territory. They have ever urged its small extent as being
inadequate to their accommodation and insufficiently for their wants.
It was only necessary for the Agent to tell them that terms had been
offered by the Government and it would be well for them to accept
to produce their entire acquiescence, on the other hand had he told
them that the Government recognized the claims of their brethren
the New York Indians they have been equally submissive. But there
were no exertions used to effect a compromise. The parties were
studiously kept asunder and in the meantime an active intercourse
was maintained through the Agent between the Government and the
Menominees.

What have we done to deserve this treatment, we have been the
friends and allies of the United States through the old and the last
war, the bones of our warriors lie mingled on many battle grounds
with those of your brave men. We have preserved the talks of
Washington to our Chiefs inviting and entreating assistance, when
we were strong and you were in trouble. These things are forgotten
while the Menominees your enemies! Who presided over the
massacres at Chicago and Fort Croghan and have ever been ready to
desolate your frontier settlements, are caressed and enriched at our
cost. We are prepared to have the worst part and ungenerous remarks
upon our course in this letter to your Excellency by men who from
party real or in difference to the federal Executive, care nothing for
our destiny. Who will probably represent that we are operated upon
by the intrigues of White men to make such a statement of our as will
throw odium on the government.

We solemnly disclaim and deny any such motive. We have no
personal feelings of hostility toward the Secretary of War, we
know that he has incautiously imbibed prejudices from false and
bane misstatements. Reposing the most implicit confidence in

the President, we are nevertheless persuaded that he does not comprehend the merits of this controversy, his pressing engagements render it impossible that all the necessary information on the subject should pass from the War Department in review before him the mind of the Secretary being preoccupied with untrue representation from men who should have been disinterested communicates its impressions to him upon which without time for proper investigation he is obligated to act. We repose too much confidence in his integrity and friendship to believe that being once fully ascertained of all the facts connected with this transaction he would sanction any proceedings defeating or improving our just claims. But we protest against this late treaty as being inconsistent with the public faith and tending to destroy our prospect of peace and a home at Green Bay.

Approaching your Excellency with a solemn convocation of the truth of this allegation we entreat that you will submit this subject to the legislature of the State of New York at the commencement of its next session with a recommendation that their Senators and Representative in Congress, be instructed to investigate the subject and to guard our rights from any violation which may be intended, further that your Excellency will take such other steps as in your wisdom may be deemed proper to promote the cause of justice, and advance the interest of the unfortunate people the undersigned represent.

Done at Brothertown in General Council this 13th day of April in the year of 1831.

Legged by

David Tower Delegate from Brothertown Tribe

John W. Quinney Delegate from Stockbridge-Munsee Tribes, and

Daniel Bread Delegate from Oneida Tribe[6]

In May 1831, the Munsee petitioned Eaton, expressing their desire to relocate to Green Bay. The acting chiefs wrote:

We John Locke and Samuel Harris, Chiefs, acting for that portion of the Munsee Nation or Tribe of Indians who reside in the vicinity of Cattaraugus Creek in the State of New York.

Represent to their father the Secretary of War, That the Munsees have long desired to remove to Green Bay to the lands allotted to their Nation with their Brethren the Stockbridge Indians.

The Munsees on Cattaraugus Creek are bout eighty in number, consisting of twelve families — They are poor — They reside upon Lands of the Sencecas and receive no monies from the State or National Governments.

We have at the request of our people called upon our father James Styker of Buffalo who is the agent for the New York Indians emigrating to Green Bay, and we have asked him to lay our case before the Secretary of War, or our great father the President.

There are with us at Cattaraugus fifteen Stockbridge Indians who desire also to remove to Green Bay but have not the means.

We have no money — no Lands in this State — no claims Upon the State, and we are living upon the favor of the Senecas.

We ask for help, and desire the Secretary to state our situation to our Great father the President, that he may direct the agent at Buffalo, whom we know, and who has our confidence to aid us in removing to Green Bay where our brethren are. If the kind hand of the Government be extended to us in this our helpless condition, we shall ever be grateful.

Dated May 12th 1831

In the Presence of John his X mark Locke

Samuel his X mark Harris

A.L. Baee

James Strykery

Signed by

Ghus karan his X mark or Walking

Capt. Brie his X mark Ellis[7]

Stambaugh met with the Menominee Nation in Wisconsin on July 18, 1831, to obtain their approval of the 1831 treaty provisions as required in the treaty. He documented the struggles between the Menominee and New York Indians in establishing boundaries, and he submitted his report to the secretary of war.

Stambaugh covers three topics within his report to the secretary of war. First is a historical overview of the issues from 1810 up to the 1831 meeting. Second, Stambaugh expresses his opinions, which do not favor the New York Indians. And third, he expresses his support for the treaty to be ratified. Stambaugh does not provide any of the interactions with the Menominee. Included as an appendix is the report of A. G. Ellis on the July 18, 1831, meeting, in which Ellis included two speeches by Menominee chiefs.

Stambaugh's report on the July 18 meetings with the Menominee begins with an introduction and with Stambaugh's instructions, received April 21, to let the Menominee know that the February 8 treaty was not acted on by the Senate, but would be considered in the next meeting of the Senate. He was instructed "to endeavor to suppress all disagreements and unkind feelings arising upon this subject, and awaken them to a disposition of living in amity with the United States, and resting satisfied and contented until the want they have signified in the concluded Treaty, can be heard, understood, and acted upon." He was to distribute presents among the Menominee when the Menominee left Washington.[8]

When Stambaugh met with the Menominee on July 18, he saw the "largest assemblage of Indians every known within this agency; and comprised every chief of the Menomine nation, with one exception." Stambaugh claimed that the purpose of this meeting was to explain the history of the dispute with the New York Indians and the treaty arrangement with the United States.

In the report, Stambaugh said he was unbiased and did not favor one tribe over the other; however, he expressed his own negative opinion of the New York Indians throughout the document. He said he just wanted to settle the issues that had been going on for ten years. He intended to submit "all proofs and allegations adduced by the New York Indians, with the simple, but earnest response of the Menominies, before the Government, for its consideration and final decision." His historical overview of events begins with 1810 and President James Madison's approval of the New York Indians' request to move to the west in 1815, and Secretary of War William H. Crawford's approval on February 16, 1816. It is quite clear that the US government sanctioned the New York Indians request to move west, as the goal of both New York State and the US government was to remove all Indians west of the Mississippi River.

Stambaugh then reviewed the August 18, 1821, treaty made between the Menominee and the Winnebago on one hand, and the New York Indians on the other. He estimated the land ceded to the New York Indians was 860,000 acres, for which the New York Indians were to pay two thousand dollars. The second treaty was made February 9, 1822, for 6,720,000 acres. Stambaugh stressed that the treaty "gives the Menomonies the right to occupy them [the lands] in common" with the New York Indians.

Another Indian nation–to–Indian nation treaty happened in January 1825, among Six Nations, St. Regis, Stockbridge, and Munsee, in which they ceded some of the lands from the 1822 treaty to the Brothertown, who paid $950 to the Menominee. This 1825 treaty offended the Menominee, who thought they were sharing the land with the New York Indians and who did not believe that the New York Indians had any right to sell some of the land. The Menominee had expressed their position, saying the principal chiefs were not present and did not sign the 1821 and 1822 treaties. A petition by the Menominee Nation in 1824 and affidavits of people living in the area who attended the treaties "prove that this tribe did not intend to sell their country."[9]

Stambaugh summarized the 1831 treaty provisions of five hundred thousand acres for the New York Indians and a payment of twenty thousand dollars to the Menominee. He described his efforts to obtain agreements to settle this matter and maintain peace, but all efforts failed, writing:

John W. Quinney pronounced the decision of that tribe [Stockbridge] not to submit the matter to the President, unless the right of an appeal to Congress was reserved, if his decision would not be found satisfactory to them. Mr. Eleazer Williams, who was also present and interpreted for the Oneidas, gave the same decisions for that tribe. Delegates from the New York tribes, you are aware, however, proceeded to Washington last winter, and were present at the treaty made with the Menomonies.

Next, Stambaugh presented his opinions. He argued that the 1821 and 1822 treaties were not legal, based on "An Act to Regulate Trade and Intercourse with Indians Tribes," passed on March 30, 1802. He quoted the section that says any purchase of Indians lands "shall be of any validity, in law or equity, unless the same be made by treaty or convention, entered into pursuant to the Constitution." A section of the US Constitution authorizes the president to make treaties with consent of two-thirds of the Senate. Next, he stated that Charles C. Trowbridge, who negotiated the 1821 treaty, and John Sergeant, who negotiated the 1822 treaty, were not appointed to negotiate these treaties. This is outright false, as there are documents affirming their appointments. Stambaugh believed that since these treaties were not sent to the Senate, they had "no validity in law or equity" and were not binding. He did not address the fact that the president signed these treaties and did not send the treaties to the Senate because they were made Indian nation to Indian nation.

Stambaugh boldly asserted that William H. Crawford, and later John C. Calhoun and Lewis Cass, were only being kind to the Indians when they approved the negotiation of these treaties. He also stated that surely the government did not think six million acres would be ceded. Stambaugh also debunked the influence of the French on the Menominee. He proposed that all treaties should be made in Washington because the government would not have to feed all the tribal members who attended and it would avoid the possibility of outside influence, and prevent the Indians asking for presents. He was very upset about the charges of "improper influence" on the Indians. He maintained the New York Indians asked to remove, were approved to do so, and that the US paid their expenses; therefore, he did not see any improper influence or actions to support the petitions of the New York Indians having been wronged. He referred to the John W. Quinney speech in which Quinney referred to "principles of law, justice and common humanity." He was adamantly opposed to these arguments. He said this was an issue between Indian tribes. The complaint of undue influence by Green Bay residents was addressed, and he condemned the military being ordered to deal with it. Stambaugh also insisted the New York Indians had been influenced by outside advisors. In an interesting chain of thought, he said he felt the New York Indians opposed the Bowyer treaty because they could obtain the land at a lower price than if it was sold to the United States.

Stambaugh supported the 1831 treaty, as it provided a "valuable tract of land" for the New York Indians, and the government would pay twenty thousand dollars for it. He acknowledged the New York Indians were not a party to this treaty, and he said they should be placed on the west side of the Fox River. He argued that if the New York Indians needed more land following the larger cession by the Menominee to the United States, then they could apply directly to the government. Stambaugh was assigned to survey the lands for suitability, and he wrote that if the lands were not sufficient for agriculture, he would recommend more lands on the south side for the New York Indians.[10]

A. G. Ellis's report on the July 18 meeting was attached to Stambaugh's report. Ellis confirmed the purpose of the meeting was to obtain agreement from the Menominees with the 1831 treaty and to distribute presents. He stated that Stambaugh addressed the Menominee as brothers. The description of the dispute between the Menominee and the New York Indians was based on the New York Indians having purchased the lands and the Menominee stating they never sold their land.

On February 9, 1831 the Menominee delegates, the president, and the secretary of war were present when the Menominee signed the treaty. Stambaugh said this treaty would help them and keep them from perishing, as

> you are destitute of a home, and strangers in your own lands; your wives and daughters are poor wanderers, pointed at and insulted as miserable beggars by those who are far beneath you in the powers of body and mind; your fine young warriors, too, are seen hungry and naked at the door of the white man; their spirits bending under those scourges of the Indian idleness and intemperance, which have been fast leading the Menominee nation to disgrace and destruction. . . . this will change, you'll be a new people and plenty of food and clothes, you will be provided with comfortable houses. . . . you can light your own council fires in your own wigwams. . . . Your great father has laid the foundation for your future comfort and happiness.

Another opinion on the treaty was offered by Reverend Cadle, who said, "You want education for your children. They will learn to read, write, and do math—the Menomonee will be proud when their children can read the prices of food, clothing, furs they sell, gun powder and be able to protect yourselves from being cheated."

One of the treaty provisions held that the New York Indians had to remove to the lands on the west side of the Fox River within three years, but when the treaty was submitted to Congress, the three-year time frame was changed to "leave it discretionary with the President."[11]

Stambaugh stated he would give some presents, and they would receive more after the Senate approved the treaty in their next session. He promised mills and houses would be built the next year, and cattle and farming tools would be given to the Menominee, saying, "comfort and happiness will surround you on every side." These items were intended to change the Menominee from a hunting people to an agricultural lifestyle.

Stambaugh stated as well that the Menominee had given part of their land to the president so that "your white brothers" may settle down among you and farm, and that in doing so "you have secured great and lasting benefits to yourselves." Stambaugh described the land boundaries as follows:

The land lies on the south and east of Green Bay and Fox River, running from southern extremity of Winnebago lake, southeast to Milwaukee River and down this river to Lake Michigan, along the shore of Lake Michigan to the mouth of Green Bay which includes all the land between the lake, Green Bay and Fox River.[12]

Stambaugh continued discussing the rumor that the Potawatomi and Winnebago had sold some of the Menominee lands and received large annuities, but he didn't believe the rumor. He stated the Menominee did not sell their land before the 1831 treaty. Stambaugh said the boundaries defined would ensure that the Menominee retained a large area of land, and "the land selected between big Butte des Morts and the little Kackalin for your farming will provide wheat, corn, potatoes." He hoped to hear the Menominee were "contented and happy."

Furthermore, Stambaugh said the United States had clearly explained the treaty and that no one was cheating them. They gave up four times larger an area for the New York Indians than previously. The Menominee were to be paid twenty thousand dollars for the land along with presents. Stambaugh reported he had been told they exchanged presents for whiskey and admonished them not to do this as offenders would no longer receive presents and would be punished.

He concluded by giving presents and provisions, and he asked the Menominee to "speak freely, and let me hear the voice of the Menomonie nation in your answer."[13]

At this time, Josette Carron, one of the two principal chiefs of the Menominee Nation, rose and addressed his people as follows:

Brothers: you have all of you, chiefs, warriors, men, women and children heard here, in open day, before all these, our white brother, everything that our father has said. When we do an act for the nation, you all know that we the chiefs, as well as our people, must be united.

Brothers: I hope your ears have been open, and everything our good father here has said to you, has gone deep into your hearts. The things which have been done for Menomonie nation, at the council-house of our great father, last winter, has now been fully explained to us. It is a plain matter, and I am well pleased with it. I hope all of you are likewise pleased, and that not one of my people would be opposed to measures so wise and good. The Menominees have heretofore been poor and unhappy; they believed their great father had forgotten them, and that they had no friends.

Brothers: we now find we have a strong friend in our father here, and that our great father far off, also loves us We have now given him a piece of our land, and he has promised to take good care of his Menomonie children, as you heard by treaty which our father just read to us. Are all satisfied? The chiefs and warriors replied with one voice, in the usual manner "Yes."

The chief then turned to Stambaugh and said:

Father: what you have said is heard by us all, and we are glad. You hear my people say so with one voice. The Menomonies all were satisfied when you went away last fall, that you knew what was best for them. You and our chiefs who went with you, have done what was good for Menomonie nation, before our great father, the President.

Father: I thank you for the whole nation; and, for them, now tell you that we want the treaty made strong.

Father: some of our friends wish to know, if the half-breeds are to settle on the land set apart for our farms. If they were permitted to settle there, by our great father, the President, I hope they will have their pieces marked out, to distinguish them from ours. Then, if they sell them, they will have no more.

Father: we are satisfied that our children, the half-breeds, should come on our land; but they want to know if there has been no place kept for them, from the land sold to our great father, the President, on the east side of Fox River.

Father: we have heard what you know about educating our children. It is good; the Menomonies wish to have their children taught like the Americans. (Then presenting a venerable looking old man, the chief said)

Father: I place this old chief before you, that you may see and remember him. The Menomonies now seem like a new people; they have a father that they all love, and we all want to be known to you. As one of our chiefs, I want this old man known to you.

Father: my friend here, Kuush-kau-nau-nien, will speak to you on behalf of the Menomonie people. We all look upon him as our counsellor with the red skin, and upon you, as our friend and counsellor with the white skin, who will always tell him what is good for the Menomonies. When I was a little boy, he was my father's friend and was a great speaker; since father died, he has been the council chief for the Menomonie people. Father, that was the reason he went with you to see our great father, last winter, because we look upon him as being wiser than our other chiefs, and we know our people would be satisfied with what he would do, under your advice. Father, I have nothing more to say.

Kuush-kau-nau-nien, or Grizzly Bear, the chief orator of the Menominee Nation, then rose and said:

Father: you have heard what the chief has said, I can now hold up my head, and am not ashamed. Let those who questioned the authority by which I acted for my people at Washington, last winter, now hear the answer of the whole Menomine nation.

Father: the heart of Kuush-kau-nau-nien is glad. Look around and see all the Menomonie tribe — chiefs, warriors, men, women, and children, all are present — they have listened with open ears, and glad hearts to what you have said, and you see no dark clouds among them: all is clear as the bright sun.

Father: you hear my voice only, but it speaks for the Menomonie nation. We understand well the provisions of the treaty, as you have explained them to us. The country pointed out as the country of the Menomonies, was ours; part of it is now our great fathers. No red or white man dare say I lie. Before last winter we sold none of our land; but our brothers the Potawatamies and Winnebagoes, have sold much of theirs, and they are getting a great deal of money from the Government every year; when the poor Menomonies get none. Now it appears that they want to claim some piece of the land we have sold, because we have suffered them, like Waubenockies [New York Indians], to sit down upon it, and did not with a strong arm drive them away.

Father: we, the Menomonies, look up to you to protect us in our rights. Our great father at Washington, promised last winter, before the Great Spirit, to take care of his Menomonie children, and not permit them to suffer wrong. We feel it in our hearts that he will keep his promise. Father, I again say that our line begins at the river, at the south end of Winnebago lake, and runs back to Milwaukee, as you read it in the treaty just now.

Father: with respect to the Waubenockies, you know our whole hearts. We have always said the same thing; the Menomonie chiefs never sold them a foot of land. Our chiefs long ago sent word to our great father to take them away, but we were not listened to. It appeared as if we had no friends; but the Great Spirit heard us speak, and we at length found our way to the ears of our great father. At Butte des Morts, some years ago, our father from Detroit, and another commissioner, held a council with our people. I was then on the Mississippi, counselling our people there on a serious subject to my red brothers. But the chiefs who are now present, were then there and stood face to face with the Waubenockies, and they then thought that all their troubles with these people were closed. Our fathers then spoke good words to us, and we rested awhile in peace. But after awhile there were other commissioners sent here, and the Waubenockies again claimed our land. Father, we told these commissioners the same truth, that we had never sold any of our country to the tribes from beyond the lakes. Then they went away, and we went straight to the house of great father, and laid the whole matter before him.

Now, my father, you know all that was done at Washington, was done in open day, and our great father was satisfied.

Father: we have given the New York Indians a large piece of land, because you said our great father wished them to have a home in our country, and we took your advice.

Father: your words to us sounded good; you told us that all our difficulties should have an end, and the Menomonies would become a new people.

Father: the hearts of the Menomonie people are one heart. You have a home in it, and we want to keep you there. Now you have heard what we have said to you. We want you to send all we say to our great father, with this Pipe. Tell him that I send it; and when he smokes with it, he will think of his Menomonie children.

Father: when we return from our hunting ground next spring, we hope to hear you gladden our hearts, by telling us that the great council-house of the nation has said the Menomonies shall have justice. Then we will sit down and be contented in our own country. I have nothing more to say.

Stambaugh then praised the Indians in attendance for making their decisions and said he is happy the Menominee accepted the treaty. He said a few of the Menominee would most likely continue hunting for a while, but all would soon settle down to farm. He promised to take their words to the secretary of war, who would in turn take their words to the president. He then conveyed the arrangement that they agreed to and stated that their acceptance of the presents given that day confirmed the treaty provisions, saying, "When you sign this paper, every article of your arrangements is made binding upon the Menominee tribe."

He then stated that land for those of mixed ancestry was not included. To this, Grizzly Bear replied:

> Father: I know the half-breeds cannot settle at this side of the river. I told them they might go with us to our farming country on the west side of the river. Father: we have nothing more to say.

Immediately following the document submitted by Ellis, there are two more documents signed by the Menominee chiefs. First is the agreement made with the Menominee on March 16, which told them the Senate would confirm the 1831 treaty in its next session. Second, Article A, is an agreement signed by the Menominee confirming the 1831 treaty as discussed in the July 18 meeting.

Article A appears as follows:

> Acceptance by the Menominee tribe of Indians, of the provisions of a treaty concluded at the city of Washington, on the 9th day of February, 1831, between John H. Eaton, Secretary of War, and Samuel C. Stambaugh, Commissioners in behalf of the United States, and the representative of the said Menominee tribe.[14]
>
> At a council held on the 18th day of July, 1831, with the chiefs and warriors of the Menominee nation, by Samuel C. Stambaugh, United States' agent, for the purpose of communicating to the nation certain arrangements entered into at the city of Washington, between the United States and representatives of the Menominee tribe, and of delivering presents to the amount of five thousand dollars to the said tribe, in pursuance of an article of agreement concluded on the 15th of March last, the following instrument of writing was explained to, and signed by said chiefs, on behalf of the nation:
>
> Whereas, certain articles of agreement were made and concluded at the city of Washington, on the 9th day of February, 1831 between commissioners appointed on behalf of the United States, and the

delegates of the Menominee tribe of Indians, whereby the said tribe ceded certain portions of their lands on the east side of Fox river and Green Bay to the United States, for the benefit of their white brothers; and another portion on west side, as a home for the New York Indians.

These articles of said treaty, with the supplement thereto, being read this day, and explained to the Menominee Indians, in full council assembled, we, the chiefs and head warriors of said tribe, holding the whole power the nation, upon full and mature consideration, do give our sanction to each and every article of said treaty, and do highly approve of all its provisions.

And whereas certain other articles of agreement, made and concluded by the said parties, on the 15th day of March last, for the purpose of preserving the provisions of the said treaty, until acted upon by the Senate of the United States at its next session, have been also read and explained to us.

Now, therefore, we, the chiefs and warriors of the Menominee nation aforesaid, having considered this agreement, do highly approve of each and every article thereof; and we hereby acknowledge to have received the full amount of presents secured to us by the said last mentioned articles, in full satisfaction and payment of all their stipulations, and for the purposes for which they were intended.

In testimony whereof, we, the chiefs and warriors of the Menominee nation, hereunto sign our respective names, at Green Bay, this 18th day of July, 1831.

Chiefs

Joseph or Jossette Carron, his X mark,
Kaush-kau-no-nien, or Ma-con-matan, or Medicine Bear
Grizzly Bear his X mark
Ah-yam-eh-tau, his X mark,
Ko-mah-ni-keen, his X mark, Big Wave.
Ko-mah-ni-keen-o-shah, his X mark, Little Wave.
O-ho-pah-shah, his X mark, Small Whoop.
Pee-way-tee-net, his X mark, The Rain.
Maw-baw-zo, his X mark
Cha-nau-pau-neh, his X mark, The one they look upon
Aleh-sheh-neh, his X mark

Kee-shee-aw-ko-teach, his X mark, Flying Cloud.

Wau-boase, his X mark, The Rabbit.

Kar-ah-shoh, his X mark The Sun.

Ah-waw-sha-nee-chee-un, his X mark, Little Bear or Infant Bear

Pah-mo-ne-kot, his X mark,

Moush, his X mark, The Moose.

Pau-mo-ge-nau, his X mark, The Big Soldier.

Sho-nee-neuh, his X mark,

Oshaw-wau-no-ma-teuh, his X mark, The South Medicine.

Ma-cha-au-nau-quit, his X mark, The Bad Cloud.

The Spaniard, his X mark.

The above paper was read and explained to the Menominee chiefs and warriors, by S.C. Stambaugh, and their names signed thereto in our presence:

N. Clark, Captain 5th Infantry.

Rob't Irwin, Jr.

St. Clair Denny, Lieutenant 5th Infantry.

J.L. Thompson, Lieutenant 5th Infantry.

Rich'd F. Cadle.

Daniel Whitney.

Henry S. Baird.

Wm. Dickson.

John P. Arndt.

J. Irwin.

John H. Whistler.

Jos. Dickenson.

Geo. Johnson.

Witnesses to the above signatures:

Jos. Jourdain, United States' blacksmith.

Eben. Childs

Rufus Hunter.

Richard Prichet, his X mark, United States' interpreter.

C.A. Grignon, Menominee interpreter.

A.G. Ellis.[15]

Also attached was the following statement from Oash-Kash, a principal chief of the Menominee Nation. Dated August 2, it reads:

Whereas the undersigned, one of the principal chiefs of the Menominee nation, being absent in the Indian country at the distribution of presents to the Menominee nation, secured to them under certain articles of agreement concluded at Washington, on the 15th day of March last, and was unable to reach Green Bay in time to be present at the council held for that purpose, on the 18th ultim; and having this day held a talk with S.C. Stambaugh, United States agent, the above, with the several articles of agreement concluded at Washington city last winter, between John H. Eaton, Secretary of War, and Samuel C. Stambaugh, Indian agent, on behalf of the United States, and the delegates of the Menominee tribe, on behalf of their nation, being fully explained to me:

Now, therefore, in confirmation of the acts of the other chiefs, I do hereby declare my full and entire approbation of each and

A longtime leader of the Menominee, Chief Oshkosh played a key role during treaty negotiations in 1827, 1831, and 1832. WHI IMAGE ID 1888

Menominee Chief Grizzly Bear as painted by George Catlin in 1831
MAH-KÉE-MEE-TEUV, GRIZZLY BEAR, CHIEF OF THE TRIBE, 1831, OIL ON CANVAS, SMITHSONIAN AMERICAN ART MUSEUM, GIFT OF MRS. JOSEPH HARRISON JR., 1985.66.218

every article said treaty or agreement, with the supplement thereto, and desire that the same may be recorded as the act of the whole Menominee nation of Indians. And I do, moreover, join with to the other chiefs in acknowledging the receipt by our nation, from Samuel C. Stambaugh, United States' agent, the sum of five thousand dollars, in presents secured to us by the articles of agreement, entered into on the 16th day of March aforesaid, in full satisfaction and payment thereof.

In testimony whereof, I have hereunto set my hand and seal,

the 2 day of August, 1831

Oash-kash, his x mark, The Brave.

The above paper was fully read and explained to Oash-kash, one of the principal chiefs of the Menominee Nation, and signed by him in our presence.

Rich'd F. Cadle, P.E. Miss'y at G. R.

J.D. Doty.

Robert Irwin, jr.

Wm. Dickinson.

Ricch'd Picket, his X mark, United States' interpreter[16]

Opposition to the Menominee Treaty

The New York Indians were opposed to the 1831 treaty, partially because they were not included in negotiating or signing the treaty, and because the boundaries were still not settled.

On November 2, 1831, Stambaugh wrote to the governor of Michigan Territory, George Bryan Porter, advising him that a delegation of New York Indians went to Washington without his permission. The standard procedure being imposed by the US was that in order for Indian nations to meet with the president, they were to make a request to the Indian agent who forwarded that request to the secretary of war for approval. The New York Indians did not follow that imposed restriction and went directly to Washington. The delegation included a missionary who lived with the Stockbridge. The purpose of the delegation was to "oppose the ratification of the treaty, made last winter."[17]

On November 8, at the Indian agency in Green Bay, Stambaugh expressed his opinion about the 1831 treaty to Cass, writing, "The Senate of the United States will not suffer an arrangement, so highly advantageous to the Government, as the Menomonie treaty, to be lost, upon objections so futile as those urged against it by the New York Indians."[18] Stambaugh was clearly opposed to the New York Indians' claim for land near Green Bay, and he expressed his negative opinions. It often happened that the US government received only one side of the story, and that's why the New York Indians wrote extensive memorials directly to the president.

The New York Indians met with Governor Porter of Michigan at Washington late in December 1831. The negotiations between Porter and the New York Indians during the month of December, regarding the provisions of the 1831 treaty with the Menominee, are documented. The New York Indians did eventually meet with the president, and Porter submitted a report detailing the negotiations.[19]

On December 19, 1831, as the New York Indians arrived in Washington, Porter received instructions from Cass to meet with them. The purpose was "endeavoring to adjust the differences which have arisen at Green Bay respecting their claims to land in that quarter." He was to report on his progress. In the meetings with Porter, the New York Indians expressed their dissatisfaction with the 1831 treaty with the Menominee. Porter wrote:

> In the course of these friendly meetings I gave them to understand what was believed to be the interest and policy of the Government: that the Indians should all remove to the North West side of Fox River and Green Bay; — thereby leaving vacant all the land on the East Side of the same, as ceded by the Menominies to the United States by the said Treaty which if put into market, as other public lands, there was reason to believe would soon sell, and thereby furnish the means for defraying the expenses incurred and paying the amount of the consideration of the purchase from the Menominies.[20]

Porter tried to persuade the New York Indians to accept the five hundred thousand acres designated in the 1831 treaty in order to end the dispute:

On the 20th of December the following was submitted to me to wit

The Deputies of the N.Y. tribes submit to the Commissioners the following modifications of their former proposals.

The Stockbridge & Brothertown tribes to relinquish their present possessions on the South East bank of the Fox River & to accept two townships to be located by them on the East shore of the Winnebago Lake, on receiving an indemnity for its full value of their improvements & the expenses of their removal.

The remaining Tribes to be located on the N.W. side of Fox River, on a tract to be defined as follows:

> Beginning at the mouth of the creek designated on the map as Shawanoegunk, being the stream next South of the . . . , thence along Green Bay & Fox River to the lower line of Grignon's farm — Thence on a N.W. course four miles, — thence on a course parallel with the course of the River & distant from it four miles to the most westerly branch of the stream which empties into the Fox River, next below the little Butte Des Morts — Thence on a N.W. course forty miles. Thence on a course due North, twenty five miles. Thence by the nearest direct course to the Shawanoegunk Creek & thence down this creek to the place of beginning. — excepting the lands occupied by the US & all confirmed private claims. Estimated to contain about 800,000 acres.[21]

Porter asked the New York Indians to define the boundaries acceptable to them. On December 24, Porter received three written documents. The first was sent by Thomas L. Ogden on behalf of the Six Nations and the St. Regis tribe. The second and third were written by Samuel W. Beall on behalf of the Stockbridge, Munsee, and Brothertown tribes. It is very interesting to note that Ogden wrote for the Six Nations and St. Regis tribe because he was a proponent of moving the entire Six Nations to the west.

First, Ogden said the population of about six thousand of the Six Nations would need at least one million acres. The land was described as follows:

They propose that this River & the waters connected with it from the mouth of Duck Creek to that of the Wolf River shall form the south eastern boundary of the tract. Wolf river it's western boundary and a line running from the mouth of Duck Creek on a N.W. course its' North Eastern boundary, and that so bounded, it shall extend. Northwardly so far as to embrace, exclusive of all exceptions, one million of acres, or so much of that quantity as may remain after deducting the quality of land which shall be elsewhere appropriated to the Stockbridge, and Brothertown Tribes.[22]

Ogden also wrote:

To testify the sincerity of their desire to meet the views of the Government, the tribes to be located on the N.W. side of Fox River, will forego all claims to the water privileges at the rapids of the Grand Kaukaulin & that these may be effectively secured they will further consent that a strip of land three miles in breadth be laid off along the shore of the River from the foot of the rapids to the Grand Chute, or that it be excepted out of the tract above defined.[23]

Beall, speaking for the Stockbridge-Munsee and Brothertown, began by explaining the loss of the White River, Indiana, lands. He reported that Calhoun used "his influence & assistance in procuring land for them in the vicinity of Green Bay, which was represented to be better and more suitable than the White River tract."[24] He also claimed, "These tribe have instructed their Delegates to receive no location, other than on the East side of Fox River, & if possible to obtain the tract at the Grand Kaukaulin, as described in their memorial of last winter to the President,"[25] and "They have resided on this tract nine years; their improvements are great, notwithstanding the difficulties they had had to contend with."[26] He added: "If the United States desire to possess the land at the Grand Kaukaulin, the Delegates will agree that their tribes shall remove to the East side of Winnebago Lake, upon being paid indemnity."[27]

Beall explained the White River situation and Calhoun's encouragement that they should join the other New York Indians to procure land near Green Bay. The Brothertown "paid $950 of the consideration stipulated by the treaty of 1822, & became owners of a tract of 153,000 acres on the East side of Fox River." Beall wrote, "This tribe has expended $7,000 in endeavouring to establish their title as acquired. A part of them are now actually settled upon the land," adding, "The Commissioners of 1830 considered it proper that they should be located on the East side of Fox River & allotted to them 20,000 acres. This allotment they are desirous to retain."[28]

Porter, however, rejected all three propositions, writing, "The government would not agree that these Stockbridge, Munsee, and Brothertown tribes should remain on & hold the lands on the East side of Fox River." The goal, according to Porter, was to remove all the New York Indians to the

> N.W. side of Fox River. . . . But they had expressed a wish to be located separate & apart from the other tribes, it was possible that if the Treaty was confirmed, the Government would consent to grant them, a small tract of land sufficient for their accommodations somewhere along the Eastern shore of Lake Winnebago.

There was a glimmer of hope that they could stay on the lands they occupied, but Porter went on to assure them that if they were removed, they would be compensated for their improvements.[29]

The Six Nations were told their requested boundaries were "wholly inadmissible." The land requested still belonged to the Menominee and the government could not sell it. Porter explained of the land,

> That it was a district of country to which they were much attached; and which were the Little and Big Butte Des Morts; the Land Big Butte Des Morts; and at the latter place were the trading houses, at which they & the Winnebagoes usually assembled. That it was a Neutral ground, where Menomonies, Chippewas, Winnebagoes and sometimes Pottawattamie, meet, and, as we believed, no consideration would induce the Menomonies to give it up. Besides which the Government of the United States have no right to this part of the territory, and of course could not undertake to grant it to anyone.[30]

On December 26, the New York Indians replied:

The deputies of the New York Tribes submit to the commissioners the following modifications of their former proposals: The Stockbridge and Brothertown tribes to relinquish their present possessions on the southeast bank of Fox river, and to accept three townships, to be located by them on the east shore of the Winnebago lake, on receiving an indemnity for the full value of their improvements, and the expenses of their removal.

The remaining tribes to be located on the northwest side of Fox river, and a tract to be defined as follows:

Beginning at the mouth of the creek designated on the map as the Shawamegunk, being the stream next south of the Oconto; thence along Green Bay and fox river to the lower line of Grignon's farm; thence, on a northwest course four miles; then on a course parallel with the courses of the river, and distant from it four miles, to the most westerly branch of the stream which empties into Fox river, next below the Little Butte des Morts; thence, on a northwest course, forty miles; thence, on a course due north twenty-five miles; thence, by the nearest direct course to the Shawamegunk creek and thence down the creek to the place of beginning; excepting the lands occupied by the United States, and all confirmed private claims — estimated to contact about 800,000 acres.[31]

On December 27, Porter replied with the same rejection of proposals. He reminded them that the 1831 treaty provided five hundred thousand acres to the New York Indians. In order to end the dispute, it had been proposed to exchange two hundred thousand on the north side of the five hundred thousand acres for two hundred thousand on the south side of Lake Winnebago, because the lands on the south side were more suitable for agriculture. He reiterated that the land requested still belonged to the Menominee Nation. However, he wrote, "If, as has been suggested, the Governments could make an arrangement with the Menomonies for a cession of a tract of land on the South side of what has been set apart in the Treaty aforesaid for the N.Y. Indians — and extending from near the Fox River to the North West, it would be at heavy expense which always attends Indian treaties."

Porter wrote as well that:

The United States Government, would, in lieu of the lands now
occupied and claimed by the Stockbridge, Munsee, Brothertown
and Oneida Tribes on the East side of Fox River, in the vicinity of the
Grand Kaukaulin, assign to said tribes two townships of land on the
S.E. side of Winnebago Lake, and to consist of one entire tract, and to
be so surveyed and laid off, that it shall have a front on the Lake of the
same extent, that will be required in depth to make 46,080 acres.[32]

Porter again offered payment, up to twenty-five thousand dollars for
their improvements, and instructed them to remove to the lands on the
south side of Lake Winnebago by May 1, 1833.

To this proposal the New York Indians made the following answer on
December 28:

The Deputies of the New York Indians are constrained to decline the
proposals submitted to them last evening by the Commissioners.

Their claims being founded on contracts which they know to have
been fairly made, & on their part faithfully executed, they believe
them to be of binding obligation. Standing upon this ground it will
be readily perceived, that they cannot yield to the force of obligations
which, in conformity with the late Treaty, assume the nonexistence
of those contacts, or in accordance with the earlier pretension of
the Menomonies, assume their invalidity, on the ground of want
of authority in the Chiefs who negotiated them & of mistake or
misapprehension in reducing them to writing.

Arguments of this kind prejudice the question on which as a
matter of right & justice the whole controversy must depend.

Of this character are all the remarks which, referring to the
provisions of the late Treaty, would deduce from them objections of
practical inconveniences to the Menomonies, by reason of any new
appropriations of lands, assigned to them by that instrument for
agricultural purposes.

The complaints of the New York Indians are based on what
they allege to be a flagrant violation of good faith on the part of
the Menomonies in selling to the United States & in retaining to
their own use lands previously purchased and paid for by the N.Y.

Tribes, and they invoke interference of the Government to rectify the injustice by a modification of the Treaty — this the United States will have an undoubted right to do, on the ground of a failure of the title of the Menomonies to a large portions of the lands, which they thereby undertook to sell.

The New York Indians, whilst indisposed to yield anything to their perfidious countrymen, are animated by a sincere desire to accommodate themselves to the view of the Government of the US. In a spirit of compromise & concession dictated by this feeling, they have consented to abandon their favourite positions & valuable improvements on the South side of Fox River, & to limit their claims to what they deem to be the essential wants of their people:

Keeping these in views, the Stockbridge and Munsee Tribes must again insist on a grant of two townships, to be laid off by them in a square form on the East side of the Winnebago Lake, with an indemnity of $25,000, & the Brothertown Tribe on a grant of one township in a like square form on the Winnebago Lake, with an indemnity of two thousand dollars & the Six Nations & St. Regis Tribes, upon an additional quantity of land on the North side of Fox River to the amount of at least 200,000 acres, to be laid off along the S.W. line of the last designated in the late Treaty & also upon the land on the North bank of Fox river, between [its] mouth and the lower line of Grignon's farm, excepting the confirmed claims.

It has been ascertained by actual examination that the greater part of that tract consists of low swampy land unfit for cultivation; To accept a seat for the future residence of these tribes destitute of the sufficiency of land adapted to agricultural purpose would be to hold out to them & to the Government hopes of improvement in their habits and conditions, which could not fail to prove delusive.
Dec. 28, 1831

On December 29, Porter replied:

We do not deem it necessary now to discuss the several remarks referring the proposals made on behalf of the N.Y. Tribes. We came at once to the point. So far as it respected the granting of three townships, instead of two as heretofore suggested, on the E. side of Lake Winnebago, for the use of the Stockbridge, Munsee, Brothertown and Oneida tribes there would be but little difficulty. He continues to talk about compensation for improvements.

Porter also wrote that the government would agree to three townships on the east side of Lake Winnebago.

On December 30, the New York Indians rejected Porter's offer:

The rejecting of this proposition was submitted on the 30th December and is as follows to wit:

The Deputies of the New York tribes, deeply reject the abortive result of their various efforts to effect an amicable adjustment of their claims. The position assumed by the Commissioners that the Menomini Tribe are in all events to be secured in the undisturbed possession of all the lands on the west side of Fox River appropriated to them by the late Treaty, and are thus to profit by their own wrong; at the expense of the N.Y. Tribes, seems of itself to interpose an insurmountable obstacle to the conclusion of any compromise by which the New York Tribes can secure a tract of Country adequate in point of extent, soil & situation to their indispensable wants.

The Stockbridge Tribe in the improvements which they have made, consisting of sixty one dwelling houses, of about one thousand acres of land, cleared & in fence, of a commodious mission house & mill, in removing from the State of New York & in travelling to & from the Seat of Government, to establish & settle their claims, have actually expended out of the proceeds of the lands constituting their former possessions upward of forty thousand dollars. They are not willing to abandon their present Seats & to encounter the hardships of a new settlement, without the presence of an indemnity such as they have proposed, nor are the Brothertown Tribe of whom a portion are settled on the tract, assigned to them by the other Tribes & in the possession of which the Commissioners of 1830 recommended that they should be confirmed, willing to relinquish that tract without an assurance of the moderate indemnity which they have proposed.

Both Tribes are unwilling to exchange these favorite Seats without a right to select within specified limits & in a specified form, the tracts to be inhabited in their place, and under all the securities proposed. It would be far more desirable to each to retain their present positions.

It only remains to the N.Y. Tribes to submit their claims to the Senate, in it constitutional action upon the Treaty, now under its consideration of that body.

30 December 1831.[33]

Despite many proposals and negotiations, the December 1831 meeting with Porter ended with no solution to the question of lands for the New York Indians, and they requested a meeting with the president. Porter understood the proposal for three townships for the Stockbridge and Brothertown, and five hundred thousand acres for the Six Nations. The request of the New York Indians was to exchange two hundred thousand acres on the north side of the proposed five hundred thousand acres for two hundred thousand acres on the south side of Lake Winnebago, which was more suitable for farming. The unsettled dispute would lead to another council meeting with Porter in 1832.

10

1832 Treaty with · the Menominee

Indian Nation to the United States

Delegates from the Six Nations, St. Regis, Stockbridge and Munsee, and Brothertown went to Washington to meet in person with President Andrew Jackson. The meeting happened on January 9, 1832. The delegates were Daniel Bread and Antoine John, who represented the Six Nations (Oneida) and St. Regis (Mohawk), respectively; John W. Quinney and John Metoxen, who represented the Stockbridge and Munsee; and David Towcee, who represented the Brothertown. Metoxen presented a lengthy speech interpreted by Quinney in which he discussed the long dispute and the wish to settle it. According to a record of the meeting written by George Bryan Porter, the governor of Michigan Territory, and delivered to Lewis Cass:

> After the usual introduction, that he was pleased to see his great Father, &c. he stated, in substance, that his people were tired and nearly worn out with the disputes which had for years past been carried on: that they had heretofore sent their young chiefs to endeavor to effect a settlement and compromise of their differences; that, as they had not been able to accomplish this, they had now sent him, and had instructed him not to return without settling everything.
> Then addressing himself to the president, he said:
> "Father, I am getting old. I want to have an end put to

these disputes. You have given us good commissioners; we
are pleased with them, and see that they are willing to do
everything in their power for us. Now, Father, we are perfectly
satisfied with the offer made us by your commissioners; we
agree to what they propose; and why cannot this dispute be
settled?"[1]

Metoxen was then told that an agreement had been reached, and the
only remaining issue was for the deputies of the Six Nations to accept the
five hundred thousand acres designated in the 1831 treaty. The record
then notes:

Daniel Bread then rose, and addressed the President quite intelligibly,
in the English language; stated that he was very anxious to have this
settled; that he did not deny but that there was land enough, and
more than enough; but he did not believe there was enough of good
land; and wished to know whether a piece of land could not be given
to them on the south side of that tract.[2]

Jackson told him this was not possible because that land belonged to the
Menominee and was reserved for agriculture. The New York Indians were
agricultural people and they knew the northern part of the allottment
was not suitable for agriculture; therefore, they requested an exchange of
two hundred thousand acres on the north side for two hundred thousand
acres on the south side, which was better suited for agriculture. Bread then
asked the president, "If we can make a bargain with the Menominees for an
exchange of lands, giving them a piece on the north of the 500,000 acres
for a small piece on the south of the tract, will you sanction it?"[3] Jackson
agreed, and Bread told him, "We are afraid, Father, that some of the white
men will interfere, and that the Menominees will not do this, unless our
Great Father will advise them; the Menominee have a high respect for
their Great Father says; and if he will advise them, we are sure they will
make this exchange."[4]

Colonel Samuel C. Stambaugh was instructed on April 23, 1831, to ascertain the quality of the soil for the New York Indians in the Green Bay
area, and his topographical report was submitted with this Senate report.

In discussions with the president on January 9, Stambaugh asked how many families there were in the New York Indians. They numbered less than one thousand, so the president figured that at two hundred acres per family for cultivation there would be three hundred thousand acres left; couldn't they find two hundred thousand acres of good land? This statement shows the president was not aware of the geographic location of these lands.

After some discussion, Bread responded:

> that he wished to have an end to their disputes; and, as his Great Father had now said, that he would send good advice to the Menominees, he would agree to the settlement, and he thought that they could make an exchange sometime with the Menominees, and get what they wanted, and they could live in peace.[5]

When it was their turn to speak, the Stockbridge asked for funding for a school and building and a mill, but they were told this should come out of the twenty-five thousand dollars agreed to for their improvements. The Brothertown agreed to accept sixteen hundred dollars for their improvements upon removal.

Eleazer Williams arrived in Washington around this time, and he acted as the interpreter for Bread. Porter recorded that

> To my great astonishment and in the face of his voluntary agreement when before the President, he [Bread] refused absolutely to consent to any arrangements unless the Government guarantee and assure to them two hundred thousand acres on the South side of the tract of 500,000 acres set apart by the Treaty of last year; In vain, did I remind him of his own voluntary agreement.

Porter again stated the government could not grant the two hundred thousand acres on the south side because those lands still belonged to the Menominee,[6] and he told Bread that he had received some bad advice, or that "bad birds have been flying about his head."

On January 14, Bread presented the following statement on behalf of the Six Nations:

The undersigned, delegates from the Six Nations of Indians, has thought proper to communicate to the commissioners in writing, his determination to decline an acceptance of the tract of 500,000 acres, (as set off by the Menominee treaty) for the accommodation of the tribes he represents — He does so, for the purpose of preventing any misunderstanding or misapprehension of the motives which have influenced him.

The situation, soil, and condition of this tract form the insuperable objections. Its limited extent, (though objectionable, would not defeat a settlement), if, in other respects, it was suitable. If the commissioners could guaranty an exchange of 200,000 acres on the north side of this tract, for a like number to be added to the south side, the undersigned would agree to a settlement.

But to effect this, the commissioners declare that they have no power — a promise, that the influence of the Executive will be exerted in persuading the Menominees to agree to this exchange, does not offer to the undersigned a sufficient security. Besides, if the purchase of these lands, under the sanction of one President, has been unavailing in perfecting a good title, what reliance can be placed upon the influence and authority of another?

The negotiation must, therefore, end here. The treaty of last winter, by assuring to the Menominees an agricultural tract of the lands they had formerly ceded to the New York tribes, and, without the consent of these tribes, appears to prevent a compliance on the part of the commissioners, with terms such as are stated above. In that treaty, the undersigned was not consulted, and, for its consequences, in rendering nugatory the efforts of the present commission, he is not accountable.

The undersigned takes this occasion to declare most solemnly, that he received no invitation to become a contract party in that treaty. It has been stated by the commissioners that the undersigned, in an interview with President, expressed his readiness to close with the terms offered by the commissioners — his meaning has certainly been misapprehended. He understood the President to say that the lands should be exchanged as desired, thereby pledging the faith of the Government to him, to effect the exchange with the Menominees.

With this, the undersigned was satisfied. His imperfect knowledge
of the English language, and his almost entire inability to express
himself intelligibly, has doubtless produced this misunderstanding.
    Daniel Bread
    January 14. A.D. 1832[7]

    In his report, Porter wrote that he "avoided a discussion of the ques-
tions involved in the alleged purchases made of the Menominees by the
New York Indians in 1821 and 1822," but in fact he continued talks with
the delegates by questioning the validity of the 1821 and 1822 treaties. He
then recapped the efforts to resolve this issue. What's clear, however, is
that Porter opposed the New York Indians' claim to land. After reviewing
the treaties and documents, he came to the conclusion that "we do not
think, from all the circumstances which have come to our knowledge, that
the Menominee Indians have been fairly treated in this business." Porter
ranted that the New York Indians had defied authority when they settled
on the Fox River and sold part of the land, referring to the agreement with
the Brothertown. He neglected to mention the fact that the Brothertown
paid the Menominee $950 as part of the amount due for the 1822 treaty.
Porter felt that because the New York Indians had defied authority, Cass
and McKenney would have to address the information in the 1827 treaty,
while referring to the journal of the 1827 treaty made by McKenney for
the "truth." He then continued discussing the 1827 treaty and the three
commissioners' attempts to settle this dispute. Porter claimed the Menominee agreed to the exchange of lands, but Bread was obstinate. Then, he
expressed his main purpose by saying that the dragging out of this dispute
had slowed the sale of these lands, which:

> calculated seriously to affect the interests of our citizens in the
> vicinity; — to retard the settlement and improvement of one of the
> most interesting portions of our Country; to formalize the exertions
> of many of our enterprising men, and to interfere not only with the
> revenue which must accrue to the Government, from the extensive
> sale of land that would undoubtedly take place, were that part of
> the Territory of Michigan put into market; but also, prevent the
> use, occupation and enjoyment of the water communications and

an uninterrupted intercourse by land, between Green Bay, and Fort
Winnebago, and thence to the Mississippi.[8]

Porter asked that the 1831 treaty be ratified, with the United States
claiming ownership of all the lands on the east side of Lake Winnebago,
the Fox River, and Green Bay.[9] In his February 3, 1832, journal, which was
eventually submitted to the US Senate, Porter elaborated on the request
to take two hundred thousand acres off the north side of the five hundred
thousand acres designated for the New York Indians in the 1831 treaty with
the Menominee, and to add two hundred thousand acres on the south side,
which was better suited for agriculture.

On February 8, 1832, Cass submitted Stambaugh's and Porter's reports
to Jackson. On the same day, Jackson referred the documents to the Senate,
writing, "I transmit herewith for information of the Senate, a report from
the Department of War, showing the situation of the country at Green Bay,
ceded for the benefit of the New York Indians, and also the proceedings of
the Commissioner, who has lately held a meeting with them."[10] Jackson
also wrote, "Mr. Macy presented a memorial of the New York Indians
in relation to a treaty with the Menomonee Indians, transmitted to the
Senate 28th of February, 1831."[11] On July 9, 1832, the Senate ratified the
February 8, 1831, treaty with the Menominee. Nine days later, the Senate
added a supplemental article, a Senate proviso that the Menominee needed
to approve. The proviso conditions were as follows:

1. Two townships on the east side of Winnebago Lake totaling
   46,080 acres for the Stockbridge and Munsee; they would also
   be paid for improvements on the east side of the Fox River,
   not to exceed $25,000.

2. One township of 23,040 acres adjoining the Stockbridge lands
   for the Brothertown. The United States would pay $1,600 for
   their improvements on their lands on the east side of the Fox
   River.

3. An exchange of land to be made by drawing a new line for the
   New York Indians on the west side of the Fox River, one mile
   above Grand Chute on Fox River of two hundred thousand

acres to be part of the five hundred thousand acres, which was to be traded for land on the northeastern side of Oconto Creek, to add these lands on the southwestern side.[12]

Efforts to obtain Menominee approval of the 1831 treaty and proviso led to a council meeting between the Menominee and the United States in October 1832. This meeting resulted in the 1832 treaty between the Menominee and the United States. Given that the Menominee treaty of 1831 was ratified with a Senate proviso that required the Menominee's consent, Cass instructed Porter to go to Green Bay to get it. If the Menominee Nation did not agree with the Senate proviso, then Porter was to "endeavor to procure their assent to the best practicable terms, short of those proposed by the Senate." Cass also said that it would be "very desirable that the New York Indians should also signify their acceptance of the modification required by the Menomonie."[13]

Porter served as the commissioner for the United States during the treaty negotiations in 1832. He was instructed to hold a council meeting from October 22 to October 26 at the Indian agency house at Green Bay. The extensive proceedings of these meetings are included here because Porter's journal includes many speeches from the Menominee.

THE COUNCIL MEETING

The council began on October 22 at the Green Bay agency. In attendance were Porter, Grignon, who served as interpreter, Boyd the Indian agent, Richard Prickett, and the chiefs and men of the Menominee Nation. The chiefs and head men of the Menominee were introduced, then Porter explained the 1831 treaty, the treaty benefits, and the Senate proviso, stating that the New York Indians had gone to Washington to oppose the treaty and that the Stockbridge-Munsee and Brothertown were to be located on the east side of Lake Winnebago and paid for their improvements. Porter noted that the "Six Nations and St. Regis insisted on quantity of land on North Side of Fox River of at least 200,000 acres to be laid off along the southwest line of the Tract designated and set apart for the New York Indians in the late Treaty and to extend up the Fox River as far as the lower line of Grignon's farm."[14] The land requested was between the Old Mill

Dam and Grignon's line, but the Six Nations and St. Regis were told that land did not belong to the United States, that it was still Menominee land and the United States could not grant approval of those lands. Nevertheless, "This did not satisfy them, and no arrangement was effected." Porter further explained,

> That he would here show them the final proposition drawn up by Samuel W. Beall (who was now present listening to what he said) and signed by Daniel Bread at Washington on the 14th of January 1832 in which it is stated that 'if the Commissioners could guarantee and exchange of 200,000 acres, on the North side of this tract (500,000 acres) for a like number to be added to the South side the undersigned would agree to a settlement. But to effect this the Commissioners declare that they have no power.

The next day, the Menominee chiefs were introduced by Grizzly Bear. He said that Oshkosh, also called the Brave or the Claws, was their first chief and he was not present, but his brother was present and "fully authorized to act for him." All their chiefs and principal men were present. One young man to speak was Skee-O-ni-ni, or Little Brave. He said:

> Father, you say you are glad to see us, we also are pleased to see you, we have waited a great while to see you, and now since you have come, we think we see in you, our Great Father the President of the United States. Many of our Chiefs and principal men have seen our Great Father and they believe he intends to do what is right for us and our people. We are a great way from him, and we hope you will say to him that we expect he will protect us and assist us, and we look to you, too to protect us, and see that we are not wronged.
>
> When the first white man came to us he said that we should not be wronged, and that they did not want to drive us away from our land, and so the white man who came with these New York Indians said, that they would not wrong us, if we would only let them sit down among us. It would be a long story to tell you all. Now if we should go away what would become of us? The hope to settle this old dispute the

New York Indians always opposed it. We ask you therefore Father to help us, so that we may get what we were to have by the Treaty.

There is one thing that we would like to have done. There are some of these half-breeds who have been brought up among us, and live among us, and we wish them to have some of our land. We will let you know what we want for them hereafter. This man (Grizzly Bear) is our speaker. He will speak for us all. My Grandfather was the 1st Chief and when he died my father was the Chief in his place, and therefore you see that I have a right to be considered a principal man. They had this man for their Orator. He was born and brought up alongside of them. And he is our Orator as all our Chiefs will inform you. He will now speak for us all. If have done.

Grizzly Bear spoke next. He said:

Father this is our custom. We smoke to please the Great Spirit before we begin any important business like this. This is our War Chiefs Pipe. Now I will begin.

Father, this man who stands in the place of our chief, has told you right. We are pleased to see you and we think we see in you our Great Father the President of the United States. We know all about this dispute and what these not go all over it. When Col. Stambaugh was here, and first talked to us about it he said, your Great Father, wants to see you. We thought we were going to settle and agreed to go and see our Great Father. But we did not think that we were to give these New York Indians a right to make Sugar on our Land, and cut down our Maple Trees. When we were with our Great Father the President, we told him that we would not allow these New York Indians anything. But he said to us My children if you like me, you must let these New York Indian have a piece of your land, as much as will be necessary for them. We then began to make the bargain. We know what we agreed to. We sold (pointing to the map) all on this side of the River (the East Side) and the Lake, because the Potawatomies had already sold a part of our Land on the same side and got a heap of money and annuities and we got none of it. We did not wish any more of our land sold by them, and we agreed to sell it ourselves to our Great Father.

Afterwards we gave away 500,000 acres for these New York Indians and when they got us to agree to that, I told our Great Father, and everyone about us heard it, that we would not give them a step more. First, we offered to give a piece on the West Side of Fox River, but not so big as it is now (pointing to the 500,000 acres as laid down on the Map). But our Great Father then said we should give more, and we agreed to do so. He said my children, I ask you to grant a piece to the New York Indians, they were satisfied too. But they stayed there to make objections. We don't know what they mean. We don't like it, that they act so. Our Great Father said to us, now my children I am pleased that you have behaved so well. If these New York Indians will not accept of what you have agreed to give them, they shall not remain two days on your land. I will send them off. You have behaved very generously. You have given more than I expected you would have done.

Our Father Col. Boyd tells us that he speaks to us with one mouth, that he had but one mouth and one heart. We say so too. We settle a matter in our hearts, and, as it is there, we all agree to it, and nothing else. Father, we have done as you have told us; we have all been together and consulted this morning; we all agree in what I tell you. It is bad enough that you have had to come so far; and bad enough that we have had to wait here, so that we cannot for so long a time get to our hunting grounds. We are anxious to get away, and have therefore, soon decided, and are all of one mind.

Father, you have Senators, who think themselves Great Men. But they do not know one place from another on this Fox River, or they never would ask us to do what is in the Paper you read, and which was explained to us. They agree to make a thing such a way. We may be considered, by them, small. But we have our War Chiefs; and we do, like your Senators, consult them all; and when we all agree on anything, it cannot be made otherwise. Now I don't see why they refuse what our War Chiefs offered. We were too generous, agreed to give them too much. But these New York Indians were not satisfied and if we had given them half as much more they would not have been satisfied. Our Great Father the President told us, when we sold to him all on the East side, you have all on the West Side of Fox River. It is your own country and you can do with it as you please.

Now, Father, I have told you what we agreed to give these New York Indians. We are not disposed to give them any more. I told our Great Father, the President so. I cannot see their object in asking us to make this exchange. True it is, there is to be the like quantity given for it below. But if this land is good for them, it is good for us too.

Father, These New York Indians have behaved so badly, and opposed everything that is right so long a time, that we begin to hate them. They are dogs. They want to take our land from us without paying for it. They hunt on our land and kill our deer. Have they any right to do so? We are becoming angry, mad. Father, we have seen these New York Indians hunting on our land above the Grand Chute. They have killed a great many of our deer. They have been hunting all the way out to the Big River or River of the Lake (Wolf River). Was this their agreement? No, they were to cultivate the land. This is what they wanted land for, they said, not to hunt deer on.

Father, If they had fulfilled the first agreement as they ought to have done, complied with the provisions of it, we perhaps might have attempted to satisfy them. But they did not do so; and we don't know how to satisfy them.

Father, Our Chief asked you to take care of us. In the name of all our people I tell you that we expect you will take care of us. We cannot do just whatever these New York Indians want. They are always wanting more.

Father, Here is this tract we agreed to give them on your map. I do not see why they should refuse it. Land is but land, nothing else. We are ignorant of the way you measure land. We do not know what you mean by the Acres you speak of. What is it? Father, there is a house put up where they want this land at the Grand Chute. So you see they made up their minds, before they went, to get the land by that house.

Father, You told us that these New York Indians said they bought a great deal of our land. I ask you, with what did they pay for it? We received nothing; nor did any of our people receive anything of consequence. How then can they say they bought our Land?

Father, you now understand me. We do not agree to the
proposition made by the Senate. We cannot agree to it. And we ask
you to tell all that we have said to our Great Father and the Senate,
and to see that we are not wronged. We look to you to help us. Father,
I am now done. If any of our Chiefs wish to speak, they will do so.

A-yah-ma-ta was the next Menominee to speak:

Father, what this young man told you is true. My father was a Chief.
He was wise and he had this man (Grizzly Bear) for his Speaker. He
was the Orator. My father's name was Kah-ro. He was a Chief. You
see, therefore, Father, that I am a principal man.

Father, all that our Orator has said is right. I approve of it all.
These are my sentiments, and he spoke for all of us. The Great Spirit
knows, and we call him to witness, that we all consulted together and
we came to the conclusion, he has told you.

Father, we, your children, do not look well; we are ragged; and we
have no good clothes. But we are all the principal men of the Nation.
Every one of us is here but one: and this young man is here in his
place.

Father, there is no use in talking the same thing over again; that is
not our custom; we consult together and when we have agreed, one of
us speaks; that is sufficient. This our custom. I have now done.

Afterward, Shawenogeshig voiced his own thoughts to the council:

Father, you see your children before you, all these here are our
principal men of the nation. I have nothing to say more than our
Speaker told you; we all approve what he said. Father, we stand in
need of clothes, and we have nothing to get them with; we have no
money, and we have waited here so long to see you, that we have lost
a great deal, which we would have had if we had gone out hunting, as
we are accustomed to do.

Father, we have been expecting the annuity which was to be paid
us for the land we ceded; we need it very much; we hoped it would
come soon, but it did not come.

Father, I tell you this, we were looking anxiously; and every Schooner we saw, we supposed brought our annuity money. Our children are in great want of clothes; they thought they would be supplied, when a vessel would come here, with our money; but all our thoughts are in vain.

Father, our families had nothing for a long time but potatoes to eat; we helped people to dig up potatoes, and got some of them. Now, Father, we would like to grease our mouths with some meat.

Next, Cheno-mu-bee-mu addressed the council:

Father, I have something to say to you, and I did not know whether to say it now, or wait until you would be done speaking. But, as you say I may speak, I will tell you, Father, I want to tell you something about the saw-mills, on our land. The object of our Great Father in granting mill privileges, we understand is, that we might derive some benefit from it; that by having sawed, we could get some of it, to have houses made for ourselves.

Father, Mr. Childs first spoke to my uncle, who died lately; he asked him for the privilege to build a mill on this river (Goose River) and said if he would grant him this privilege his Great Father would give him permission to do it. He afterwards built the mill, and while he had it, he gave us a present every year as he had promised he would do. But since he gave his right to another or sold it to another, we never got anything. This I wanted to tell you the first opportunity; and I thought I could not have a better chance. I went to Mr. Arndt, the present owner of the mill, and spoke to him about it, and he said that several of his cattle had been killed, and that the loss he had sustained thereby, was more than would pay for these last 4 years. Now, Father, is that a good answer? The pay is coming to me in right of my uncle, and am I to be wronged out of it because others may have done wrong? Now, Father, look at all these new buildings you see in this country; all the lumber for them was made at Arndt's mill. He must make a great deal of money; will get rich; should not he give us something? He could very well afford to do it. He promised to do so; and he does not do it. I hope, Father, you will see that justice is done to us. We do not complain of his having the mill. We only complain that he does not pay us as he promised.

This, Father, is all I have to say, I wished to wait until all about the Treaty was over. But as you asked if any of us had anything more to say, I thought I would tell you of this matter.

Pewaitenau, or the Rain, then spoke:

Father, I come from the Menominee River; I am glad to see you here, and I have something to say. I hope you will listen to me. I have a story what this (last) young man told you. I am a Chief: I sprung from the family and am related to this young man (alluding to the Little Brave) I was brought up at Menominee River; my Grandfather's home was there, and so was my father's and so is mine.

Father, I do not like to have the Menominee River dammed up. Is this what our Great Father gave them permission to do? Did he direct this? I ask you Father is it the word of our Great Father that our river should be dammed the whole way across? We used to catch plenty of fish; it was our principal means of subsistence. Father, I think these men should be satisfied with cutting down all our best timber, and sawing it up without stopping the fish. I have nothing to say against the grant. Our Chiefs gave their permission — sent it to their Great Father. But have these men the right to dam the river so that the fish cannot go up the River? Father, did we ever sell all the fish? I have no recollection of doing this. Father, this man says he owns all the fish in the River and all the cranberries. We never sold all these. Did we?

Father, all I wish is that the channel of the River may be left open, so that the fish can go up and down and that we catch them as heretofore, to subsist on.

After this speech, Porter and Colonel Boyd conferred in private. When they returned, Grizzly Bear spoke again:

Father, I wish you to listen to me, as this young man (Little Brave) told you, there are several of these half-breeds — a great many of them half Menominee — they have been brought up with us, and we have a good

feeling for them; we are favorable them; they are part of our blood. I
mentioned this when we were at Washington and a provision, in their
behalf, was to have been inserted in the Treaty. It was understood so;
we intended it; but somehow it was omitted, they forgot to put it in.
Now Father, I want you to write down, where these people are each
to have a track a piece. It is below the Grand Butte, and all along down
the river on the west side. I told this to our Great Father when I saw
him at Washington, and when we were making the Treaty.

Father, I hope you will have pity on us; our Great Father has pity
on his Menominee children. He said he would give us farmers to live
among us, and to raise for us corn and all kinds of vegetables. Now,
Father, about these farmers I have something to say. We do not like
the idea of having them among us; we would rather have the money;
the valuable consideration to be paid to them would do us good.
Father, these Farmers will eat up all the flour and give the bran to
their hogs. We never will get anything they raise; you must tell Our
Great Father about all this. He also wished us to have mills, and to
make these, it will require millwrights, and carpenters. And we are
told that with their mills, the boards will be sawed to make houses
for us. Now, Father, we do not want these mills; nor any mechanics
among us. We can build our own houses. Do you tell our Great Father
to give us money — the Cash — and it will do us more good, or if he
wishes to gives us more money than all these things will cost, we will
take it; our people know what to do with money.

Our great father has pity on us; we know this. But, Father, I wish to
ask you — is he a merchant? He sent us goods, why did he do this? We
want him to send us the pewter, and then we can buy our blankets,
and everything we need. We can do this ourselves. Our Great Father
promised to send us money, too, but we have never seen it yet. Our
People are poor as you see, and they should have some.

I told our Great Father, the President, that my village was at the
Butte des Morts, and that these half-breeds were with us there, and
I wished them to have their land there, and from thence down the
River. My Father lived and died there. I live there; and the principal
Chief lives there too — the Brother of this young man (Little Wave).

Father, you know we always take the advice of our Great Father;

and we do what he tells us to do; we, therefore, expect he will
have pity on us, and protect us. You know, when the Sac and Foxes
killed some our people, our Great Father said we must not raise the
Tomahawk and kill them; and, although it was very hard to restrain
our war Chiefs and young warriors, we obeyed; and afterwards when
our Great Father sent us word to go after these Sacs and Foxes, we
went at once, and had our satisfaction — our revenge.

Then, Father, at the time that three Menominees were killed, near
Prairie du Chien, by the Chippewas, we did not go after them; when
we were told we must not, we did not mind it; and so, Father, you will
find that we will do. If any more of our people should be killed, we
will do just as our father here (Col. Boyd) may tell us to do.

Now, father, we are done; and we are anxious to go home, after we
hear what you have further to say to us. We understood all you said;
and we cannot agree to give these New York Indians what is proposed
by the Senate.

After many Menominee representatives had taken their turns before
the council, Porter spoke. He claimed he didn't know why the provision
of land for the "half breeds" was left out of the treaty and he did not have
the authority to put the provision back in the treaty. Boyd, Porter assured
them, would eventually be instructed to deal with the issues of the mill and
the dams that stopped the fish in the Menominee River. Then Arndt spoke,
saying he had paid the annual sum but last year he did not because the person he had paid died and he didn't know whom to pay. Porter said he would
caution the New York Indians that they couldn't hunt on Menominee lands
or "injure your Sugar Camps." Finally, he again asked the Menominee to
approve the treaty with the Senate provisos.

At this, Grizzly Bear became upset and said "they never would consent
to any such thing." The exact speech is not quoted in Porter's journal, only
the substance of it. Grizzly Bear said that some of their people lived above
and some lived below Grand Chute. They went up and down the river
with their canoes, and the traders lived there. "They never would consent
to give up the ground, & if these Wabenockies intended to rob them of it,
they would defend themselves. They had their guns."

At this point, Porter interrupted Grizzly Bear and ordered him to stop speaking and listen to the rest of what Porter had to say. Porter said he would send honest men to be millers and farmers. However, he added that "Until the Treaty be ratified you cannot expect to receive any benefit from the several provisions . . . the whole Treaty must fall to the ground, and what then will be your situation. I beg you to reflect on this." This sounds like a threat, indicating that the Menominee must sign the Senate proviso or they would not receive the provisions in the treaty.

Porter then told the Menominee to discuss these ideas among themselves and come to an agreement. He said the treaty was for their own good as well as the good of the New York Indians. Porter said that the previous winter in Washington he told Daniel Bread and the other deputies that he thought the Menominee would agree to

give up the land along the Fox River from the Old Mill Dam to the lower line of Grignon's tract at the Big Kaklin and sending thence on a parallel line with the present south west line of the 5000,000 acres set apart by the Treaty for these New York Indians, as far as to include 200,000 acres, in exchange for an equal quantity of land on the North Eastern side of the Tract.

Nevertheless, Porter could not guarantee this because the Menominee weren't there. His task was to obtain agreement from the Menominee Nation. Porter encouraged the Menominee to agree to the proposed boundaries for the treaty. If they agreed, it would show they were not obstinate, "but willing to make a great sacrifice for the sake of peace. Besides thus, it is reasonable to suppose that these New York Indians will assent to it." If they agreed, it could be finalized and go to the Senate.

With the council still assembled, Grizzly Bear spoke again:

Father, it seems to take you a long time to do business — you white men. It is many years that this matter has been unsettled; we have waited a long time to see you; you have given us good reason why you could not come sooner. You could not control the winds and the sea. You now see all the principal men of our nation here; we ask you to take care of our nation, to protect us, and to be good to our children after we are dead.

Father, it does not take us so long to do our business. It would take us a long time to talk this matter all over. We do not talk much — we are so brought up. The forest is our life, and, as you perceive, we do not like to part with it, or any of our land, as we said to you before.

But, Father, you are sent here; we take you to be a good man, and that you would not advise us to anything that is not for our good. Your words have gone into our ears. We hold you fast by the hand. We never refuse good advice from our father. We hope you will tell us the truth. We expect that what we have agreed to do will satisfy the Senate. You must understand me, Father — there must be no mistake — you have been very particular in making us understand all you have said; that is all right. Now understand what we agree to do.

We agree to give the land from the old mill — Dam up along the River to the Big Kakalin, where one of our Traders lives (Augustus Grignon) at the lower line, and then to extend back as you said (on a line parallel with the South West line of the tract of land described in the treaty) so far as will include 200,000 acres; and we are to receive an equal quantity of land on the North Eastern side of Tract, on the Oconto Creek.

But we have one exception to make, Augustus Grignon has Sugar Camps at which he makes Sugar, we do not know exactly where they are so as to describe them to you. They are back from the River, on the land which we agree to give up. He must have the privilege to make Sugar as heretofore at his camps. And there are some of our Friends, the Traders, who have Sugar Camps back here, and it is our wish that they may not be interfered with either.

Now, my father, I hope it will be as we have told you. And it must be understood that these New York Indians shall not hunt on our lands, we forbid them to do so — have told them so. And besides this it must be understood that the communication shall not be stopped where we let them have the lands. The road is open to all, and we must have the right to pass along, as other people will do.

Father, you should know, too, that we granted a tract of land to one man, and the Secretary of War, gave him permission to hold it. It is Apple Creek (Here governor Porter enquired the name of the person to whom it was granted. The answer was, to Charles A. Grignon)

Father, I do not see why this was not included in Treaty, because I told our Great Father before we signed the Treaty that he (Charles A. Grignon) was to have this section of land, and it appears it was not included in the Treaty. You must also tell the New York Indians that they must not spoil these Sugar Camps.

We hope what we have agreed to do, will be satisfactory to our Great Father, the President, and to the Senate of the United States, and to you. And after this, if the New York Indians hunt upon our lands, we will break their Guns. This is our custom; and besides this, which is the practice of all your red Children, the New York Indians will now have notice of what we will do, if we catch them hunting on our lands. Father, you must not be angry with us for this. We are determined to do so, and we rely on you to protect us and to help us along. These New York Indians are hard to be satisfied. They are made like you are. They have education, and pride themselves upon it. But, Father, they have no ears; they are like Dogs; when we give them a piece they want more. They have no hearts or souls, and I told you before, they behave so badly that we hate them. What we agree to do now, is for our Great Father's sake and for your sake — you advise us to do, and we never refuse good advice coming from our Father. They have no right to ask or expect anything from us. I have told you all, except this which I tell you, that you may let them know it; that we now agree to fix a line and if we find a house of the New York Indians over this line, we will pull it down and put it back on their ground. Father, you must not be angry with us. You see we have, in pursuance of your advice, agreed to do so much for peace, and having done this, we are determined on what I last told you.

Father, we told you before about the half-breeds; that what we agreed to give them ought to have been included in the treaty, and that we told our great father, and all of them around us, this before we signed the Treaty. I need not say anything more. I am done.

Pe-wait-e-naw then spoke for the Menominee:

Father we are all of the same opinion. Our great Speaker has told you what we agreed to do. We are now all done.

Grizzly Bear then consulted with the other chiefs before saying:

We do not agree to grant anything to please the New York Indians;
we do not care whether they like this or not. We have done so much
to please you, under the hope that it will be satisfactory to our Great
Father and the Senate; and these little privileges we insist on.

On Wednesday, October 24, another council meeting was held, this
time with Porter, the interpreters, and citizens. Since none of the New
York Indians attended, Porter sent them a written notice that clarified
that his assignment was to acquire approval of the Senate provisos, and
if agreement was not reached, he was to identify a solution in the best
practicable terms.

The next day, Porter met in council with the New York Indians. According to Porter, John Quinney made a neat address in the English language,
welcoming their father to this country, and hoped the Great Spirit would
aid and assist him in putting an end to this perplexing affair. He said from
what he had seen during the last winter at Washington, he was convinced
the president would do everything in his power to effect an adjustment of
their differences on fair and just principles, and, being now assembled,
they were anxious to hear what proposition he had to make to them.

Porter told the New York Indians that the Menominee absolutely refused to accept the treaty with the Senate provisos, but after many meetings the Menominee finally agreed to the proposition. He asked them to
accept the proposition he was going to submit to them. The New York
Indians said they would give their answer at 4 p.m. the same day. Quinney
then asked that the proposition made by the Menominee and the Great
Father's instructions be given to them in writing. Porter advised the New
York Indians to accept the Menominee modifications. In reply to the request of New York Indians to see the Menominee modifications in writing,
the New York Indians were shown the following:

They agree to give up and cede the land along Fox River, from the
Old Mill Dam to the lower line of Augustin Grignon's tract, at the Big
Kakalin, and, extending thence on a northwest line, or a line parallel

with the present South western line of the tract of 500,000 acres,
set apart by the treaty for the New York Indians, so far as to include
a tract of 200,000 acres, without including any of the confirmed
private land claims;

and in lieu of this, the New York Indians to give in exchange an
equal quantity (200,000) acres of land, on the northeastern side
of the tract on the Oconto creek, being a part of the same tract of
500,000 acres, as aforesaid.

Porter then explained that other parts of the agreement included the
tract of land with the mill to Charles Grignon's land on Apple Creek. The
issue of the sugar camps was to be allowed, and the New York Indians were
not to hunt or build houses on Menominee land.

At 9 a.m. on October 26, the council again assembled, but no Indians
attended because Samuel W. Beall, a land speculator and lawyer, advised
them not to. Beall was being paid six hundred dollars a year as long as the
dispute continued, so he had a reason to keep the conflict unsettled. Then
at 10 a.m., Samson Marquis (Stockbridge) appeared and addressed the
council as follows:

Governor, in the English language remarked, the rest of the Indians
who had met us in Council yesterday, were at Mr. Beall's office; that
he was writing up a paper for them to sign by which they refused to
accept of the proposition made by the Menominee; and as soon as it
should be completed, a Commuter or Deputation would bring to the
council room.

That Mr. Beall had told them not to meet again in Council; but
to let him advise them and draw up in writing an answer to any
proposition which might be made to them. That he; Sampson
Marquis and many more of their people, were dissatisfied with this
mode of doing business; that their Chiefs and head men did not
understand what Mr. Beall would write down; that he would write
it his own way and not as they wanted it; and that it was hard when
all the Stockbridges, Brotherton and Munsee were perfectly satisfied
with the proposition made to them last winter at Washington and

which was still within their power, that Mr. Beall should prevent
them from coming to a settlement; that he was astonished at their
people for being blind, not only to their own interest, but to the
motives of Mr. Beall conduct.

That the contract entered into long ago with Mr. Beall, was, to
pay him six hundred dollars per year, for his services so long as the
dispute remained unsettled; that this sum was principally paid to
him out of their money; that the Six Nations paid little or none of
it; and now, when they (Stockbridge &c.,) had got all they wanted,
it was asked that they should pay to keep up a dispute, to their great
prejudice, and seriously affecting their true interests; that he thought
it his duty to come and state these facts, and to ask their Father
whether something could not be done to prevent Mr. Beal from
interfering in their concerns.

At 1 p.m. on October 26, Quinney and others presented their response
to Porter in writing:

We, the undersigned Chiefs and principal men of the several tribes of
New York Indians, now resident in the vicinity of Green Bay, having
received and considered the proposition of the Menominee tribes, (as
contained in the letter of your Excellency of October 25th) to amend
the modification of the Senate to the Treaty of February 1831, and
being advised by your Excellency to accede to said amendment of the
Menominees, beg leave respectfully, but explicitly, to state the we
have neither the power nor inclination to close with any terms other
than those expressed in the foresaid modification of the Senate.

We cannot express the surprise we feel that an obstruction
should be offered from any quarter, to prevent a settlement of the
matter, as it stood upon the final and impartial action of the Senate
of the United States; and we are mortified to find that, after all
our sacrifices, we should again be called on by the officers of the
Government to make further concessions.

We intreat your excellency, as the general father and head of all
the Tribes of the north west, to review the past history of this long
and distressing contest; and if you can then find it in your heart to

term us obstinate and unyielding, we erred in attributing to you feeling towards us you do not possess.

If, in the course of the few remarks we shall make to your excellency at this time, an expression should escape us which may be wounding to your ear, or unbecoming the red man, when addressing his Father, our apology will be found in the necessity of asserting our rights respectfully but firmly, and in the feelings we must possess our present, unparalleled condition.

In the course of the various negotiations regarding our claims in Territory, we have constantly retreated and yielded up our rights when called upon by the Government, until this spirit of concessions seem to have rendered us contemptible in the eyes of the Menominee. How else can they now ask more of us?

If a desire of peace, and an attachment to the Government of the United States, has exposed us to privations and losses, we should otherwise have avoided, it cannot, therefore, be supposed that we will now, or any time, yield anything to the perfidy of our Menominee brethren.

No good reason exists, why they should not cheerfully have yielded to the will of the Senate. We believed that, to the band residing on the Oconto, the tract in that vicinity is more valuable than the land on the South, and that they would gladly have closed with the offer of exchange, if left free to express an opinion.

There is no weight in the remark, that the proviso of the Senate, by granting to the Six Nations the course of the river from the Mill Dam to the Grand Chute, worked any injury to the mill or farm of the Menominees.

The water power of the outlet of the Winnebago Lake is great — is included in their tract, and would be useful and available for the Menominees as that at the Grand Chute. Besides, from the reports of Col. Stambaugh, we are to believe that the Oconto, and the streams in its vicinity, abound with excellent mill seats. Equally unfounded is the consideration that, if the Six Nations possess the river above Grignon's line, to the Grand Chute, the Menominees will have no privileges of encampment and portage. With what nation of the world, and with what Indian Tribe, is the permission of temporary rest, for the peaceable traveler withheld? And why does not the objection, if good, hold the more strongly, for the difference in distance between the Rapids des Peres and Grignon's Line, now proposed to be allowed to the New York Indians?

But upon the assumption that the modification was of real injury to the milling operations of the Menominees, as intended by the treaty to be centered at the Grand Chute, would it not be preferable that, by a subsequent arrangement the Government should select the Winnebago Rapids, or some other water power for that purpose, instead of jeopardizing the welfare of both parties in opening the door for another contest more bitter and obdurate from duration?

It is manifestly so impossible that the exceptions in the proposition of the Menominees, in favor of their traders, and some of the French inhabitants of the country, should be acceded to, that we would not refer to them, but that the attention of your excellency may be called to the quarter from whence all our difficulties have sprung, and that you may personally attest the influence which this part of the white population exercise upon the movements of the Menominees.

From our knowledge of the easy means by which Government effectuates it's plans with Indians generally, and from all which has met our notice during the present negotiation with the Menominees, justice to ourselves requires us to express the decided belief that, if the same persevering efforts which were exerted in obtaining the assent of the Menomonies to the proposition now submitted us, had been employed in procuring their unconditional concurrence in the modification of the Senate, your excellency would have accomplished what we are informed has been the main object of your Mission. As it is, we have the consoling reflection that whatever may be the result of the present violation of will and expressed intention of the Senate by the non-acceptance of the Menominees; however injurious to the interests of the country and the rights of individuals, no dispassionate tribunal will attribute to us any portion of folly or obloquy which may be attached to the transaction.

Green Bay October 26th 1831

Attest S.W. Beall

Oneidas: Henry his X mark Powles
            John his X mark Anthony
            Nathaniel his X mark Neddy
            Cornelius his X mark Stevens
            Neddy Autlequette

Seneca   Geo his X mark Jamieson

St Regis & Tuscarora   E. Williams

Brotherton   Randall Abner

Stockbridge   John Metoxen
            Jacob Checkthancon
            Rob't his X mark Konkapot
            John W. Quinney

Munsee   Capt. Porter X mark

Porter told them he expected these comments since Samson Marquis had told them about Beall's getting paid six hundred dollars yearly to keep the dispute going. He told them he knew that they signed the paper that Beall wrote without fully understanding what was in it and that it contained "insinuations and falsehoods." Porter stated that he and twenty people, some of whom were present, could attest to the false information that had been told to the New York Indians.

The governor pointed out several of the statements and asked if this was true, "To what they answered that they could not say it was. That they had no knowledge of it, and some remarked that they did not know that such a thing was in the paper." He advised them to speak for themselves and give him an answer. He would wait in the council room until they returned with an answer, and if they didn't appear they would not be in good standing with the president and the Senate. Porter wrote, "Soon afterwards, the Chiefs and Head men of the Stockbridge, Munsee, and Brotherton tribes, returned and wished to hear as they express it, their father's advice."

Porter told them they now had the opportunity to settle this problem, and he seemed to threaten that if they refused, they might "not advance their interests." He wanted them to accept the proposition; "the assent of the Menomonies had been obtained." Porter said that he believed they were in agreement with the offer, and they should "have the effect of inducing Daniel Bread and the other principal men of the Six Nations to come into the measure, and thus and all further trouble and enable them to set down in peace and harmony."

The New York Indians then held a meeting and agreed to sign the agreement the Menominee had made. The agreement appeared as follows:

> For the purpose of settling and adjusting this long, protracted dispute, we hereby acknowledge that we will accept the modifications required by the Menominees. Done at the Agency house at Green Bay this 26th day of October in the year of our Lord One thousand eight hundred and thirty-two.
> Signed Sealed and delivered in the presence of us.
> George Boyd — U.S. Indian Agent
> Sam Abbott
> Joshua Boyer — Secretary
> Henry S. Baird
> Charles A. Grignon
> A.J. Irwin
> Eben Childs
> William Dick
> John Metoxen
> Jacob Chicks
> Robert Konkapot his X mark
> Thos. J. Hendrick
> Austin Quinney
> Sampson Marquis
> Capt. Porter his X mark
> Elkanah Dick his X mark

John W. Quinney, however, objected to signing. Instead he had another statement drawn up, which he signed:

> I hereby signify my acceptance of the modifications required by the Menominees, as set forth in their proposition within stated, with

this exception that, I am of opinion that the reservations which they wish to make of the privilege of Charles A. Grignon and of the sugar camps, ought not to be made. My opinion is, that the Menominees have agreed to grant a sufficient quantity of good land, and suitable in its location, for the New York Indians, but that the land should be clear of these incumbencies.

Done at this Agency house at Green Bay this twenty seventh day of October one thousand eight hundred and thirty-two.

J.W. Quinney

Signed Sealed & delivered in presence of us.

George Boyd — U.S, Indian Agent

Samuel Abbott

Joshua Boyer — Secretary

Charles A. Grignon

Eben Childs

At this point, Porter saw the opportunity to get the agreements signed, so he sent for the Menominee and told them that if they would agree to drop their requirements regarding Grignon and the sugar camps and agree that the two hundred thousand acres be higher up the Fox River, then it would be settled.

In response, Grizzly Bear said:

Father, you do not seem to know us; we do not change our mind so soon as this; we have already told you that when we have anything to do, we consult together and decide, and when done, so it must be. We have also told you that we do not care anything for the New York Indians; whether they are pleased or not, we will not do anything for them. We would not take all the money our Great Father has, nor all the good things you have offered, to give the New York Indians any more of our Land. You tell us that if we do not agree to do something now by which settlement will be effected, the treaty will fall to the ground, as we will lose all the advantages secured to us by it. We say, no matter, let it fall to the ground; we will not do anymore; we are willing to do what is right. We take you and our father, Col. Boyd, by the hand, believing that in so doing we take our great father by the hand; but we know that our Great Father would not ask us, for his sake, to do more. What you want us to do is for the New York Indians and we say no! we will do nothing more.

It was obvious to those present that Grizzly Bear was upset, even "enraged," according to Porter, as he gave this speech. The journal says something was said to soothe those feelings. Everyone left because it was late, and "It being understood that an agreement for them to sign would be prepared in the course of the next day, and that when it should be completed and signed, they might return home."

Eventually, Porter put his request in writing. On October 27, he sent a note to the New York Indians:

> To the Chiefs and principal men of the New York Indians as well
> of the Stockbridge, Munsee and Brothertown Tribes, as of the Six
> Nations & St. Regis Tribe.
>   Previously to closing with the Menominees, by obtaining their
> signatures to the agreement which I have drawn up, I think it right
> to invite you to meet me at the Agency house, that you may have
> an opportunity once more of saying whether you will all accept the
> proposition made by the Menominees, or whether you have anything
> further to say or propose to me when assembled in Council. It is
> Saturday and I must close my labors here today. The sooner you can
> come to the Agency house to meet me, the better. The Menomoniees
> are very impatient and threaten to go home immediately.
> G. B. Porter

Eleazer Williams responded the next day on behalf of the New York Indians:

> Father, to show you that we are willing to make a sacrifice, for the
> sake having this dispute settled, we attended agreeably to your
> notice of this morning and I am instructed by the New York Indians
> to make this, as their last and final propositions, viz. The New York
> Indians will agree to settle this controversy, on condition that they
> have granted to them in exchange for 200,000 acres on the North
> Eastern Side of the tract of 500,000 described in the Treaty, and equal

quantity of the South West Side, to be laid off as follows:

Beginning at the old mill-dam, and thence extending up Fox River to the Little Rapid Croche, thence running back from the River three miles, thence in the direction of the course of Fox river, keeping back three miles from the same until it shall intersect the first stream which empties into Fox River above the Grand Chute, and thence running on a line parallel with the south west boundary line of the tract of 500,000 acres, described in the Treaty; the necessary distance to include 200,000 acres.

Porter said these boundaries were not acceptable, and "That in no event could the line extend further up Fox River than where it would intersect a line running N. W. commencing one mile above the Grand Chute, which was the point mentioned in the Resolution of the Senate, and which had been pointed out again and again to the Menominees." He explained the line for the New York Indians should not get closer to the Fox River than three miles. If this was agreed to, the Menominee objections for their "postage ground and trading post would remain free to them."

Porter asked for the New York Indians to change the line so "that the line should not run higher up than where it would intersect a northwest Line, commencing one mile above the Grand Chute, it was possible that the Menominees could be induced to accept it." The New York Indians consulted and agreed to this, saying now their only objections were the reservation for Charles A. Grignon and that the sugar camps should not be in the treaty.

Daniel Bread was informed that Cass had given Grignon the permission and the governor could not change it. Grignon was present and after discussion agreed he would release that tract, if another tract would be designated. Bread, however, continued to be opposed to the reservation for the sugar camps. Porter made sure everyone understood the terms, that the line would run:

Beginning on the said treaty line at the Old Mill Dam on Fox River; and thence extending up Fox River to the Little Rapid Croche, from thence a line running North West course three miles, thence on a line running parallel with the several courses of Fox

River and three miles distant from the river, until it will intersect a line running on a northwest course, commencing at a point one mile above the Grand Chute; thence on a line running northwest so far as will be necessary to include, between the said last line and line described as the southwestern boundary line of the 500,000 acres in the Treaty aforesaid, the quantity of 200,000 acres, and thence running northeast until it will intersect the line forming the south western boundary aforesaid; and from thence along the said line to the old mill dam or place of beginning, containing 200,000 acres.

They did allow the tract of land on Apple Creek for Grignon, which was approved by the Department of War on April 22, 1831. The five hundred thousand acres was to be marked off "without delay" by a commissioner whom the president would appoint. He reaffirmed the agreement and "that in exchange for the above quantity of land equal to that which was added to the southwestern side should be taken off from the northeastern side of said tract, described in that article, on the Oconto Creek, to be run, marked, and determined by the commissioner to be appointed by the President of the United States as aforesaid, so that the whole number of acres to be granted to the Six Nations and St. Regis tribe of Indians, shall not exceed the quantity of 500,000 acres."

The New York Indians assented to this. Afterward, Porter met with the Menominee and explained the boundaries the New York Indians had agreed to, which kept them three miles back from the river so the Menominee would have use of that area. Grizzly Bear had the governor present a map showing the boundaries. After much discussion, Grizzly Bear said he "wished to be distinctly informed whether the Governor would give them what he had said he would viz. Presents in clothing to the amount of $1,000, 500 bushels of corn, ten barrels of pork, and ten barrels of flour." The governor affirmed these items would be given.

Grizzly Bear then said:

Father, I shake hands with you all, I hold you fast by the hand; listen, I am now about to speak for all our Nation; I am talking to you, but still I think I am talking to my Great Father with whom I had the pleasure of shaking hands when we were at Washington. When I spoke with our Great Father he did not ask us to do this. But as it cannot be settled otherwise and you have been sent here by our Great Father we must take your advice. You are strong we are weak, I am not talking to these New York Indians, but to you; representing, as you do, our great father, and I am willing to [do] what is thought right by him and you; I am willing to leave the whole matter to him, and do as you say.

I hope our Great Father will have pity on us; when I shook hands with him I thought I would be happy. He told me we would be made comfortable; you have told us all, and how it is that we have so long kept out of money and everything else. We leave it all to our great father; only put an end to it now, and let us go home.

I wish you would not intrude on our Traders; they take care of us, and when they have a right, they should be permitted to hold it.

(He here shook hands with all present)

Now, Father, I leave it altogether to my great father and you; if you think it right, we are perfectly willing to do so, as you explained it. We wish to get through it to-day; tomorrow is your Sunday, and if it is not finished tonight, we will be kept two days longer here.

We do not want to [talk] more about it today.

Father, I have a sore throat. Our Father here (Col. Boyd) gave me something for it. I want you to do so too. You understand me. I am dry. And all our people here want to grease their mouths.

Porter replied that it would be impossible to have the document written and ready for signing before night came. Nevertheless, the Menominee said they would sign that evening. Porter then met with the New York Indians, and their part "of the agreement being made ready, all present signed it." On October 29, a dinner was held, with Porter writing,

The Chiefs and head men of the Menominee Nation, and of the several Tribes of New York Indians dined with the Governor at the public house of John P. Arndt; much good feeling existed; they shook hands and parted as friends, determining to forget and forgive all that had passed, and to live hereafter in peace and harmony with each other.

1832 Treaty with the Menominee, October 27, 1832[15]

The treaty begins by summarizing the February 8, 1831, treaty agreements and the February 17, 1831, supplemental articles made to the treaty. This treaty was submitted to the Senate, but no action was taken. In the March 15, 1831, session it was agreed the treaty would be dealt with at the next session of the Senate.

The Senate supplemental articles and the proviso contained the following provisions:

1. Two townships equal to 46,800 for the Stockbridge and Munsee and twenty-five thousand dollars for their improvements on current lands, which the Stockbridge and Munsee relinquished.

2. One township of 23,040 acres for the Brothertown, with the US government to pay sixteen hundred dollars to the Brothertown for improvements on the east side of Fox River, which the Brothertown relinquished.

3. A new line for the Six Nations and the St. Regis, a boundary of five hundred thousand acres for the New York Indians that designated two hundred thousand acres (part of five hundred thousand) to "commence at a point on the west side of the Fox river, and one mile above the Grand Shute, on Fox river, and at a sufficient distance from the said boundary line as established by the said first article, as shall comprehend the additional quantity of two hundred thousand acres of land on and along the west side of Fox River." (See map on page 231.)

This action traded lands on the north side for lands on the southwestern side. This agreement had been "conditionally" ratified in the 1831 treaty and was now agreed upon with the Menominee in the 1832 treaty.

The treaty referred the reader to Porter's journal to view the disagreements and discussions. A modified agreement was made with the Menominee, and the New York Indians accepted:

First, the Menominee agree to the townships for the Stockbridge, Munsee, and Brothertown nations.

Second, the Senate proviso boundary lines which were rejected, are replaced and both the Menominee and New York Indians "agree, in lieu of this proposition, to set off a like quantity of two hundred thousand acres as follows: The said Menominee nation hereby agree to cede for the benefit of the New York Indians along the southwestern boundary line of the present five hundred thousand acres described in the first article of the treaty as set apart for the New York Indians, a tract of land; bounded as follows.

Beginning on the said treaty line, at the old mill dam on Fox River, and thence extending up along Fox river to the little Rapid Croche; from thence running a northwest course three miles; thence on a line running parallel with the several courses of Fox river, and three miles distant from the river, until it will intersect a line, running on a northwest course, commencing at a point one mile above the Grand Shute; thence on a line running northwest, so far as will be necessary to include, between the said last line and the line described as the southwestern boundary line of the five hundred thousand acres in the treaty aforesaid, the quantity of two hundred thousand acres; and thence running northeast until it will intersect the line, forming the southwestern boundary line aforesaid; and from thence along the said line to the old mill dam, or place of beginning, containing two hundred thousand acres.

The treaty confirmed the "privilege of Charles A. Grignon, for erecting a mill on Apple creek"; and the private land claims were confirmed:

And that in exchange for the above, a quantity of land equal to that which is added to the southwestern side shall be taken off from the northeastern side of the said tract, described in that article, on the Oconto creek, to be run, marked and determined by the commissioner to be appointed by the President of the United States, as aforesaid, so that the whole number of acres to be granted to the Six Nations and St. Regis tribe of Indians, shall not exceed the quantity of five hundred thousand acres.

Article 3. The Menominees agree to the treaty, with modifications, will be binding and obligatory on them. Porter delivered to chiefs, headmen, and the people of the said Menominee:

clothing up to $1,000
500 bushels of corn
10 barrels of pork
10 barrels of flours, &c. &c.

The treaty was signed on October 27, 1832 at the Indian Agency house at Green Bay.

G.B. Porter, Commissioner of the United States
Kausk-kan-no-naïve, grizzly bear, his X mark,
Osh-rosh [?], the brave (by his brother fully empowered to act,)
Osh-ke-e-na-neur, the young man, his X mark,
A-ya-mah-ta, fish spawn, his X mark,
Pe-wait-enaw, his X mark,
Che-na-po-mee, one that is looked at, his X mark,
Ko-ma-ni-kin, big wave, his X mark,
Ke-shee-a-quo-teur, the flying cloud, his X mark,
Wain-e-saut, one who arranges the circle, (by his son, Wa-kee-
    che-on-a-peur,) his X mark,
Ke-shoh, the sun, (by his son, A-pa-ma-chao, shifting cloud,)
    his X mark
Ma-concee-wa-be-no-chee, bear's child, his X mark,
Wa-bose, the rabbit, his X mark,
Shaw-e-no-ge-shick, south sky, his X mark,
Ac-camut, the prophet, his X mark,
Mas-ka-ma-gee, his X mark,
Sho-ne-on, silver, his X mark,
Maw-baw-so, pale color, his X mark,

Paw-ako-neur, big soldier, (by his representative, Che-kaw-mah-
    kee-shen,) his X mark,
Sealed and delivered, in the presence of —
George Boyd, United States Indian agent,
Charles A. Grignon, interpreter,
Samuel Abbott,
Joshua Boyer, secretary,
James M. Boyd,
Richard Pricket, his X mark, interpreter,
Henry S. Baird,
R.A. Forsyth, paymaster U.S. Army,
B.B. Kercheval,
Ebenezer Childs.[16]

The following appendix was attached to the 1832 treaty.

Appendix: October 27, 1832, 7 Stat. 409
To all to whom these presents shall come, the undersigned, Chiefs
and headmen of the sundry tribes of New York Indians, (as set forth
in the specifications annexed to their signatures,) send greeting:

WHEREAS a tedious and perplexing and harassing dispute and
controversy have long existed between the Menominee nation of
Indians and the New York Indians, more particularly known as the
Stockbridge, Munsee and Brothertown tribes, the Six Nations and
St. Regis tribe. The treaty made between the said Menominee nation,
and the United States, and the conditional ratification thereof by the
Senate of the United States, being stated and set forth in the within
agreement, entered into between the chiefs and headmen of the
said Menominees, and George B. Porter, Governor the Michigan,
commissioner especially appointed, with instructions referred to in
the said agreement. And whereas the undersigned are satisfied, and
believe that the best efforts of the said commissioner were directed
and used to procure, if practicable, the unconditional assent of the
said Menominees to the change proposed by the Senate of the United
States in the ratification of the said treaty: but without success.

And whereas the undersigned further believe that the terms stated in the within agreement are the best practicable terms, short of those proposed by the Senate of the United States, which could be obtained from the said Menominees; and being asked to signify our acceptance of the modifications proposed as aforesaid by the Menominees, we are compelled, by a sense of duty and propriety to say that we do hereby accept the same.

So far as the tribes to which we belong are concerned, we are perfectly satisfied, that the treaty should be ratified on the terms proposed by the Menominees. We further believe that the tract of land which the Menominees in the within agreement, are willing to cede, in exchange for an equal quantity on the northeast side of the tract of five hundred thousand acres, contains a sufficient quantity of good land, favorably and advantageously situated, to answer all the wants of the New York Indians, and St. Regis tribe. For the purpose, then of putting an end to strife, and that we may all sit down in peace harmony, we thus signify our acceptance of the modifications proposed by the Menominees: and we most respectfully request that the treaty as now modified by the agreement this day entered into with the Menominees, may be ratified and approved by the President and Senate of the United States.

In witness whereof, we have hereunto set our hands and seals, at the Agency House at Green Bay, this twenty-seventh day of October, in the year of our Lord one thousand eighteen [sic] hundred and thirty-two.

G.B. Porter, commissioner on behalf of the United States,

For, and on behalf of, the Stockbridge and Munsees:

John Metoxen,

John W. Quinney,

Austin Quinney,

Jacob Chicks,

Robert Konkopa, his X mark,

Thos. J. Hendrick,

Benjamin Palmer, his X mark,

Sampson Medyard,

Capt. Porter, his X mark,

For, and on behalf of, the Brothertowns:
  William Dick,
  Daniel Dick
  Elcanah Dick, his X mark

For and on behalf of, the Six Nations and St. Regis tribe:
  Daniel Bread
  John Anthony Brant, his X mark,
  Henry Powles, his X mark,
  Nathaniel Neddy, his X mark,
  Cornelius Stevens, his X mark,
  Thomas Neddy, his X mark

Sealed, and delivered, in the presence of—
  George Boyd, United States Agent,
  R.A. Forsyth, paymaster U.S. Army,
  Charles A. Grignon, Interpreter,
  Samuel Abbott,
  Joshua Boyer, secretary
  B.B. Kercheval,
  Eben. Childs,
  Henry S. Baird,
  Peter B. Grignon,
  Hanson Johnson,
  James M. Boyd,
  Richard Pricket, his X mark, interpreter.

This treaty was ratified March 13, 1833.

—ıı—

George Bryan Porter, the governor of Michigan Territory, was sent to get the Menominee to agree to changes to the 1831 treaty proposed by the Senate. His goal was to procure unconditional assent, or if they wouldn't agree then, to procure their assent to the *best practicable terms.* The New York Indians were asked to accept the modifications required by Menominees.

The issue of boundaries went back and forth as discussed in speeches by the Menominee, Stockbridge, and Oneida leaders. This treaty was designed by the United States to obtain more Menominee lands and put those lands for sale. The treaty provides an overview of Porter's attempts to persuade the Menominee to accept the Senate proviso, their refusal, discussions with the New York Indians, and modifications made. The voices of both the Menominee and the New York Indians were documented during these intense negotiations. An ironic issue raised was that a mill had been built that dammed the Menominee River, and the fish couldn't get upstream. This parallels contemporary issues of a proposed open-pit mine that would pollute the river; the Menominee have been strong in their opposition to the mine.

11

THE ONGOING THREAT OF REMOVAL

What happened in the years following the 1832 treaty between the United States and the Menominee Nation, which guaranteed five hundred thousand acres to the New York Indians, and the final Oneida treaty with the United States, signed in 1838, which allowed for only 65,400 acres? In 1836, a commissioner from the United States, John Schermerhorn, was sent to meet with the Menominee and the New York Indians to negotiate another move west. Schermerhorn promised lands in the west and funding to survive the first year. Immediately after this meeting, Schermerhorn had two removal treaties drawn up, one with the Oneida and another with the Stockbridge, but neither treaty was ever ratified.

Removal policies created divisions within the Oneida and Stockbridge Nations. Some favored removal, feeling they had no choice and would ultimately be removed no matter what. Others opposed, stating they had already been forced to relocate once and would not do so again.

1832–1836

Between 1832 and 1836, the United States attempted to implement the 1831 and 1832 treaties with the Menominee. Letters indicate the payment of annuities for the treaties and problems with those payments, as well as arrangements made on behalf of farmers, blacksmiths, and teachers. These were not always beneficial.

The Oneida chiefs wrote a letter to Lewis Cass in January of 1833, informing the secretary of war that they had not yet received their annuity payment. The Stockbridge also wrote to Cass to inform him that they had delegated power of attorney to Daniel Whitney, and the Oneida at Duck Creek requested funds from George Boyd, the Indian Agent, for a school. The Oneida chiefs wrote:

> Dear Sir,
> We have not as yet received our goods from the Indian Agent of the
> United States. The Agent on the part of the general government
> has heretofore furnished us goods every year in the early part of
> November. We had heard nothing from him this year. It is now about
> the middle of Winter and the naked children of our Tribe feel sharply
> the inclemency of the season. Please let us know the cause of this
> delay. —
> Oneida, 4th of Jany. 1833
> Witness of
> David [?] Thomas
> Yours
> Christian X his mark Beachtree
> August his X mark Cornelius
> Abraham his X mark Schuyler
> Chiefs of the Oneida Tribe
> The above are Chiefs of the Oneida Indians
> . . . Lunhis [?] Atty for the Oneida Indians[1]

The Stockbridge letter to Cass, dated January 31, 1834, read as follows:

> Father,
> We the undersigned are Chiefs and Head men of the Stockbridge
> Tribe of Indians. We have given to our friend Daniel Whitney of
> Green Bay, who is known to you, a power of attorney to receive for us,
> from the proper office, whatever sums of money may be appropriated
> by Congress for our benefit, in consideration of improvements which
> we hold on the Fox river.

The sum of twelve-thousand seven hundred and eight dollars is due from us to Mr. Whitney, which we desire to be paid to him at the earliest date possible. The remainder of the money we wish paid to him under the conditions specified in the power of attorney. The power was given him in full council & with the understanding of the Tribe, and He holds our agreements and evidences of the debt as stated above.

Father, We take the liberty of requesting your good offices both for W. Whitney and ourselves.

John W. Quinney
Thos J. Hendrick
John N. Chicks
John his X mark . . .
Sampson Marquis
James his X mark Plomer [?]
Capt. his X mark Porter
Josiah Miller
Timothy his X mark Jourdan
John Metoxen
Robt his X mark Konkapot
Jacob his X mark Chicks
Austin E. his X mark Quinney[2]

The Oneida at Duck Creek wrote a letter to Boyd regarding construction of a school appears here as written:

Father,
We your children, Chiefs of the Oneida Tribe, desire to say a few words to you.

Father,
We are exceedingly anxious that our children should be educated as White children are. We wish for this purpose, that a school might be regularly kept in our settlement. But Father we are poor and unable to bear the expense of paying a teacher — May we therefore, ask of our Father that he would . . . to our Great Father at Washington

requesting that a small portion of the fund for the civilization of
Indians be appropriated annually for the benefit of the First Christian
Party of Oneida Indians settled at Duck Creek, Green Bay, of which
party we are the chiefs and representatives.

Father, We take this occasion to thank you for all your friendship
to your children and to assure you that we do now, and ever shall hold
your foot by the hand.

Father, We think it right to inform you that we are now building a
school house. May we therefore request you to lend us your . . . with
our Great Father at Washington, in furtherance of the object we have
in mind.

Father, It would give us great pleasure to see you at our Settlement
that you may observe with your own eyes our improvement, and the
benefits of granting us this favor we now ask.

Witness S.W. Beall, John V. Suydam
Elijah Scanando
Henry his X mark Powlis
Adam his X mark Swamp
Cornelius his X mark Steivens
Neddy his X mark Archiquet
Cornelius his X mark Bear
Thos his X mark King
David his X mark Williams
Daniel Bread[3]

A council was scheduled to be held in August 1836 at Green Bay between Boyd and the Stockbridge, Oneida, Brothertown and St. Regis, and
Munsee. Its exclusive purpose was to discuss removing the New York Indians from Wisconsin to lands west of the Mississippi. The Brothertown and
the Oneida sent letters beforehand to define parameters for the meeting to
be held on August 30. The Brothertown letters indicate that the time period
to arrive was too short. Evidence of division within the Oneida was also
written down, as the Orchard Party would no longer meet with the other
New York Indians, as they were a distinct and separate nation. This was
refuted as a misunderstanding by the Oneida chiefs of the First Christian
Party. These discussions and letters took place and were written at the

treaty grounds of Cedar Point, on the Fox River near Little Chute, before the meeting. The actual meeting was held at Green Bay.

The letter from the Brothertown to Boyd, dated August 27, 1836, reads as follows:

Dear Sire,

We received your note informing us that Gov. Dodge was desirous to have an interview with the principal men of the Brothertown Tribe of Indians as soon as possible 3 miles below the Grand Shute. The late arrival of which will not permit us to be at that place before & sometime on Monday next.

Statesburgh August 27, 1836

George Boyd, Esq. US I. A.

Elhand Dick,

David Fowler,

Thomas Commuch [?],

Alonzo Dick

On August 29, Daniel Bread wrote the following to Henry Dodge, the governor of Wisconsin Territory, to voice his opposition to the council:

Sir, on behalf of my Nation allow me to express to you our determination not to attend the council to be held in the present week at the Little Shute. We say to you in the most respectful manner that we not only now refuse but will forever hereafter refuse to sitting in Council with the Menomonee, Stockbridge & Brothertown Tribes. We have nothing to do in conjunction with them.

The Oneida Nation must therefore be regarded as standing alone. Any communication coming from the Government to them shall be respectfully considered. Should there be a proposition for us to dispose of any tract of our country however, it must be expected that our answer will be more in accordance with what may be deemed in strict regard to our own interest than with feelings and views of your Excellency. (Signed) Daniel Bread

A true copy from the original. John M. McCammon, Sec.[4]

Boyd responded with the following letter to the Brothertown:

A letter of which the following is a copy was addressed & immediately
sent by an Oneida as a messenger to the Oneida Chiefs . . .
     Treaty Grounds Cedar Point, on Fox River, near Little Shute,
August 30, 1836
To Cornelius Stevens, Cornelius . . . , Adam Swamp, Elijah
Scanandoe, Thomas King & Henry Powlis, Chiefs & Head men of the
Oneida Nation—
George Boyd the Indian Agent said he is relaying instructions from
the Great Father to hold these meetings and in response to the
Oneida letter, he states that he "expects this request to be complied
with without delay as the chiefs of the other tribe are now in
attendance at this place." H. Dodge (Gov.)[5]

The same letter was sent to the Brothertown.
    A letter was attached to the report made by Boyd. It showed that the
government met with the individual nations and parties separately as
requested. The Indigenous nations kept their individual nation identities,
despite the United States lumping them together and labeling them the
New York Indians. This letter reads as follows:

To His Excellency Gov. Dodge,
The Chiefs of the First Christian Party of Oneida Indians are now
on the ground & will bring an attentive ear to what you have to
say. By refusing to comply with your request, they did not intend
any disrespect to your Excellency individually nor to their Great
Father, whom you represent. They were governed in their conduct
by a mutual agreement entered into with the Orchard Party that as
we knew of no business of interest to our Nation we would decline
attendance. If our course in this affair has caused any unpleasant
feelings it is to us a matter of sincere regret. Father, this is the Truth!
Daniel Bread
Elijah Skenando
Adam Swamp[6]

1836 TREATY COUNCIL WITH THE NEW YORK INDIANS, AUGUST 30 TO SEPTEMBER 6

The treaty council was held at Green Bay with the New York Indians and Governor Dodge, who served as one of the commissioners. The purpose of this treaty council was to present the government's proposal to move the Stockbridge, Oneida, and Brothertown west of the Mississippi. The journal from this treaty council documents speeches of the Stockbridge, the Brothertown, and the Oneida's two parties: the First Christian Party and the Second Christian Party (the Orchard Party). The letters show the opposing opinions within the tribes on the removal. The government met with the nations separately.

Those present for the council included the following men:

Stockbridge:
   John Metoxen
   John Quinney
   Austin Quinney
   Thomas Reudsel
   Jacob Chicks
   Captain Porter
   Anthony Jourdan
   A. Konkapot

Brothertown:
   Randall Abner [?]

Oneida:
   Jacob Cornelius
   John Cornelius
   Thomas Lodowich
   Honyous Smith

On August 30, the council meeting began. The Stockbridge and Brothertown were the first to deliberate. The commissioners addressed them as "friends and brothers," and praised them for their improvements in agriculture. Then the commissioners said they could not stop the number of whites moving to the area, and advised them that it would be better for the Stockbridge and Brothertown to move "west of the Mississippi and South of the Missouri River, where you can live unmolested." Dodge continued and in a paternalistic manner assured the Stockbridge and Brothertown that the Great Father was looking out for them and would provide them a safe place so as to prevent "the remnants of Indian nations, once powerful, from becoming extinct."

Immediately after this, a council was held with the Oneida Nation. The following chiefs and head men were present: Jacob Cornelius, John Cornelius, Thomas Lodwick, Honyost Smith, and Christian Peachtree.[7] According to the journal kept at this treaty council, Dodge "addressed the Chiefs & headmen present, in substance as to the same effect as he had previously done to the Stockbridge & Brothertowns. Those part of the Treaties of 1831 & 1832 relative to the New York Indians, were then read & explained to the Indians, in their own language." The chiefs were told that they could take time to consider and deliberate and give an answer at a convenient time. Then Dodge described the

> disposition of the President as being kind & friendly, and that he
> was surprised that a part of the chiefs had refused to attend & he
> expressed himself well pleased with those who had attended, but
> displeased with those who had refused, whose conduct should be
> fully explained to their Great father the President.[8]

The following day, the Oneida at Duck Creek sent Dodge a brief and deliberate letter in response:

> To His Excellency & Gov. Dodge
> Your talk of the 30th has been received. The Chiefs met in council
> and after seriously deliberating upon the same have come to
> the conclusion not to comply with your request. The letter you
> acknowledge to having received from Daniel Bread is a fair expression
> of our view. We have nothing more to say.

Witness Teionohiathe [?]

Cornelius his X mark Stevens

Addy Atsequette

Elijah his X mark Skenando

Thomas his X mark King

Daniel his X mark Williams

P.S. Henry Powlis & Adam Swamp are absent from the talks.[9]

On September 1, Jacob Cornelius spoke for the Orchard Party of Oneidas to again assert their position. Addressing the council, he said:

We want you to listen. Yesterday we heard what you wanted & we
have come to tell you what we think of it. We are very glad we heard
all we did yesterday & that President thinks of his red children. We are
glad & well pleased at heart to hear that he wishes to us as well, and of
his instructions, as we think he intends to do us good.

We have counselled together here & our Great father has expressed
his wish to remove us west of the Mississippi, & south of the Missouri,
and thinks it would be better for all of the New York Indians, to
remove them there: we understand this and will let him know what
we think. We are not afraid to tell our minds for we know our Great
Father likes us — When we left N.Y, we came to G. Bay intending
to live in a great woods, because where we lived we were being
surrounded by too many white people, we are much pleased with
the land we have now & the manner in which we work & live. Want to
keep the land which the President agreed to give us here, and not sell
it: we think if we do not stay here we will never stop moving, and we
do not like to move from place to place. We are different now in mind
from our forefathers. They knew how to hunt, but we see our white
brethren farming near us like to do so too: we are very hopeful since
we commenced farming. We ask the favor of our Great father the
President, that we may stop here. We think we will not have so good
a chance to farm if we remove west of the Mississippi. Another thing,
we do not want [to] follow the footsteps of our forefathers, hunting is
no good to us: & we want to live by farming: we have said but little &

in such a way as is proper for us: we want to farm & we want a school for our children so they may be educated, & become a part of the people of the United States. Such is our mind, and when we become fit to be citizens, we will tell our great father, the president: we only want to have our land secured so that no one shall interfere with us: we want all the land which we are entitled to set apart in one body: so that we may know how much we are entitled to.

The other party, called the First Christian Party, of our tribe, do not wish to become citizens: we must be governed by the treaty & when the president pleased to apportion the land we must submit: we are willing to abide by the treaty. We wish to ask of our Great Father the favor that he wouldn't again ask us to go west of Mississippi. That is all we have to say on the subject—

Father, we wish to say to you that we are very glad to see you here & we feel in our hearts that you are as well & that you do so: we have faith in you: we believe you are doing good here and we believe the president has faith in you. We ask of you to endeavor to settle the difficulties between our nations.

We have two denominations of Christians, & they do not agree. Our party (the Orchard party) live about four miles from the other (First Christian Party). We are all Methodists: In the other party there are some Methodists. We the Orchard party are poor and unable to buy a house for school because Mr. Clark the Methodists Superintendent gave us a schoolhouse which is situated in the part of our country occupied by the other party.

Some of the female missionaries of our party held school in that house: and the other party do not wish to have us occupy it. The chiefs of that party objected to our having the house there so they wanted to have school of their own. All other Methodists that belong to the first Christian party say that they want the Methodist school as they like it best.

The chiefs of the other party & their warriors held a council, and went to the house & tore it down and have not left one log standing: they also took leave to remove the teachers & their things. She refused to go: and they then took away without her consent, all her clothes, furniture & provision & carried them to the place where she formerly lived at the mission house, is all they have done: and we ask you to regulate the matter in your own way & settle it as you think best: we look upon you as the representative of our Great Father the President — & we leave it with you.

Dodge advised the Orchard Party Oneidas to meet with him to discuss the disputes and advised them be friendly with each other, and that the Stockbridge, Brothertown, and Oneida should live as brothers. Dodge had been meeting separately with each nation and wanted them to negotiate together.[10]

On the same day, at noon, the Brothertown met with the commissioners to further discuss removal. In a letter addressed to Dodge, they wrote:

Father, in answer to the propositions made to the delegates of the Brothertown Tribes of Indians to dispose of these lands and remove west of the Mississippi and south of the Missouri River, we would respectfully reply that we are very happy to hear that our great father the President of the United States is so mindful and solicitous for the welfare of us his children. We cannot but express heartfelt gratitude to him for his benevolent feelings towards us.

Father, but as we have long since laid aside those arms made use of in war for the peaceful implements of agriculture and husbandry, and as our great Father the President of the United States was pleased to grant to us this tract of land on which we now reside, with which we are so pleased & suited with both as to soil & climate that we could not at present feel a proposition or a desire to make the exchange.

Father, We would further state that as we have so far progressed in the arts of civilization and husbandry and having for several generations past been brought up among & in the neighborhood of white people in the State of New York where the Legislature was pleased to enact laws for our benefit and protection and as we have lost the Language, manners and customs of our forefathers and can and speak no other language than the English, it would not in our opinion ameliorate our condition to be removed into a Country where its inhabitants are almost wholly uncivilized and entirely an Indian Country, the Brothertown Indians would have to receive a new Language & new manners and customs which they fear would not increase their happiness.

Father, we would further state as one of our reasons for removing from the State of New York that as our reservations was too small and under a deep sense of this, we were influenced by a very small degree of that spirit so common to our Brethren the white people which induces them to provide and establish their children so that they may be enabled to live comfortably. We thought that with these means in our possession, we could purchase a sufficient quantity of land so that all of our children individually could have comfortable farms, but after all the tract which we now occupy is hereby . . . & sufficient to answer our necessities, but if hereafter the Brothertown Indians should have a desire to sell their lands here and remove to some other country, they feel it their duty to inform their great father the President and petition for his approbation for the same. We would now after having given a civil reply to the before mentioned propositions express our deep sense of the high estimation we still sustain for our great Father the President of the United States as also to your excellency: We would wish that you may enjoy the blessing of a long and prosperous life.

We are with the most profound respect you most obedient servants.
Signed Sept 1st 1836, Cedar Point Treaty grounds
Peacemakers & Principle Men of the Brothertown Tribe
Randall . . .
Elhabeth [?] Dick
Thomas Commach
Alonso D. Dick
Daniel Fowler
Solomon Paulis
David Dick
William Fowler[11]

The journal notes that in response,

The Commissioner said he had read their answer which should be communicated to their great Father, and told them that as they had lost their Language, they could perhaps be incorporated with their white brethren — That he did not know what might be the decision of the Government. That he was well pleased with their conduct while present which had been moral and correct, and that he should. . . .

Here the microfilm stops and a page seems to be missing. The signatures present, however, would indicate that a speech was given by the Stockbridge leaders:

us by the hand in Friendship — We are also pleased to hear that he has the welfare of all his red Children greatly at heart and wishes to make them prosperous and happy.

We therefore thank the Great Spirit above for including in his heart to have compassion for us & all his red Children in this western country. We likewise thank our great father for it.

With respect to the proposition made to us for the Country we now occupy and our removal west of the Mississippi and South of the Missouri. We would most respectfully and frankly reply that as important a movement is worthy of the greatest and most careful consideration, and that we have given it the same — We do not say that we will not comply with his request of our Great father — But Father, before giving our consent & before agreeing to give our place, we have a wish to visit the Country west of the Mississippi and South of the Missouri. We wish to go in a company of six or seven persons and examine the Country proposed, and this we would do if our great father would shew us the way this present fall or a year from this time. Should we find a Country west better suited to our wants than this where we are now where we could be sure of a peaceful permanent home then we would leave our present possessions

We thank you Father & . . . you and Great Father for the kind expression of regard for us, and we hope that this kindness & good will, will always be continued to us —

Signed at the Treaty Ground on the West Bank of the Fox River — this 2nd day of September (1836) for and in behalf by your excellencies most obt. & dutiful children.

John Metoxin
Austin Quinney
Jacob Chicks
Timothy Jourdon
Robert Konkapot
Thomas J [?] Hendrick
Captain Porter
. . . W. Quinney
Hendrick Aupaumont
Peter Sherman
Andrew Miller[12]

The commissioner, Dodge, said he had read their letter and was pleased they "express an inclination favorable to their removal." He stated he would forward their letter and their request to visit the lands west of the Mississippi to the president, and he commended them on their "good character and moral conduct."

Next, the commissioner held a separate council with just the First Christian Party of the Oneida and advised them to live in peace with the other party.

Elijah Scanando said:

Father we are very happy that the great spirit has permitted us to meet you here: I think it necessary to say that we wish to address you through our principle speaker.

Daniel Bread then spoke:

Friends & Father as this is the last day of the Council, we wish to say a few words in answer to your propositions. We have long since heard that this proposition would be made to us. We believe the President to have good feelings for his red children this day has brought forth an expression of that kind. I have heard it, some know that . . . have a kind feeling for their children. We believe the great father has the same feeling for us.

He has told us that the Country South of the Missouri and west of the Mississippi is a place calculated to make us happy. You have heard a few words from your red children, the Oneida, in regard to our land. This thing has discouraged as well, those who are here & those who have not removed here; our removal toward the setting sun. It is a hard case and proves the report to be true, that our great father to remove us farther. We have hardly laid down our packs or cleared land enough to live on, when word comes for us to go on — As to the advice of the President we have long been prepared to answer such a demand.

We have gone about far enough. We expected to have a chance to remain where we are. We are sorry we cannot answer you as you did ask. It is hard to find a place where we can be at rest. Wherever we go whites come also, and to get away from them is impossible. We beg you to let us rest here where we are. If you see us improving, why cannot we be left alone until we choose to change our residence and go farther. You are rich enough. You can cause rivers to flow the contrary way and cause the hills to be leveled down and great Father and Creator has given you riches and religion. We wish the President to look at his wealth. We hope he will consider former Treaties.

He possesses all the land of the Indian except a few spots and we hope he will let us rest for the sake of the good he has already rec'd from us. We thank you for the good wishes and the example set us in cultivating Land. We understand now. —

Our great Father thinks the proposed country is better for us than our own. We have the bad effects of moving often to be like feather to be driven by the wind is bad, it is better to be of a heavier substance and it sticks close to the ground. If we move often we will at last land on some mountain. —

We have no doubt that the President has good feeling towards his children. He is endowed with powers of the great spirit & is the guardian of his Red Children. We are in great trouble. We work hard to live. Once there appears to be a whip over us. We do not see of the benefit of our labor — every one is for his own interest — we think we have shew our kind feeling to our white brethren & have given them sufficient land to live on. This country is not so thickly peopled as many others. The whites do not disturb us, and we want to remain where we are. We are happy to read what the President had to say. We will now be better satisfied as we have been in suspense. We now know his wishes. We thank him for his former good wishes but we think this climate is better for us. Those that would be removed soon cause us to become . . . and we could not live with our red Brethren.

By the Treaty of Peace we have declared to be his children & that he was to take care of us. That treaty was sealed by shaking of hands & a silver Seal. As token of friendship & peace between us — the silver seal of that Treaty is getting rusty. We have not had it for many years. We are not discouraged by its failure — for we have confidence in our great Father and believe he will pay us our back annuities and the interest. We believe you will put in the President his mind of his promises perhaps he has forgotten them & we hope you will remind him of it. We feel thankful to the great Spirit that he has not forgotten us and that a man of good feeling has been chosen to meet us here. We wish to say in regard to the School House as this is important. We wish time to answer it in writing. The Chiefs have taken pains to provide for themselves & children. This was open for all. We hope all may live in peace as you recommend. We will let you know as soon as possible.[13]

The proceedings picked up again on September 6. In the journal, it states that on that day, "A council was held at Green Bay by the Commissioners with certain of the Chiefs of the Oneida Nation, to wit—Daniel Bread, Adam Swamp, Henry Powlis, Elijah Scando & Thomas King. The several treaties were read and fully explained in their own language." Then Daniel Bread said:

We understand the treaty and know its provisions and we wish
your advice and also what you will state is the instruction [and]
the goal of the President & if they wanted to take those lands — the
Commissioner told them the treaty was very plain and that as far as
he was interested. He would see a liberal construction of the treaty —
he would always lean towards the weaker party as they were less able
to protect themselves — and that such he knew to be the disposition
and intentions of their great father the President.

You have shewn your tender feelings to us — We endeavored to give the views of chiefs & Nation what were their wishes and wants — they have always been willing to give their attention to matters of such . . . as those proposed. It appears that the whites and Indians always want the same tracts of land, and that they have suffered for want of friends, but they see in you a friend of the weak. It is the minds of the Chiefs of your party that we have long sought for a place of rest and security. We think we should now look only to our interest and not to that of other Tribes & hope our Great Father will look to our interest as this is a matter of great moment. We think no decision should be made without consideration. We think the rest of the Tribes now in New York should be again invited to come here and if they refuse then we will make other arrangements with the government.

As we consider you as our father and state your good feelings towards us, we wish you to understand that we are the only Tribe who own the land here. We are the only Tribe who have paid anything towards its purchase & we think after they refuse to come here that we are the only Tribe who should be contracted with for its purchase.

We have confidence in you and we hope as we have honorably obtained the land the president will not resort to dishonorable means to take from us our lands. We hope he will only get it in a proper way — We hope that you will see we have our rights and that we may not be wronged. We wish to let you know all the land was for the six nations & we think they should be notified and if they refuse to remove the President may be informed of it. We have confidence in your ability & as you are endowed with power — and wish you to use it for the benefit of us the weaker which will acquire our gratitude.

Some say allow to the Indians a few acres which is enough for them, but we hope and rely upon you that you will use your influence to see ample justice done to us. That is all we have to say at present.

The commissioners assured the Oneida that their words would be taken to the president and "that the sooner their rights under the treaty was defined the better for all parties."[14]

Only ten days after the conclusion of the treaty council, Schermerhorn was appointed commissioner for the United States, and he wrote a treaty with the Oneida and the Six Nations on September 16, 1836. Three days later, he wrote a treaty with the Stockbridge. The treaty with the Oneida begins, "Articles of a Treaty made and concluded at Duck Creek, Wisconsin Territory, September 16, 1836, by John F. Schermerhorn, Commissioner on the part of the United States and the Chiefs Head men and Warriors of the several Tribes of New York Indians." In the first article, the Oneida "cede, relinquish, and convey to the United States" all their rights to the lands, including the five hundred thousand acres from the treaties with the Menominee in 1831 and 1832. Nevertheless, they did reserve the land where they lived:

> Beginning at the south westerly corner of the French Grants at Green Bay and running thence southwardly to a point on a line to be run from Little Cacalin (Little Chute) parallel with the line of the French Grants and Six miles from Fox River, from thence on said parallel line northwardly Six miles, from thence eastwardly to a point on the Northeast line of the said lands and being at right angles with the same.

For this cession of land, the United States would provide the Oneida the same amount of land in Indian Territory, located west of the state of Missouri, adjoining the lands of the Cherokee and Osage. The treaty did acknowledge there were other Native nations living in those territories, and the Oneida should select land not designated for other Native nations.

The financial provision, for three hundred forty thousand dollars, was designated as compensation for lands ceded and funds for the removal of the portion of the Six Nations who were to remove to the west. The funds were to be spent as follows:

> $250,000 for removal and subsistence for one year after their removal west

> 50,000 for a school and assistance of the "aged, infirm, orphans." The amount was to be invested in stocks in the state of New York, and the annual interest would be given to those who removed.

$1,500 allowed for the Tuscarora Tribe

$5,000 for the St. Regis Tribe

$3,500 to the First Christian Party of the Oneida at Green Bay to pay for "services rendered by their Chief and Agents" in obtaining the lands.

Article 3 of the treaty states that "If they don't all remove, the balance of unexpended funds can be disposed of by the President for their benefit," while Article 4 states that when the Oneida notified the government that they were ready to remove, the funds would be furnished, "And any chief conducting a party of not less than One Hundred Souls shall be allowed five Hundred Dollars for his service." If the person was "judged competent to remove the party" he would be paid "$20 per head for each person belonging to his party." Furthermore, "The emigrant will be permitted to commute their one year's subsistence for thirty-three & one third Dollars in cash if they prefer it."

Article 5 is significant because it recognized the right for the New York Indians and Oneida to govern themselves in Indian Territory, and it confirmed "perpetual peace and friendship with the US and New York Indians or the Six Nations of the Ancient Iroquois Confederacy." The United States also

guarantees to protect and defend them in the peaceful enjoyment of their new homes and hereby secure to them in said country the right to establish their own form of Government, appoint their own officers, administer their own laws, subject however to the Legislation of the Congress of the United States for regulating trade and intercourse with the Indians. The Land secured to them by Patent under this Treaty shall never be included without their consent within any State or Territory of this Union. They shall also be entitled, in all respects, to the same political, civil rights and privileges that are granted, and secured by the United States to any of the several Tribes of Immigrant Indians residing and settled in the Indian Territory.

Article 6 stated that no land could be "conveyed or relinquished" without the consent of both the First Christian and Orchard Parties of the Oneida. This article stopped any more Oneida from removing from New York State to Green Bay. Finally, Article 7 stated the treaty had to be ratified and confirmed by the president and the Senate.

The treaty was signed by the following individuals:

George Boyd, US Ind Agt.	J.F. Schermerhorn
John P. Arndt	Henry X Powlis
Solomon Davis	Elijah X Scanandoa
M.L. Martin	
A.G. Ellis	Adam X Swamp
John Dana	Jacob X Cornelius
US Interpreter	Neddy X Atsiqwot
	Thomas X Lodwick
	Cornelius X Stevens
	Thomas X King
	John X August
	David X Williams
	John X Cornelius
	John X Cooper
	Daniel Bread
	James Cusick
	William Mount Pleasant
	Daniel X Peter
	Eleazer Williams[15]

Indorsed: "J.F Schermerhorn's Treaty with the Oneida at Duck Creek, Sept. 16, 1836."

From the signatures on this treaty, it appears Oneida representatives from the First Christian Party and the Orchard Party signed. The Oneida relinquished the five hundred thousand acres they received in the 1831 and 1832 treaties with the Menominee, but they reserved the land on which they were living, which seems to be close to the present-day reservation boundaries.

Three days later, Schermerhorn made almost the same treaty with the Stockbridge and Munsee. He referred to the lands provided for them in the treaties with the Menominee in 1831 and 1832. In Article 2, the Stockbridge and Munsee agreed to cede their lands on the "East side of Winnebago Lake." The United States was to sell these lands, and the funds would be used for the benefit of the Stockbridge and Munsee minus the expenses incurred by the US for the sale and survey of the lands. In order to sell the land, the commissioner would obtain a "just and fair value" for the land and any improvements to it. Funds were to be set apart for the Stockbridge and Munsee's removal and their subsistence for one year. Twenty thousand dollars was designated for the tribe for its expenses and the services rendered by the chiefs and agents, and these funds were to be invested in stocks for the New York Indians. The interest on these stocks would be paid to the chiefs of the tribe. Their removal and one year of subsistence were to be paid to them from the sale of their lands, "and any Chief who removes his Tribe or any party not less than 100 persons shall be allowed & paid $500 for his services."

In Article 3, the United States agreed to provide the funds for delegates of the Stockbridge and Munsee to go and examine the lands southwest of the Missouri River. They were to receive land equal to two townships. If they couldn't find suitable land, however, "then it is expressly understood and agreed that only the East half of the said tract on Winnebago Lake is hereby ceded to the United States: and the remaining half shall be held by them in common, but the Munsees shall not be permitted to sell or relinquish their right to the United States without the consent of the Stockbridge Indians." If only one township was sold to the US, eight thousand dollars out of the sale of the lands would be for the removal of the Munsee from New York State, plus one year of subsistence. If funds were not all spent, the balance would go to the Stockbridge per the second article of the treaty. Article 4 provided a commissioner to establish the value of the Stockbridge lands. This commissioner was to sell the Stockbridge lands and supervise removal and payments. Article 5 assured peace and friendship, and it provided directions to establish a sovereign government, with assurances given that their land would not become part of any state. Last, Article 6 stated that the treaty must be approved and ratified by the US Senate and the president.

The signees to this treaty were:

In the presence of	J.F. Schermerhorn
George Boyd, US Ind Agent	John Metoxen
R.S. Seattles L. M	
Leeyun U.S Army	
John L Arndt	Austin Quinney
In the Presence of:	
Cutting Marsh	Jacob Chicks
M.L. Martin	
W.L. Newberry	T. Jourdan
Mr B Llaughter . . .	
[Illegible]	J.W. Quinney
A.G. Ellis	Hendrick Aupaumont
D. Giddings	Jacob his X mark David
	Jonas his X mark Thompson
	Joseph M. Quinney
	Simon S. Metoxen
	Capt. Porter his X mark

The aforesaid Treaty having been submitted & explained, by J. L. Schermerhorn Commissioner; it is hereby assented to agreed unto, in all its provisions and . . . , in the presence of W. G. Brodhead, Commissioner or the . . . State of N. York on the behalf of the Munsee now residing in the State of New York.
Oct. 15th, 1836

In the presence of
W.G. Brodhead   John his X mark Wilson
George Turkey — Interpreter [16]

Despite opposition to removal, requests to have the Schermerhorn treaties ratified were submitted by some of the Oneida and Stockbridge. In February 1838, they wrote:

To: Rev. Davis
From: Chiefs of Oneida Tribe
Date: Feb. 7, 1838
Oneida Indian Affairs, Green Bay
Rev. Davis
Washington, Feb. 7, 1838

A memorial signed by 60 of the Oneida Nation of Indians dated 6th October, 1837, praying the ratification of Mr. Schermerhorn Treaty of September 1836, and empowering Daniel Bread, Elijah Skenandore, and Adam Swamp, to act for them in regard to said treaty.

Received 13th, February 1838

We the undersigned Chiefs and Headmen, Warriors, and others of the Oneida Nation of Indians residing at Duck Creek. The Territory of Wisconsin in full Council Assembled, and constituting a large majority of the Oneida Nation, and whose names are offered to this instrument. Most respectfully and earnestly request that the Treaty signed . . . the . . . John S. Schermerhorn and the Oneidas on the 16th day of September 1836 at Duck Creek may be confirmed and ratified in every particular as therein agreed between the Parties to the said Treaty by the President and the Senate of the United States. And for the better, carrying into effect our wishes and making known our intentions. We having full faith and confidence in the ability and intensity of Daniel Bread, Jacob Cornelius, Henry Powless, and Elijah Skenandore and Adam Swamp, (chiefs and headmen of our said Nation) have made constituted and appointed, and in our peace and stead put, deputed, and delegated them our true lawful and only alterners, for us and in our name and in the name of the Oneida Nation to do make perform and execute all things that shall and may be necessary to be done made performed and executed in and about said treaty as foresaid, as fully, firmly and effectually as if we and everyone were personally present aiding and assisting.

Hereby ratify and confirming all and what so ever the said attorneys shall so in and about premises for the benefit of the said Oneida Nation.

Done at Duck Creek the 6th day of October 1837
John Denny has been appointed by the Chiefs of the Nations as special
interpreter to accompany the Delegation approved by me.
Witness:

George Boyd Indian Agent
A.G. Ellis
T. Davis
Chet. C. P. Arndt

John August
Cornelius Stephens
Neddy Archequette
Thomas Loadwich
Daniel Williams

Warriors
Thomas Neddy
John Louis
Elijah Powless
William Anthony
John Cornelius
Peter Cooper
Cornelius Hill
Moses Cornelius
Jacob Cornelius, Jr.
Peter Neddy
Arron Hill
Cobus Hill
Anthony Archequette
John Dauthford
John Smith
Cornelius Doxtator
Peter Skenandore
George Hill
Thomas Powless
Mailiness Denny
Cobus Cornelius
Joseph Powless

John Cornelius
John Copper
Paul Powless
Thomas Schuyler
Baptes Skenandore
Moses John
Baptist Peter
Joseph Wheelock
Abraham Powless
Daniel Powless
Abraham Webster
Peter Webster
Peter Green
Daniel Doxtater
Baptist Doxtator
Daniel Ludwick
Joseph Cockelt
Daniel Hill
William Bread
William Jourdaui
Baptist Smith
Peter Stephens
Baptist Stephens
Isaac Stephens
John Stephens

Cornelius Stephens
Harry Stephens
Honyoust Stephens
Abram John
Wina Anthony

Territory of Wis.   Be it remembered that on the 6th day of
                        Oct. 1837

before
County of Brown   me the undersigned Notary Public at
                        Brown County,
                        Green Bay Cha C.P. Arndt
                        Notary Public
                        Charles C. Sholes Clerk of District Court
                            of US also
                        Signed Oct. 26, 1837
                        William C. Frazer Judge of US District
                            Court also signed[17]

Again, it appears that members of both the First Christian Party and the Orchard Party signed this letter, despite the division across the two parties regarding removal.

The Stockbridge and Munsees wrote:

This Petition of the undersigned being the Chiefs, Warriors and head men of the Stockbridge and Munsee Tribes interested in and owning land on the East side of Winnebago Lake in the County of Brown and Territory of Wisconsin, would respectfully show that in the year 1836 — in the month of September the Chiefs and warriors of the said Tribes held a treaty with John F. Schermerhorn, Commissioner of the part of the United States at Green Bay with the aforesaid Chiefs Warriors and head men at which Treaty the aforesaid Chiefs Warriors and head men ceded to the Government a tract of land eight miles long and four mile wide containing twenty three thousand and forty acres be the same or less, and as it is understood that the Treaty was not ratified at the last Session of Congress, your petitioners would beg leave to represent to their Great father, the President, and the

Honorable the Senate of the United States that they are desirous of
having the aforesaid Treaty ratified as there is a considerable number
of the Tribe who wish to remove to the Indian Country west of the
State of Missouri and as those who wish to remove . . . Poor and
indigent circumstances. Therefore it [is] our wish as there is about
100 souls of the Munsee Tribe who wish to emigrate to the Indian
Country west of the State of Missouri. It is also the wish and desire
of your petitioners to accede to the modifications and stipulation of
the aforesaid Treaty. It is also the wish and desire of your petitioners
that Henry Dodge, the present governor of the Territory of Wisconsin
may be appointed a special commissioner, and also to settle the
concerns of those who emigrate, and if this our most earnest and
humble request, can be granted, your petitions as in duty bound will
ever pray.

Stockbridge December 4, 1837

Stockbridge Chiefs & Warriors	*Munsee Chiefs and Warriors*
Robert his X mark Konkapot	John his X mark . . .
Thomas J. Hendrick	Isaac his X mark Thomas
John M. Badwin [?]	Patrick his X mark Samuel
Peter Littleman	Capt. His X mark. . .
Jonas Konkapot	Job his X mark Nathan [?]
Thomas his X mark Skenandoah	Job his X mark Samuel
. . . his X mark Peters	Capt his X mark Henry
Thomas S. . . .	Daniel his X mark Jacob
Simon Konkapot	Stephen his X mark Abram
Brother of Clavins [?]	Levi his X mark Jack
Eli Hendricks	Leonard his X mark Drake
Jonas his X mark Littleman	Jessee his X mark Williams
Levi his X mark Konkapot	Gibson [?] his X mark Williams
Daniel David	Aaron his X mark Hendrick
John his X mark Yooccum [?]	John his X mark Bubbrige
Eliska Konkapot	Jacob his X mark Weat [?]
Thomas Hendrick, Jr	Samuel his X mark Peter
David . . .	William his X mark Kilbuck
Timothy his X mark Towsy	Col his X mark Joseph

Peter his X mark Sharman [?]	Simon his X mark Peter
Moses his X mark	Charles Job his X mark Gilewa [?]
Isaac his X mark Littleman	Little his X mark Fish
David his X mark	Calvin John his X mark Young
John W. Quinney, Jr.	Buffalo his X mark Hill
Ben Jaman his X mark Bye	James his X mark Logan
John his X mark Moonhoas	John [his X mark] Logan[18]

There is no evidence that the Schermerhorn treaties with the Oneida and the Stockbridge were ever ratified. But the disputes and disagreements between those who wanted to remove and those who did not continued to plague the history of these nations as the threat of removal did not end in 1837.

Buffalo Creek Treaty, 1838

The next removal treaty council was held at Buffalo Creek, New York, in 1838. The sole purpose of this treaty was to remove all of the Six Nations west of the Mississippi River. Each nation had a section in the treaty defining its agreements. The Oneida reserved a portion of land near Green Bay in this treaty, but some also agreed to remove west. In the 1838 Buffalo Creek Treaty, the New York Indians ceded all their lands, except one tract near Green Bay, from the 1831 treaty with the Menominee.

The treaty begins with an overview of the history, according to Commissioner Ransom H. Gillet, from the time of the American Revolution to the move to Green Bay and the controversy over the five hundred thousand acres for the New York Indians in the 1831 and 1832 treaties with the Menominee. Gillet's interpretation states that, according to him, the Six Nations saw the advantages of going west. He acknowledged the agitation this proposal had caused among the Six Nations. The treaty begins:

> And whereas, with the approbation of the President of the United
> States, purchases were made by the New York Indians from the
> Menomonie and Winnebago Indians of certain lands at Green
> Bay in the Territory of Wisconsin, which after much difficulty
> and contention with those Indians concerning the extent of that

purchase, the whole subject was finally settled by a treaty between the
United States and Menomonie Indians, concluded in February, 1831,
to which the New York Indians gave their assent on the seventeenth
day of October 1832: And whereas, by the provisions of that treaty,
five hundred thousand acres of land are secured to the New York
Indians of the Six Nations and the St. Regis tribe, as a future home,
on condition that they all remove to the same within three years, or
such reasonable time as the President should prescribe.

It goes on:

And whereas, the President is satisfied that various considerations
have prevented those still residing in New York from removing to
Green Bay, and among other reasons, that many who were in favour
of emigration, preferred to remove at once to the Indian territory,
which they were fully persuaded was the only permanent and
peaceful home for all the Indians. And they therefore applied to the
President to take their Green Bay lands, and provide them a new
home among their brethren in the Indian territory.

Article 1. The several tribes of New York Indians, the names of
whose chiefs, head men, warriors and representative are hereunto
annexed, in consideration of the premises above recited, and the
covenants hereinafter contained, to be performed on the part of the
United States, hereby cede and relinquish to the United States all their
right, title and interest to the lands secured to them at Green Bay
by the Menomonie treaty of 1831, excepting the following tract, on
which a part of the New York Indians now reside:

> beginning at the southwesterly corner of the French
> grants at Green Bay, and running thence southwardly to a
> point on a line to be run from the Little Cocaclin, parallel
> to a line of the French grants and six miles from Fox River;
> from thence on said parallel line, northwardly six miles;
> from thence eastwardly to a point on the northeast line of
> the Indian lands, and being right angles to the same.

Article 2. In consideration of the above cession and
relinquishment, on the part of the tribes of the New York Indians,

and in order to manifest the deep interest of the United States in the
future peace and prosperity of the New York Indians, the United
States agree to set apart the following tract of country, situated
directly west of the State of Missouri, as a permanent home for
all the New York Indians, now residing in the State of New York,
or in Wisconsin, or elsewhere in the United States, who have no
permanent homes, which said country is described as follows, to wit:
Beginning on the west line of the State of Missouri, at the northeast
corner of the Cherokee tract, and running thence . . .
. . . to include one million eight hundred and twenty-four
thousand acres of land, being three hundred and twenty acres for
each soul of said Indians as their numbers are at present computed.

This treaty was intended to provide lands for all of the Six Nations upon
their arrival in Indian Territory:

It is understood and agreed that the above described country is
intended as a future home for the following tribes, to wit: The
Senecas, Onondagas, Cayugas, Tuscaroras, Oneida, St. Regis,
Stockbridges, Munsees, and Brothertowns residing in the State of
New York.
Article 4. Perpetual peace and friendship shall exist between the
United States and the New York Indians; and the United States hereby
guaranty to protect and defend them in the peaceable possession and
enjoyment of their new homes, and hereby secure to them, in said
country, the right to establish their own form of government, appoint
their own officers, and administer their own laws; subject, however,
to the legislation of the Congress of the United States, regulating
trade and intercourse with the Indians. The lands secured to them
by patent under this treaty shall never be included in any State or
Territory of this Union.

Articles 9 to 14 provide special provisions for the St. Regis, Seneca,
Cayuga, Onondaga, and Oneida residing in the State of New York, and
Tuscarora. Article 9 includes a specific section referring to Eleazer Williams's lands near Green Bay, which are identified as:

beginning at a point in the west bank of Fox River thirteen chains above the old mill dam at the rapids of the Little Kockalin; thence north fifty-two degrees and thirty minutes west, two hundred and forty chains; thence north thirty-seven degrees and thirty minutes east, two hundred chains, thence south fifty-two degrees and thirty minutes east, two hundred and forty chains to the bank of Fox river; thence up along the bank of Fox river to the place of beginning.

Article 10 provided land in the west for the Seneca, who were to move within five years. The continued presence and influence of Thomas L. Ogden is evident as he and Joseph Fellows claimed the preemptive right to purchase, with the approval of the United States, a portion of Seneca lands. In Articles 11 and 12, a pattern emerges in that the United States designated funds that were to be kept in "safe stocks," and told Indigenous nations that the proceeds on the interest would be given to them in their new homes. The United States would also pay $2,500 to the Cayuga chiefs for their removal. The Onondaga, residing on the Seneca reservation, were to receive $2,500 when they removed, and these funds were to be invested in safe stocks. Upon their removal, $2,000 would be given to the chiefs for distribution as they saw fit.

Article 13 identified special provisions for the Oneida living in New York State:

The United States will pay the sum of four thousand dollars, to be paid to Baptista Powlis, and the chiefs of the first Christian Party residing at Oneida, and the sum of two thousand dollars shall be paid to William Day, and the chiefs of the Orchard party residing there, for expenses incurred and services rendered in securing the Green Bay country, and the settlement of a portion thereof; and they hereby agree to remove to their new homes in the Indian territory as soon as they can make satisfactory arrangements with the Governor of the State of New York for the purchase of their lands at Oneida.

Article 14 called for special provisions for the Tuscarora that offered them three thousand dollars for their removal within five years. Specific lands, "lying in Niagara County, in the State of New York," were to be conveyed to the United States. The land developers, Thomas L. Ogden and Joseph Fellows, "the assignees of the State of Massachusetts," would be allowed to purchase Tuscarora lands.

In Article 15, the United States appropriated four hundred thousand dollars for removing to the west and first year expenses in the new lands, including education, cultivating land, erecting mills, purchasing domestic animals and farming utensils, and "acquiring a knowledge of the mechanic arts." These funds were for the entire Six Nations.

Signatures of Seneca, Tuscarora, Oneidas residing the State of New York, Oneida at Green Bay, St. Regis, Oneidas residing on the Seneca Reservation, Onondaga, Cayuga, and witnesses.
Signatures:
Oneida residing in the State of New York, for themselves and their parties:
    Baptiste Powless
    Jonathan Jordan
Oneidas at Green Bay:
    John Anthony,
    Honjoit Smith,
    Henry Jordan,
    Thomas King

On August 9, 1838, the Oneida of New York agreed to the treaty "as amended by the resolution of the Senate of the United States on the eleventh day of June 1838." The divisions within the Oneida Nation, with some agreeing to remove and others not, continued to be evident. The signatures list included First Christian Party, Orchard Party, and Second Christian Party members. Some 620 Oneida remained in New York at this time, and about 654 had moved to the Green Bay area.[19]

There was a great deal of controversy over this treaty and whether it was valid. According to one author, "Asher Wright and the Society of Friends produced evidence of fraud, bribery, and forgery, and objections were raised in Congress; but the transaction occurred during the Jackson administration at the height of the clamor for Indian removal, and the treaty was ratified."[20]

NEW YORK INDIANS V. THE UNITED STATES (1892)

The controversy over the legality of the 1838 Buffalo Creek treaty continued into the court case *New York Indians v. the United States* (1892).
The court provided a historical overview and referred to the 1821 treaty
with the Menominee, who "ceded to the Stockbridge, Oneida, Tuscarora,
St. Regis, and Munsee nations two large tracts of land in Wisconsin for
a small money consideration. The title the land in the 1821 treaty was
confirmed in the New York Indians by the President March 13, 1823."[21] In
Article IV of the judge's decision, the court cited the 1831 treaty with the
Menominee, which included five hundred thousand acres for the New
York Indians, two townships for the Stockbridge, and one township for the
Brothertown. The articles of the case provided more historical references
and the numbers of actual removals.

Article V reads:

> The title of the New York Indians as set forth in the fourth finding
> has since been acknowledged by the United States; as in the treaty
> with the Menomonees of September 3, 1836; in the treaty with the
> Stockbridge and Munsees, of September 3, 1839; in the treaty with
> the New York Indians concluded at Buffalo Creek January 15, 1838

Article XV provided the actual numbers of those who removed. Only
260 applied for funds under the 1838 Buffalo Creek Treaty, and of that
number, "only 32 ever received patents or certificates of allotment of any
of the lands mentioned in the first article of the treaty, and the amount
allotted to those 32 was at the rate of 320 acres each, or 10,240 acres in all."
In 1845, a group of 271 was designated to remove to Kansas. Of those, 73 did
not go, which left 198 who "arrived in Kansas June 15, 1846; 17 other Indians arrived subsequently; 62 died, and 17 returned to New York." Out of the
$400,000 designated for removal and first year expenses, only $9,464.08
was every appropriated, and it did not "appear that any of the 32 Indians
to whom allotments were made settled permanently in Kansas."

Yet Article XVI stated that after the 1838 Buffalo Creek Treaty, the
lands at Green Bay were "made part of the public domain . . . and sold or

otherwise disposed of and conveyed." Here they are referring to the five hundred thousand acres for the New York Indians from the 1831 and 1832 Menominee treaties. The lands to the "west of the Mississippi secured to the claimant by the treaty of Buffalo Creek were, afterwards surveyed and made part of the public domain, and were sold or otherwise disposed of by the United States."

Article XXII provided a financial overview of the Buffalo Creek Treaty that amounted to $2,247,000.00. After expenses were deducted, the balance was $1,971,295.92. This account was filed on January 16, 1892.[22]

It is clear that the United States benefited from the 1838 Buffalo Creek Treaty, as it did throughout the era, by annexing lands it designated as surplus and then selling it.

The move west brought with it a large tract of land for a permanent home and the promise of self-government for the New York Indians, which must have been appealing to some. But, to those who didn't want to move any farther, it was another broken promise in a series of promises made to have a permanent homeland in the area near Green Bay. Daniel Bread expressed the angst many were feeling about removal:

> We have gone about far enough. . . . Our great Father thinks the proposed country is better for us than our own. We have the bad effects of moving often to be like feather to be driven by the wind is bad, it is better to be of a heavier substance and it sticks close to the ground. If we move often, we will at last land on some mountain.[23]

Only some of the Stockbridge, Oneida, and Brothertown removed from the Green Bay area. The Six Nations did not remove west of the Mississippi, and they continue to have reservations, except for the Cayuga, in New York State.

12

ESTABLISHING CURRENT
RESERVATION BOUNDARIES

Treaties established the final boundaries of the Oneida reservation in 1838, the Menominee reservation in 1854, and the Stockbridge-Munsee reservation in 1856. Pressure to remove west continued, however, and caused divisions within these Indigenous nations. Later, when Congress passed the General Allotment Act in 1887, it divided Indigenous lands across the United States into individual and family parcels. Surplus lands were sold to white settlers and land speculators, and Indigenous nations lost millions of acres of tribal lands in the process.

Nineteen days after the January 15, 1838, Buffalo Creek Treaty tried to remove all of the Six Nations to the west, a separate treaty was made with the Oneida First Christian and Orchard Parties on February 3. It is important to note that this treaty was held and signed in Washington, DC. The United States preferred to hold treaty negotiations there because these treaties involved only a few chiefs and head men of the nation. Treaties conducted on or near the Native nations involved many people from those nations attending. This meant the United States had to feed all of them, and the government did not like the additional expense. Thus, the February 3 treaty was signed by four chiefs from the First Christian Party and one chief from the Orchard Party in Washington.

In the treaties with the Menominee Nation in 1831 and 1832, the United States designated five hundred thousand acres for the New York Indians. The 1832 treaty designated lands for the Stockbridge and Brothertown on the east side of Lake Winnebago. In the 1838 Buffalo Creek Treaty, 500,000 acres of land were ceded, with the Oneida reserving only a small portion of the lands near Green Bay. In the February 3 treaty, it was again stated that the Oneida ceded the lands—500,000 acres from the 1831 and 1832 treaties—and the Oneida reserved a portion of the lands that became the February 3, 1838, treaty boundaries. One has to wonder why the Oneida would be willing to give up 500,000 acres for only 65,400 acres in return. Was this due to the intense pressure to remove the New York Indians to Indian Territory in the west? As in all previous treaties, even though large areas were ceded, the Oneida reserved land for their nation.

TREATY BETWEEN THE UNITED STATES AND THE FIRST CHRISTIAN AND ORCHARD PARTIES OF THE ONEIDA INDIANS AT GREEN BAY

The February 3, 1838, treaty negotiated in Washington, DC, was made to ensure and confirm lands for the Oneida in Wisconsin because the January 15, 1838, treaty with the Six Nations made provisions for all of the Six Nations to move west. Despite the Oneida division into two parties, leaders of both parties signed the treaty. The treaty reads:

> Articles of a treaty made at the City of Washington between Carey A. Harris, thereto specially directed by the President of the United States and the First Christian and Orchard parties of the Oneida Indians residing at Green Bay, by their chiefs and representatives.
>
> ART. 1. The First Christian and Orchard parties of Indians cede to the United States all their title and interest in the land set apart for them in the 1st article of the treaty with the Menomonies of February 8th, 1831, and the 2d article of the treaty with the same tribe of October 27th, 1832.
>
> ART. 2. From the foregoing cession there shall be reserved to the said Indians to be held as other Indians land are held a tract of land containing one hundred (100) acres, for each individual, and the lines of which shall be so run as to include all their settlements and improvements in the vicinity of Green Bay.
>
> ART. 3. In consideration of the cession contained in the 1st article of this treaty, the United States agree to pay to the Orchard party of

the Oneida Indians three thousand (3000) dollars, and to the First Christian party of Oneida Indians thirty thousand five hundred (30,500) dollars, of which last sum three thousand (3,000) dollars may be expended under the supervision of the Rev. Solomon Davis, in the erection of a church and parsonage house, and the residue apportioned, under the direction of the President among the person having just claim thereto; it being understood that said aggregate sum of thirty-three thousand five hundred (33,500) dollars is designed to be in reimbursement of monies expended by said Indians and remuneration of the services of their chiefs and agents in purchasing and securing a title to the land ceded in the 1st article. The United States further agree to cause the tracts reserved in the 2d article to be surveyed as soon as practicable.

ART. 4. In consideration of the sum of five hundred (500) dollars to be paid to him by the chiefs and representatives of the said parties of Oneida Indians, John Denny (alias John Sundown,) their interpreter, agrees to relinquish to them all his title and interest in the tract reserved in the 2d article of this treaty.

ART. 5. It is understood and agreed that the expenses of this treaty and of the chiefs and representatives signing it, in coming to and returning from this city, and while here, shall be paid by the United States.

ART. 6. This treaty to be binding upon the contracting parties when the same shall be ratified by the United States.

In witness whereof, the said Carey A. Harris and the undersigned chiefs and representatives of the said parties of Oneida Indians have hereunto set their hands at the City of Washington, this third day of February 1838.

C.A. Harris

First Christians:
   Henry Powles,
   John Denny, alias John Sundown,
   Adam Swamp,
   Daniel Bread.

Orchard:

    Jacob Cornelius.

    In the presence of —

    Geo. W. Jones, Delegate Wisconsin Territory.

    Solomon Davis.

    Alfred Iverson.

    O.S. Hall.

    Jas. P. Maury.

    Charles E. Mix.

    Charles J. Love

    John Denny, alias John Sundown, Interpreter

(To the Indian names are subjoined marks.)[1]

In this treaty, the Oneida relinquished the 500,000 acres from the treaties of 1831 and 1832. There were 654 members of the Oneida living near Duck Creek on the lands to be surveyed, so 100 acres times 654 determined the final acreage of 65,400. The land continued to be held in common by the Oneida Nation. The reservation boundaries are not described in the treaty, so one has to wonder why they would sign the treaty. In all previous treaties, boundaries were listed. However, a rough map of the current reservation boundaries was presented to the Oneida chiefs at the treaty signing in Washington, DC. This map is known as the John Suydam 1838 plat of the Oneida reservation. As stated in the treaty, the lands were to be surveyed as soon as "practicable" after the treaty signing. Written notes on the Suydam map state:

MAP of ONEIDA RESERVATION, containing 65,400 acres of land. — surveyed Dec. 1838 under the direction of H.S. Baird, US Commissioner. By J. V. Suydam, Dist. Surv.[2]

The final Oneida reservation boundaries are basically the same as shown in the Suydam map. A notation on the map listing the boundaries is not legible. Written in the lower corner is a piece of writing that dates to at least 1872:

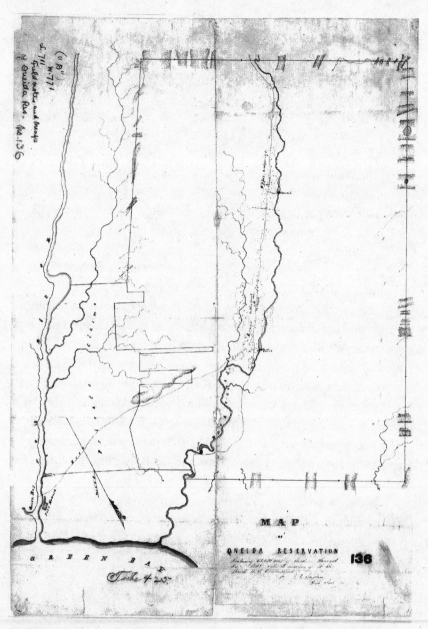

Suydam's 1838 rough map presented to Oneida on February 3, 1838. The Oneida signed
the treaty based on this rough map.
RG 75, NATIONAL ARCHIVES, RECORDS OF THE BUREAU OF INDIAN AFFAIRS, CENTRAL MAP FILE,
MAP 136

Colored Annotations made at the General Land Office. Course
and distances taken from field notes on file in Indian Office. Course
and Distances on . . . W Boundary of Private Claims taken from a
diagram of the same on file in the General Land Office. I.B. Sur. Dir,
March 1872.

On February 5, 1838, a letter was sent to Commissioner of Indian Affairs C. A. Harris from the Oneida chiefs as they were about to return to
Green Bay from Washington, DC. In the letter, they delegated Reverend
Johnson Davis to conclude their business, including collecting expenses
incurred during the trip and future annuities. The letter reads:

Sir, the undersigned Chiefs and representatives of the Oneida Indians
at Duck Creek in the Territory of Wisconsin being now about to leave
the seat of Government and return to their homes beg leave to inform
you that all their business affairs with the Government and especially
with your department are left in charge of the Rev. Johnson Davis
who will remain at Washington till all our concerns are adjusted.

And he is hereby authorized by us to settle with United States for
our expenses agreeable to stipulations in the Treaty of February 3,
1838, and to receive all monies which may be due us on account of
the same or that may be due pr . . . account of annuities which are due
from the United States, and to transmit all other matters that may
be necessary to be for us in our behalf with the Government of the
United States as fully as we ourselves could do were we present.

The Delegation call this opinion Annuity to express to you, Sir,
where in sincere thanks for your kind attention to them during
their stay in this city. Dated at Washington city, this fifth day of
February 1838.

Witness

    Geo. N. Jones

    Daniel Bread

    Jacob Cornelius

    Henry Powless

    Adam Swamp[3]

The Missouri Party

The Missouri Party was established by the Oneida who were willing to remove to Missouri, and they requested President Jackson to ratify the September 16, 1836, removal treaty with Schermerhorn, which was never ratified. In the *Proceedings of the Council held by Henry Dodge/Comm. To treat with the Oneida Indians at Duck Creek on the 19th 20th & 21st days of November 1845*, the Oneida said, "In 1837, J. F. Schermerhorn visited us, and since that time there has been a Missouri Party among the Oneidas at Green Bay." Schermerhorn's goal was to remove all the Oneida west of Missouri. The Missouri Party wrote to the president to express its concerns about the distribution of $33,500 in the 1838 treaty and confirm the party's wish to remove west of the Mississippi.

The petition from the Missouri Party reads:

October 23, 1838
To His Excellency the Presi[dent] of the United States
    The Petition, and Remonstrance, of the Undersigned, Head Men, Chiefs, and Individuals, of the Oneida Nation of Indians being near Green Bay, humbly complaining, Sheweth unto your Excellency that they have dully and seriously, considered the situation in which they find, themselves placed, as well in relation to their condition among themselves as a mixed nation, as to their obligations to with the General Government of the United States.
    Your Excellency, knows that, a Treaty was made and confirmed, with the first Christian and Orchard Parties of the Oneida Tribe of Indians on the 23 of February [the treaty was actually made on February 3] 1838 (7 STAT. 566-67) by which Treaty [said] Tribe of Indians sold to the United States all their Lands, in the Vicinity of Green Bay; reserving 100 acres of said land to each Individual Indian, That the Treaty aforesaid, although; made by a part and a minority of the Head men and Chiefs of said Tribe, Your Petitioners are willing to carry out in good faith as far as it goes; but they were then, and are now, willing, as they then, and now, consider it their interest,

and that of the entire Tribe, to make and effect, stipulations and agreements, beyond the terms & provisions of the said Treaty; and such is now the opinion and desire of a large majority of the first Christian and Orchard parties of the Oneida Tribe.

In the first place your Petitioners believe it to be their interest (as it is the policy of their Great Father) that they go, West of the Mississippi, to land to be assigned them out of the reach of the White Settlements; and those malign influences which overcome and overreach the half civilized Indian relative to their property and Moral habits.

Your Petitioners further state that, the Undersigned Chiefs and Head men of the First Christian and Orchard parties of the Oneida Tribe of Indians, are willing and hereby propose to exchange all their right and title to the lands they are separately or in a national point of view intitled to under the Treaty 3rd of February 1838; that is to say, that each Indian who owns 100 acres, of land near Green Bay, is to have in exchange for them, 320 acres of Land West of Missouri, or on such terms as have heretofore granted to Indians emigrating to the West; being on or near the Osage River; The Government of the United States agreeing to pay the cost and reasonable charges of our transportation during the summer of 1839.

Your Petitioners also state that great injustice, oppression & fraud has been heretofore practiced on a great portion of the tribe, by misapplication of the principal of the sum of money, to which they are intitled from the State of New York, by an unequal and unjust distribution of the same; They fear and apprehend the same injustice in the distribution of the $33,500 to be paid to the Orchard and first Christian Parties under the 3rd article of the aforesaid Treaty.

Your Petitioners therefore make known to your, Excellency their grievances, in their behalf, with their fears of repetition of the same; They therefore pray that your attention and that of the War Department, be specially called to the fair & Equitable distribution of the aforesaid Sum of $33,500, among the first Christian and Orchard Parties of the Oneida Tribe of Indians, by a Commissioner duly and specially instructed to deal out justly the aforesaid sum of money, equally among all the Chiefs of the Nation, & not as heretofore to four Chiefs, to the exclusion of Six other Chiefs and [manuscript torn] People.

Your Petitioners further state that the Six Chiefs whose names are hereunto annexed represent the Missouri Emigrating Party, and only four Chiefs, two of whom are old and infirm and superannuated men entirely under the influence of a certain Daniel Bread who is not a Chief; represent the adverse party who are a Minority of the Tribe and who have heretofore and will particularly hereafter by the aid of certain interested persons, deprive your Petitioner of their just rights unless your Excellency promptly interfere in the premises.

To the End, therefore that our wants and desire may be known, and our grievances redressed; We, the Undersigned appoint the following Head Men & Chief as our delegation to Washington to visit your Excellency, viz John Anthony, Thomas King, Thomas James of the first Christian Party, and Honyost Smith, of the Orchard Party to be associated with J.M. Cutts of the city of Washington, to whom we have been recommended as a Special Agent to assist and advise our Delegation in their behalf.

In Testimony whereof the Undersigned Chiefs, Head Men and Individuals hereunto set their Hands and Seals this 23rd of Oct. 1838.

John his X mark Anthony Chief (Seal)   Henry his X mark John

Thomas his X mark King Chief (Seal)   Louis his X mark Denny

Thomas his X mark James Chief   Nicholas his X mark
     Wheelock

Honyost his X mark Smith Chief   Henry his X mark Bear

Christian his X mark Beechtree Chief   Adam his X mark King

Cornelius his X mark Bear Chief   John his X mark Matoxen

John his X mark House   James his X mark Ninham

The above signed in Presence of Jno L. Watson John S. Horner

Cornelius his X mark Bain   William his X mark Nickols

Matinas his X mark King   Sally her X mark John

Aaron his X mark Smith   Mary her X mark Hill

Thomas his X mark Nickols   Sarah her X mark Hill

William his X mark Hill

Henry his X mark Nickols

Thomas his X mark Bain

Isaac his X mark John

Jane her X mark John

Esqr his X mark Daniels

Abram his X mark Bain

Henry his X mark Bain Jun

Mary her X mark Bain

Elizabeth her X mark Bain

Jerusia her X mark Jourdin

Katy her X mark Jourdin

Adam his X mark King 2d

Peggy her X mark Green

Thomas his X mark Green

Jane her X mark Green

Betsy her X mark Green

Margaret her X mark House

Thomas his X mark House

Electa her X mark House

Peggy her X mark House

Hendrick his X mark John

Katy her X mark John

Woreon his X mark Smith 2nd

Baptist his X mark Smith

Abram his X mark Smith

Elizabeth her X mark Jourdin

Cefas his X mark Hill

Henry his X mark Antony

Katharine her X mark Antony

John his X mark Antony Jun

Sara her X mark Antony

Hannah her X mark Antony

Gero her X mark Antony

Richard his X mark Antony

Adam his X mark Antony

Margaret her X mark Antony

Antony his X mark King

Mary her X mark Smith

Mary Ann her X mark Smith

Adam his X mark Smith

Hannah her X mark Denny

Nancy her X mark John

Thomas his X mark John

Baptist his X mark Denny

Jane her X mark Dockstader

Polly her X mark Dockstader

Elizabeth her X mark Dockstader

Hannah her X mark Dockstader

Katy her X mark Smith

John his X mark Tompson

Henry his X mark George[4]

Several months later, in March 1839, the Missouri Party chiefs and head men wrote a letter to T. Hartley Crawford, the commission of Indian Affairs, to object to stipulations granted to Daniel Bread and the Oneida at Duck Creek:

We the undersigned Chiefs & Head men of the Missouri or emigration party of the Oneida Indians of Green Bay, respectfully represent that we & those whom we represent, are not satisfied with the distribution proposed to be made of the sum of money set apart

for the Oneidas at Green Bay, as we have been informed it has been
made. The money was for the Indians & not for white men, & no
white man should have a dollar of it. We also object to Daniel Bread's
having so large a share as is said to be awarded to him. His claims
are not better than ours, nor do we think as good, because while he
opposes the policy of the Government concerning emigration, we
have sustained that policy & are in favor of going west of Missouri to
the Lands set apart for the New York Indians.

If Governor Dodge can attend to the distribution of said money we
wish him to be directed to do so, but if he cannot, then we desire that
some other person may be sent, who is not connected with Daniel
Brad [Bread] or any of the white men acting with him, who will
thoroughly investigate the whole matter & make proper disposition
of the money & report to you for your consideration & final decision
thereon.

We are your obt. Serv
JOHN ANTHONY his X mark
THOMAS JAMES his X mark
HONYOST SMITH his X mark
Dated Albany March 12, 1839
P.S. Any reply to this should be directed at Green Bay.[5]

John Anthony (Oneida), a representative of the Missouri Party who
was not present at the treaty made in 1838, expressed his approval of 1838
Buffalo Creek Treaty in a separate letter:

The undersigned delegates from the Missouri party of the Oneida
Indians at Green Bay who were authorized by a certain power of
attorney now on file in the office of the Commissioner of Indian
Affairs at Washington, not having been present at the City of
Buffalo when Honyost Smith & Thomas James, the other delegates
for themselves & for us executed a treaty with R. H. Gillct, the
Commissioner for the release of our lands at Green Bay to the United
States, & for receiving others west of Missouri, having had the same
fully explained to us by the said Commissioner, do hereby ratify &
confirm the same & do hereby make the same and every part thereof

our act & deed, as fully & perfectly as if we had been at Buffalo & then
& there signed the same with our own hands.
Done at ALBANY the 12th day of March 1839
John Anthony his X mark
Signed in presence of [blank][6]

John Anthony and Honyost Smith refer to the 1838 Buffalo Creek
Treaty as being enacted in the fall; however, it was completed on January
15, 1838. There were 654 Oneida at Green Bay in 1838, and Anthony and
Smith, in the following letter, wrote that 280 of them were ready to move
west. They wrote to protest the division of the $33,500 from the February 3
treaty because they had previously seen misallocation of funds. In a March
18, 1839, letter to Secretary of War Joel R. Poinsett, they wrote:

Sir;
     You have been informed by Mr. Gillett Commissioner to treat with
the Six Nations, that he made a treaty last fall, with that part of the
Oneida Indians living at Green Bay, in favour of emigration to the
south west of the Missouri River in the Indian Territory. We saw Mr.
Gillett a few days ago at Albany, N.Y., who told us there was nothing
done about our treaty, because it was not signed by all the Chiefs
authorized to make it. We could not all attend at Buffalo last fall. We
are disappointed, but our minds and the needs of our people are not
changed; for we are all of the same mind state.
     We want to move to the country for the Six Nations west of the
State of Missouri. Our people want to go this summer. There are
280 of them now ready and willing to emigrate. We must move. We
cannot live in Green Bay any longer. Our people there are divided,
pretty near equally, but when we are ready to start, then many more
will go than stay behind. If the treaty we made with Mr. Gillett is not
right we want to make it right. One of Chiefs John Anthony who was
authorized and empowered by the people to make the treaty, he is
here now and ready to sign it, and Thomas King the other delegate
told John Anthony to sign for him. They all want a treaty and cannot
live in Green Bay any longer in peace with Daniel Bread and his party,
who want to stay in Green Bay and become as white men citizens of

the Country, and he opposes us because we want to emigrate. We come to see our Great Father to know what he says on the subject whether he will stand to his treaty or not, and whether we can move this summer; we are all ready to go this summer.

We also want our Great Father to know that the Missouri party, or emigration party, make half of the people now at Green Bay, and we do not want that a few Chiefs and white men shall have all the money under our Treaty of last year $33,500, and the poor Indians to have nothing. We all suffered loss in moving from New York. We want this money to be divided between Daniel Breads party and the Missouri party according to their numbers. If the other party want Daniel Bread and a few white men to have all the money let them give their share to them; but our party want their share to be divided among all this party. They have not given Honyost Smith who had a just claim for $250 any thing because he was so warm for emigration, and secured a large party of his people and therefore Daniel Bread and Jacob Cornelius said he should not have any. We want the President our Great Father to see justice done him. He was absent when the Commissioner was there to Buffalo and Albany on business for his people. We hope he will not be left to suffer for being a friend to the Government and in favour of emigration.

We want also to know if we emigrate whether we can have our share of the annuities from the Government paid us in the Indian Country west of Missouri.

We have come here to fix the treaty right if it is not right we want to know what our Great Father means to do about, whether he will stick to it or not? We do not want to stay here long. We want to know soon what is to be done. We will also tell our Great Father we are poor, we have had to borrow a little money to come here and we want some for our expenses here and to go home. We hope our Great Father will remember us his poor children and help us to get home and to remove to the country of the Six Nations west. We are all ready we want to go very soon.

We are here now waiting to hear what our Father will say to comfort and encourage us, and our friends and women and children at home.

With respect we sign ourselves your friends
And the friend of the Government
    John Anthony
    Honyost Smith
In the presence of
    Baptist Cowles — Interpreter
    J.F. Schermerhouse[7]

In June 1839, the Missouri Party was still making the list of names to submit to the government of those Oneida who wanted to remove to the west. They wrote:

> To Mr. James Cain, Esq. Agent on Indians Affairs for the State of New York.
> Sir, We the undersigned Chiefs of the Missouri party in the Oneida Nation of Indians do hereby wish to inform your honour that there has been a mistake made in making the list of the names of our said party by forgetting to enter the names of heirs of one Adam Skenando (now deceased) of our said Tribe or Nation & their names are as follows, Mrs. Catherine Mills [Hills?], Thomas Skenando, Mary Hendrick, on account of the said error we now make it known & manifest to your honour that the said person do lawfully belong to our said party, agreeable to the rules & regulations of our people & we do further acknowledge & own the said persons as members of our nation & tribe entitled to receive an equal share with us of the money due to our said party from the people of State of N. York.
> Dated at Oneida settlement at Duck Creek, Wisconsin Territory, June 24, 1839.[8]

Cornelius Hill (1834–1907) became a Bear Clan chief at the age of thirteen and presented the views of those Oneida who did not want to remove. The following excerpt is from an article Chief Hill wrote "many years ago" when the Oneida were being pressured to remove to the West:

> The civilization which I and the greater part of my people aim at is one of truth and honor; one that will raise us to a higher state of

existence here on earth, and fit us for a blessed one in the next world. For this civilization we intend to strive — right here where we are — being sure that we shall find it no sooner in the wilds beyond the Mississippi.

'Progress' is our motto, and you who labor to deprive us of this small spot of God's footstool will labor in vain.

We will not sign your treaty; no amount of money can tempt us to sell our people. You say our answer must be given today. You can't be troubled any longer with these Council meetings. You shall have your wish — and it is one that you will hear every time you seek to drive us from our lands — No![9]

In July 1845, the Oneida who stayed in Wisconsin at Duck Creek wrote to the commissioner of Indian Affairs to protest the replacement of their Indian agent:

Father, The Chiefs of the Oneida Nation of Indians take the liberty to speak a few words to you and they hope you will listen to what they say.

Father, We hear an effort is being made to remove Col. Jones from this Sub. Agency, and that Albert G. Ellis, of Green Bay, is recommended to take his place. We know both of these men. We have long known them. And we should be sorry to be taken from the hands of one and placed in the hands of the other. Col. Jones has been kind and faithful; during his Agency he has watched over our best interests and advised us for our good. Mr. Ellis, should he be appointed, is not the man who will do this. We have no confidence in him. We do not believe him to be honest. He has smooth words; but, we fear, a bad heart. These are two bad things, when united in one man it will not be good for such a man to stand between our Nation and the President of the United States. We can never know through him how to understand each others words; and it will require a great deal of rubbing & scouring to keep the chain of friendship bright between you and us.

Father, It will be a great and good thing for us, if you will allow

Col. Jones, our present Agent, to remain where he is. We are all well satisfied with him. We know him to be our friend.

Father, We are sorry to trouble you with our words, for we know you are much perplexed in managing Indian affairs. We could not help speaking, however, tho' our voice may not be heard; We are fearful of going into the hands of such a man as Mr. Ellis.

Father, We know the Secretary of War. He is our friend. We love him. He is honest. He hates rogues. If Col. Jones must be taken away from us, will you have the kindness to ask him not to appoint Mr. Ellis, but some man whom he knows to be honest. This is all we have to say.

Done in council at Duck Creek. This 14th day of July 1845.

Signed in the presence of Solomon Davis

Henry X Powless

Cornelius X Stevens

Adam X Swamp

Daniel Bread

Jacob Cornelius

John Cornelius[10]

In November 1845, the Oneida at Duck Creek held a council with the governor of Wisconsin Territory, Henry Dodge. The following excerpt is from the journal of the proceedings as submitted by Dodge, who negotiated with the Oneida on behalf of the United States. The journal reads:

Council convened at the Council house, at Duck Creek, on the Oneida Reservation. Present Hon Henry Dodge, Governor of Wisconsin, Commissioner on part of the United States, and the Chiefs and principal men belonging to the 1st Christian & Orchard Parties of the Oneida Nation. Also present A. G. Ellis. US Sub Indian Agent. Henry S. Baird appointed Secretary to the Commissioner.

Council opened.

Jacob L.W. Doxtator and Peter . . . was appointed interpreters & Peter Denny assistant interpreter.

The Commissioner said he wished to be informed who were the

chiefs and principal men of the nation, and whether all, or how many of them were present. The following were named

Of the First Christian Party	Of the Orchard Party
Daniel Bread	Jacob Cornelius
Henry Powlis	John Cooper
Cornelius Stevans	Moses Cornelius
Adam Swamp	John Cornelius
Elijah Skenandoah	Isaac Johnson
Daniel Williams	Cornelius Metoxin
John August	Thomas Lodwick
Neddy Autahiquette	
Thomas King	

All of whom were present, except Elijah Skenandoah & Neddy Autahiquette of the Christian Party and John Cornelius and Isaac Johnson of the Orchard Party.

The Commissioner stated the object of the council as it had been represented to the President of the United States, was the wish of a part of the Oneida Nation to sell their lands, and that he was sent by their Great Father the President for the purpose of treating with them; and there upon read the treaty of Buffalo Creek of 1838 and explained it to them. He further stated that the same reason which operated for their removal from New York now did, or soon could, exist for their removal from Wisconsin. That their Great Father was governed by benevolent and kind motives in sending him to treat with them. That they were entitled to 320 acres according to the treaty of 1838, west of Missouri — and that the Government of the US will pay them a fair value for their lands; and a fair equivalent for their improvements. That he, the Comr., was a friend to the Indians, and would never consent to make an unjust treaty, or take any advantage of them. He wished them to consult together and give him an answer.

Daniel Bread said, — "Father, we feel very thankful to hear why you have come and also to hear what were the wishes and feeling of our Great Father, the President. We are well pleased and are glad to see you. We will consult together and meet you again tomorrow, and give you an answer; as we shall be as well prepared then, as any time, to come to a decision.

I wish to enquire if the Government wishes to purchase and pay for our lands here, or only to exchange for lands south of Missouri; and whether the lands west of the Mississippi would be given to them in addition?"

The Commissioner stated that they would be paid for their lands and improvements here, and get the land west of the Mississippi also, if they made a treaty.

Henry Bear said he was the one who applied to Washington for a Commissioner to treat with the Oneidas. He was glad to hear what the Commissioner said, that he was pleased at it, and it suited his views. He wanted to sell and go West — and tomorrow he would bring a list of all the people who were willing to emigrate. They wanted to emigrate because they were poor. It was his wish to hold the council hereafter at Green Bay rather than at this place.

—||—

November 20, 1845

Council opened — present same as yesterday

Jacob Cornelius said — "You can now hear the few words I have to say. God has permitted us to meet here in good health. I will now tell you our wishes and what we have agreed upon. We thank the President for his friendship, and we thank you also. It pleased us to hear what was told us yesterday, also that you have taken so much trouble to explain all this to us. We hope you will excuse our want of knowledge, but we will explain ourselves as well as possible.

We now refer to old times; we have always been friends to the President and know that he is a friend to us. In the Revolution our people were friends to the United States. We can remember when our fathers fought & shed their blood; and we have then become friends. We have always remembered this and have ever since been friends to the US Government. We remember that the United States then became independent, and we also considered ourselves free; We have been satisfied with all the transactions which we have had with the US Government, — and we have always thought that when we bought the lands at this place, we had a right to them. All our business has been done by the Chiefs. We are perfectly satisfied with this our home, and know no other. We did not leave New York because the whites surrounded us, but because our lands there were too small — and the use of ardent spirits caused many of our people to. . . . We were told we should have permanent homes here, and on this promise we came here to Duck Creek, and made improvements, and feel at home.

We have been told heretofore, that if we would build churches we should do right, and we think so, now as the country and its climate are good we do not want to leave it. We think this the proper place for us; that a warm climate would not agree with us.

Yesterday we were told that $400,000 has been given for our removal from this place. — also that a part of the money would be given to us if we would remove, for our support.

We would be thankful if our Great Father would educate our children here; we only want schools, to make us happy.

We are satisfied with these lands, and have all agreed not to sell; and we hope you will not think hard of us in refusing to sell. We have spent a great deal and have had much trouble in getting this land and don't want to sell it — we value it much. If we should sell we could not escape the Whites, for we would be surrounded by them even at the Rocky Mountains. We take the Whites to be our friends and do not object to being near them — We are now taught and instructed by the Whites, there is good and bad among all. The good advise us to remain, and the bad alone advise us to remove. We have now got land cleared and cultivated, and if we should remove, we should be compelled to move again before many years.

Once more we repeat — we have been assisted by the Whites, in getting this land, and are pleased that we can cultivate it.

The Chiefs say we made a fair treaty; They are satisfied, and think the Government should be, — and for that reason we are unwilling to sell.

The Oneidas here had nothing to do in making the Treaty at Buffalo, it was made by those in New York. We are governed by the treaty which we made with the United States. This is all he has to say."

The Commissioner inquired if this was the answer of all the

Chiefs, and whether Jacob Cornelius was authorized to speak for all; and whether all were present that were here yesterday. The names of the Chiefs were then called and all answered that they approved Cornelius's answer.

The Commissioner inquired if any were present who went to Washington and requested to have a treaty made. Thomas King replied that he requested the appointment of a Commissioner. The Commissioner stated that from the account of these delegates the President was induced to believe that a part of the Oneidas were willing to remove; and from these statements this Council is held. The feelings of the President are of the kindest nature. He believes that some are willing to remove and therefore sent his Commissioner — and this has caused the assembly of this Council; He has no disposition to force Indians to sell; but they should be cautious how they send or permit their people to go to Washington and make representations. It should never be done except in Council and this by the Chiefs.

Thomas King said he wants to make known his reasons for doing as he has done. He would express himself as well as he can.

In 1837, J. F. Schermerhorn visited us, and since that time there has been a Missouri Party among the Oneidas at Green Bay. Since then, inducements were let out relative to money matters about going to Missouri. Next year Schermerhorn returned here and took a party to Missouri, without the consent of the Nation. The next season a delegation of Oneida chiefs was sent to Washington, who made a treaty. Schermerhorn went to Buffalo and made a treaty there. Two Chiefs now absent (Elijah Skenandoah & Adam Swamp) persuaded him to go to Buffalo Treaty. — He was always with the leading Chiefs, but these two men induced him to leave the Chiefs. Afterwards these men deserted him and went back to the Chiefs. What has been said today by the Chiefs is agreeable to him. He is now glad that one has just come in who was with him at Washington (Baptiste Powlis). They went there not to make a treaty, but to make inquires of the President and Secretary and Commissioner relative to the removal of a few. They gave their papers to a gentleman who was there, to assist them. The President then said he wants to take the paper & consider upon the subject and give them an answer the next day. The next day they met the President, Secretary and Commissioner of Indian Affairs, who told them if 250 people [were] for remove, they would remove them, and said to them that they had better send a Commissioner to make a treaty with the Oneidas at Green Bay; They told him they have come to get an appropriation for the removal of some. They told the President it would be difficult to make a treaty, as so many were opposed it and wished to know how they could manage that. The President said he would manage it in some other way. They . . . appropriate that you, (the Commissioner) has come on with some such instructions.

When he was about leaving Washington he told the President, it was in his mind very doubtful whether a treaty could be made at Green Bay, and wanted to know how those wishing to go could go. The whole of this matter of separating themselves from the Chiefs was caused by the bad management of Schermerhorn.

The Commissioner inquired how many were in favor emigrating when he went as a Delegate last winter.

He replied that when he went as a Delegate, Powlis was sent with him, and the power of attorney was signed when he was absent, and he does not know how many signed it. He examined it and understood it. It was said, at Washington, to them by the President that they could not make a treaty unless they could control a majority of the nation.

The Commissioner inquired if the power of attorney was accepted by the consent and with the knowledge of the Chiefs. He answered that the power of attorney was made by consent of some of the Chiefs who were in favor of emigrating — namely John August, Thomas Lodwick, and Metinus King, but not by consent of those opposed to selling.

The Commissioner inquired how many were represented to be willing to emigrate by them at Washington. Baptist Powlis (another Delegate to Washington) represented to the President that there were 300 Oneidas willing to emigrate; and that this number of names was taken down by Thomas Bain and were on the paper which they left with the President.

The Commissioner then inquired of the Chiefs and other present how many were willing to Emigrate to Missouri.

Henry Bear, said, you make the inquiry only of the Chiefs and not of those who wish to emigrate; we know the number of those who want to go. 100 would go this fall or 200 next season, as we calculated. I have a few words to say. I have listened to the other party. I will now explain. King has told how we came to be divided into two parties. It has always been delayed, but now you have come to make us a visit. As far as we are called the Missouri Party it is not our wish to take anything from our Chiefs; we only want to sell what belongs to us 100 acres each. As you have come so far, we hope you will treat with us. These are the same men and Chiefs who were once sent for to visit you at Cedar Point. He further said that he wished to make a treaty with the Commissioner and would meet him tomorrow at the Bay — That he has a right to make a Treaty; he has himself forgot on the . . . one, and thought he had a right to sell his own lands.[11]

—◁||▷—

Friday, Nov. 21, 1845

Council opened at 12 o'clock — Present as yesterday.

Baptist Powlis said, he would speak if the Commissioner, would hear him. The Commissioners, said that as he has been to Washington and his name was on the Treaty of 1838, he would hear him.

Powlis said he wished to state the number of the Chiefs, who were willing to emigrate. He said that Henry Bear and John Antony were Chiefs (their names not being entered on the list made of the first day of the Council.) The Commissioner, called upon all now present to say whether these men were Chiefs, and if so, why their names were not given in?

Daniel Bread, for the Chiefs, said, we wish you to understand our customs; and the reason why these men are not put on the list as Chiefs. John Antony was formerly a Chief of the Oneidas; but has been removed by the people, which removal was confirmed by the Chiefs of the Nation, and approved by Col. Boyd, then US Indian Agent at Green Bay, in the year 1833: and since this Chief has been deposed we have done business without him. Another was appointed

a Chief in place of Antony, whose name is Adam Swamp; and he has
since acted as a Chief.

Bread further stated that Henry Bear never was recognized as
a Chief, by the other Chiefs, or by the Nation. He has always been
opposed to the Chiefs, and has tried to make a party against them;
and with this only, and because he calls himself a Chief, is he one? He
also stated that Baptista Powlis was not a Chief, nor has he ever been
considered as one. His brother, Henry Powlis is a head Chief, and
Baptista was merely appointed by his brother as head of this (Henry
& family) at one time while being in New York, and on consequence
he called himself a Chief. Baptista has nothing to do here, nor any
interest in the place. He further said that there was an old Chief in
New York, called "Big Knife", who is now dead. The Oneidas expected
that this old man would have come here, but he did not come. The
band of this Chief is now without a Chief; and it is entitled to one.
Henry Bear & some others made John Metoxin and Metinus King
Chiefs, but not in the regular way. — These men have not yet been
recognized as Chiefs by the other Chiefs; but they would not object to
these two being Chiefs if they would act with the others. — They have
never met in Council or acted as Chiefs.

Bread further stated, that he believed the Missouri Party also
claimed Isaac Wheelock as a Chief; but the Chiefs did not consider
him one, for the old Chief whom he pretends to represent or succeed
(Christian Beachtree) is still alive in New York. All he has now said
has been on behalf of all the Chiefs now present.

Henry Bear said, — he wished to explain in relation to those whom
the other Chiefs deny to be Chiefs. He said that Antony Big Knife
left the Oneidas and went to the Onondagas, and that his band was
entitled to a Chief, — that the Missouri Party then had a regular feast
and called the people together and made a Chief in place of Big Knife.
John Metoxen was put in his place as a Chief. Metoxen was made a
Chief at the same time by the same party. The band then agreed that
as these two were young men, he (Bear) should act as a speaker and
leading man to do business. He thinks nothing can be said against
them being Chiefs. He then gave notice to all the Chiefs holding the
feast and told them he wanted them to come. After these Chiefs were
made, he called upon the Chiefs for their approval; They were at the

feast and took dinner, but said they would have nothing to do with these men as they were not properly made Chiefs. Bear said, he told them he would have them Chiefs, even if it was in Missouri.

The list of heads of families being called it approved that there was 87 persons who . . . of selling and emigrating a schedule of whom is attached to these proceedings.

William Schuyler & ten other Oneidas residing at Green Bay for 3 years, and having no interest here, wished for means to take them to Missouri, and asked the Commissioner for some provision for this purpose. Baptista Powlis and some others made the same request purpose. The Commissioner told them he would make inquiry of their great Father the President on the subject.

Daniel Bread said he would say a few words. — We are very glad you have come to see us; and hope you are pleased with the Chiefs. I believe everything has been done on a just and proper manner, and through the Chiefs. — They are thankful that we have all met here, and hope that we may see you often and that friendship may long continue between yourself and the Oneidas; and the peace will continue between us and the United States. We are glad to see so many white friends. They have always been friendly, and we hope you will be fully satisfied with us. The Chiefs have now united together and intend to remain so. The warriors are all satisfied. I thank you on behalf of the Chiefs for your kindness, and hope you will remember us, — and we hope ask that our Great Father will give us a flag to put on a tree as an evidence of our friendship to the United States, and a remembrance of the 4th of July, the Birth-day of Independence. We are glad our Great Father has sent so good a man for Commissioner.

The Commissioner answered explaining the motives of their Great Father, the President. He (Comr.) was sent here to ascertain their wishes and to know how many wished to sell. He told them that all which had been said here should be reported — that he knew the friendly feelings of the Oneidas, and their patriotic conduct in the late war. He advised them to cultivate the soil; raise stock, and to cultivate the peaceful art of Husbandry that they might all be united and remain true to themselves and their own interests — that he would be glad to see them happy and united as a people.

He told them he was glad to see their improvements & that as

Superintendent he would always serve them faithfully. He
recommended to them their Agent (A.G. Ellis) as a faithful officer
and one high in his confidence. He said he was pleased to hear that
good opinion expressed by them yesterday of their missionaries, and
that they deserved their confidence and esteem — and that he parted
with them with kind feelings, and asked for them the blessing of their
creator.

The council concluded and a list was submitted of the numbers of
Oneida who were still intent on moving to the West:

Schedule of Heads of Families of Oneida Indians residing at Duck
Creek, Wisconsin Territory, with the number of persons in each
family and who expressed a wish to sell their lands at Green Bay
and remove West of Missouri, at the Council held at Duck Creek, by
Governor Dodge in November 1845:

Squire David	11 persons
Isaac Beachtree	1
John Antony	9
Adam King	3
John Antony	4
John Stevens	2
Harvey Bear	8
Henry Stevens	4
Honyus Smith	5
Peter Cooper	1
Susan Hendrick	6
Adam Williams	1
Green family	3
David Bear	7
John House	8
Catharine Peter	1
John Denny	4
Isaac Wheelock	4
Polly Smith	5
Total	87[12]

FINAL RESERVATIONS FOR THE BROTHERTOWN, STOCKBRIDGE-MUNSEE, HO-CHUNK, AND MENOMINEE NATIONS

The final reservation boundaries for the Brothertown, Stockbridge-Munsee, Ho-Chunk, and Menominee Nations were established through treaties and congressional acts.

Brothertown Nation

The Senate proviso to the 1831 treaty with the Menominee provided one township, on the east side of Lake Winnebago, for the Brothertown, and it was confirmed in the 1832 Menominee treaty. However, under the threat of further removal to Kansas, the Brothertown made the decision to become citizens in 1839. That meant they would no longer be recognized by the United States as a Native nation.

The Brothertown applied for citizenship believing this would prevent removal and establish their community's "permanently resting place for [themselves] and posterity"[13] The Brothertown became citizens in 1839, but still spoke of "their own nations" and "continued to see themselves and their community as set apart by their unique history and rich culture." Congress passed an Act for the Relief of the Brothertown Indians in the Territory of Wisconsin, on March 3, 1839. The act states "their rights as a tribe or nation, and their power of making or executing their own laws, usages, or customs, as such tribe, shall cease."[14] This act set up a different form of government, as the Brothertown were now to elect a five-member board of commissioners from the tribe to transact the business of allotting the lands. The Brothertown lands were divided among the people, and patents were issued, and land was now held in fee simple. This means private, individual ownership of land, which made it possible to sell the land. This act is a boilerplate document with the same terms that were applied to the Stockbridge years later in 1843.

The Brothertown tribal headquarters are located in Fond du Lac, Wisconsin. They continue to conduct tribal council meetings as the Brothertown Indian Nation and have extensive tribal rolls. The US has turned down every attempt they have made to regain recognition as an Indian nation, but the Brothertown have not stopped their quest.[15]

In 1990, I was honored to interview June Ezwold, who had been the tribal chairperson for many years. She spoke with great strength about the Brothertown Nation's continued effort to regain the United States recognition as an Indian nation. June Ezwold sent me a document titled, "Where Did All the Montauks Go?," by Rudi and Will Ottery. Enclosed in the document was the genealogy of Montauk, starting with the first-generation Wyandanch, dated 1659, through eleven generations. I found my grandmother on the Stockbridge side, Eureka Jourdan, along with her sisters, Wilda and Julia, listed in the ninth generation.

In 1995, a collection of Brothertown documents was found in a steamer trunk by a man who had inherited a farm. He was willing to sell the documents to the Brothertown for a million dollars. Of course, that amount of money was not available. The negotiations went back and forth for years. Loretta Metoxen, the Oneida historian, was able to convince the owner to let her see and catalog the documents. The documents include brochures, pamphlets, books, a bible, hymns, ledgers, notebooks, a register, binders, an original manuscript of a play about the Brothertown, meeting minutes, pensions, lists of orphans, correspondence, leases, land allotments, lists of veterans of the Civil War, the War of 1812, the Mexican War, and World War I, newspaper clippings, deeds, land contracts, military listings, agreements, letters, mortgages, marriage certificates, death records, birth records, affidavits, quit claim deeds, warranty deeds, tax deeds, claims against the US, lists of correspondence, postcards, and pictures.

Again, negotiations went on for years. Finally, the purchase price was greatly reduced and the Oneida Nation agreed to pay for the documents and take care of them until the Brothertown Nation had its own museum or place to store the documents.

The Brothertown Nation has sought to reestablish federal recognition as an Indian nation for years. The United States has established a process for Indian nations that are no longer federally recognized as such, but continue to function as Indian nations, to obtain federal recognition. In April 1980, the Brothertown filed a letter of intent for federal recognition. Ten years later, in 1990, they were informed by the Department of Interior that they were not eligible for recognition. Yet the Brothertown continued their battle. In 2012, The Department of Interior issued its final determination saying that the 1839 congressional act acknowledging them as US citizens terminated their rights to their own governance and that they "lacked the authority to recognize the Brothertown." Since it was a congressional act that terminated the Brothertown, they would have to obtain a congressional act to reinstate their recognition by the government as an Indian nation.

The Brothertown released a statement of response:

> We do not take lightly the fight ahead of us. It will take time that
> many of us do not have, and it will take money that none of us have.
> However, because we know the fights behind us, we are confident
> that restoration of the government-to-government relations between
> the United States and the Brothertown Nation will be forthcoming.[16]

At the state level, the governor of Wisconsin, Tony Evers, issued Executive Order 50 on October 8, 2019, recognizing the Native nations in Wisconsin, and he included the Brothertown in his list.[17]

Stockbridge-Munsee

In the Senate proviso to the 1831 treaty with the Menominee, two townships of land totaling 46,080 acres were granted to the Stockbridge. These lands were confirmed in the 1832 Menominee treaty.

Just seven years after the 1832 treaty, another treaty was made with "the Stockbridge and Munsee tribes of Indians, who reside upon Lake Winnebago in the territory Wisconsin." In Article 1, the Stockbridge and Munsee ceded "the east half of the tract of forty-six thousand and eighty acres land, which was laid off for their use, on the east side of Lake Winnebago." The US recognized there were those who wanted to emigrate and those who wanted to stay, and a roll or census was made according to these divisions. The emigrating parties' share of land to be ceded was 8,767 ¾ acres, and they were to be paid $8,767.75, which amounts to one dollar per acre. The following describes Stockbridge removal:

> A group of Stockbridge Mohicans, fearing the inevitable, moved
> to Indian Territory in 1839. Many died while making this journey.

Some reached Kansas and Oklahoma and married into other tribes. Most simply gave up and returned to Wisconsin, which had gained statehood in 1848.[18]

Just as the Oneida Nation experienced divisions over removal to the west, the Stockbridge were also divided. The Stockbridge had an Indian party opposed to removal and a citizens party willing to become citizens and to remove. This division into parties would determine, influence, and disrupt the Stockbridge-Munsee Nation and government for years. Each party claimed it was the real government and had authority. This predicament bounced political leadership back and forth and impacted treaties, acts of Congress, and land allotments.

In 1843, Congress passed an Act for the Relief of the Stockbridge Tribe of Indians in the Territory of Wisconsin. Stockbridge lands were to be allotted to individual members of the tribe, "and their rights as a tribe or nation and their power of making or executing their own laws, usage, or customs, as such tribe shall cease." A method was set up to elect five commissioners from the tribe who would divide the lands for allotment. They were made citizens of the United States.

Thus, the Stockbridge lands were allotted, their government changed to an elected system, their members made citizens, and the nation terminated all in one congressional act.

After three years of lobbying by the Stockbridge-Munsee, the 1843 act was repealed, and "the said Stockbridge tribe or nation of Indians is restored to their ancient form of government, with all powers, rights, and privileges, held and exercised by them under their customs and usages, as fully and completely as though the above-recited act had never passed." This act divided the Stockbridge lands on the east side of Lake Winnebago into an Indian District and a Citizens District. The allotted lands that were sold between 1843 and 1846 continued to be a source of conflict for many years.

Just two years after the repeal, in 1848, another treaty was made with the intent to remove the Stockbridge to the west. The preamble to this treaty acknowledged the 1843 act and the repeal of that act in 1846, saying, "that such of said tribe as should enroll themselves with the subagent of Indian affairs at Green Bay, should be and remain citizens of the United

States, and the residue of said tribe were restored to their ancient form of government as an Indian tribe."[19]

Article 2 stated that a roll or census would be taken with the names of the Stockbridge tribal members who would benefit from the treaty. If a person separated from the tribe, their share or portion would cease.

Article 3 required ceding all of the Stockbridge lands on the east side of Lake Winnebago, while Article 4 stated the lands of those who had become citizens of the United States would have their land surveyed into lots and issued patents.

Article 5 stated that six months after ratification of the treaty, the United States would pay the Stockbridge $16,500 to settle their affairs and prepare themselves to move to a new home. Article 6 stated that upon ratification of the treaty, the US would pay within six months $14,504.85 to the Stockbridge for their improvements on the lands ceded. In Article 7, the Stockbridge were guaranteed they could stay on their lands for one year, but then they would have to move to the lands beyond the Mississippi River. Article 8 assured the Stockbridge that if they moved to the west, they would be paid subsistence for one year.

Article 9 explained that the US would invest $16,500 in stocks with interest at five percent interest. The interest would be paid to the Stockbridge. Article 10 provided for a survey, and in Article 11, the United States agreed to pay $3,000 to cover the expenses of sachem and head men in attending to the business of the tribe since 1843.

Article 12 stated this treaty would be binding upon ratification of the government of the US. Signers of the treaty included the following men:

Morgan L. Martin	John Metoxen Councillor
Albert G. Ellis	John W. Quinney Councillor
Augustin E. Quinney, sachem	Samuel Miller
Zeba T. Peters, Councillor	*David Palmer
Peter D. Littlemen, Councillor	Ezekiel Robinson
*Abram Pye, Councillor	*James Joshua
Joseph M. Quinney	*Garrett Thompson
Samuel Stephens	Jeremiah Slingerland
*Benjamin Pye, 2d	*Thomas Schanandoah
Simon S. Metoxen	*John W. Quinnery, Jr.

Daniel Metoxen
*Moses Charles
*Benjamin Pye, 3d
*Jacob Jehoiakim
*Laurens Yocron

*Nicolas Palmer
John P. Quinney
*Washington Quinney
*Aaron Turkey

To each of the names of the Indians marked with an asterisk is affixed his mark.

In Presence of
Charles A. Grignon, US Interpreter
Lemuel Goodell
Eleazer Williams
Charles Poreuninozer

The supplemental article to the 1848 treaty stated that the United States would pay the Stockbridge for their claims on lands in Indiana and Wisconsin, as follows:

$5,000 to chiefs and head men
$20,000 to be paid in 10 installments when they have removed

Within two years, the president would obtain land for the Stockbridge west of the Mississippi River in Minnesota. The purpose of this treaty was removal to the west of those who wanted to move and had been made citizens, and ceding of their lands east side of Lake Winnebago.

Three documents are attached to the supplemental article. The first is the census of the Stockbridge, which lists their names and gender, with a total of 177 names. This census was taken by M. L. Martin, Albert G. Ellis, and Austin E. Quinney at Stockbridge on November 24, 1848. The second document was the "Schedule of land to be patented to individuals under the 4th article of the above agreement." Listed are the names, number of lots, and number of acres.[20] The third document, "List: Valuation of improvements (vide Art.6)," with the names, acres, and dollar amounts with a total of $14,504.85, was signed by M. L. Martin and Albert G. Ellis.

In 1855, an unratified treaty was made to unite the Indian Party and
Citizens Party of the Stockbridge into one tribal organization. It appears
from this document the Stockbridge "relinquished" the seventy-two
sections of land designated for them west of the Mississippi. They provided for the improvements of white settlers who purchased land from
the Stockbridge. All annuities from the 1794 Six Nations treaty and the
September 3, 1839, treaty were to apply to education and improving their
circumstances.

This final treaty, in 1856, acknowledged the two townships for the
Stockbridge in the 1831 treaty with the Menomonee, and that in the 1839
treaty, the "east half of said two townships was retroceded to the United
States." When

> they refused to move, they were offered a location in Minnesota, and
> applied for a retrocession to them of the township of Stockbridge,
> which has been refused by the United States; and Whereas a majority
> of the said tribe of Stockbridge and the Munsees are adverse to
> removing to Minnesota and prefer a new location in Wisconsin.

In Article 1 of the treaty, the Stockbridge relinquished all lands east of
Lake Winnebago, as well as the seventy-two sections of land in Minnesota
from the 1848 treaty. They further relinquished the $20,000 in stocks and
the $16,500 in cash from 1848 treaty.

Article 2 reads in part:

> In consideration of such cession and relinquishment by said
> Stockbridges and Munsees, the United States agree to select as soon as
> practicable and to give them a tract of land in the State of Wisconsin,
> near the southern boundary of the Menomonee reservation, of such
> sufficient extent to provide for each head of a family and others lots
> of land of eighty and forty acres.

Payments for improvements totaled $40,100, while $20,550 was promised
"to enable them to remove" and $18,000 ($12,000 for Stockbridge and
$6,000 for Munsees) "in the purchase of stock and necessaries, [for] the

discharge of national or tribal debts, and to enable them to settle their affairs."

Article 3 provided the tract of land selected, near the southern boundary of the Menominee reservation, that was to be surveyed and allotted:

Head of family 80 acres, if more than 4 members another 80 acres
Single male over 18, 80 acres
Single females over 18, and orphans, to be given 40 acres

The land was to be held in trust until the United States issued patents, and the Stockbridge could not sell this land.

Article 6 addressed the issue of Stockbridge who had emigrated to the west under 1839 treaty, stating if they returned, the remaining Stockbridge were to "receive them as brethren." Article 7 stated that the annuities from the treaties of November 11, 1794, August 11, 1827, and September 3, 1839, were to be used for education. Article 8 provided $150 for a school house, while Article 9 provided land for a cemetery.

Article 10 read: "It is agreed that all roads and highways laid out by authority of law shall have the right of way through the lands set aside for said Indians, on the same terms as are provided by law for their location through lands of citizens of the United States."

Article 11 stated that the United States was to "advance the welfare and improvement of said Indians," noting that the US president could "with the advice and consent of the Senate, adopt such policy in the management of their affairs, as in his judgment may be most beneficial to them; or Congress may, hereafter, make such provision by law, as experience shall prove to be necessary."

In Article 12, the Stockbridge agreed to "suppress the use of ardent spirits" and keep alcohol out of their lands.

Articles 13 and 14 provided measures to examine the validity of sales by the Stockbridge under the 1843 act, which allotted lands but was repealed. If the sales were not valid, and by the 1848 treaty receded to the United States, then the United States could sell the lands. Meanwhile, Article 15 provided payment to the Stockbridge for improvements made on the ceded lands, and Article 16 provided for those Stockbridge who relinquished all their rights as Stockbridge Indians and wanted to stay on their lands near

Lake Winnebago. For those people the United States would issue fee-simple patents (ownership) to them. The treaty document includes a list of names and the lots to be patented to them.

Under Article 17, the treaties of 1839 and 1848 are "hereby abrogated and annulled."

Article 18 reads that the treaty to be ratified and signed by Francis Huebschmann, commissioner, and chiefs, headmen, and members of the "said Stockbridge and Munsee tribes, and the said delegates of the Munsee of New York, have hereunto set their hands and seals."

The following signatures appear on the treaty:

Ziba T. Peters, sachem
John N. Chicks

Counselors:
   Jeremiah Slingerland
   John W. Abrams
   Levi Konkapot
   Joshua Willson, his X mark

Delegates of Munsee of New York
   Thomas S. Branch
   Jacob Davids, his X mark
   John W. Quinney Jr., his X mark
   Timothy Jourden, his X mark
   John Yoccom, his X mark
   William Mohawk, his X mark

The treaty included the names of 107 Stockbridge people.

A letter was attached to this treaty from the northern superintendency, Milwaukee, and dated February 23, 1856, written by Francis Huebschmann, a superintendent. He transmitted the 1856 treaty but said, "one-fifth of the Indians, headed by Austin E. Quinney, and most consisting of members of the Quinney family, did not sign the treaty." It is clear from the letter that he did not like Quinney because he was a leader in the Indian Party of the tribe. Huebschmann accused him of mismanagement of money.

Some Stockbridge people did not sign for either the Citizens Party or the Indian Party because they were not aligned with either party or actually were against one of the parties.

The 1856 treaty with the Stockbridge-Munsee was the final treaty for lands in Red Springs, which was on the southern boundary of the Menominee reservation. Allotments of land to individuals in this treaty happened long before the 1887 General Allotment Act was applied to all other Native nations. With their land having been allotted in the 1839, 1843, and 1848 treaties, and in acts of Congress, the Stockbridge-Munsee wanted to reorganize their government and acquire land for their people. In the final treaty, two townships on the southern boundary of the Menominee reservation were assigned to the Stockbridge-Munsee. These lands were allotted to the tribal members but eventually were lost through debts, taxes, and mortgages.[21]

After the 1934 Indian Reorganization Act, the Stockbridge wrote their own constitution, but it was rejected by the Bureau of Indian Affairs (BIA). The BIA had created a boilerplate constitution to fit across all Native nations, and wanted the Stockbridge-Munsee to have the same format. Thus, the voices of the Stockbridge-Munsee, stating what they wanted for themselves, were not included.

In 1937, the Stockbridge-Munsee lands totaled 15,327 acres, which was much less than the original two townships from the 1856 treaty. The Department of Interior "recognized the tribe's understanding that its community — its homelands — extended to the full two townships [46,060 acres]," which forms the boundaries of the Stockbridge-Munsee.[22]

The first land purchased for the Stockbridge Nation through the 1934 Indian Reorganization Act was near Bowler, Wisconsin. The land became the new village, Moh-he-con-nuck, which was the original name of the Stockbridge and which means "people who live by the waters that are never still." You can drive on Moh-he-con-nuck Road today. This became the main and largest settlement, with some staying in Red Springs and Morgan Siding, as well as on Big Lake. My grandfather's homestead was on Big Lake, but he lost it in the 1930s due to not being able to pay the taxes. This land could have been one of the allotments made in 1856 treaty and owned by the Citizens Party. It was issued a patent and passed through several owners, eventually becoming taxable. My grandfather moved the family to Moh-he-con-nuck to establish a new home. I grew up listening to my elders talk about pressuring the BIA to put the Farm Security Administration lands—13,077 acres—into a trust, which finally happened in 1972.[23] One relative stayed on Big Lake and as children we would go through a trail on their land to swim in Big Lake. Later, my Aunt Dot, Dorothy Davids, purchased part of my grandfather's lands near Big Lake. Through all of this history, disputes, treaties, acts of Congress, removals, and allotment, the Stockbridge-Munsee continued their identity as a nation.[24]

Treaties with the Menominee

The approximately ten million acres of Menominee homelands were reduced through treaties from 1821 to 1856, to a final reservation of 235,000 acres.[25]

In 1817, the first Menominee treaty of peace and friendship was made with the United States. In 1819, John Bowyer, an Indian agent, made a treaty with the Menominee for a major portion of their lands. This treaty was a matter of debate and controversy and was never ratified.

The first Menominee treaties that ceded land were made in 1821 and 1822 with the New York Indians. The 1821 treaty ceded 860,000 acres, and the 1822 treaty ceded 6.72 million acres.[26] These treaties were made Indian nation to Indian nation and were approved and signed by President James Monroe. Because these treaties were between Indian nations, Monroe did not submit them to Congress, as the United States was not involved and the treaties did not require congressional approval. This became a point of controversy that was not settled well into the 1830s. The 1825 United States treaty at Prairie du Chien, made with the Sioux, Chippewa, Menominee, Ioway, Winnebago, and a portion of the Ottawa and Potawatomi tribes, established boundaries between these nations. The Menominee boundaries were left open because it wasn't clear which lands were for the New York Indians.

Land was also ceded in the 1827 Treaty of Butte des Morts, made between the United States and the Chippewa, Menominee, and Winnebago. Yet the controversy about lands for the New York Indians was not settled, and the treaty referred the final decision to the president of the United. States. In both the 1825 and 1827 treaties, the New York Indians were not included in the final treaty. Three commissioners were sent in 1830 to meet with the Menominee and New York Indians to settle the dispute over lands for the New York Indians. The commissioners were not successful.

In the US treaties with the Menominee in 1831 and 1832, an estimated 2.5 million acres were ceded to the United States. The New York Indians received five hundred thousand acres, the Stockbridge-Munsee received two townships, and the Brothertown one township.

In another treaty with the United States, the 1836 Treaty of Cedars, the Menominee ceded approximately four million acres.[27] These lands included "most of their land in northeastern Wisconsin and a small strip along the Wisconsin River."[28] The boundaries were defined as

Beginning at the mouth of the Wolf river, and running up and along the same, to a point on the north branch of said river where it crosses the extreme north or rear line of the five hundred thousand acre tract heretofore granted to the New York Indians: thence following the line last mentioned, in a northeastwardly direction, three miles: then in a northwardly course, to the upper forks of the Menomonie river, at a point to intersect the boundary line between the Menomonie and Chippewa nation of Indians: thence following the said boundary line last mentioned, in an eastwardly direction as defined and established by the treaty of the Little Bute des Mort, in 1827, to the Smooth rock of Shos-kin-aubie river: thence down the said river to where it empties into Green bay, between the Little and Great by de Noquet: thence up and long the west side of Green bay, (and including all the islands therein, not heretofore ceded) to the mouth of Fox river: then up and along the said Fox river, and along the west side of Winnebago lake (including the islands therein) to the mouth of Fox river, where it empties into said lake: thence up and along said Fox river to the place of beginning (saving and reserving out of the district of country above ceded and described, all that part of the five hundred thousand acre tract, granted by the treaties between the Menomonies and the United States, made on the eighth day of February A.D. 1831, and on the twenty-seventh day of October A.D. 1832, which may be situated within the boundaries hereinbefore described) the quantity of land contained in the tract herby ceded, being estimated at about four millions of acres.[29]

This treaty clearly builds on previous treaties with the intention of obtaining all of the Menominee lands.

The United States continued its removal policy in the 1848 US Treaty of Lake Pow-aw-hay-kon-nay-Poygan with the Menominee, with the aim to remove the Menominee from Wisconsin. This was part of the larger continuing movement to remove all Indian tribes to the west. The Menominee ceded 5.5 million acres in exchange for 600,000 acres at Crow Wing Territory in Minnesota. They were given two years to explore the new lands and to remove. Article 4 provided "to the chiefs, as soon after the same shall be appropriated by Congress as may be convenient, to enable them to arrange settle the affairs of their tribe preparatory their removal to the country set apart for and given to them as above, thirty thousand dollars."[30] But the Menominee refused to remove, as they found the lands unsuitable, and they petitioned the president to stay in Wisconsin.[31]

As a result of their "great unwillingness" to remove to Minnesota, the president consented to "their locating temporarily upon the Wolf and Oconto rivers." The Menominee agreed to relinquish the lands designated in Minnesota in the 1848 treaty.

The Menominee made their final treaty with the United States in 1854. This treaty established the current 270,000-acre Menominee Indian Reservation, which ended the removal to Minnesota from the 1848 treaty. The boundaries were described as follows:

to said Indians for a home, to be held as Indian lands are held, that tract of country lying upon the Wolf River, in the State of Wisconsin, commencing at the southeast corner of township 28 north of range 16 east of the fourth principal meridian, running west twenty-four miles, thence north eighteen miles, thence east twenty-four miles, thence south eighteen miles, to the place of beginning — the same being townships 28, 29, and 30, of ranges 13, 14, 15, and 16, according to the public surveys.[32]

The treaty established a manual-labor school, grist and saw mills, $15,000 for a person to run the mills for fifteen years, and $9,000 for a blacksmith ship, with iron and steel for twelve years beginning 1857 at $11,000. The $40,000 for their removal to Minnesota, which did not happen, was to be paid to them "under the direction of the President." The Menominee were to be paid for the lands in the 1848 treaty the sum of $242,686 in installments, annually over fifteen years, again under the "direction of the President . . . as he shall judge necessary and proper for their wants, improvement, and civilization."

The treaty was signed by Francis Huebschmann, a superintendent of Indian Affairs overseeing the Menominee, along with the following signatories:

Wau-ke-chon, his X mark
Wis-ke-no, his X mark
Way-tan-sah, his X mark
Carron, his X mark
Sho-e-niew, his X mark
Lamotte, his X mark
Pe-quo-quon-ah, his X mark
Shaw-poa-tuk, his X mark
Wau-pen-na-nosh, his X mark
Sho-ne-on, his X mark
Shaw-wan-na-penasse, his X mark
Ta-ko, his X mark
Ko-man-ne-kin-no-shah, his X mark
Wau-pa-mah-shaew, his X mark
Auck-ka-na-pa-waew, his X mark
Ah-way-sha-shah, his X mark
Check-e-quon-way, his X mark
Nah-pone, his X mark
Mo-sha-hat, his X mark
I-yaw-shiew, his X mark
Kah-way-sot, his X mark

Signed and sealed in the presence of us:
John V. Suydam, sub-agent
Chas. A. Grignon, United States Interpreter
H.W. Jones, secretary to the commissioner

Chas. H. White, deputy United States marshal
Herman M. Cady, United States timber agent
William Powell
John Wiley
H.L. Murray[33]

In the 1856 treaty between the United States and the Menominee, two of the Menominee townships on the south line of their reservation were ceded to the US government for the Stockbridge-Munsee. The United States agreed to pay the Menominee sixty cents per acre for the two townships. Article 2 stated that the money from the sale "shall be expended in a like manner, to promote the improvement of the Menominee, as is stipulated by the third article of the treaty May twelfth, eighteen hundred and fifty-four." The paternalism of the United States is shown in the statement that "the President of the United States may, by and with the advice and consent of the Senate, adopt such policy in the management of the affairs of the Menomonees as in his judgment may be most beneficial to them." This treaty stated the Menominee should "suppress the use of ardent spirits," and that their annuity monies would be paid in semiannual or quarterly payments. All roads and highways "laid out by authority of law, shall right of way through the lands of the said Indians." The treaty reads in part:

> In testimony whereof, the said Francis Huebschmann, commissioner as aforesaid, and the chiefs and headmen of the Menomonee tribe, in presence and with the consent of the warriors and young men of the said tribe, assembled in general council, have hereunto set their hands and seals at the place and on the day and year hereinbefore written.

The treaty was signed by Francis Huebschmann, as well as the following representatives:

Osh-kosh, his X mark
Sho-ne-niew, his X mark

Ke-she-na, his X mark
La-motte, his X mark
Pe-quah-kaw-nah, his X mark
Car-ron, his X mark
Wau-ke-chon, his X mark
Ah-kamote, his X mark
Ah-yah-metah, his X mark
Osh-ke-he-na-niew, his X mark
Kotch-kaw-no-naew, his X mark
Sho-no-on, his X mark
Wa-pa-massaew, his X mark
Naw-no-ha-toke, his X mark
Match-a-kin-naew, his X mark
Oken-a-po-wet, his X mark
Way-taw-say, his X mark
Naw-kaw-chis-ka, his X mark
Wa-ta-push, his X mark
Py-aw-wah-say, his X mark
Way-aich-kiew, his X mark
Ay-oh-sha, his X mark
Mo-sha-hart, his X mark

Signed and sealed in presence of—
Benja Hunkins, Indian agent
Talbot Pricket, United States interpreter
Theodore Koven, secretary to commissioner
John Wily
R. Otto Skolla
H.L. Murny
Benjamin Rice
John Werdchaff
Stephen Canfield
Thomas Heaton[34]

The millions of acres of Menominee land was reduced in this final treaty to the existing Menominee reservation of only 235,000 acres.

The Ho-Chunk Nation

The history of the Ho-Chunk tells of many, many removals, of the people's resistance, and of their survival as an Indigenous nation in Wisconsin. According to Andy Thundercloud, a Ho-Chunk elder, "The Ho-Chunk Nation's ten million acres of ancestral land, between the Mississippi and Rock Rivers, were recognized in treaties between the United States and the Ho-Chunk Nation." He described their land as stretching from the Door Peninsula south to Chicago and west to the Mississippi.[35] Despite many attempts by the United States to remove the Ho-Chunk from Wisconsin land, many refused to leave or later returned to their homelands and now live in twelve counties in southeastern Wisconsin. As a result of the treaties and removals, there are Ho-Chunk reservations in Wisconsin and Nebraska.

In the 1820s, lead miners began intruding on Ho-Chunk lands. Despite repeated trips and petitions to Washington, the invasion of lead miners and the loss of land did not stop. This led to a number of treaties between the Ho-Chunk and the United States, by which the Ho-Chunk's land base dwindled and they were removed to sites in Iowa, Minnesota, South Dakota, and finally Nebraska. Each treaty of removal promised a place to remove to and provisions, but the US government did not uphold its treaty obligations, and many Ho-Chunk people were forced into removal through not only treaties, but also starvation. *Winnebago Oratory: Great Moments in the Recorded Speech of the Hochungra, 1742–1887*, compiled by Mark Diedrich, contains documents and speeches of Ho-Chunk leaders referring to their repeated attempts to stop the removal and prevent the starvation of their people.

In the 1825 Treaty at Prairie du Chien, the Ho-Chunk signed a treaty for peace and friendship and to establish land boundaries. In 1827, they signed another treaty to establish boundaries. However, these treaties did little to stem invasion of thousands of lead miners on their lands.

In 1827, the Ho-Chunk Red Bird retaliated for the execution of Ho-Chunk warriors at Fort Snelling in Minnesota by attacking and killing white squatters near La Crosse and miners near Prairie du Chien. In 1827, Red Bird surrendered, and Ho-Chunk leaders went to Washington to negotiate his release. This resulted in their losing their lands in Illinois that were being mined for lead. In 1828, the United States pushed to acquire all of the Ho-Chunk's mineral lands south of the Wisconsin River.

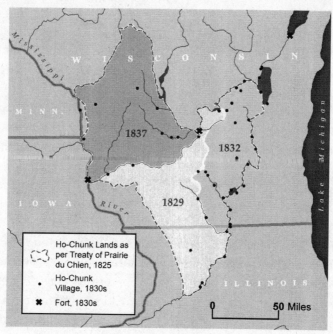

Cessions of the Ho-Chunk Homelands: 1829, 1832, 1837
MAP BY COLE SUTTON

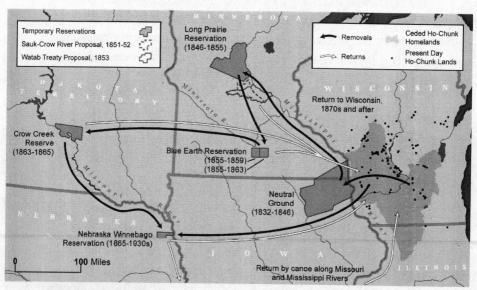

Relocations of the Ho-Chunk Tribe
MAP BY COLE SUTTON

Entire villages of Ho-Chunk people attended the treaties, but tradition allowed only certain people to sign treaties. The United States violated this custom by appointing Native people who were in favor of the treaty. Eventually the Ho-Chunk people became divided as "treaty Indians" versus those who resisted removal and stayed in Wisconsin.

In 1829, the United States and the Ho-Chunk signed a treaty at Prairie du Chien. The original treaty had a wampum string attached at the top. In the treaty, the Ho-Chunk ceded lands for the promise of annual payments of eighteen thousand dollars for thirty years. It was signed by Ho-Chunk living at Prairie du Chien and Fort Winnebago. The 1829 treaty was ratified and signed by President Andrew Jackson on February 13, 1833.

In the 1832 treaty concluded September 15, 1832, at Fort Armstrong, Rock Island, Illinois, the Ho-Chunk ceded all their lands east of the Mississippi and south of the Wisconsin River. The US government's goal was to obtain all of the Ho-Chunk land and remove the people to "neutral ground" west of the Mississippi River. This neutral ground included lands in southeastern Minnesota and northeastern Iowa. Article 2 of the treaty directed that by June 1833 "All the Winnebagos now residing within the country ceded by them, as above, shall leave the said country." They were told that after the first day of June, 1833, no Ho-Chunk persons could plant, fish, or hunt in the ceded territory. This devastated their economy.[36]

Because the land ceded was more valuable than the lands where they were designated to remove, the Ho-Chunk people were to be paid ten thousand dollars a year for twenty-seven years; however, they were required to give up certain Ho-Chunk people accused of crimes, or they wouldn't be paid. Many Ho-Chunk people refused to remove to the neutral land.

At the August 29, 1833, meeting with United States government representatives, the Ho-Chunk asked to stay one more year. Whirling Thunder said, "We are all very anxious to remain on our lands for this season that we may be able to raise wherewith to keep us from starving the ensuing winter."[37]

White Crow stated, "Many of my nation appeared to seem to be dissatisfied; but I think that can be easily settled. A great deal of provisions has been promised to us, a part only has been delivered to us. If we were well supplied with provisions we would not think it hard to remove from our country, but we know we will suffer; and it is for this reason we would like to remain, for this season, in this country."[38]

General Dodge spoke at the gathering about the earlier treaty which, he said, was designed by the United States to separate the Ho-Chunk from the whites with a great river as the boundary. He discussed prisoners and those who had been delivered but escaped, and he accused the village of Rock River of allowing them to stay there. He stated there were twenty thousand rations of pork and flour at Fort Winnebago that he would have delivered to the Ho-Chunk, along with two hundred bushels of corn "in order to expedite your removal." He stated that only those Ho-Chunk who were willing to remove would receive the rations that that the rations should support them for that summer.[39]

Because so many Ho-Chunk refused to remove, another treaty in 1837 ceded all the Ho-Chunk lands east of the Mississippi River and relocated those who lived on those lands to Long Prairie, Minnesota, but let them retain the right to hunt on some of the lands. The Ho-Chunk were given eight months after ratification to remove to the lands west of the Mississippi per the 1829 Treaty. It is interesting to note that in this treaty the United States would pay one hundred thousand dollars for those friends and relations who were less than one-quarter Ho-Chunk. Additional funds would be provided for removal expenses, goods and horses, provisions, and construction of a grist mill. The US would invest "eleven hundred thousand dollars [$1,100,000] at interest rate 5%." The interest of $55,000 would be spent on education, an interpreter for the school, a miller, agricultural supplies, medical services, and medicine. The 1837 treaty also included a stipulation that previous treaties were no longer valid. Only twenty Ho-Chunk people signed the treaty.[40]

In 1840, a farmer who also worked as an interpreter for the government told the heart-wrenching account of the removal of the Ho-Chunk by troops sent to Portage. "[Pierre] Meneg was sent after Yellow Thunder and Black Wolf's son inviting them to Portage to get provisions; but instead of that, as soon as they arrived, they were put in the guardhouse, with ball and chain, which hurt the feelings of the Indians very much, as they had done no wrong to the Government." When General Dodge arrived, the captives were released and the Ho-Chunk people "all promised faithfully to be at Portage, ready for removal, in three days." They went down the Rock River in two large boats. The account continued,

We went down to Rock River, to look for Masimanikaka; from there we went to Madison, and thence to Fox River. We picked up 250 Indians, men, women and children, and we took them down to Prairie du Chien. Before we got there, at the head of the Kickapoo river, we came to three Indian wigwams. The Captain directed me to order the Indians to break up their camp and come along with him. Two old women, sisters of Black Wolf, and another one came up, throwing themselves on their knees crying and beseeching Captain Summer to kill them; that they were old, and would rather die, and be buried with their fathers, mothers and children, than be taken away, and that they were ready to receive their death-blows. Capt. Summer had pity on them and permitted them to say where they were, and left three young Indians to hunt for them."[41]

When the group arrived at the camp of Kejiqueweka, the captain told the people there to break camp and go with the troops. The people headed to the south, saying "they were going to say good-bye to their fathers, mothers and children." The interpreter followed and "found them on their knees, kissing the ground and crying very loud, where their relations were buried. This touched the Captain's feelings, and he exclaimed 'Good God! What harm could those poor Indian do among the rocks.'"[42]

According to the same interpreter, in 1844, Captain Summer and his troops asked him to help hunt for the Ho-Chunk Chief Dandy. After he was found and in chains on horseback, Chief Dandy demanded to see Governor Dodge at Mineral Point. When he met Dodge, Dandy pulled a Bible from his shirt and requested to meet in council. In the council meeting, Dandy asked if the Bible was a good book, and the governor said yes. "Then, said Dandy, if a man would do all that was in that book, could any more be required of him?" The governor replied no. "Well, said Dandy, "look that book all through, and if you find in it that Dandy ought to be removed by the Government to Turkey River, then I will go right off; but if you do not find it, I will never go there to stay." Dandy's argument did not sway the governor, and Dandy was put back on the horse, chained, and taken to Prairie du Chien. His feet and legs were blistered, and he couldn't walk for weeks. Then, the order came to send Dandy to Turkey River. When the corporal went to find his whip, Dandy jumped out of the buggy and escaped. He was not captured and lived to be seventy-seven years old.[43]

In 1846, the United States made another treaty with the Ho-Chunk at Washington, DC. The treaty began mentioning peace and friendship but went on to have the Ho-Chunk cede all their lands, specifically in the neutral ground assigned in the 1832 Treaty. In it, the US agreed to purchase 800,000 acres for the Ho-Chunk north of St. Peters and west of the Mississippi in Long Prairie, Minnesota (but only if it could be obtained "on just and reasonable terms"!) The United States would pay the Ho-Chunk $150,000 for the land and $40,000 for release of hunting and fishing rights. The $190,000 was to be paid for the expense of exploring and finding their new homes and "for removal and subsistence, for breaking up and fencing lands at their new home, and including ten thousand dollars of it for manual labor schools, and five thousand dollars and for grist and saw mills. The remaining eighty-five thousand dollars was to be put in trust with 5 percent interest for thirty years to be paid to the tribe. The Ho-Chunk were to remove within one year of the ratification of this treaty, and no amount of money would be paid to the Ho-Chunk until they arrived at their new home. It was signed by twenty-five Ho-Chunk.[44]

Land cessions and removal of the Ho-Chunk continued in succeeding treaties. A treaty made on February 27, 1855, at Washington, DC., required the Ho-Chunk to cede lands allotted to them in the 1846 treaty at Long Prairie, Minnesota, for lands at Blue Earth, Minnesota.[45]

A treaty was made with the Ho-Chunk in Washington, DC., in 1859 for allotment of their lands to individuals. The head of family would receive eighty acres; other males over eighteen would receive forty acres; the Indian agency received 160 acres; and "surplus" lands could be sold by the United States.[46]

In the winter of 1863, the Ho-Chunk were moved once again to Crow Creek, South Dakota, to an environment that was unsuitable for them. A quarter of the tribe perished on the journey.[47] Some survivors went into hiding, and many others fled south to take refuge on the Omaha reservation in Nebraska. An 1865 treaty carved out a portion of that reservation for the Ho-Chunk, and Ho-Chunk people remain there today, though that tribe is politically separate from the Ho-Chunk of Wisconsin. According to historian Patty Loew, "The 'renegades,' the tough survivors who hid out in Wisconsin or returned from reservations in the west, were rounded up again and again and on one occasion were put into boxcars and shipped to Nebraska. Again, they made their way home. In 1874, as a little girl, Mountain Wolf Woman (Xehaćiwiŋga) heard her mother's account of the last of the government's forced removal of the Wisconsin Ho-Chunk."[48]

Under the 1862 US Homestead Act, some of the Ho-Chunk who had resisted removal were able to acquire homesteads in Wisconsin. In 1875, the Ho-Chunk were recognized as permanent residents of Wisconsin and a census was conducted regarding annuities due to them. In 1881, Congressional legislation allowed the Ho-Chunk forty-acre homesteads. In 1963, the Ho-Chunk Nation ratified its first tribal constitution, which led to federal recognition of the nation. Their lands would now be trust lands. In 1974, the Ho-Chunk won a judgment of $4.6 million from the Indian Claims Commission to "compensate the tribe for its lands lost through fraudulent treaties."[49]

Today, the Ho-Chunk Nation's main headquarters is in Black River Falls, Wisconsin. Their land base comprises 3,535 acres of trust lands and 5,328 "fee simple" (individually owned) acres. The nation maintains four gaming sites and has expanded its business enterprise to include hotels, restaurants, and gas stations. The Ho-Chunk continue to revitalize their language, obtain land, strengthen their culture, and grow their economy.[50] A thriving Indigenous nation, they state, "Our cultural ways, songs and stories guide us with values of how to respect the land, the animals and how to live in balance with nature."[51]

MORE LOSS OF LAND

One might think after the reduction of Indigenous lands from millions of acres to a few thousand acres that the small amount of land that remained would be left alone and be secure. However, in 1871, the United States stopped making treaties with Indigenous nations, and congressional legislation became the way to deal with Native issues. In 1887, the US Congress passed the General Allotment Act, which led to more loss of land. This act was passed despite opposition by Indigenous nations.

Allotment divided reservation lands into individual ownership to break up the Native lands that were considered to belong to everyone, or held in common. The US government believed that individual land ownership would hasten assimilation. Around one hundred million acres of tribal land across the United States was lost due to allotment. The lands were allotted to the membership of the Indigenous nation, and if there was land left, it went to the United States. Indigenous people did not have any experience with the concept of private land ownership. Lands were now lost due to being taxed, mortgaged, and sold by individuals, so that the land base of each Native nation dwindled to only a fraction of what it once was.

Somehow the Menominee lands were not allotted. In dealing with Stockbridge lands, the US government "divided up the reservations and allotted the parcels to individual Native people."[52] At the Oneida Geographic Land Information Systems office, there is a map of the Oneida reservation allotments to individual tribal members made in 1892. This map has the names on each allotment. The courts have ruled that the General Allotment Act did not diminish the reservation boundaries. However, the Oneida reservation is what is called a checkerboard of reservation lands, and lands were lost.[53]

In 1934, Congress passed the Indian Reorganization Act (IRA) to stop the allotment and sale of Indian lands. This act would buy back a few acres of land for the Stockbridge and Oneida. The IRA produced boilerplate constitutions with elected forms of government, which were sent to Indigenous nations for signatures. The purpose was to end traditional governments through clans and tribal council meetings. Even though there was opposition to signing these constitutions, many felt that signing was the only way to continue their recognition as Indigenous nations and obtain some land.

INDIGENOUS NATIONS BUY BACK THE LAND

Treaty after treaty with the United States took Indigenous nations' lands. The United States continued its removal attempts by making treaties with the goal to remove all the Indigenous nations west of the Mississippi River and thereby obtain their land.

Treaty council meetings over many years featured speeches by Menominee, Ho-Chunk, Oneida, Stockbridge, and Brothertown chiefs that were made to both protest the taking of land and preserve some land for their people.

The survivance of Indigenous nations in Wisconsin shows the strength of Indigenous people. Despite the loss of land, through treaties and the false promises of a permanent homeland, Indigenous people have survived as nations. In spite of the United States' determination to obtain all Indigenous lands, and to dissolve our nations, we have survived with dignity. Today, Indigenous nations have government-to-government relationships and govern their own nations.

With economies reestablished with bingo and gaming, the Indigenous nations in Wisconsin have been able to repurchase parcels of land within their original boundaries. The goal is to buy all the land within the boundaries. It is a slow but steady process to once again have the lands specified in treaties with the United States.

US GOVERNMENT OFFICIALS DURING THE REMOVAL ERA

US President

James Madison 1809–1817

James Monroe 1817–1825

John Quincy Adams 1825–1829

Andrew Jackson 1829–1837

Secretary of War

William H. Crawford 1815–1816

John C. Calhoun 1817–1825

James Barbour 1825–1828

Peter B. Porter 1828–1829

John H. Eaton 1829–1831

Lewis Cass 1831–1836

Governor of Michigan Territory

Lewis Cass 1813–1831 (negotiated 1825 and 1827 treaties)

George Bryan Porter 1831–1834

Indian Agent at Green Bay Agency

John Bowyer 1816–1821

John Biddle 1821–1822

Henry Brevoort 1822–1830

Samuel Stambaugh 1830–1832

George Boyd 1832–1842

George W. Lawe 1842–1843

David Jones 1843–1845

Albert G. Ellis 1845–1849

Indian Agents in New York

Jasper Parrish, subagent for Six Nations in New York State

Thomas Dean, Indian Agent for New York Indians for 1827 treaty

US Commissioners Appointed to Negotiate Treaties

Charles C. Trowbridge, 1821

John Sergeant Jr., 1822

William Clark, 1825

Thomas L. McKenney, 1825 and 1827

James McCall, 1830

Erastus Root, 1830

J. T. Mason, 1830

Notes

The following abbreviations are used for frequently cited sources:

M15: *Letters Sent by Secretary of War Relating to Indian Affairs 1800–1824*, National Archives, Washington, DC. Microfilm M15.

M221: *Letters Received by the Secretary of War, Registered Series, 1801–1870*, National Archives, Washington, DC. Microfilm M221.

M234: *Letters received by Office of Indian Affairs, 1824–1881, 962 rolls, Green Bay Agency, 1824–1881*, Brown County Library, Green Bay, WI. Microfilm M234.

M271: *Letters Received by the Office of Secretary of War Relating to Indian Affairs 1800–1823*, National Archives, Washington, DC. Microfilm M271.

S. Doc. 189: *Memorial of Stockbridge Nations of Indians of Wisconsin*, 27th Cong., 2d sess. (1842), Senate, Serial set 397, S. Doc. 189, National Archives, Washington, DC.

S. Doc. 512: *Correspondence on the subject of the emigration of Indians between the 30th November, 1831, and 27th December 1833, WITH ABSTRACTS OF EXPENDITURES BY DISBURSING AGENTS, in the Removal and subsistence of Indians &c &c furnished in answer to a resolution of the Senate, of 27th December, 1833 by the Commissary General of subsistence. Vol. I–V.* 23rd Cong., 1st sess. (1834), US Serial set 246, S. Doc. 23-512. US War Department, Washington, DC: Printed by Duff Green, 1835.

T494: *Documents Relating to the Negotiation of Ratified and Unratified Treaties with various Tribes of Indians, 1801–1869*. Records of the Bureau of Indian Affairs, National Archives, Washington, DC. Microfilm T494.

Introduction

1. Porter Report to Cass, 3 February 1832, vol. III, Serial set 246, 173–88, in S. Doc. 23-512, *Correspondence on the subject of the Emigration Of Indians between the 30th November, 1831, and 27th December 1833, With Abstracts Of Expenditures By Disbursing Agents, in the Removal and subsistence of Indians &c &c furnished in answer to a resolution of the Senate, of 27th December,*

1833 by the Commissary General of subsistence, 23rd Cong., 1st sess., Special Collections, Resources Related to the Treaty Era, vertical file folder, box 1, College of Menominee Nation, Menominee, WI (hereafter cited as S. Doc. 23-512); S. Doc. 23-512, vol. IV, 27–52; Oneida History Conference papers, tab 13 (29–39), Oneida Library, Oneida, Wisconsin.

2. For detailed information on the Menominee creation story and clan system, see University of Wisconsin–Stevens Point, "The Menominee Clans Story," www4.uwsp.edu/museum/menomineeClans. The interactive map at this site shows traditional Menominee territory, current reservation land, and ancestral place names of Menominee villages in the Menominee language.

3. Jedidah Morse, *A Report to the Secretary of War of the United States on Indian Affairs, Comprising a narrative of a tour performed in the summer of 1820, under a commission from the President of the United States, for the purpose of ascertaining, for the use of the government, the actual state of the Indian Tribes in our county: by Jedediah Morse, 1822. Late Minister of the Frist Congregation Church in Charlestown, near Boston, now resident in New Haven* (New York: Augustus M. Kelly, 1970), 51.

4. *Tribal Histories: Ho-Chunk History,* Wisconsin Public Television, video, 26:45, Wisconsin First Nations, https://wisconsinfirstnations.org/tribal-histories-ho-chunk-history.

5. Paul Lauter, ed., *Heath Anthology of American Literature,* vol. A, *Colonial Period to 1800* (Boston: Houghton-Mifflin, 2005).

6. A. G. Ellis, *Advent of the New York Indians into Wisconsin,* vol. 2 (Madison: State Historical Society of Wisconsin, 1903), 416, in Eleazer Williams papers, Wisconsin Historical Society, Area Research Center at Green Bay.

7. Ellis, *Advent,* 417.

8. Paul Lauter, ed., *Heath Anthology of American Literature,* vol. B, *Early Nineteenth Century, 1800–1865* (Boston: Houghton Mifflin, 2014).

9. "Brothertown Indians," *Wisconsin Enquirer,* June 15, 1839, 3, quoted in Alanna Rice, " 'To procure a Residence Amongst Their Brethren to the West': The Relocation of the Brotherton Tribe in Territorial Wisconsin," *Wisconsin Magazine of History* 92, no. 2 (Winter 2008/2009): 28–41.

10. J. S. Whipple, *Report of Special Committee to Investigate the Indian Problem of the State of New York,* February 1, 1889, vol. 1 (Albany, NY: Troy Press, 1889).

11. Charles J. Kappler, *Indian Affairs: Laws and Treaties.* Vol. 2, *Treaties.* Washington, DC: Government Printing Office, 1904.

12. Richard Hill, "Oral Memory of the Haudenosaunee: Views of the Two Row Wampum," in José Barreiro, *Indian Roots of American Democracy* (Ithaca, NY: Akwe:kon Press, 1992), 154–56.

Chapter 1

1. For more on Oneida land loss and for a comprehensive overview of Oneida history, see Alexander Von Gernet, *The Historical Context of the Oneida Treaties with the State of New York*, Department of Anthropology, University of Toronto at Mississauga, Ontario, Canada. Report prepared for the State of New York Office of the Attorney General, February 2004.

2. Eleazer Williams papers, box 1, folder 10, page 2, Wisconsin Historical Society, Area Research Center at Green Bay. Hereafter cited as Williams papers.

3. *Petition of Six Nations of New York Indians relating to Kansas lands*, 47th Cong., 2d sess. (1883), No. 38, Native Americans Reference Collection, pt.1, reel 5, frame 77.

4. Wm. H. Crawford, Secretary of War, *Petition and Appeal of the Six Nations, Oneida, Stockbridge &c to the Government of the United States*, signed February 13, 1816. 1829, War Dept. Library; *Petition to the Hon. the Senate of the US from the Chiefs of the Six Nations, and other Indian tribes, asking Congress to confirm them in the possession of certain lands guaranteed to them by treaty*, 1829, 7–9, https://catalog.hathitrust.org/Record/100137108.

5. *Journal of a Treaty made & concluded at Butte Des Morts, on Fox River, in the Territory of Michigan, between Lewis Cass and Thomas McKenney, Commissioners of the United States of America and the Menominee, Winnebago, Ottawa & Munsee Tribes of Indians. Treaty of August 11, 1827*, No. 148, in *Documents Relating To The Negotiation Of Ratified And Unratified Treaties With Various Indian Tribes*, comp. John H. Martin, Special List No. 6 (Washington, DC: National Archives, 1949), 39; S. Doc. 23-512, vol. II.

6. Charles C. Trowbridge to Lyman C. Draper, September 21, 1821 [?], box 4, folder 8, Williams papers.

7. Ellis, *Advent*, 416.

8. *Ta Luh Ya Wa Gu: Holy Apostles Church Mission to the Oneidas 1822–1972* (privately published, 1972), 3; Ellis, Advent, 415–16.

9. Clarence Edwin Carter, comp. and ed., *Territorial Papers of the United States* vol. X, *The Territory of Michigan, 1805–1820* (Washington, DC: Government Printing Office, 1943), 876–77.

10. Morse, *Report to the Secretary of War*, 26.

11. Williams papers, box 1, folder 10, p. 5.

12. Ellis, *Advent*, 421.

13. Ellis, *Advent*, 421.

14. Ellis, *Advent*, 420.

15. Ellis, *Advent*, 421.

16. Ellis, *Advent*, 421.

17. Ellis, *Advent*, 421.

18. Williams papers, box 1, folder 10, p. 9.

19. Williams papers, box 1, folder 10, p. 3.

20. Trowbridge to Lyman C. Draper, Williams papers, box 4, folder 8.

21. Williams to D. A. Ogden, September 1833, Williams papers, box 1, folder 10.

22. Williams to "Respected Madam," Williams papers, box 1, folder 10, p. 5–6.

23. Williams papers, box 1, folder 10, p. 3.

24. Williams papers, box 1, folder 10, p. 7.

25. Williams papers, box 1, folder 10, p. 6–7.

26. See Arthur C. Parker, *Parker on the Iroquois*, Book 2, 5–145 (Syracuse, NY: Syracuse University Press, 1968).

27. Oneida petition to DeWitt Clinton, *Assembly Journal of New York State*, 42nd sess., January 1819 (Albany, NY: New York State Assembly), 33–34.

28. Williams papers, box 1, folder 10, p. 24.

29. Williams papers, box 1, folder 10.

Chapter 2

1. Carter, *Territorial Papers*, vol. XI, 3.

2. Carter, *Territorial Papers*, vol. XI, 14–16.

3. Carter, *Territorial Papers*, vol. XI, 14–16.

4. Morse, *Report to the Secretary of War*, 23.

5. Richard K. Cadle, ed., *Reports and Public Letters of John C. Calhoun*, vol. 5 (New York: D. Appleton and Company, 1874), 102–3.

6. Letter from the Secretary of War to the Rev. Jedediah Morse, February 7, 1820, in Cadle, *Reports and Public Letters*, vol. 5, 102–3.

7. Cadle, *Reports and Public Letters*, vol. 5, 106.

8. Cadle, *Reports and Public Letters*, vol, 5, 107.

9. Cadle, *Reports and Public Letters*, vol. 5, 107.

10. Fort Howard was established by the US government in 1816 in Green Bay.

11. Carter, *Territorial Papers*, vol. X, 834–35.

12. Carter, *Territorial Papers*, vol. X, 834–35.

13. Carter, *Territorial Papers*, vol. X, 852.

14. Carter, *Territorial Papers*, vol. X, 852.

15. Williams papers, box 1, folder 10, 16–17.

16. *Interview with the Chiefs and principal men of the Menomine Indians*, summer 1820, in Morse, *Report to the Secretary of War*, Appendix, 53–56.

17. Williams to "Right Rev. Father," May 16, 1820, Williams papers, box 1, folder 1; Ellis, *Advent*, 422.

18. Ellis, *Advent*, 422n.

19. C. C. Trowbridge Manuscripts, Detroit Public Library, Detroit, Michigan, Burton Historical Collection.

20. *Letters Received by the Secretary of War, Registered Series, 1801–1870* (Washington DC: National Archives, 1965), M221, reel 90, frames 6936–38 (hereafter cited as M221 with reel and frame).

21. M221, reel 90, frames 6937–38; Correspondence 1801–1830 folder, 3 pages, Williams papers. There is an original handwritten version of the letter in the Eleazer Williams papers with a chunk of the paper missing.

22. Carter, *Territorial Papers*, vol. XI, pt. 8, 69–70.

23. Carter, *Territorial Papers*, vol. XI, pt. 8, 69–70.

24. Carter, *Territorial Papers*, vol. XI, pt. 8, 69–70.

25. M221, reel 90.

26. Carter, *Territorial Papers*, vol. XI, pt. 8, 69–70.

27. Edwin W. Hemphill, ed., *The Papers of John C. Calhoun*, vol. VI, 1821–1822 (Columbia, SC: University of South Carolina Press, 1972), 13.

28. Trowbridge to Lyman C. Draper, September 21, 1821, Williams papers.

Chapter 3

1. M221:90, frames 6943–48.

2. *Papers of John C. Calhoun*, vol. VI, 30; M221:90, frames 6943–48.

3. *Papers of John C. Calhoun*, vol. VI, 30; M221:90, frames 6943–48.

4. M221:90, frames 6943–48.

5. *Papers of John C. Calhoun*, vol. VI, 49. The November 6, 1820, letter referred to is in the National Archives.

6. *Letters Sent by Secretary of War Relating to Indian Affairs 1800–1824*, 6 rolls, M15-5, National Archives, Washington, DC (hereafter cited as M15 with roll numbers); *Papers of John C. Calhoun*, vol. VI, 169.

7. *Letters Received by the Office of Secretary of War Relating to Indian Affairs*

1800–1823, (National Archives, Washington, DC, 1963), M271, roll 3, frames 941–944 (hereafter cited as M271 with roll and frame).

8. *Letters Received by the Secretary of War Registered Series 1801–1860* (National Archives, Washington, DC), M221, roll 8, frames 288–291 (hereafter cited as M221 with roll and frame); M15:5, 72.

9. M221:92.

10. Carter, *Territorial Papers*, vol. XI, 128; M221:92.

11. Trowbridge to Lyman C. Draper, September 21, 1821, Williams papers.

12. Carter, *Territorial Papers*, vol. XI, 128.

13. Ellis, *Advent*, 422–23.

14. Ellis, *Advent*, 424.

15. *Documents Relating to the Negotiation of Ratified and Unratified Treaties with various Tribes of Indians, 1801–1869*, Record Group 75, Records of the Bureau of Indian Affairs, National Archives, Washington, DC, Microcopy Number T494, Roll 8, Unratified Treaties 1821–1865 (hereafter cited as T494 with roll and frame).

16. Ellis, *Advent*, 425.

17. Ellis, *Advent*, 425–26.

18. T494, roll 8.

19. T494.

20. *Memorial of Stockbridge Nations of Indians of Wisconsin*, February 10, 1842, 27th Cong., 2d sess. (1842), Senate, Serial set 397, S. Doc. 189, National Archives, Washington, DC (hereafter cited as S. Doc. 189). The map was not attached to the document.

21. *Map of the Fox River and the part of the Winnebago Lake as contained within the limits of the cession of 1821 by the Menominee and Winnebago Indians to the New York Tribes* [1832?], Map, www.loc.gov/item/2009580303.

22. Ellis, *Advent*, 425.

23. *Papers of John C. Calhoun*, vol. VI, 452; letter with enclosures in T494, r oll 8, frames 1–11; M1:4, 322–23.

24. *Papers of John C. Calhoun*, vol. VI, 524.

25. M221:94; *Papers of John C. Calhoun*, vol. VI, 543.

26. *Papers of John C. Calhoun*, vol. VI, 578; M221:92; M221:4, 351.

27. There are two columns of signatures with seventeen X marks, but they are so faint that only the X marks are visible. *Papers of John C. Calhoun*, vol. VI, 326; letter with enclosures in M221:0–24; see also M221:93.

28. M221:93.

29. Ellis, *Advent*, 426.

30. Ellis, *Advent*, 336.

31. M221:93, frames 9181–83; *Papers of John C. Calhoun*, vol. VI, 438.

32. M221:93; letter with their marks in M221, 0–57; *John C. Calhoun Papers*, vol. VI, 632.

33. Ellis, *Advent*, 424–25.

34. Ellis, *Advent*, 423.

35. Ellis, *Advent*, 425.

36. James W. Oberly, *A Nation of Statesmen: The Political Culture of the Stockbridge-Munsee Mohicans, 1815–1972* (Repr., Norman: University of Oklahoma Press, 2008). Oberly translated from the French (or reprinted a translation) in note 44.

37. Oberly, *Nation of Statesmen*, 287.

38. Oberly, *Nation of Statesmen*, 35–36.

39. Oneida to Bishop Hobart, November 12, 1821, in *The Reformer* 4 (1823): 55–57.

40. M15:5; *John C Calhoun Papers*, vol. VII, 523–24. This letter is dated November 22, 1821. President Monroe's signature on the treaty is dated February 19, 1822.

Chapter 4

1. Letter (with his mark) in M221:92; Solomon Hendrick to Calhoun, February 5, 1822, in *Papers of John C. Calhoun*, vol. VII, 633. See also letter in M221:92; this may be the same as the January 25, 1822, letter.

2. Calhoun refers to a letter of February 5, 1822, which may be the same letter of January 25, 1822.

3. M15:5, 215–16; *Papers of John C. Calhoun*, vol. VI, 695–97.

4. M221:93, frames 9194–96.

5. *Papers of John C. Calhoun*, vol. VII, 162–63.

6. Oneida to President Monroe, January 22, 1822, in M221:93, frames 9187–89.

7. Letter in M221:93, frames 9189–90; *Papers of John C. Calhoun*, vol. VI, 723.

8. Letter in M221:96.

9. M221:96; *Papers of John C. Calhoun*, vol. VII, 311–12.

10. Letter in M221:96, frames 921–23; *Papers of John C. Calhoun*, vol. VII, 201–2.

11. *Papers of John C. Calhoun*, vol. VII, 311–12; letter in M221:96.

12. Tuscarora Nation to Stockbridge Nation, August 12, 1822, Williams papers, box 1, folder 5.

13. Benjamin Franklin, *Indian Treaties Printed by Benjamin Franklin, 1736–1762* (Philadelphia: Philadelphia Historical Society of Pennsylvania, 1938).

14. A. G. Ellis, *A journal 1822 fragment of A. G. Ellis in which he described his travels to Green Bay and Negotiations of a treaty with the Menominee and Winnebago Indians in 1822*, Williams papers, box 5, folder 2.

15. Ellis, *Advent*, 427.

16. Ellis, *Journal fragment*.

17. Ellis, *Journal fragment*.

18. "True Extract from the 1st Copy., Per J.W. ——, Extract of a communication from S.U. Hendricks to Calhoun, made at Washington City the 20th of Feb., 1823," Miscellaneous Files, Indian Office MS Records, quoted in *Annual Report of the American Historical Association for the Year 1906*, vol. 1 (Washington, DC: Government Printing Office, 1908), 320; *Papers of John C. Calhoun*, vol. VII, 485; M271:4.

19. *Annual Report of the American Historical Association for the Year 1906*, 319n–320n; John Sergeant report to Territorial Governor Lewis Cass, February 28, 1831, in *In the Senate of the United States, Feb. 28 1831, A Treaty with the Menominee Tribe of Indians, The Documents accompanying it, and a remonstrance of John W. Quinney and others, delegates from certain tribes of New York Indians, against the provisions of this treaty*, 21st Cong., 2d sess. (1831), Appendix 14, p. 41.

20. No. 13, September 22, 1822, in *In the Senate of the United States*, 31–35. On page 35, this document continues with No. 14, which is the journal dated October 16, 1822, of the events occurring during the 1822 treaty event, submitted by John Sergeant Jr. The treaty is also located in Ellis, *Advent*, and is referred to as an attachment in the McKenney journal.

21. S. Doc. 189, p. 3.

22. Williams to D. A. Ogden, May 15, 1823, in *Papers of John C. Calhoun*, vol. VIII, 229.

23. M221:96; *Papers of John C. Calhoun*, vol. VII, 386.

24. "Journal of a Treaty made & concluded at Butte Des Morts, on Fox River, in the Territory of Michigan, between Lewis Cass and Thomas McKenney, Commissioners of the United States of America and the Menominee, Winnebago, Ottawa & Munsee Tribes of Indians. Treaty of August 11, 1827,"

in *Ratified treaty no. 148, Documents relating to the negotiation of the treaty of August 11, 1827, with the Chippewa, Menominee and Winnebago Indians* (Washington, DC: National Archives, August 11, 1827), 20. Hereafter cited as *McKenney Journal*.

25. *McKenney Journal*, 2.

26. *McKenney Journal*, 11–12.

27. *McKenney Journal*, 20.

28. *Papers of John C. Calhoun*, vol. VIII, 239.

29. *Papers of John C. Calhoun*, vol. VIII, 324–25.

30. *Letters received by office of Secretary of War relating to Indian Affairs 1800–1823* (National Archives, Washington, DC), 4 rolls, M271, roll 4, frames 769–71; also in S. Doc. 189.

31. *Papers of John C. Calhoun*, vol. VIII, 338–39.

32. The second version of this agreement or treaty was found in the footnotes on pages 29–31 of *A Petition and Appeal of the Six Nations, Oneida, Stockbridge &e to the Government of the United States in 1829*, January 8, 1825. See also John C. Adams papers, 1792–1932, Wisconsin Historical Society, manuscript HP1/15/file, 1825 Jan. 8 (hereafter cited as Adams papers).

33. *Documents relating to the negotiation of an unratified treaty of August 12, 1821, with the Menominee, Winnebago, and New York Indians*, in T494, reel 8, 1–22.

34. Stockbridge and Munsee Indians Treaty, January 8, 1825, Adams papers.

Chapter 5

1. M221:96. This document is dated August 2, 1822, and the treaty of 1822 was made September 23, 1822, so these delegates may have been on their way to make the treaty. It makes it clear the Oneida already had two parties in 1822.

2. *Map of the Fox River and that part of the Winnebagoe Lake as contained within the limits of the cession ofby the Menominie and Winnebago Indians to the New York tribes.* [1832?] Map. www.loc.gov/item/2009580303.

3. A. G. Ellis, *Fifty Four Years' Recollections of Men and Events in Wisconsin*, vol. VII, 225, Williams papers.

4. Ellis, *Advent*, 429.

5. Ellis, *Advent*, 418.

6. Ellis, *Advent*, 429.

7. Ellis, *Advent*, 430.

8. Ellis, *Advent*, 429.

9. Ellis, *Advent*, 428.

10. Ellis, *Advent*, 428.

11. Letter in M221:96, frames 0941–0943; *Papers of John C. Calhoun*, vol. VII, 178.

12. *Memorial to Congress from the inhabitants of Green Bay, To the Honorable the Senate of the United States*, in Carter, *Territorial Papers*, vol. XI, 337–39.

13. A portion of this first sentence is not legible on the microfilm.

14. M271:4, 755–61; S. Doc. 23-512, vol. 3, 1841–1842; H. Doc. 127.

15. Carter, *Territorial Papers*, vol XI, 657–58.

16. Carter, *Territorial Papers*, vol. XI, 673.

17. *Papers of John C. Calhoun*, vol. VIII, 229–230.

18. *Papers of John C. Calhoun*, vol. VIII, 229–230; emphasis in original.

19. *Papers of John C. Calhoun*, vol. VIII, 229–230.

20. The cited document refers to President James Madison, but the president at the time would have been James Monroe.

21. *Papers of John C. Calhoun*, vol. VIII, 227.

22. *Papers of John C. Calhoun*, vol. VIII, 228.

23. *Papers of John C. Calhoun*, vol. VIII, 227–229.

24. *Papers of John C. Calhoun*, vol. VIII, 239.

25. Stambaugh Report, 1831, Attachment C, in S. Doc. 23-512, vol. II, 536–37.

26. Grignon, in Stambaugh Report, 537.

27. Grignon, in Stambaugh Report, 537.

28. *In the Senate of the United States, February 9, 1832, 22nd Congress, 1st session (Green Bay Lands Ceded to New York Indians) Confidential*. "Transmits War Department report, Indian commissioner report, and related documents concerning Green Bay, Mich. Terr., lands ceded by the Menominee Indians for the benefit of various New York tribes," Appendixes 3 and 4, pgs. 30–36 (hereafter cited as Senate Report, 22nd Cong.).

29. Appendix 3 and 4 of Senate Report, 22nd Cong., 31–32.

30. Appendix 3 and 4 of Senate Report, 22nd Cong., 32.

31. Appendix 3 and 4 of Senate Report, 22nd Cong., 32.

32. Appendix 3 and 4 of Senate Report, 22nd Cong., 33.

33. Senate Report, 22nd Cong., 33.

34. S. Doc. 23-512, 538–39.

35. S. Doc. 23-512, 538–39.
36. Senate Report, 22nd Cong., 36–37.
37. Senate Report, 22nd Cong., 36–37.
38. *Letters received by Office of Indian Affairs, 1824–1881, 962 rolls, Green Bay Agency, 1824–1881*, M234, roll 315, Brown County Library, Green Bay, WI (hereafter cited as M234 with roll number).
39. M234:315.
40. M234:315.
41. M234:315.
42. M234:315.

Chapter 6

1. "1825, August Treaty Prairie Du Chien, between the United States and the Sioux, Chippewa, Sac and Fox, Menominee, Winnebago, a portion of the United Tribes of Ottawas, Chippewas, and Potawatomis, and Other Tribes," in Kappler, *Indian Affairs*, vol. 2, 250–255.
2. Kappler, "1825 Treaty," article 8.
3. Kappler, "1825 Treaty," articles 8 and 11.
4. Kappler, "1825 Treaty," article 8.
5. Carter, *Territorial Papers*, vol. XI, 1063–64.
6. Thomas L. McKenney, *Memoirs, Official and Personal* (New York, 1845; repr., Lincoln: University of Nebraska Press, 1973), 81.
7. Kappler, *Indian Affairs*, 2:281–283.
8. *McKenney Journal*; Senate Report, 22nd Cong., 34–35, in S. Doc. 23-512, 539–41.
9. *McKenney Journal*, 2.
10. *McKenney Journal*, 2.
11. *McKenney Journal*, 4.
12. *McKenney Journal*, 5. The warning of a possible war refers to the Winnebago. The Winnebago were mistakenly informed that two of their men were put to death at Fort Snelling for a murder they did not commit. A series of events, including the intrusion by lead miners, led Red Bird and several others to murder two Americans in retaliation for the murder of two of their members. During the 1827 treaty, the McKenney journal cites the surrender of Red Bird as one of the issues. Red Bird did surrender to prevent a major war, and was imprisoned, where he died. Two others were

later pardoned. See "The Surrender and Captivity of Ho-Chunk Warrior Red Bird" at www.wisconsinhistory.org/Records/Article/CS294.

13. *McKenney Journal*, 5.

14. The list of documents included (1) A letter from Mr. Crawford, Secretary of War, dated Feby 12, 1816. To the Six Nations, authorizing their migration to Green Bay. Marked exhibit A. (2) A letter from Mr. Calhoun, Secretary of War, dated Feby 13, 1822, authorizing them to extend their purchase. Marked B. (3) A Duplicate of the Report of John Sergeant, dated Oct. 16, 1822 of a negotiation with the Menomonie, accompanied by a Treaty. Marked C (4) A letter from Mr. Calhoun to the Six Nations, dated Oct. 27, 1823, exhibiting the views of the government with respect to both treaties. Marked D (5) A Treaty, dated Aug. 18, 1821, transmitted by the Commissioners. (6) The Treaty submitted by Sergeant, dated Sept. 23, 1822, transmitted by the Commissioners.

15. *McKenney Journal*, 6.

16. *McKenney Journal*, 7.

17. *McKenney Journal*, 7.

18. *McKenney Journal*, 8.

19. *McKenney Journal*, 8.

20. *McKenney Journal*, 6.

21. *McKenney Journal*, 8.

22. *McKenney Journal*, 12.

23. *McKenney Journal*, 12 (speeches are in Appendix F, 7–8).

24. *McKenney Journal*, 14.

25. *McKenney Journal*, 13.

26. *McKenney Journal*, 15–17.

27. *McKenney Journal*, 18.

28. *McKenney Journal*, 19.

29. *McKenney Journal*, 18–20.

30. *McKenney Journal*, 20–21.

31. *McKenney Journal*, 21.

32. *McKenney Journal*, 21–22.

33. *McKenney Journal*, 24.

34. *McKenney Journal*, 25.

35. *McKenney Journal*, 25.

36. *McKenney Journal*, 27.

37. *McKenney Journal*, 27.

38. *McKenney Journal*, 18–19.

39. *McKenney Journal*, 18–19.

40. Kappler, *Indian Treaties*, 2:281–83.

Chapter 7

1. *Petition to the Hon. the Senate of the U.S. from the Chiefs of the Six Nations, and other Indian tribes, asking Congress to confirm them in the possession of certain lands guaranteed to them by treaty*, n.p., 1829, https://catalog .hathitrust.org/Record/100137108.

2. *Petition to the Hon. Senate*, 7.

3. *Petition to the Hon. Senate*, 7.

4. *Petition to the Hon. Senate*, 7–8.

5. *Petition to the Hon. Senate*, 7.

6. *Petition to the Hon. Senate*, 12–13.

7. *Petition to the Hon. Senate*, 13.

8. *Petition to the Hon. Senate*, 19.

9. *Petition to the Hon. Senate*, 20; capitals in original.

10. *Petition to the Hon. Senate*, 25.

11. *Petition to the Hon. Senate*, 26–27.

12. *Petition to the Hon. Senate*, 29–30.

13. *Petition to the Hon. Senate*, 30–31; capitals in original.

14. *Petition to the Hon. Senate*, 29–32. Pages 29–31 contain the 1824 treaty between the Muhheconnuk or Stockbridge, St. Regis, First Christian Party of Oneida, Tuscarora, and Munsee with the Brothertown.

15. *To the Honorable the House of Representatives and Senate in Congress convened, Done in General Council held at Green Bay, Michigan Territory. Dec. 4, 1829 Submitted by John Metoxen and Austin Quinney*, M234, roll 315, frames 190–94, Brown County Library, Green Bay, WI; Oneida History Conference papers, vol. 3, document 6.

16. On the microfilm there is an additional page of signatures, with the first list being Stockbridge.

17. McKenney to Eaton, in Carter, *Territorial Papers*, vol. XII, 170; underline in original.

18. McKenney to Eaton, in Carter, *Territorial Papers*, vol. XII, 170.

Chapter 8

1. Carter, *Territorial Papers*, vol. XII, 170.
2. S. Doc. 23-512, 2:8–9.
3. Eaton to Lewis Cass and Thomas L. McKenney, June 9, 1830, S. Doc. 23-512.
4. John Eaton to Lewis Cass and Thomas L. McKenney, June 9, 1830, S. Doc. 23–512.
5. S. Doc. 23-512, 2:10–13; complete letter found in M234:15, frames 395–400; Oneida History Conference papers, vol. III, document 8.
6. S. Doc. 23-512, 2:141.
7. M234:315, 133.
8. S. Doc. 23-512.
9. Emphasis added.
10. S. Doc. 23-512, 2:142–44.
11. M234:315, 256–57.
12. M234:315, 421.
13. M234:315, 254.
14. M234:315, 251–52.
15. M234:315, 424–25.
16. M234:315, 425.
17. M234:315, 425–26.
18. M234:315, 426–27.
19. M234:315, 428–29.
20. It would appear this document was written in 1830, based on the content, and may have been a rough draft due to crossed-out lines and some repetitive paragraphs. The draft has been edited using the actual submission to the three commissioners appointed by the president to go to Green Bay to end the controversy over land between the Menominees and the New York Indians. This document appears to have been submitted on August 27, 1830, as the next entry is for August 28. (M234:315, frames 266–85; Quinney Communication). The final document is part of the *Journal of a Council Meeting, AUGUST 24, 1830–Sept 1, 1830*, M234:315, frames 421–69, which is forty-six pages, and the Quinney Communication, frames 431–46, in which Quinney confirmed that he wrote the document contained therein.
21. M234:315, 447–48.
22. M234:315, 448–50.

23. M234:315, 455–56.
24. M234:315, 457.
25. M234:315, 459–60.
26. M234:315, 461–62.
27. M234:315, 461–67.
28. M234:315, 261–64.
29. S. Doc. 23-512, 2:105.
30. S. Doc. 23-512, 2:107–10
31. S. Doc. 23-512, 2:131
32. M234:315, 160–75.
33. S. Doc. 23-512, 2:198–200; M234:315, 204–5.
34. S. Doc. 23-512, 2:206–9.

Chapter 9
1. S. Doc. 23–512, 2:390.
2. M234:315, 197–203; Oneida History Conference, pt. 3.
3. S. Doc. 23-512, 2:405.
4. Kappler, *Indian Affairs*, 2:319–22.
5. S. Doc. 23-512, 2:551–52.
6. Oneida History Conference, tab 3, item 14.
7. S. Doc. 23-512, 2:455; M234:315, 629–31.
8. S. Doc. 23-512, 2:523.
9. S. Doc. 23-512, 2:20.
10. Stambugh report, November 30, 1831, and December 27, 1833, in S. Doc. 23-512, 2:523–36 and Supporting Documents in S. Doc. 23-512, 2:536–54; Senate Report, 22nd Cong., 40–42; Oneida History Conference.
11. S. Doc. 23-512, 2:545.
12. S. Doc. 23-512, 2:545–46.
13. S. Doc. 23-512, 2:548.
14. Senate Report, 22nd Cong., 38–40; also in Stambaugh report as attachment A; M234:315, 523–24.
15. S. Doc. 23-512, 2:552–53; Senate Report, 22nd Cong., 38–40; M234:315, 523–24.
16. Senate Report, 22nd Cong., 38–40; Exhibit B in Stambaugh report, August 1831, S. Doc. 23-512, 2:554.
17. S. Doc. 23-512, 2:686.

18. S. Doc. 23-512, 2:655–76.
19. Porter Report to Cass, 3 February 1832, vol. 3, Serial set 246,; M234:315, 710–43.
20. M234:315, 711–12.
21. M234:315, 717; Senate Report, 22nd Cong., 1–3.
22. Porter Report to Cass, M234:315, 710–43.
23. Porter Report to Cass, M234:315, 714; Senate Report, 22nd Cong., 3.
24. M234:315, 714.
25. Porter Report to Cass, M234:315, 714; Senate Report, 22nd Cong., 4.
26. Senate Report, 22nd Cong., 4.
27. Porter Report to Cass, M234:315, 714; Senate Report, 22nd Cong., 4.
28. M234:15, 715.
29. Porter Report to Cass, M234:315, 715, 716; Senate Report, 22nd Cong., 4–5.
30. Porter Report to Cass, M234:315, 710–43; Senate Report, 22nd Cong., 6–7.
31. Senate Report, 22nd Cong., 5.
32. Porter Report to Cass, M234:315, 710–43; Senate Report, 22nd Cong., 6–7.
33. Porter Report to Cass, M234:315, 710–43; Senate Report, 22nd Cong., 7–8.

Chapter 10

1. Senate Report, 22nd Cong., 8–9; M234:315, 726.
2. M234:315, 727.
3. Senate Report, 22nd Cong., 10.
4. Senate Report, 22nd Cong., 10.
5. Senate Report, 22nd Cong., 10; M324:315, 727–28.
6. M234:315, 729–30.
7. Senate Report, 22nd Cong., 12.
8. M234:315, 741.
9. M234:315, 741.
10. United States Congress, Senate, "February 8, 1832," in *Journal of the Executive Proceedings of the Senate of the United States of America, 1829–1837* (Washington, DC: Government Printing Office), 209, The Center for Legislative Archives, RG 287, Library of Congress, Washington, DC.
11. Senate, "February 8, 1832," *Journal of the Executive Proceedings*, 210.
12. The Senate proviso was attached to the 1831 treaty.
13. S. Doc. 23-512, 4:23–52; S. Doc. 23-512, 2:20–21; Oneida History Conference, tab 13.

14. This and all quoted material to follow in this section appear in the Porter journal in S. Doc. 23-512.
15. Charles J. Kappler, *Indian Affairs: Laws and Treaties*, vol. 2, *Treaties* (Washington, DC: Government Printing Office, 1904), 377–81.
16. Kappler, *Indian Affairs*, 377–82.

Chapter 11

1. M234:316, 21–22.
2. M234:316, 169.
3. M234:316, 51–52.
4. M234:316, 422.
5. M234:316, 423.
6. M234:316, 445.
7. M234:316, 434.
8. M234:316, 427.
9. M234:316, 426.
10. M234:316, 427–29.
11. M234:316, 430–32.
12. Above signatures seem to be Stockbridge; M234:316, 433–34.
13. M234:316, frames 436–40. Some portions of this document were published in the booklet *Oneida: The People of the Stone: The Church's Mission to the Oneidas* (Oneida, Wisconsin: Oneida Indian Reservation: 1899).
14. M234:316, 440–43.
15. Lyman Draper, ed., "Some Wisconsin Indian Conveyances, 1793–1836," *Wisconsin Historical Collection* 15 (Madison: State Historical Society of Wisconsin, 1900), 20–24.
16. John H. Martin, comp., *List of Documents Concerning The Negotiations Of Ratified Indian Treaties, 1801–1869* (Washington, DC: National Archives, 1949); "Unratified Treaty of September 19, 1836" in *Documents Relating to the Negotiation of Ratified and Unratified Treaties with various Tribes of Indians, 1801-69*, RG 75, Records of the Bureau of Indian Affairs, Microcopy No. T494, Roll 8, Unratified Treaties 1821–65, National Archives and Records Service, General Services Administration, Washington, DC: 1960; "Articles of a Treaty, made and concluded at Green Bay, Wisconsin Territory, September 19, 1836 by John F. Schermerhorn, Commissioner on the part of the United States, and the Chiefs and head men of the Stockbridge

and Munsee Tribes of Indians," in Annual *Report of the American Historical Association for the Year 1906*, vol. 1 (Washington, DC: Government Printing Office, 1908), 409n.

17. Letter to President Van Buren, February 7, 1838, in Oneida History Conference papers; M234:317.

18. See To Col. Geo. Boyd, US Indian Agent, September 19, 1837, M234, roll 316, frames 528–29. In this letter, the Stockbridge living on the east shore of Winnebago Lake request provisions for 230 of "our friends" who are moving to the "Indian Country south of Missouri River to join theirs friends the Delaware tribe at that place."

19. Kappler, *Indian Treaties*, 2:517–18.

20. Francis Jennings, quoted in *Classroom Activities on Wisconsin Indian Treaties and Tribal Sovereignty* (Madison: Wisconsin Department of Public Instruction, 1996), 408.

21. Findings Filed by the Court of Claims in the Case of the New York Indians vs the United States, S. Misc. Doc. No. 46, 52nd Cong., 1st Sess. (1892), Article III.

22. S. Doc. No. 46, 52nd Cong., 1st Sess. (1892).

23. *Oneida: The People of the Stone*, 28–29.

Chapter 12

1. Kappler, *Indian Affairs*, 2:517–18.

2. Cartographic maps and plans, National Archives Microfilm Series, M-236, roll 122, frame 003.

3. Oneida Committee Treaty Workshop, May 12, 1999, Oneida History Conference papers.

4. John Porter Bloom, ed., *Territorial Papers of the United States*, vol. 27, *Wisconsin Territory 1836–1839* (Washington, DC: National Archives, 1969), 1078–87; Missouri Party in *Chief Daniel Bread and the Oneida Nation of Indians of Wisconsin*, Laurence Hauptman and Gordon McLester, eds. (Norman, OK: University of Oklahoma Press, 2002), 107–109, 113–115, 178n.32. See also John Anthony entry in *Chief Daniel Bread*.

5. *"The letter may have been delivered by hand, for on this day in Washington John Anthony and Hanjost Smith addressed a letter to Secretary of War, Poinsett, saying in part: "We have come here to fix the treaty (of December 1838) right if it is not right . . ."* Bloom, *Territorial Papers*, 27:1212–13.

6. Bloom, Territorial Papers, 27:1213.
7. Letter found in Oneida History Conference papers, tab 3.
8. Missouri Party to Mr. James Cain, Esq., June 24, 1839, Williams papers, box 1, folder 5.
9. *Oneida: The People of the Stone*, 29.
10. M234:319.
11. M234:319.
12. M234:319.
13. "Brothertown Indians," *Wisconsin Enquirer*, June 15, 1839, 3, quoted in Alanna Rice, "'To Procure a Residence among Their Brethren in the West': The Relocation of the Brotherton Tribe in Territorial Wisconsin," *Wisconsin Magazine of History*, 92:2, 39.
14. Act for the Relief of the Brothertown Indians in the Territory of Wisconsin, 25th Cong., 3d Sess., Ch. 83 (1839).
15. Rice, *Wisconsin Magazine of History*.
16. "Eeyamquittoowauconnuck 'Brothertown' Day," Brothertown Indian Nation website, https://brothertownindians.org.
17. For more information, see Thomas Commuck, *Sketch of Calumet County*, Collections of State Historical Society of Wisconsin, vol. 1, 1903, pp. 103–5; and David J. Silverman, *Red Brethren, the Brothertown and Stockbridge Indians and the Problem of Race in Early America* (New York: Cornell University Press, 2010).
18. "Origin and Early History," Stockbridge-Munsee Community Band of Mohican Indians website, www.mohican.com/services/cultural-services/our-history/origin-and-early-history/.
19. *Ratified Indian Treaty 254: Stockbridge – Stockbridge, Wisconsin, November 24, 1848*. Record Group 11, General Records of the US Government, 1778–2006, Indian Treaties Series, National Archives, Washington, DC, https://catalog.archives.gov/id/176204523.
20. Kappler, *Indian Affairs*, 574–82.
21. The 1934 Indian Reorganization Act (IRA) included provisions to stop the loss of land caused by the 1887 Allotment Act. It proposed to reacquire lands for Native nations and to reorganize their governmental structure. There are both positive and negative views on the IRA. It stopped the loss of land and provided funds to purchase a small amount of land previously lost in treaties. It also required a US-standard type of government by re-

quiring constitutions instead of traditional governments. These constitutions began recognizing tribal membership by blood quantum, which was a foreign concept to Native peoples and continues to be controversial to the present day.

22. James W. Oberly, *A Nation of Statesmen: The Political Culture of the Stockbridge-Munsee Mohicans, 1815–1972* (Repr., Norman: University of Oklahoma Press, 2008), 181.

23. Interview with Leah Miller, June 2020.

24. See also Oberly, *Nation of Statesmen.*

25. Menominee Indian Tribe of Wisconsin, *Facts and Figures Reference Book* (Keshena, WI: Menominee Indian Tribe of Wisconsin, 2004), Appendix B.

26. Menominee, *Facts and Figures*; "Menominee Treaties and Treaty Rights," Milwaukee Public Museum website, www.mpm.edu/content/wirp/ICW-108.

27. Menominee, *Facts and Figures*, 46.

28. "Menominee Treaties and Treaty Rights," www.mpm.edu/content/wirp/ICW-108.

29. Kappler, *Indian Affairs*, vol. 2, 572–74.

30. Kappler, *Indian Affairs*, vol. 2, 572–74.

31. Kappler, *Indian Affairs*, vol. 2, 572–74.

32. Kappler, *Indian Affairs*, vol. 2, 626–27.

33. Kappler, *Indian Affairs*, vol. 2, 755–56.

34. Kappler, *Indian Affairs*, vol. 2, 755–56.

35. *Tribal Histories, Ho Chunk History,* Wisconsin Public Television, video, 26.45, Wisconsin First Nations, https://wisconsinfirstnations.org/tribal-histories-ho-chunk-history.

36. "Treaty Between the United States and the Winnebago Indians Signed at Fort Armstrong, Rock Island, Illinois." Treaties and Cessions (related to) HoChunk Nation of Wisconsin. Treaty 169. Indigenous Digital Archive's Treaty Explorer, https://digitreaties.org/presenttribe/HoChunk; Kappler, *Indian Affairs*, 2:690–93.

37. S. Doc. 23-512, 203.

38. S. Doc. 23-512, 203.

39. S. Doc. 23-512, 204.

40. "Ratified Indian Treaty 228: Winnebago–Washington, DC, November 1, 1837." Treaties and Cessions (related to) HoChunk Nation of Wisconsin.

Indigenous Digital Archive's Treaty Explorer, https://digitreaties.org/presenttribe/HoChunk.

41. John T. de La Ronde, "A Personal Narrative," Wisconsin Historical Collections, vol. 7 (1876; reprint, Madison: State Historical Society of Wisconsin, 1908), 362–5.

42. de La Ronde, "A Personal Narrative."

43. de La Ronde, "A Personal Narrative."

44. "Treaty between United States and the Winnebago, October 13, 1846." Treaty 249. Treaties and Cessions (related to) HoChunk Nation of Wisconsin. Indigenous Digital Archive's Treaty Explorer, https://digitreaties.org/presenttribe/HoChunk.

45. Kappler, *Indian Affairs*, 2:690–93.

46. Kappler, *Indian Affairs*, 2:690–93.

47. Patty Loew, *Indian Nations of Wisconsin* (Madison: State Historical Society of Wisconsin, 2001), 47.

48. Loew, *Indian Nations*, 50.

49. Loew, *Indian Nations*, 51.

50. Wisconsin Department of Public Instruction, "Ho-Chunk Nation," https://dpi.wi.gov/amind/tribalnationswi/ho-chunk.

51. Great Lakes Intertribal Council, "Ho-Chunk Nation," www.glitc.org/tribes-served/ho-chunk-nation.

52. *The History of the Stockbridge-Munsee Band of Mohican Indians* (Stockbridge-Munsee Historical Committee, 1993), 21.

53. See Loretta Metoxen, "Subdivide and Conquer: The Dawes Allotment Act," Oneida Cultural Heritage Department, https://oneida-nsn.gov/wp-content/uploads/2016/04/SUBDIVIDE-AND-CONQUER-THE-DAWES-ALOTTMENT-ACT-9.13.pdf; and Kirke Kickingbird, *One Hundred Million Acres* (New York: Macmillan, 1973).

BIBLIOGRAPHY AND SOURCE NOTES

Archival Collections

Adams, John C. Papers. 1792–1932. Wisconsin Historical Society, Madison, WI.

Calendered Treaty of Green Bay, August 18, 1821, between the New York Indians and the Menominees and Winnebagos. WHi Image ID 27037 (front of treaty) and WHi Image ID 100345 (back of treaty). Wisconsin Historical Society, Madison, WI.

Documents Relating to the Negotiation of Ratified and Unratified Treaties with various Tribes of Indians, 1801–1869. National Archives and Records Administration, Washington, DC. Record Group 75. Records of the Bureau of Indian Affairs. Microfilm. Microcopy No. T494. Roll 8, Unratified Treaties 1821–69.

> Includes the handwritten August 18, 1821, treaty; the letter from Lewis Cass to Secretary of War Calhoun submitting the 1821 Treaty October 22, 1821; the Charles C. Trowbridge report of September 1821; papers relating to an arrangement with the Stockbridge and other tribes of Indians . . . the Brothertown tribe . . . for a portion of the lands of the former at Green Bay for the latter June 16, 1824. Acknowledges that the Six Nations of Indians, Stockbridge tribe or nation, St. Regis tribe or nation, and Munsee tribe or nations . . . on August 18, 1821, held a treaty with and purchase of the Menomonee tribe or nation of Indians and the Winnebago tribe or nation of Indians in the Territory of Michigan and acknowledges both the 1821 and 1822 treaties.

Letters received by the Office of Indian Affairs, 1824–81. Green Bay Agency. Brown County Library, Green Bay, WI. Microfilm. Microcopy No. M234. 962 rolls.

roll 315	1824–32
roll 316	1833–37
roll 317	1838–39
roll 948	1836–40
roll 949	1841–48

Letters Received by the Secretary of War. Registered series, 1801–1870. National Archives and Records Administration, Washington, DC. Microfilm. Microcopy No. M221. Rolls 90, 91, 92, 93, 96.

Letters Received by the Office of Secretary of War Relating to Indian Affairs, 1800–1823. National Archives and Records Administration, Washington, DC. Microfilm. Microcopy No. 271. 4 rolls.

Letters Sent by Secretary of War Relating to Indian Affairs, 1800–1824. National Archives and Records Administration, Washington, DC. Microfilm. Microcopy No. M15. 6 rolls.

Map of the Fox River and that part of the Winnebagoe Lake as contained within the limits of the cession of 1821 by the Menominie and Winnebago Indians to the New York Tribes. Map. Library of Congress Geography and Maps Division, Washington, DC. http://hdl.loc.gov/loc.gmd/g4122f.ct002451.

Oneida History Conference papers. Oneida Library, Oneida, WI.

    Includes Oneida History Committee Treaty Workshop, May 22, 1999.

Records of Wisconsin Superintendency of Indian Affairs and Green Bay Subagency, 1836–1848. Brown County Library, Green Bay, WI. Microfilm. Microcopy No. M295. 4 rolls.

Resources Related to the Treaty Era. S. Verna Fowler Academic Library and Menominee Public Library, College of Menominee Nation, Keshena, WI. Special Collections.

Royce, Charles C., comp. *Indian Land Cessions in the United States.* 1899. Map. Library of Congress Geography and Map Division. Washington, DC. www .loc/gov/item/13023487.

Trowbridge, C. C. Manuscripts. Burton Historical Collection. Detroit Public Library. Detroit, MI; Wisconsin Historical Society. Madison, WI. Area Research Center at University of Wisconsin–Green Bay.

Williams, Eleazer Papers. 1634–1964. Box 4, folder 8. Wisconsin Historical Society, Madison, WI. Area Research Center at University of Wisconsin–Green Bay.

Published Works

A brief exposition of the claims of the New-York Indians to certain lands at Green Bay in the Michigan Territory. January 20, 1831 [n.p.]. Wisconsin Historical Society Library Pamphlet Collection, 56-1672.

Annual Report of the American Historical Association for the Year 1906. Vol. 1.
Washington, DC: Government Printing Office, 1908.

Barreiro, José. *Indian Roots of American Democracy.* Ithaca, NY: Akwe:kon
Press, 1992.

Beck, David R. M. *Siege and Survival: History of the Menominee Indians, 1634–
1856.* Lincoln: University of Nebraska Press, 2002.

Bloom, John Porter, ed. *Territorial Papers of the United States.* Vol. 27, *Wisconsin Territory 1836–1839.* Washington, DC: National Archives, 1969.

Campisi, Jack. *The Brothertown Indian Nation of Wisconsin: A Brief History.*
Pamphlet, privately published. Brothertown Indian Nation.

Cadle, Richard K., ed. *Reports and Public Letters of John C. Calhoun.* New York:
D. Appleton and Company, 1874.

Calhoun, John C. *The Papers of John C. Calhoun.* 27 vols. University of South
Carolina. Vol. 8, *1821–1822.* Edited by W. Edwin Hemphill. Columbia:
University of South Carolina Press, 1972.

Carter, Clarence Edwin, comp. and ed. *The Territorial Papers of the United
States.* Vol. XI, *The Territory of Michigan, 1820–1829.* Washington, DC:
Government Printing Office, 1943.

Classroom Activities on Wisconsin Indian Treaties and Tribal Sovereignty. Madison: Wisconsin Department of Public Instruction, 1996.
  Includes the 1821 treaty, President Monroe approval, and receipts.

Cleland, Charles E. *Faith in Paper: The Ethnohistory and Litigation of the Upper
Great Lakes Indian Treaties.* Ann Arbor: University of Michigan Press, 2011.

*Correspondence on the subject of the emigration of Indians between the 30th November, 1831, and 27th December 1833, WITH ABSTRACTS OF EXPENDITURES BY DISBURSING AGENTS, in the Removal and subsistence of Indians
&c &c furnished in answer to a resolution of the Senate, of 27th December,
1833 by the Commissary General of subsistence.* Vol. I–V. 23rd Cong., 1st sess.
(1834). US Serial set 246, S. Doc. 23-512. US War Department, Washington, DC: Printed by Duff Green, 1835.
  Includes Stambaugh report, Vol. II pages 522–54; A. G. Ellis report, Vol. II pages 543–51; Porter Report to Cass, Feb. 3, 1832, Vol.
III pages 173–88; Daniel Bread statement, Vol. III pages 183–84;
Porter Journal notes on the meeting of October 22–23, 1832, Vol.
IV pages 27–52 ; and account of August 29, 1833, meeting of US
and Ho-Chunk at Rock River, Vol. IV pages 203–05.

Davidson, John Nelson. "The coming of the New York Indians to Wisconsin," in *Proceedings of the State Historical Society of Wisconsin* (1899). Also in Pamphlet Collection: 80-2919, Wisconsin Historical Society, Madison, WI.

Davids, Dorothy W. *A Brief History of the Mohican Nation, Stockbridge-Munsee Band*. Bowler, WI: Stockbridge-Munsee Historical Committee, 2001.

de la Ronde, John. "A Personal Narrative," in *Wisconsin Historical Collections*, Vol. 7. Madison: State Historical Society of Wisconsin, 1876.

Deloria, Vine, Jr., and Raymond J. DeMallie. *Documents of American Indian Diplomacy, Treaties, Agreements, and Conventions, 1775–1979*. Vol. 1. Norman: University of Oklahoma Press, 1999.

    The 1821 treaty is on page 686.

Diedrich, Mark. *Winnebago Oratory: Great Moments in the Recorded Speech of the Hochungra, 1742–1887*. Rochester, MN: Coyote Books, 1991.

Draper, Lyman, ed. "Some Wisconsin Indian Conveyances, 1793–1836," in *Wisconsin Historical Collections*, Vol. 15. Madison: State Historical Society of Wisconsin, 1900.

Ellis, A. G. "Advent of the New York Indians into Wisconsin," in *Wisconsin Historical Collections*, Vol. 2. Madison: State Historical Society of Wisconsin, 1856.

Ellis, A. G. "Fifty-four Years Recollections of Men and Events in Wisconsin," *Wisconsin Historical Collections*, Vol. 7. Madison: State Historical Society of Wisconsin, 1876.

Franklin, Benjamin. *Indian Treaties Printed by Benjamin Franklin, 1736–1762*. Philadelphia: Philadelphia Historical Society of Pennsylvania, 1938.

Grignon, Augustin. "Seventy-two years' recollections of Wisconsin," in *Wisconsin Historical Collections*, Vol. 3. Madison: State Historical Society of Wisconsin, 1857.

The History of the Stockbridge-Munsee Band of Mohican Indians. Stockbridge-Munsee Historical Committee, 1993.

In Senate of the United States, February 28, 1831. A Treaty with the Menomonee Tribe of Indians, The Documents accompanying it, and a remonstrance of John W. Quinney and others, delegates from certain tribes of New York Indians, against the provisions of this treaty. 21st Congress, 2d sess. (1831). US Serial set 204.

    Includes the text of the 1831 treaty of the Menomonee with United States (pages 1–7); "Memorial of John W. Quinney and Others,

Delegates from certain tribes of New York Indians, relative to their lands at Green Bay, and remonstrating against the provisions of a treaty recently concluded with the Menominee Indians," February 15, 1831, addressed to the Senate by the New York Indians (pages 12–16); letter to the president of the United States signed by delegates from Stockbridge, Munsee, Brothertown, Oneida, and St. Regis, January 20, 1831 (pages 16–19); "A brief exposition of the claims of the New York Indians to certain lands at Green Bay, In the Michigan Territory," pages 19–28; August 18, 1821, treaty made between Menominee, Winnebago and Six Nations, St. Regis, Stockbridge, and Munsee (appendix 7, pages 31–33, receipt on page 33; Trowbridge report to Governor Cass describing the negotiations of the 1821 Treaty, September 7, 1831 (appendix 8, pages 34–36); text of 1822 treaty between Menominee and New York Indians, September 23, 1822, and President James Monroe approval (appendix 13, pages 38-41); John Sergeant report on 1822 treaty, submitted October 16, 1822 (appendix 14, page 41); treaty made at Butte des Morts between United States and Chippeway, Menomonee, and Winnebago, August 11, 1827 (appendix 16, pages 42–44). Text of this document can also be found at https://treaties .okstate.edu/treaties/treaty-with-the-menominee-1831-0319.

Journal of the Assembly of the State of New York. 42nd Sess. Albany, NY: New York State Assembly, 1819.

Journal of a Treaty made & concluded at Butte Des Morts, on Fox River, in the Territory of Michigan, between Lewis Cass and Thomas McKenney, Commissioners of the United States of America and the Menominee, Winnebago, Ottawa & Munsee Tribes of Indians. Treaty of August 11, 1827. In Ratified treaty no. 148, Documents relating to the negotiation of the treaty of August 11, 1827, with the Chippewa, Menominee and Winnebago Indians. Washington, DC: National Archives.

Kappler, Charles J. *Indian Affairs: Laws and Treaties.* Vol. 2, *Treaties.* Washington, DC: Government Printing Office, 1904.

Keesing, Felix. *The Menomini Indians of Wisconsin: A Study of Three Centuries of Cultural Contact and Change.* Madison: University of Wisconsin Press, 1987 (1939).

Lauter, Paul, ed. *Heath Anthology of American Literature.* 5th ed. 5 vols. Boston: Houghton-Mifflin, 2005.

Loew, Patty. *Indian Nations of Wisconsin: Histories of Endurance and Renewal.* Madison: Wisconsin Historical Society Press, 2001.

Lurie, Nancy Oestreich. *Mountain Wolf Woman, Sister of Crashing Thunder: The Autobiography of a Winnebago Indian.* Ann Arbor: University of Michigan Press, 1961.

Lurie, Nancy Oestreich. *Wisconsin Indians.* Revised and expanded edition. Madison: Wisconsin Historical Society Press, 2002.

Martin, John H., comp. *List of Documents Concerning The Negotiations Of Ratified Indian Treaties, 1801–1869.* Washington, DC: National Archives, 1949.

"McCall's Journal of a Visit to Wisconsin, 1830," in *Wisconsin Historical Collections,* Vol. 7. Madison: State Historical Society of Wisconsin, 1892.
> Journal covers June 30, 1830, to September 3, 1830.

McKenney, Thomas L. *Memoirs, Official and Personal.* New York, 1845. Repr., Lincoln: University of Nebraska Press, 1973.
> Abbreviated *McKenney Journal.* Contains the text of the 1822 treaty and states that there is a duplicate of the John Sergeant report, October 16, 1822, of the negotiation with the Menominies *(sic),* accompanied by a treaty (but these attachments are not contained in the journal). A footnote contains the text of the 1822 treaty.

Memorial of Stockbridge nation of Indians in Wiskonsin, for remuneration for the expenses of their removal from New York; and that the title to their lands be guarantied to them by the United States. December 3, 1839. 26th Cong., 1st sess. (1840). US Serial set 365, H. Doc. 127.

Memorial of Stockbridge Nations of Indians of Wisconsin. 10 February 1842. 27th Cong., 2d sess. (1842.) Senate US Serial set 397, S. Doc. 189.
> Includes *Indian Nation to Indian Nation Treaty between Muhheconnuk or Stockbridge, St. Regis tribe, first Christian party of the Oneida tribe or nation, and the Tuscarora tribe or nation, and Munsee tribe or nation with the Brothertown* and receipts for payments related to the 1821 and 1822 treaties.

Menominee Indian Tribe of Wisconsin. *Facts and Figures Reference Book.* Appendix B, Felix Keesing, 1987 List of Treaties. Keshena, WI: Menominee Indian Tribe of Wisconsin, 2004.

Menominee Clans Story. University of Wisconsin–Stevens Point website, https://www4.uwsp.edu/museum/menomineeClans.

Menominee Treaties and Treaty Rights. Milwaukee Public Museum website, www.mpm.edu/content/wirp/ICW-108.

Morse, Jedidah. *A Report to the Secretary of War of the United States on Indian Affairs, Comprising a narrative of a tour performed in the summer of 1820, under a commission from the President of the United States, for the purpose of ascertaining, for the use of the government, the actual state of the Indian Tribes in our county: by Jedediah Morse, 1822. Late Minister of the First Congregation Church in Charlestown, near Boston, now resident in New Haven.* New York: Augustus M. Kelly, 1970.

Oberly, James W. *A Nation of Statesmen: The Political Culture of the Stockbridge-Munsee Mohicans, 1815–1972.* Repr., Norman: University of Oklahoma Press, 2008.

 Appendix B includes the 1822 treaty but omits the first paragraph stating who was present and omits the signatures.

Oneida: The People of the Stone: The Church's Mission to the Oneidas. Oneida, WI: Oneida Indian Reservation, 1899. Repr., Forgotten Books, 1902.

Original Menominee Homeland. Menominee, WI: Historic Preservation Office, 1994.

Parker, Arthur C. *Parker on the Iroquois.* Syracuse, NY: Syracuse University Press, 1968.

Payment of interest to Orchard party and First Christian party of New York Indians. 1864 (n.p.). Proquest US Serial set digital collection; 1178 S. rp.66.

Petition to US Senate. *Petition of Six Nations of New York Indians relating to Kansas lands.* S. Misc. Doc. No. 38, 47th Cong., 2nd Sess. (1883.)

Petition to US Senate. *Petition to the Hon. Senate of the US from the Chiefs of the Six Nations, and other Indian tribes, asking Congress to confirm them in the possession of certain lands guaranteed to them by treaty.* 1829 (n.p.). Hathitrust.org.

Petition to US Senate. *The New York Indians having, by renewed application to the Executive, ineffectually sough: to obtain through its interposition such modifications of the treaty lately concluded with the Menomonie tribe.* 1831 (n.p.). Wisconsin Historical Society Library Pamphlet Collection 52-1532.

Public Law 90–93. *Disposition of Funds Appropriated to pay a judgement in favor of the Emigrant New York Indians in Indian Claims Commission Docket Numbered 75.* House and Senate Unpublished Hearings (Proquest Congressional US serial set digital collection, 12753-4 H.rp. 636) 1967.

Rice, Alanna. " 'To procure a Residence Amongst Their Brethren to the West':

The Relocation of the Brotherton Tribe in Territorial Wisconsin." *Wisconsin Magazine of History* 92, no. 2 (Winter, 2008/2009): 28–41.

Silverman, David J. *Red Brethren, the Brothertown and Stockbridge Indians and the Problem of Race in Early America*. New York: Cornell University Press, 2010.

Speck, Frank G. *Celestial Bear Comes Down to Earth: The Bears Sacrifice Ceremony of the Munsee-Mahican in Canada as Related by Nekatacit*. Reading, PA: Reading Public Museum and Art Gallery, 1945.

Tanner, Helen Hornbeck. *Atlas of Great Lakes Indian History*. Norman: University of Oklahoma Press, 1987.

Treaties and Cessions (related to) HoChunk Nation of Wisconsin. Indigenous Digital Archive's Treaty Explorer, https://digitreaties.org/presenttribe/HoChunk.

Tribal Histories: Ho-Chunk History. Wisconsin Public Television. Video, 26:45. Wisconsin First Nations. https://wisconsinfirstnations.org/tribal-histories-ho-chunk-history.

Von Gernet, Alexander. *The Historical Context of the Oneida Treaties with the State of New York*. Department of Anthropology, University of Toronto at Mississauga, Ontario, Canada. Report prepared for the State of New York Office of the Attorney General. February 2004.

Whipple, J. S. *Report of Special Committee to Investigate the Indian Problem. of the State of New York: February 1, 1889*. Vol. 1. Albany, NY: Troy Press, 1889.

Acknowledgments

"Land, land, it's always about the land" was a statement often repeated by Loretta Metoxen, Oneida historian and elder who recently went to the Creator's world. This quote guided me in my research for this book and proved to be a most accurate description of what happened.

I am merely the gatherer of the documents in this book. Many, many people encouraged me to continue this research to gather the words of our ancestors.

A huge thank-you to my family for their patience as I spent so many hours, days, and weeks over ten years researching, writing, and editing.

To Wanda Antone and Kim Cakowski at the Oneida Library for being so patient with me and for searching and obtaining obscure books on interlibrary loan.

To the Brown County Library's Mary Jane Herber, for patiently listening, encouraging, and helping me identify documents, and Dennis Jacobs, for his assistance in finding maps.

To Troy Parr, Oneida Nation, for assisting with the removal map.

To Leah Miller, Stockbridge Historical Committee, for information on the Mohican Nation.

To J P Leary, Lisa Poupart, and Forrest Brooks, University of Wisconsin–Green Bay First Nations Studies, for encouraging me in my writing and listening patiently when I was frustrated with the publishing process.

To the University of Wisconsin Archives and Area Research Center staff for their assistance with the Eleazor Williams papers.

To Thomas Krause for patiently editing and Kate Thompson and the staff of the Wisconsin Historical Society Press for helping me move this project along to completion.

Index

Names of Native people were frequently spelled multiple ways in source documents. The most common spellings are used here.
Page numbers in *italics* refer to illustrations.

ernment/missionaries/land
companies, xvii, 4–5, 7, 14; first
arrival of New York Indians in
Detroit, 23–28; Ho-Chunk resistance, 385–387; missionaries'
support for, 4–5, 7, 14; Oneida
opposition to, 11–13; removal
efforts (1832-1836), 309–314; requests for from tribes, 1–3
reservation boundaries: Brothertown
(Brotherton) Nation, 367–369;
establishment of, 342–343;
Ho-Chunk Nation, 383–389;
and Menominee land, 377–382;
Missouri Party, 348–366;
Oneida Nation, 345–347, 390;
Stockbridge-Munsee Nations,
369–377; treaties with Oneida
Nation, 343–347; US government
allotment plans, 389–390
Revolutionary War, American, and
Indian cooperation, xx, xxii, xxiii
Rogers, B. W., 88–89, 111–112
Root, Erastus, 168, 177–179, 198,
199–200, 212, 219
Rouse, Lewis, 114–115, 136, 142

Sac and Fox Nation, 121–127
Sagowitha (Jonathan Printup), 80
Sampson (Owwohthommaug), 80
Sampson/Samson, George, 94, 96
Scanando/Scando/Skenandoah, Eli-
jah, 322, 324, 358
Schermerhorn, John F., 309, 325–
329, 333–335; Missouri Party,
348, 361
Schermerhorn treaties, 325–335
Schoolcraft, Mr., 142
schools, US government, for Indians,
17, 310, 311–312
Schuyler, Alfonse, 50

Schuyler, William, 365
Scipio, George, 96
Second Christian Party (Orchard
Party), 312, 315, 317–319, 342;
Buffalo Creek Treaty (1838),
339; council with Dodge (1845),
357–366; Treaty (1838), 343–
347; treaty council at Green Bay
(1836), 317–319, 328, 333
Secretary of War. See Calhoun, John
C.; Crawford, William H.; Eaton,
John H.; Poinsett, Joel R.; War
Department
Senate, US: Committee on Indian
Affairs, xv; and Indian nation–
to–Indian nation treaties, 250;
petitions to, 147; provisos to trea-
ties, 276–277, 286, 290, 308;
treaty ratification, 28, 34, 145,
154, 223, 236, 248, 276–277,
302
Senate Committee on Indian Affairs,
xv, 163
Seneca Nation, 11, viii, 29, 38–42,
89, 224–229, 338
Sergeant, John, Jr., 60, 65, 73, 78–
79, 103, 154–155, 250
Sganawaty (Thomas Christian), 43
Sha-kaut-che-o-ke-maw (Menominee
chief), 20–22
Shawenogeshig, 282–283
Shounk-Whunk-siap (Black Wolf),
198, 386
Silver Chain Treaty (1613),
xxvii–xxviii
Sioux Nation, 121–127, 377
Six Nations, viii, xvii, 1-3; Buffalo
Creek Treaty (1838), 335–339,
342–343; as "civilized" Indians,
187–188, 190; delegations to
District of Columbia, 261–270,

327; delegation to District of Columbia (1832), 271–275; Indian nation–to–Indian nation treaties, 60; memorial to Monroe, 104–109; Treaties of 1824 and 1825, 90–99; Treaty of 1822, 79–84; Treaty of Green Bay (1821), 29, 38–42

Styker, James, 247

sugar camps, 288–289, 291, 297, 299–300

Summer, Peter, 55

Superintendent of Indian Affairs. *See* Huebschmann, Francis; McKenney, Thomas L.

surveying. *See* boundaries

Suydam, John, 345; Suydam 1838 map, 345–346

Swamp, Adam, 324, 358

Tahnongotha (John Skenando), 43

Tahyantanekea (John Anthony), 43, 350, 352–355

Tegaweiatiron/Tegaiweiatiron, Daniel, 25–27, 31–34

Tekarihonentee (Neddy Atsiguet/Autahiquette), 80, 102

Thomaw (Menominee chief), 20

Thoo-tshopp (Winnebago chief), 180

Thundercloud, Andy, xix, 383

Toucee/Towcee/Towcey, David, 96, 225, 271

Trade and Non-Intercourse Act (1790), xvi, 15

Treaties: and boilerplate language, 367, 376, 386; Constitutional basis for, xiv, 250; and diplomatic protocols, xiv–xv, 60, 71–73; and doublespeak, 90; Indian nation–to–Indian nation, xii–xiii, xv, 60, 90–99, 377; location for negotiations, 342; and specific land boundaries, 3

treaties of 1822: Indian report (Solomon U. Hendrick), 77–78; Indian speeches, 74–77; John Sergeant Jr. report, 78–79; legality of, 249–250; negotiations, 71–73; receipts for payment, 155; text of, 79–84

Treaty between US and Oneida at Green Bay (1838), 343–347

treaty council at Green Bay (1836), 312–314; attendees, 315; compensation for lands ceded, 326–327, 329; proceedings, 315–325; Schermerhorn treaties, 325–335; signatories to Schermerhorn treaties, 328, 330

Treaty of 1821. *See* Treaty of Green Bay (1821)

Treaty of 1822, 184–186

Treaty of 1824, 90–95, 212

Treaty of 1825 (Indian nation–to–Indian nation), 95–99

Treaty of 1825 (US with Indian nations), 121–127, 212, 377, 383; boundaries, 124–127; illustration of, *125*; maps, *122–124*

Treaty of 1827. *See* Treaty of Butte des Morts (1827)

Treaty of Butte des Morts (1827), 87–88, 377; boundaries, 87–88, 130, 145–146, 168, 179, 275; negotiations, 128–142; remarks on by 1830 Council, 191–193, 212; signatories, 142–145. *See also* petition of 1828

ABOUT THE AUTHOR

DR. CAROL A. CORNELIUS, Oneida / Stockbridge Munsee and Montauk, Turtle Clan, earned her PhD in cross-cultural curriculum and American Indian history from Cornell University. She has taught at the University of Wisconsin–Green Bay, where she helped build the First Nations Studies undergraduate program, and the College of the Menominee Nation. She is a former area manager for the Oneida Cultural Heritage Department and the author of *Iroquois Corn in a Culture-Based Curriculum: A Framework for Respectfully Teaching about Cultures*.